The Computer as an Educational Tool

Productivity and Problem Solving

Fourth Edition

Richard C. Forcier
Western Oregon University

Don E. Descy
Minnesota State University, Mankato

PEARSON

Merrill
Prentice Hall

Upper Saddle River, New Jersey
Columbus, Ohio

Library of Congress Cataloging-in-Publication Data

Forcier, Richard C.
  The computer as an educational tool: productivity and problem solving / Richard C.
Forcier, Don E. Descy.—4th ed.
    p. cm.
  Includes bibliographical references and index.
  ISBN 0-13-113885-5
    1. Education—Data processing—Study and teaching (Higher) 2. Computers—Study and
teaching (Higher) 3. Computer managed instruction. 4. Computer-assisted instruction.
  I. Descy, Don E. II. Title.

LB1028.43.F67 2005
378.1'734–dc22

2004044542

Vice President and Executive Publisher: Jeffery
W. Johnston
Executive Editor: Debra A. Stollenwerk
Developmental Editor: Kimberly J. Lundy
Assistant Editor: Amy Nelson
Editorial Assistant: Mary Morrill
Production Editor: Kris Roach
Production Coordination: Carlisle Publishers Services

Design Coordinator: Diane C. Lorenzo
Cover Designer: Jim Hunter
Cover image: Getty One
Photo Coordinator: Cynthia Cassidy
Production Manager: Pamela D. Bennett
Director of Marketing: Ann Castel Davis
Marketing Manager: Darcy Betts Prybella
Marketing Coordinator: Tyra Poole

This book was set in Garamond by Carlisle Communications, Ltd. It was printed and bound by R.R. Donnelley &
Sons Company. The cover was printed by Phoenix Color Corp.

Photo Credits: Ariel Skelley/Corbis/Stock Market p. 2; Anthony Magnacca/Merrill pp. 11, 32, 42, 54, 120, 190; Scott
Cunningham/Merrill p. 14; Photo courtesy of palmOne, Inc. p. 16; Courtesy of Wacom p. 60; Courtesy of Canon, Inc.
p. 61; Courtesy of Hewlett Packard p. 63; Courtesy of InFocus p. 64; Courtesy of Apple Computer, Inc. p. 77;
© LWA-JDS/CORBIS p. 86; © Digital Vision Ltd. p. 166; Patrick White/Merrill pp. 224, 322; © Jose Luis Pelaez, Inc./
CORBIS p. 258; Ken Karp/Prentice Hall School Division p. 290; Kathy Kirtland/Merrill p. 354.

Pearson Education Ltd.
Pearson Education Singapore Pte. Ltd.
Pearson Education Canada, Ltd.
Pearson Education—Japan

Pearson Education Australia Pty. Limited
Pearson Education North Asia Ltd.
Pearson Educación de Mexico, S.A. de C.V.
Pearson Education Malaysia Pte. Ltd.

10 9 8 7 6 5 4 3 2 1
ISBN: 0-13-113885-5

Chapter:	Ch 1	Ch 2	Ch 3	Ch 4	Ch 5	Ch 6	Ch 7	Ch 8	Ch 9	Ch10	Ch11	Ch12
5. Tech Research	✓	✓	✓		✓		✓	✓	✓		✓	✓
Locate, Evaluate, Collect									x		x	x
Process and Report	x		x		x		x	x	x		x	x
Evaluate and Select		x			x				x			x
6. Tech PbS/Decision	✓	✓			✓			✓	✓		✓	✓
Solving Problems, Informed Dec.					x			x	x		x	x
Develop Strategies	x	x			x			x	x		x	x
Performance Indicators	Ch 1	Ch 2	Ch 3	Ch 4	Ch 5	Ch 6	Ch 7	Ch 8	Ch 9	Ch10	Ch11	Ch12
Grades PreK-2												
1. Use Input Devices (1)			✓			✓	✓	✓	✓	✓	✓	
2. Directed/Ind learning (1,3)			✓	✓	✓	✓	✓	✓	✓	✓	✓	✓
3. Terminology (1)	✓	✓	✓	✓	✓	✓	✓	✓	✓	✓	✓	✓
4. Multimedia (1)			✓	✓	✓						✓	✓
5. Coop/Collaborate (2)				✓	✓							
6. Positive Social/Ethical (2)	✓	✓		✓		✓	✓	✓	✓	✓	✓	✓
7. Responsible Use (2)	✓	✓	✓	✓		✓	✓	✓	✓	✓	✓	✓
8. Create Multimedia (3)					✓						✓	
9. PbS/Com/Illus (3,4,5,6)			✓	✓	✓	✓		✓	✓	✓	✓	
10. Telecom (4)											✓	✓
Grades 3-5												
1.Inpt/Otpt Devices (1)			✓			✓	✓	✓	✓	✓	✓	
2. Discuss Adv/Dis (1,2)	✓	✓	✓	✓	✓	✓	✓	✓	✓	✓	✓	✓
3. Discuss Resp Use (1,2)	✓	✓		✓		✓					✓	✓
4. Gen Product Tools (3)		✓	✓		✓	✓	✓	✓	✓	✓	✓	✓
5. Tech Tools (3,4)			✓		✓	✓	✓			✓	✓	
6. Telcom Info/commun (4)											✓	✓
7. Telcom Colab Pds (4,5)											✓	✓
8. Tech Resour Pbs/lrng (5,6)					✓						✓	✓
9. Determ Prop Tech (5,6)			✓	✓	✓	✓	✓	✓	✓	✓	✓	✓
10.Eval Elec Info (6)											✓	
Grades 6-8												
1. Routine Repair (1)												
2. Workplace & Society (2)	✓	✓	✓	✓	✓	✓	✓	✓	✓	✓	✓	✓
3. Legal/ethical behavior (2)	✓	✓				✓					✓	✓
4. Contnt-specific Tools (3,5)				✓	✓						✓	
5. Prod/MM/Perfs (3,6)			✓	✓	✓	✓	✓	✓	✓	✓	✓	
6. Des/Dv/Pb/Prsnt (4,5,6)						✓	✓	✓	✓	✓	✓	
7. Collab/Telcom/Tools (4,5)					✓						✓	✓
8. Select Tools/Tech (5,6)			✓	✓	✓	✓	✓	✓	✓	✓	✓	✓
9. D&S Underlying Cnsp (1,6)		✓	✓		✓	✓	✓	✓	✓	✓	✓	
10. Res/Eval ElecInfo (2,5,6)		✓									✓	✓
Grades 9-12												
1. Ident Cap and Lim (2)	✓	✓	✓	✓	✓	✓	✓	✓	✓	✓	✓	✓
2. Informed Choices (1,2)	✓	✓	✓	✓	✓	✓	✓	✓	✓	✓	✓	✓
3. Adv/Dis of Tech (2)	✓	✓			✓	✓	✓	✓	✓	✓	✓	✓
4. Legal/Ethical (2)	✓	✓				✓	✓	✓	✓		✓	✓
5. Man/ComPer/Prf Info (3,4)			✓		✓	✓	✓	✓	✓		✓	
6. Eval options (5)			✓	✓		✓	✓	✓	✓			
7. Use Online Info (4,5,6)						✓	✓	✓	✓	✓	✓	✓
8. Sel/App Tools (4,5)		✓	✓	✓	✓	✓	✓	✓	✓		✓	
9. ExpSys/IntellAg,Sim (3,5,6)					✓							✓
10. Contrib Cont Knowled (4,5,6)				✓	✓	✓					✓	✓

Preface

The Computer as an Educational Tool: Productivity and Problem Solving, Fourth Edition, is based on the authors' long-held view that technology should be as transparent as possible—that is, that the use of technology should not call attention to itself but rather should be a means to an end. The computer should empower the user to solve problems effectively and efficiently.

The goal of this book is to lead teachers and those aspiring to be teachers to become proficient at applying the computer to solve problems, to infuse the computer into the curriculum in order to help students do the same, and to encourage both teachers and learners to integrate technology into their professional, academic, and personal lives in useful and meaningful ways. Those who are successful in doing this will indeed come to see the computer as an extension of their human capability. The computer will allow them to do more, to do it faster, and to do it more creatively and more accurately.

A PROBLEM-SOLVING FOCUS

The Computer as an Educational Tool: Productivity and Problem Solving, Fourth Edition, provides a current, comprehensive look at the computer's role in education, as well as the application of the computer as a tool of the mind. As the text examines the computer's various roles in education, topics are organized into specific areas of interest to encourage an understanding of the computer's contribution to solving problems. Problem-solving models are included in the text to encourage an increase in computer productivity and to clarify the application of the computer in a thoughtful and deliberate manner, reinforcing the concept of the computer as a mind tool.

A LINK TO NATIONAL STANDARDS

Three sets of national/international standards for developing computer competencies in schools are explained and used in this fourth edition. The 18 foundation standards developed (revised in 1998) by the International Society for Technology in Education (ISTE) and adopted by the National Council for the Accreditation of Teacher Education (NCATE) for integration throughout teacher education programs are one set. The other two sets consist of standards again developed by an ISTE project cosponsored by the U.S. Department of Education, NASA, and computer industry representatives that became known as the National Educational Technology Standards for Students (NETS•S) and the National Educational Technology Standards for Teachers (NETS•T). Applicable standards are listed at the beginning of each chapter. Also, NETS•S and NETS•T standards as well as chapter correlations are listed on the inside front and rear covers.

NEW IN THIS EDITION

Teachers and students will find that the strengths of the book in its fourth edition remain:

- A balance of factual information, research, theory, and application
- Highly readable, student-friendly prose
- Technical matters explained clearly for the nonexpert audience
- Full NETS•S and NETS•T integration
- Examples drawn from both PC-based Windows and Macintosh platforms

With the help of feedback from professors and student users delivered via e-mail and in an extensive review process, this book has been revised significantly. Meaningful changes have been made to more effectively demonstrate the computer's capacity as an educational tool for problem solving and to show to a greater extent the range of classroom applications of computer technology available to teachers and learners. Highlights of this revision include:

- ISTE NETS Standards
  - ISTE NETS•S Standards are printed on the inside front cover along with a matrix that shows where the standards are addressed in the textbook.
  - ISTE NETS•T Standards are printed on the back inside cover along with a matrix that shows where these standards are addressed in the textbook.

- *The text is divided into two parts.* The first deals with foundational issues and underlying theory. The second addresses practical classroom applications of the computer.

- *A reorganized table of contents reflects a deeper integration of problem solving in various aspects of the curriculum* and better contextualizes computer use in educational settings.

- *Chapter 3 presents a practical explanation of computer equipment,* and appropriate equipment is discussed in context with its school application.

- *Chapter 10, one combined chapter on multimedia and multimedia authoring,* provides information on classroom applications of multimedia and the use of multimedia authoring tools.

- *Chapter 11, on Internet resources,* offers strategies for using search tools, including filtered search engines. The basics of Web page construction are presented, including the use of commonly found editors.

- *Chapter 12, a chapter on curriculum applications of the Internet,* focuses on integrating Internet-based tools into the curriculum. Applications for both teachers and students are suggested, using numerous Websites. Information is also given on how to critically evaluate Websites.

- *Curriculum applications receive even greater emphasis* with numerous examples, model lessons, and suggestions for integrating the computer into educational curricula.

- *A new bundled CD-ROM* contains a database manager demo copy along with Microsoft Office™ files of the actual examples used in the word processing, spreadsheet, and database chapters. Students can have a hands-on experience with the examples and can modify and extend them.

- Students using this text will be exposed to and interact with all NETS•S and NETS•T Standards. Complete NETS•S and NETS•T chapter correlations are listed on the inside front and rear covers. No other text can make this statement.

- *An improved Companion Website* serves as a resource to the instructor and as a reference for the student. It includes PowerPoint™ presentations related to material covered in the text. It also includes:
  - sample software evaluation forms
  - a sample parental permission form for telecommunications
  - a practical listing of Internet resources and their addresses
  - field definitions for a software database
  - a list of software publishers, in a form that allows the authors to constantly update the information and add new features as needed with a statement of each one's sales and support policies, and lots more.

TEXT ORGANIZATION AND SPECIAL FEATURES

Woven throughout this text is the use of the computer as a personal productivity and problem-solving tool for the teacher in an instructional role, as well as for the student in a learning role. The text, therefore, is organized with the following thematic frameworks:

- *Issues in information technology.* A number of issues are examined, including copyright, intellectual property, equitable computer access, and gender equity.
- *Learning theory and instruction.* Theoretical structures are established to look at the computer's role in teacher-centered instruction and to examine student-centered learning. Both *behaviorist* and *constructivist* perspectives are examined. Underlying principles and theories of education are reviewed and applied to discussions of computer applications in instruction and learning.

- *Strategies for computer use*. The computer as a productivity tool is applied to tutorial, drill and practice, simulation, and multimedia formats. The Internet, word processing, graphics, databases, and spreadsheets are seen as problem-solving tools in the curriculum. Furthermore, the text is organized to provide thorough coverage of computer knowledge and educational applications, including the following:
  - *Word processing*. Curriculum applications are suggested and sample lessons are presented to illustrate them.
  - *Graphics*. Bit-mapped and vector graphics are explored and examples given. Instruction on the use of the computer to generate display graphics for charts and graphs, signs, posters, bulletin boards, and projected presentations is given.
  - *Spreadsheets*. Problem-solving models are applied to the development of spreadsheets. Detailed instructions on the creation of spreadsheets are presented. Curriculum applications are suggested and sample lessons are presented to illustrate them. Proper selection of chart types and the interpretation of data represented by graphs are analyzed.
  - *Databases*. The organization and retrieval of information are examined. Problem-solving models are applied to the development of databases. Detailed instruction on the creation of databases is presented. Curriculum applications are suggested and sample lessons are presented to illustrate them.

CHAPTER FEATURES

This edition maintains the style of the third edition, which drew acclaim from students for presenting important and useful information in a highly readable format. The following features are included in each chapter:

- Each chapter begins with an *advance organizer* and *applicable NCATE and NETS standards*.
- *Into the Classroom* features connect chapter information directly to real-life classroom situations.
- *Charts* and *line drawings* are used to illustrate concepts in a concrete manner.
- *Screen displays* illustrate application software in, as much as possible, a nonspecific hardware platform.
- *Exercises* allow the student the opportunity to process the information presented in the chapter and apply it in a practical manner, using higher-order thinking skills.
- *Important terms are printed in boldface* when they are introduced to the reader. They are then defined in the chapter glossary and are included in the index at the end of the book to facilitate reference.

ACKNOWLEDGMENTS

We would like to acknowledge the significant contributions that the following people made to the creation and development of this text:

- Glenna Descy, for her wonderful support and thoughtful suggestions.
- Peggy Forcier, for her unflagging support and careful consideration and discussion of the ideas presented in the manuscript.
- Richard J. Forcier, R&D Section Manager, Core Technologies Lab, Hewlett Packard, Boise, for his thoughtful review of Chapter 3 and a number of good suggestions.
- Pam North of the Sherwood Public Library, a reference librarian *par excellence,* for her cheerful willingness to assist in the search for information.
- Users of our previous editions, both instructors and students, who accepted our suggestion and e-mailed us their thoughtful comments.

We would also like to express our gratitude to the reviewers who so thoughtfully read and offered constructive criticism to the work in progress. Their expertise contributed greatly to the strength of this book and to its potential usefulness in a course dealing with computers in education. They include Rosemary Buteau, Chicago State University; Mary Green, The University of Southern Mississippi; Taralynn Hartsell, The University of Southern Mississippi; Bruce Lewis, Freed-Hardeman University; Patsy Reon, The University of Southern Mississippi; Dr. Margaret L. Rice, The University of Alabama; Lawrence A. Tomei, Duquesne University; George Weimer, University of Indianapolis; Ellen W. Wiley, Valdosta State University; Dr. Steve Yuen, The University of Southern Mississippi; and Yixin Zhang, McNeese State University.

Educator Learning Center: An Invaluable Online Resource

 Merrill Education and the Association for Supervision and Curriculum Development (ASCD) invite you to take advantage of a new online resource, one that provides access to the top research and proven strategies associated with ASCD and Merrill—the Educator Learning Center. At www.EducatorLearningCenter.com you will find resources that will enhance your students' understanding of course topics and of current educational issues, in addition to being invaluable for further research.

HOW THE EDUCATOR LEARNING CENTER WILL HELP YOUR STUDENTS BECOME BETTER TEACHERS

With the combined resources of Merrill Education and ASCD, you and your students will find a wealth of tools and materials to better prepare them for the classroom.

Research
- More than 600 articles from the ASCD journal *Educational Leadership* discuss everyday issues faced by practicing teachers.
- A direct link on the site to Research Navigator™ gives students access to many of the leading education journals, as well as extensive content detailing the research process.
- Excerpts from Merrill Education texts give your students insights on important topics of instructional methods, diverse populations, assessment, classroom management, technology, and refining classroom practice.

Classroom Practice
- Hundreds of lesson plans and teaching strategies are categorized by content area and age range.
- Case studies and classroom video footage provide virtual field experience for student reflection.
- Computer simulations and other electronic tools keep your students abreast of today's classrooms and current technologies.

LOOK INTO THE VALUE OF EDUCATOR LEARNING CENTER YOURSELF

A four-month subscription to Educator Learning Center is $25 but is FREE when used in conjunction with this text. To obtain free passcodes for your students, simply contact your local Merrill/Prentice Hall sales representative, and your representative will give you a special ISBN to give your bookstore when ordering your textbooks. To preview the value of this Website to you and your students, please go to www.EducatorLearningCenter.com and click on "Demo."

Discover the Companion Website Accompanying This Book

THE PRENTICE HALL COMPANION WEBSITE: A VIRTUAL LEARNING ENVIRONMENT

Technology is a constantly growing and changing aspect of our field that is creating a need for content and resources. To address this emerging need, Prentice Hall has developed an online learning environment for students and professors alike—Companion Websites—to support our textbooks.

In creating a Companion Website, our goal is to build on and enhance what the textbook already offers. For this reason, the content for each user-friendly Website is organized by chapter and provides the professor and student with a variety of meaningful resources.

For the Professor

- **Professor Resources**—This password-protected instructor resource includes downloadable copies of the following:
  - **PowerPoint Presentations**—Over 25 presentations ranging from software tutorials to chapter content.
  - **Instructor's Manual**—An electronic copy of the Instructor's Manual that includes chapter overviews, chapter outlines, key terms, suggested activities, and self-assessment questions.
- **Digital Portfolio**—Guides students through the design and development of a digital portfolio for themselves and their students.
- **Message Board**—Virtual bulletin board to post or respond to questions or comments from a national audience.

Every Companion Website integrates **Syllabus Manager™,** an online syllabus creation and management utility.

- **Syllabus Manager™** provides you, the instructor, with an easy, step-by-step process to create and revise syllabi, with direct links into Companion Website and other online content without having to learn HTML.
- Students may log on to your syllabus during any study session. All they need to know is the Web address for the Companion Website and the password you've assigned to your syllabus.
- After you have created a syllabus using **Syllabus Manager™,** students may enter the syllabus for their course section from any point in the Companion Website.

- Clicking on a date, the student is shown the list of activities for the assignment. The activities for each assignment are linked directly to actual content, saving time for students.
- Adding assignments consists of clicking on the desired due date, then filling in the details of the assignment—name of the assignment, instructions, and whether or not it is a one-time or repeating assignment.
- In addition, links to other activities can be created easily. If the activity is online, a URL can be entered in the space provided, and it will be linked automatically in the final syllabus.
- Your completed syllabus is hosted on our servers, allowing convenient updates from any computer on the Internet. Changes you make to your syllabus are immediately available to your students at their next log on.

For the Student

Common Companion Website features for students include:

- **Chapter Objectives**—Questions for the student to think about as they read the chapter.
- **Chapter Overview**—Introduction to the chapter's content.
- **Web Resources**—List of Websites for students to visit for more information, including Supplemental Information resources for assessment, portfolio development, and standards.
- **Tutorials**—Step-by-step guides on chapter software, how to, and possible projects to create.
- **Professional Development**—Lists Websites, professional organizations, magazines and journals contact information
- **Web Extensions**—Provide a topic or situation related to chapter content, includes a designated web link or links, along with meaningful activities/questions.
- **Self-Assessment**—Includes multiple choice and true and false questions for each chapter, complete with hints and automatic grading that provide immediate feedback for students.

  After students submit their answers for the interactive self-quizzes, the Companion Website **Results Reporter** computes a percentage grade, provides a graphic representation of how many questions were answered correctly and incorrectly, and gives a question-by-question analysis of the quiz. Students are given the option to send their quiz to up to four e-mail addresses (professor, teaching assistant, study partner, etc.).
- **Portfolio Activities**—Taken from the text, these activities allow students to complete the activities online and submit them electronically to the professor.
- **Message Board**—Virtual bulletin board to post or respond to questions or comments from a national audience.

To take advantage of the many available resources, please visit the *The Computer as an Educational Tool* Companion Website at http://www.prenhall.com/forcier.

Brief Contents

Contents

NOTE: Every effort has been made to provide accurate and current Internet information in this book. However, the Internet and information posted on it are constantly changing, so it is inevitable that some of the Internet addresses listed in this textbook will change.

A Message to the Reader

"We are living in the Information Age" is a saying that has been overused to the point that we don't appreciate what it really means. The authors believe, though, that each one of us will have our own "aha!" moment, where we will reach a personal understanding of the true impact of its meaning. We venture to guess that this personal understanding will relate in some manner to shifting paradigms associated with teaching and learning and to the effective use of technology. We will fully realize that we cannot teach in the manner that we ourselves were taught.

Do not take the term *Information Age* at face value, but dig deeply to derive your own personal understanding. Let this insight guide your teaching behaviors. It is our fervent hope that each and every one of you, as readers of this text, will sharpen your skills related to this Information Age—skills dealing with the creation, storage, access, retrieval, analysis, synthesis, and dissemination of information—and pass those skills along to your students.

We have carefully chosen the title of this book. We view the computer as a tool— a tool to increase our productivity and problem-solving abilities. We hope that the title alone will challenge you to seek a deeper definition of productivity than the one based on the old factory-model meaning of the efficient creation of products. Think of productivity as encompassing effectiveness as well. Include quality, quantity, time, and space in your definition.

In our profession, change not only is inevitable but also is rapid and significant, and it is upon us all, both as a new generation of teachers and as seasoned professionals. Two quotes come to mind as we close this message: "It takes all the running you can do, to keep in the same place" from *Through the Looking Glass and What Alice Found There* and "Who dares to teach, must never cease to learn" carved above the entrance to the instructional technology building at Western Oregon University. The computer places us in a looking glass of change: a place that is rapidly changing even as you read this. Change is not something to fear but something to embrace. We must always seek the unknown so that we will grow and be able to provide the information and the guidance necessary to allow our students to create new knowledge and understanding. Let us allow the computer to become for us the productivity tool that extends our human capability as we teach and continue to learn.

Richard C. Forcier
Don E. Descy

Part
1
Foundations and Theory

CHAPTER 1

Impact of the Computer on Education

1. What are computer and technology standards and why are they needed for preservice teachers in today's society?

2. How are shifting paradigms of computer use affecting the classroom?

3. What are the primary processes involved in a computer system (input of data, operations performed on the data, and output of information)?

4. How has computer technology evolved and what is its potential impact on us?

5. What are some of the current and future trends in information technology?

6. How do portfolios aid in the authentic assessment of our students?

7. What are some steps in developing a useful digital portfolio?

A list of the ISTE/NCATE standards addressed in this chapter is available in the Standards Module on the Companion Website www.prenhall.com/forcier

In Chapter 1 we cover several parts of NETS•S *Category 1: Basic operations and concepts* by discussing computers as they relate to information, communications, human beings, and society. We discuss the computer as a tool that helps us work fast and efficiently. We also discuss some history and basic parts of this tool. NETS•S *Category 2: Social, ethical, and human issues* is also covered. We introduce the chapter with a discussion of the history of computer competencies and the need for competencies in our classrooms. We discuss the development of the computer and how it affects society now and in the future. We look at the technology and how it is employed during a typical day in a typical school. We also introduce the concept of using a computer to create a digital portfolio. The use of digital portfolios by students to highlight, evaluate, and reflect upon their work and how well they achieved competencies and standards, decide on what to include as artifacts, construct the portfolio and present it to various publics allows us to introduce several more NETS•S standards in *Category 3: Technology productivity tools, Category 4: Technology communications tools, Category 5: Technology research tools,* and *Category 6: Technology problem-solving and decision-making tools.* This is an important chapter. It lays the groundwork for your understanding of the computer in society and sets the stage for our further discussions of the computer as an educational tool.

Chapter 1 serves as a general introduction to computers and their place in society by starting off with a brief history of the development of the computer. We then turn to a discussion of obligations and expectations we have as we infuse more and more computer technology into the classroom. The chapter closes with a discussion of digital portfolios.

NETS•S Standards Addressed in This Chapter

1. Basic operations and concepts
   - Students demonstrate a sound understanding of the nature and operation of technology systems.
   - Students are proficient in the use of technology.
2. Social, ethical, and human issues
   - Students understand the ethical, cultural, and societal issues related to technology.
   - Students develop positive attitudes toward technology uses that support lifelong learning, collaboration, personal pursuits, and productivity.
3. Technology productivity tools
   - Students use technology tools to enhance learning, increase productivity, and promote creativity.
   - Students use productivity tools to collaborate in constructing technology-based models, prepare publications, and produce creative works.
4. Technology communications tools
   - Students use a variety of media and formats to communicate information and ideas effectively to multiple audiences.
5. Technology research tools
   - Students use technology tools to process data and report results.
6. Technology problem-solving and decision-making tools
   - Students employ technology in the development of strategies for solving problems in the real world.

COMPUTER COMPETENCIES FOR EDUCATORS

Computers and computer technologies have dramatically changed the face of society as we move into the twenty-first century. It would be hard to find one corner of our world that has not been changed substantially by them. Why is this? When used properly, computers and computer technologies help save us time, and allow us to do things that we never could have imagined. We can design and test cars on computers before we even start to build them. We can crash planes on computers to evaluate their design and redesign them when potential problems emerge.

Computers can do more mathematical calculations in a fraction of a second than a person can do in several hundred lifetimes. We are sure that many of you own or have seen "smart" microwave ovens where you simply put in the food, enter the food type, turn on the microwave, and take out the food perfectly cooked. Sensors read temperature and humidity in the air inside the microwave and feed data into the microwave's computer, and the computer does all the rest. The first astronauts had less computer power in their space capsules than you have in the car parked in your driveway. It is next to impossible to buy a major appliance whose operation is not governed by an onboard computer. Your cell phone is even a handheld computer taking and sending pictures, and surfing the web; e-mail, address book, date book and all the functions of a Palm™ handheld computer are now rolled into one unit. Computers are everywhere.

Just as computers are integrated throughout society, computers should also be integrated throughout the curriculum. This places a special burden on the educator. Fortunately, the burden of integrating computers across the curriculum is far outweighed by the rewards to students and teachers.

Since the first computers arrived in schools in the 1950s and 1960s, much has changed. From the beginning, computers were tools. They are tools to help students and teachers perform tasks faster and more efficiently, but as illustrated in the shifting paradigms in Figure 1–1, the first computers were big, off-site, and operated by specially trained individuals. Now, computers are small desktop, laptop or handheld models that can be used with little training.

Roblyer (1992) states that educational computing was given a boost between 1960 and 1975, because proponents believed that computers could revolutionize education the same way that computers revolutionized business. As the 1970s came to a close, though, it became apparent that this would not be the case. The introduction of microcomputers in schools in 1977 initiated a change in attitude. Microcomputers brought computer power directly into the classroom. In the 1983 National

Figure 1–1
Shift in computer paradigms (Adapted from Greene, 1988)

Commission on Excellence in Education report, *A Nation at Risk* even recommended that high school students be required to take a computer course.

Over the years, teachers, administrators, school boards, and parents have all grappled with the place of computers in the classroom and the curriculum. How should the computer be integrated to learn? What computer skills are really necessary for students? What skill level should teachers have? These questions and others have been discussed and addressed by many professional organizations that have published computer competencies for students and teachers. The organization that preservice teachers in any curriculum area or at any level may be most affected by is the National Council for Accreditation of Teacher Education (NCATE). NCATE delineates standards used to measure and accredit teacher education programs throughout the United States. In its "Vision of the Professional Teacher for the 21st Century," NCATE states that "Accredited schools, colleges, and departments of education should . . . prepare candidates who can integrate technology into instruction to enhance student learning. . . ." "Likewise, the new professional teacher who graduates from a professionally accredited school, college, or department of education should be able to . . . integrate technology into instruction effectively" (NCATE, 2002, p. 4). The International Society for Technology in Education (ISTE) developed computing and technology competencies that have been adopted by NCATE for integration throughout teacher preparation programs (ISTE, 1998).

In the early 1990s, ISTE called together a group of distinguished educators to develop technology standards for teachers. This group, the ISTE Accreditation and Professional Standards Committee, released the very first edition of these standards in 1993, *ISTE Technology Standards for All Teachers*. This first edition contained 13 indicators designed to measure technology competencies of teachers. Because of the fast growth of technology and its spread throughout society, a second edition was published in 1997. This edition contained 18 indicators organized into three broad categories: (1) basic computer/technology operations and concepts, (2) personal and professional use of technology, and (3) application of technology in instruction. Many schools, districts, universities, and states base their current technology standards on this revision. NCATE adopted these standards to measure the effectiveness of technology instruction in teacher education programs it evaluates for accreditation.

The ISTE Accreditation and Professional Standards Committee continued its work and published the National Educational Technology Standards (NETS) for students (NETS•S) in 1998, for teachers (NETS•T) in 2000, and finally for school administrators (TSSA: Technology Standards for School Administrators) in 2001. These standards reflected the results of the NETS project initiated by the ISTE committee and cosponsored by Apple™ Computer, the Milken Exchange on Education Technology, the National Aeronautics and Space Administration (NASA), and the U.S. Department of Education. "The primary goal of the ISTE/NETS Project is to enable stakeholders in PreK–12 education to develop national standards for educational uses of technology that facilitate school improvement in the United States" (ISTE, 2000a).

The NETS project features a three-pronged approach: NETS•S, NETS•T, and TSSA. It is important that you know and understand these standards. As of this writing at least 48 of the 51 states have adapted, adopted, and/or referenced at least one

A complete list of the ISTE/NCATE standards is available in the Standards Module on the Companion Website www.prenhall.com/forcier

For more information on the latest NETS·S and NETS·T information go to the Standards Module on the Companion Website www.prenhall.com/forcier

of the above sets of standards for certification, licensure, and/or in assessment, curriculum, and/or state technology plans. This includes 17 for TSSA, 24 for NETS•S, and 30 for NETS•T.

NETS•S

NETS•S (for students) contains 14 standards consolidated into six broad categories:

1. Basic operations and concepts
2. Social, ethical, and human issues
3. Technology productivity tools
4. Technology communications tools
5. Technology research tools
6. Technology problem-solving and decision-making tools. (ISTE, 2000a)

 Review the inside front cover to examine where, in the various chapters, each standard and grade level performance indicator is addressed in this textbook.

Since students are expected to develop and reinforce each of the 14 standards throughout their education, "Profiles for Technology Literate Students" are included for grades PreK–2, 3–5, 6–8, and 9–12. These profiles contain performance indicators, curriculum examples, and teaching/learning scenarios to help teachers and students track student learning.

INTO THE CLASSROOM:
Technology Enhanced Lessons
Make Learning Fun*

This is a unit where I have my students learn about the states east of the Mississippi River; however, it can easily be adapted to all 50 states or to the region your students are studying. It would be easy to send my students to the library to look up this information in encyclopedias and atlases, but using technology, in this case word processing and the Internet, introduces and reinforces skills that will help them throughout their educational experiences and their life. Technology, when properly used, also seems to make learning more interesting and current and holds the interest of many students who would have been lost or bored just using printed materials.

Students will be involved in an imaginary journey that will take them through the 28 states. They may start in the state of their choice; however, they may not visit any state more than once. The object is to travel to all 28 states in the least number of miles possible. Careful planning is very important. Students will set up a table in Word to help them keep track of their information. Students will also find interesting "factoids" (small facts)

(Continued)

about each state using an Internet site with state information. Once a student has completed his/her trip they will also:

1. Determine how much money would be needed in order to buy gas for the trip (using an average of 23 miles per gallon at $1.57 per gallon). Of course, gas prices may change.
2. Using 60 miles per hour as an average and driving seven hours per day, they will determine how many days it would take to make the trip.
3. Using the answer to #2, students will determine how much money will be needed for food if breakfast cost $4.50, lunch cost $5.25, and supper cost $7.35 (per person).

The students might present their findings using PowerPoint or HyperStudio, write it up using a word processing application, make a spreadsheet, produce a travel or state brochure or even map their trip on a bulletin board map with yarn. This is also a great group learning lesson.

Internet Sites

MapQuest: Find the distance from one city to another
http://www.mapquest.com
Factoids about the states
http://www.homeschooling.about.com/library/blstateunit.htm

What Might a Finished Product Look Like?

1. Your **table** will have the following information (20 points):
   - City-to-city route with full state name (no abbreviations)
   - Factoid for each state—the factoids will be for the state listed in the "from" column
   - Miles for each city-to-city entry
2. A **map** of the United States with the following (10 points):
   - Put a #1 in the "starting" state, #2, #3, etc. until you arrive at your final state (#28)
   - States labeled with their two-digit postal abbreviations
   - Map colored following cartographer's rules
   - Mississippi River marked from its headwaters in Lake Itasca, Minnesota, to the mouth at New Orleans, Louisiana
   - Mississippi River labeled
   - Title
3. A **chart** with your total miles traveled with the following computations completed (15 points):
   - How much money would be needed in order to buy gas for the trip (using an average of 23 miles per gallon at $1.57 per gallon).
   - Using 60 miles per hour as an average and driving seven hours per day, compute how many days it would take to make the trip.
   - Using the answer to the bullet above, determine how much money was spent on food if breakfast cost $4.50, lunch cost $5.25, and supper was $7.35 (per person).

4. A **cover sheet** with the following information (5 points):
   - Your name, student number, and date
   - Title of project "Trip Through the 28 States East of the Mississippi River" (or other appropriate name)
   - Border

Evaluation

Your finished product will be evaluated on the following (see grading rubric for details):

1. Did you travel to all 28 states without visiting any state more than once?
2. Did you travel to contiguous states?
3. Are computations correct?
4. Did you use correct grammar and punctuation?
5. Are your words spelled correctly?
6. Did you follow the directions for this project?
7. Are all parts of the project included?
8. What is the overall quality and appearance of your final project?

Paula Conley
Skyway Elementary School
Coeur d'Alene, Idaho
THE RUBRIC CREATED TO GRADE STUDENTS FOR THIS EXERCISE IS FOUND IN THE INTO THE CLASSROOM FEATURE IN CHAPTER 4.

NETS•T

NETS•T (for teachers) contains 23 standards grouped into six categories:

1. Technology operations and concepts
2. Planning and designing learning environments and experiences
3. Teaching, learning, and the curriculum
4. Assessment and evaluation
5. Productivity and professional practice
6. Social, ethical, legal, and human issues. (ISTE, 2000b)

NETS•T may be particularly important to you since they contain "Technology Performance Profiles for Teacher Preparation" for general, professional, student teaching, and first-year teaching.

TSSA (for administrations) contains 31 standards grouped into six categories:

1. Leadership and vision
2. Learning and teaching
3. Productivity and professional practice
4. Support, management, and operations

5. Assessment and evaluation

6. Social, legal, and ethical issues. (ISTE, 2002)

Unless you decide to continue your studies in the field of educational administration, you will have little contact with these standards but knowing that they exist may be important to you.

Because ISTE, NCATE, the Association for Educational Communications and Technology (AECT), other professional organizations, the authors, most states, and your instructor (by choosing this textbook) believe that computer and technology standards are important, we have aligned the text with these standards.

The use of technology standards allows teachers to strive for a common goal agreed on by a wide variety of fellow educators. Standards allow us to define a product, in this case the competent use of technology and the underlying knowledge that supports that use, and to recognize the evidence of that knowledge and use when we see it. The NETS•S standards are included in performance indicator groupings for each series of grade levels to aid educators in assessing student progress. We as teachers use a number of standards of performance and behavior in our classrooms.

The technology standards identify a computer competent person. We have chosen to focus on the NETS•S standards in this text so that as preservice teachers you will recognize what knowledge, skills, and attitudes will be expected of students in your classes. You will be preparing citizens of the twenty-first century—citizens who will need to understand and be prepared to deal with serious cultural and ethical issues and who will be expected to extend their capabilities as they create, evaluate, store, and communicate information. The NETS•S standards provide a blueprint to develop that knowledge and build the necessary technology skills in your students.

The complete list of NETS•S and NETS•T is available on this book's Companion Website. The relevant NETS•S standards are listed at the beginning of each chapter. We do not include the NETS•T at the beginning of each chapter because the full implementation of these standards is beyond the scope of a single course.

No Child Left Behind Act

Proper infusion of technology is also a national priority. On January 8, 2002, President Bush signed the No Child Left Behind (NCLB) Act into law. This act affects almost every facet of education as we know it. In order to improve student achievement through the use of technology, U.S. Secretary of Education Rod Paige announced the new "Enhancing Education Through Technology" (ED Tech) initiative shortly after the signing. The goals of ED Tech are to:

- Improve student academic achievement through the use of technology in elementary schools and secondary schools.
- Assist students to become technologically literate by the time they finish the eighth grade.
- Ensure that teachers are able to integrate technology into the curriculum to improve student achievement. (NCLB, 2002)

Title II, Part B *Enhancing Education Through Technology* (E_2T_2) of NCLB further consolidates the former Technology Literacy Challenge Fund and local Technology

A goal of the No Child Left Behind Act is to improve student achievement through the use of technology.

Innovation Challenge Grants into a single state-run ed tech grant program entitled *Enhancing Education Through Technology.* The primary objectives include:

- Encouraging innovative uses of technology in education.
- Full integration of technology into the curriculum.
- Broadening access to technology across the community and within the school.
- Reaching underserved students and areas.
- Establishing a stronger home–school connection.
- Increasing staff development including training of administrators.
- Providing ongoing funding and maintenance of technology.
- Evidence-based evaluation of the use of technology. (T&L Editors, 2002)

MEDIA AND TECHNOLOGY LITERACY

All media are extensions of some human faculty.

—Marshall McLuhan (1967)

The word *media* has been defined in many ways. Its most popular definition in our culture refers to the mass media of communications: radio, television, newspapers, and magazines. Some teachers think of media as **educational media,** meaning audio-visual aids; some believe media is related to library and **information technology.**

A definition gaining favor in recent years identifies media as a tool. Consider the word *media* itself. *Media* is the plural form of the word *medium,* a term broadly understood as being in the middle. Medium implies in the middle or between two extremes or two points. Something is medium if it is neither hot nor cold, neither fast nor slow, neither large nor small. This understanding is the ideal foundation for defining a medium as a tool between (in the middle of) the user and **information** that is to be created, received, stored, manipulated, or disseminated. A tool is in the middle between the user and the task being addressed. A hammer is the tool in the middle of, or between, a carpenter and the nail that is manipulated. Information technology is the application of the tool to solve problems related to information. Information technology is "not just hardware, wires and binary code, but also the effective use of digital information to extend human capabilities" (Milken Exchange on Educational Technology, 1999, p. 3). We agree with this definition of media as a tool and will come back to it time and again throughout the book.

Tools are what McLuhan was referring to as extensions of our human capability. From the study of archeology, we know that humans have always been toolmakers and tool users. Consider how we have created and adapted physical tools, such as the lever, the wheel, and the pulley, to amplify and extend our physical abilities, and figurative tools, such as language and mathematics, to enhance our cognitive abilities. Some would define *technology* as this deliberate ingenious effort to create, select, adapt, and apply tools to a task or problem at hand. Among our ancestors the use of technology by both women and men was essential for the well-being and growth of culture and society. Women were some of the earliest technologists because they fashioned agricultural and homemaking tools, whereas men used technology to fashion tools for the hunt.

Media literacy, on the other hand, has to do with the ability of an individual to encode information into and decode information stored in some form of media, some media tool. A media literate individual is able to use a media tool to produce a product that contains information stored (encoded) in such a way that the information would be easily and efficiently retrieved (decoded) and used by another media literate individual. Likewise, a media literate individual is able to easily and efficiently retrieve and use the information stored in a mediated product. Media literate individuals are able to separate the message from the medium and not be influenced by the particular qualities of the medium. I am sure that we have all been brought to tears or cheers when we decoded the message in a particular media tool (such as a recording or a film). Was this because of the medium or the message or both? If the message were delivered using another media tool (a book for example), would it have the same emotional impact?

When we consider technology in education, we include, among other things, the computer as one of our most recent tools. Even though the computer began to enter the educational field after the launch of the Soviet satellite *Sputnik* in 1957, most computers were not used in classrooms in significant numbers until the late 1970s and early 1980s. The application of the computer as a multifaceted tool makes it a unique form of educational technology. Not being limited to a single tool, we select from a variety of tools, perhaps adapt the tool, and then apply the tool to the problem at hand. The way we view computing has shifted in at least four significant areas. Figure 1–1 on page 5 illustrates this shift radiating outward from the past, shown in the innermost circle, through the present and the near future, represented by the outermost circle. Beginning in the upper left quadrant and progressing in a clockwise fashion, the areas represented may be summarized by the words *where, how, who,* and *what.*

The *where* has been a transition from a computer room to users' desktops in the classroom, in the office, or at home. The transition has progressed to users themselves as they transport computers with them wherever they go as personal assistants in the form of **laptops, handheld computers, personal digital assistants (PDAs),** and **web-enhanced cell phones** (that might even double as an audio player, video camera, or global positioning system).

The *how,* or under what conditions, has shifted from a tightly controlled, centralized, and institutionalized environment, such as a school district office or a service bureau providing computer services, to the school to a highly personalized environment with the user in command of the computer, and, increasingly, to a truly interpersonal environment that lets users interact with one another at almost any time and almost any location worldwide.

In addressing the *who* of computing, we have seen a distinct move from the **computer operator** (often a technician somewhat remote from the problem) to the **end user** (the person deriving direct benefit) interacting directly with the computer and then to a networked community of users interconnected electronically, though not necessarily by wires, with one another. Teachers and students can communicate with peers around the globe.

Finally, the *what* presents the move from a fascination with huge amounts of stored **data** to a concern for the value of the information that can be extracted from it. And finally, to teachers and students developing increasingly sophisticated skills in the access, manipulation, and creation of information and knowledge. These shifting paradigms have facilitated the students' and teachers' ability to personally interact and exchange information with other users in the same neighborhood or around the world. The goal of this chapter is to help educators gain perspective on current computer use by understanding historical contexts (past, present, and future trends in information technology).

EVOLUTION OF COMPUTER TECHNOLOGY

Yesterday

Rapid changes in computer technology have resulted in greatly improved and expanded applications. As we briefly review significant technology events of the twentieth century, we become aware of a tremendous simplification in computer operation, a vast improvement of the machine and human interface, and a dramatic reduction in equipment size that has taken place. These elements contribute significantly to the expanding computer utilization in society in general and in education in particular. A few milestone historical events are worth noting.

At one time, computers took up whole rooms. Now the same computer power may take up the space of a 3 or 4 drawer file cabinet.

The 1880 census took seven years to process manually and, with a growing population, the 1890 census posed a serious problem. It appeared that it would take more than 10 years to process the census data unless some new method was used. A mammoth computer was invented to process the census data by reading holes punched on cards. The machine also sorted and counted the cards. Because of this new invention, the 1890 census was processed in only three years. The inventor manufactured this device and then merged with another company. The new firm was named International Business Machines (IBM).

Sixty-five years later, the first general-purpose electronic digital computer was introduced in 1945. The ENIAC (Electronic Numerical Integrator and Calculator) occupied 3,000 cubic feet of space, weighed 30 tons, contained more than 18,000 vacuum tubes, and drew 140,000 watts of power when it was running. The lightbulb-size **vacuum tube** acted like an electronic switch or gate, passing or blocking an electrical current in a **digital** circuit. As current was passed or blocked, it was translated into a binary code of 1s (on) and 0s (off). The ENIAC could do only simple addition, subtraction, multiplication, and division operations in a programmed sequence. To change the sequence to address a new problem, the ENIAC had to be rewired by hand. Six years later, in 1951, the first electronic computer to use **transistors** and a stored program entered the market. The half-inch square transistor replaced the vacuum tube, allowing the computer itself to be reduced from building size to room size and then to the size of several large file cabinets.

Programs stored in computers were written in machine language as **binary** code. Think of the vacuum tube for a moment. It can be "on," passing current, or it can be "off," blocking current. This on or off state could be represented by a 1 or by a 0. Zeroes and ones, called **bits,** are often gathered in groups of 8, 16, 32, or more and are referred to as **bytes,** representing an alpha (letter) or a numeric (number) character. Although today's computers still understand only binary code, we fortunately, do not have to use this code to communicate with them. Computer languages have been developed that allow us to use English-like words, which are then translated into a binary form. As a side note, around this time in 1969, the U.S. Department of Defense created a network of military computers called ARPAnet (Advanced Research Projects Agency network), which evolved into the present-day **Internet.** It was a Cold War attempt to develop a nonlinear method of linking governmental installations throughout the United States in the hope that such a diffuse network would survive a nuclear attack on the United States. More about the Internet discussed later.

Microcomputers marketed in kit form for hobbyists were introduced in 1975. By 1977, Apple, Commodore™, and RadioShack™ microcomputers were on the market and the microcomputer explosion was under way. The **integrated circuit,** or **chip,** found in those microcomputers was approximately one-quarter-inch square and contained millions of transistors.

Time magazine proclaimed 1982 "The Year of the Computer" because of the significant contributions that personal computers made in complementing human abilities. This is also the year that Microsoft released the MS-DOS operating system for IBM and compatible computers. The term *microcomputer* faded in favor of the term *personal computer.*

Apple Computer introduced the Macintosh computer in 1984. The Mac™, as it became known, featured a **graphic user interface (GUI)** that was first developed by Xerox® complete with a mouse, icons, screen windows, and pull-down menus. Until this time, computers had used a text-based interface.

The **World Wide Web,** an Internet navigation system, was developed at CERN, the European Particle Physics Laboratory in Geneva, Switzerland, in the mid-1980s.

HyperCard®, a program created in 1987 at Apple Computer, is said to have opened the door to multimedia as we know it today. The program has now been supplemented by a number of others, most prominent among them is HyperStudio, a program that works on both the Macintosh and Windows platforms.

After a few setbacks (Windows® 1.0 and 2.0), Microsoft released Windows 3.0, a successful GUI competitor to the Macintosh operating system, in 1990. Windows, in its recent versions, has become the best-selling computer program, or software, of all time and the dominant operating system in almost all market segments. Unlike the 30-ton ENIAC that occupied 3,000 cubic feet of space, laptops, such as the PowerBook® introduced in 1993, weighed about seven pounds and occupied less than one-seventh of a cubic foot of space. The ENIAC had an internal memory capacity of 12 K, storing about 12,000 characters in its memory. In comparison, laptops introduced in 1993 had a memory expandable to 36 MB (about 36 million bytes)—about 3,000 times greater than the ENIAC, and 100,000 times more reliable. Today's laptops are significantly more powerful yet.

In 1993, another graphical interface called Mosaic™ was developed. It allowed World Wide Web users almost instantaneous transfer of information in the form of text, graphics, sound, and video through the simple click of the mouse. Applications such as mosaic used to access the World Wide Web are called **browsers.** Mosaic later evolved into the Netscape® Web browser. Internet Explorer™ developed by Microsoft™ is now the dominant Web browser.

In 1997, Intel Corporation began marketing a supercomputer capable, for the first time, of breaking the trillion-calculations-a-second barrier. The computer can perform 667 million calculations in the time it takes a bullet to fly one foot.

Those astonishing developments have taken place in a little more than 50 years. At present, computing power doubles every 18 months! What astounding advances in technology will the next 50 years (or even the next 5 years) bring?

Today

How do learners of today differ from learners of yesterday? It could be argued that the most dramatic changes are the amount of information available and the greatly enhanced access to it. Much of this information is packaged in a visual form and pre-

More and more faculty, students, and administrators are turning to handheld computers because of their size, computing power, and convenience. This Palm Zire even takes color digital photos.

sented in an interactive manner at a rapid rate. Consider how television, magazine, billboard, and radio ads bombard our senses as consumers. As viewers, readers, and listeners, we have adapted to "consume" information differently. We no longer have to communicate in the old ways. We don't have to go to knowledge; it comes to us through electronic fingertip access to databases, libraries, people, and places. We don't have to go to people; they come to us over satellite cell phones that allow us to talk with anyone, anywhere; via meeting software that connects several people at different physical locations in a meeting on our computers, be it on a desktop or in a cave in a mountain five thousand miles from nowhere; by video over IP (Internet Protocol) that moves instructional television and distance learning classes from one point to another through the Internet. Similarly, as the amount of information available to learners multiplies, the process of learning must evolve. Consequently, schooling is changing dramatically and, with it, the role of the teacher.

Yesterday, learners were generally seen as containers, or vessels, needing to be filled with factual information. Teachers were dispensers of information, and memorization was equated with learning. An "educated person" was well read and knew facts in a variety of fields. With the explosion of information and widespread, immediate access to it, today's learners are faced, like never before, with the need to develop problem-solving skills. Today's educated person knows how to access information efficiently, evaluate it, and apply it effectively as that individual constructs appropriate knowledge.

How do changes in schooling relate to the paradigm shifts in computing previously described? Centralized information dispensed by the teacher has shifted to individualized information retrieval by the student. The evolution of computer technology has enabled those paradigm shifts as equipment has become smaller, more portable, more affordable, more powerful, and easier to use. As new technology is making vast amounts of information available to teachers and students, a need for highly developed information literacy skills has been recognized. Teachers and students must learn how to conduct effective searches, how to critically evaluate the results of the search, and how to create new knowledge from the information distilled. The American Association of School Librarians (AASL) and the Association for Educational Communications and Technology (AECT) have jointly developed national guidelines for information literacy. Several states have adopted their own in conjunction with the national guidelines.

Change seems to be the hallmark in the twenty-first century. Social and economic struggles of the present have thrust educational and school reform from the theoretical realm of educators into the public arena. Legislators, businesspeople, parents, and other taxpayers are demanding fundamental changes from schools, teachers, and administrators. Each has a unique interpretation of what these changes should be and how they will best occur. Businesses have created, have funded, and are managing for-profit schools, some within the public school system. School choice is an issue that has been the subject of both political rhetoric and informed debate. Some parents advocate more government support of homeschooling, whereas others expect help from the school system with childcare, parenting advice, and social services. Taxpayers are dissatisfied with the performance of public schools in relation to the amount of tax money spent. Significant changes in the whole structure of the educational system and our philosophies of education and learning are occurring, a paradigm shift that is discussed in greater detail in the next chapter.

As schools have gradually adopted the use of computers and related technology, they have undergone some degree of instructional change. According to Allan Collins (1991), these trends, identified more than 10 years ago and continuing today, include the following:

1. A change from whole-class to small-group instruction.
2. A move from lecture to coaching.
3. A move from working with better students to spending more time working with weaker students.
4. A shift toward students becoming more engaged in their learning.
5. A change to assessment based on products and outcomes.
6. A shift from a competitive to a cooperative atmosphere in the classroom.
7. A shift from all students attempting to learn the same thing at the same time to different students learning different things at their own rate.
8. A move from an emphasis on verbal thinking to the integration of visual and verbal thinking.

The computer is an ideal tool shaping and molding all of these trends. It is convenient, powerful, and small in size. Students and teachers alike are now able to carry with them powerful assistants allowing them to access information from around the world, categorize and assess this information at their own rate and in their own learning style, summarize and encode this information, and deliver it in a variety of ways in audio, video, multimedia, and printed formats through themselves or electronically to any place around the world.

Tomorrow

What the authors talked about as the future as they prepared for the last edition of this text two short years ago is now the present or even the past as we prepare this edition! A computer is no longer just a tool to be used in an educational setting, in a library, or at home but is turning into an appliance that students carry around in their backpacks like a day planner, a book, or a pen. There are even schools around the country that have opted to replace textbooks with computers, the Internet, "e-books," and CD-ROMS (Associated Press, 2002). We find ourselves in the midst of a powerful information revolution. With the significant restructuring in education occurring in the United States, the way we use computers in the classroom is changing. What role might the computer play in school restructuring? Much will depend on you and teachers like you who recognize the potential of the computer as an intellectual tool. You are in a crucial role. Myron Pincomb, a technology consultant and trainer from Jacksonville, Florida, says that ". . .95% of educators under-utilize technology. In a lot of schools, the computer is used as a game or a reward—but it has so many other educational uses" (in Hill, 2002, p. 29).

In order for schools to keep up with the demands of the students, the demands of the community, and the demands of the government, there will have to be a philosophical shift in the public's perception of education. Often the public's perception is based on the past, on what education was like for them or even how it was like for one of their older children, rather than the reality of what it is like today or its present and future potential. Technology, with its frequent innovations and pervasive influence, provides an impetus for that shift. It also provides the tools educators need to implement change now.

The U.S. Department of Education has adopted four national technology goals, and funding is being provided from a variety of sources to help schools install the necessary infrastructure and to train teachers in the use of technology to meet those goals. The goals are:

- All teachers and students will have modern computers in their classrooms.
- Every classroom will be connected to the information superhighway.
- Effective and engaging software and on-line resources will be an integral part of every school curriculum.
- All teachers will have the training and support they need to help all students learn through computers and through the information superhighway.

Any lasting changes and reforms will need to be preceded by a vision of what future learning environments will be like. What expectations will be placed on the learner? What will the role of the teacher be? What will the physical structure of the learning environment be? How will library media centers fit into this new environment? How will technology affect learning?

The basic curriculum will change as schools focus on information and thinking skills, and as the use of tools, such as computers, sophisticated information storage and retrieval systems, holograms, and virtual reality simulations, becomes the norm rather than the exception. Teaching methods will change as these tools are incorporated. Instructional materials will reflect the tools being used in learning. Expectations and outcomes will be different for children, teachers, parents, and administrators. The physical structure and internal organization of the school will certainly differ as these changes are assimilated.

In the future, the amount of time children spend in school may well become more flexible as technology provides new tools and inspires new teaching and learning methods. Networking will allow students to work at multiple sites while interacting with the class or the teacher. As students begin taking more responsibility for their own learning, the pace of that learning will have a more natural rhythm dictated by the individual student's needs instead of an imposed district-wide schedule. Some students may choose to work in the early morning, at night, or on weekends. Even young children may choose to work on absorbing projects for extended periods of time rather than having the day divided into predetermined segments of learning.

Technology will provide students with access to information and the tools to produce substantial work. Each student will have a computer available at school. This may be a personal computer workstation, a shared terminal for database and networking access, a portable, or a handheld computer. The computers will all have wireless networking capabilities and be linked by a network to teachers, parents, homes, databases, electronic bulletin boards, library and information centers, and other people all over the world.

The most exciting use of technology by the students of the future will be an enhancement of their production of authentic, meaningful work. Students will write, illustrate, publish, program, and create models, movies, music, stories, poetry, art, and other products of research and learning. They will use integrated technologies involving CDs and DVDs, computers, multimedia, virtual reality, and holographic imaging. Given access to information and technology, the skills to use them, and the freedom to learn and explore, children will be able to produce work that is barely imaginable to adults today. One of the authors of this text was taught claymation animation by two first graders who later burned their demonstration onto a DVD for him to have with no teachers present as the author looked on in amazement. Reread this last section titled "Tomorrow". . . It really is "Today."

Schools are under pressure to provide more than simply a limited-use building with a single mission. Taxpayers complain about expensive buildings and equipment that are virtually deserted for up to a fourth of the year and are available only during school hours during the rest of the year. Teachers find themselves unable to teach academics when children are more in need of a nurse, counselor, social worker, or parent. The school of the future will have to address those needs. A multiple-use neighborhood facility combining education with the traditionally separate fields of childcare, health care, social services, and fitness will more successfully meet the needs of the children and the community. Professionals in each of those fields would staff the facility, working as a team to provide the best possible environment for children and their parents.

INTO THE CLASSROOM:
The Networked School

Teachers and students arriving at Lakeville High School walk through the halls casually observing the day's schedule of activities displayed by a presentation program running on video monitors throughout the building. In their classrooms, the teachers sit down at their desktop computers that are programmed to automatically boot-up each morning at 7:00 A.M. They are prompted to log into the server. They retrieve the morning's mail and notices from the e-mail system. Messages may be from the office, colleagues in the building, other employees in the district, and from parents and community members sent via the district-wide area network or the Internet. Next, they check their voice mail and prerecord the day's assignments for absent students on specially programmed phone lines. The teachers are alerted of any important meetings during the day through the use of a scheduling program.

Activity sheets also may need copying before the day begins. Teachers open their files stored on the server and select the pertinent activity sheets. After completing the details of a cover sheet, they send it via the network to the central, networked copier for processing. Before leaving to pick up their copies from the copy center, they may schedule part of the day in one of the school's 12 computer labs. These Macintosh or Windows labs are also networked to the school's server, which enables students to access on-line materials and retrieve or save their work in their own network files. All of the labs have word processing, spreadsheet, and database programs; Internet access; library access; and specialized programs (e.g., high-end graphics, CAD, world language, music, career resources, writing, business) depending on the function of the particular lab. After working in the labs, some students may move to the video production studio or industrial technology areas and work with computer imaging, three-dimensional modeling, animation, and digital editing to create digital videos or Websites for class.

Before classes begin, a teacher may turn to the control panel next to the computer to select a CD-ROM, DVD or video for the day's lesson from the centralized video retrieval system. In addition, teachers may bookmark Websites to display using the local input connection between the computer and video monitor. Teachers easily switch among commercial/satellite television inputs, presentation programs, videotapes, CD-ROMs, DVDs, and Websites using the system's remote control, while moving around the classroom. When classes begin, teachers take attendance for each student using the on-line student information system.

Teachers are able to check pertinent student records for various health concerns, test scores, and directory data in the student information system. Teachers use the system to keep track of student attendance, record grades, and track portfolio progress of curriculum standards. At the central office, school district officials are able to check all student and resident data across grade levels. With the help of a geographic information system, district officials quickly assimilate data and display that data on maps. Maps of interest to staff, parents, and community members are then posted on the school and district Websites.

Parents are able to access information about their children, school notices, and events via the Internet. Building and district Websites provide information on school and district events, courses, schedules, lunch menus, and staff. Individual teachers have course outlines and assessments posted on-line.

When the teachers leave for the day, paperwork doesn't always have to follow them home. Students are able to hand in their work on the network in special folders. Teachers access these folders on-line in school or at home when needed.

Laurie Quinlan
Communications Instructor
Lakeville High School
Lakeville, Minnesota

DIGITAL PORTFOLIOS

The school reform movement that has been gaining momentum over the past years is changing some of the basic ways schools and students interact. One way is through the implementation of national standards for teaching and learning as described previously. In many school systems, evaluation of student learning using paper-and-pencil tests and quizzes is being supplemented with more authentic means of assessment. The use of portfolios is one of the popular means of authentic assessment. Many educators believe that a portfolio is a truer representation and documentation of learning. Portfolios fit into the constructivist view of learning because they contain representations of knowledge that the students themselves have synthesized and constructed. A portfolio is not simply an assortment of a student's work used as examples to show how they met specific requirements. Rather, it is a selected collection of student work designed to demonstrate the degree to which a student achieved specific standards (Figure 1–2). An important component of this collection is the inclusion of reflective commentary and self-assessment articulated by both the teacher and student as they fit each piece of the portfolio into the larger framework of standards and achievement. This creates a much richer tool, adding insight into the abilities of the student. True portfolios are never completed but rather continue to grow and change as the student continues to grow and learn. Barrett

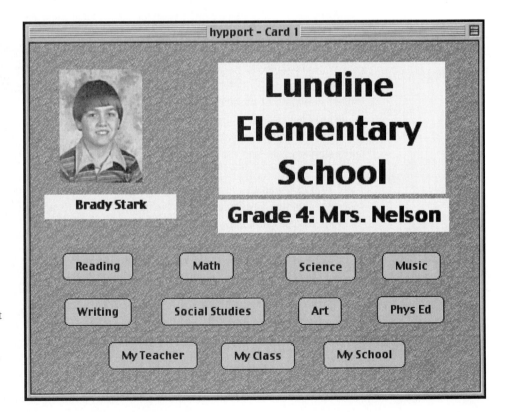

Figure 1–2
Elementary schools are using digital portfolios to demonstrate student growth and achievement. This one, on a CD-ROM, also acts as a yearbook for the student to treasure.

(2000) sums it up, "An electronic portfolio is not a haphazard collection of artifacts (i.e., a digital scrapbook or multimedia presentation) but rather a reflective tool that demonstrates growth over time" (p. 41).

Computers have proven themselves to be useful tools in the collection, development, and presentation of portfolios. Their power enables individuals to compactly store and quickly locate information at the click of a mouse. We use the term **digital portfolio** to designate one stored on a computer disk, CD-ROM, or DVD. You may encounter the term **electronic portfolio** elsewhere. Electronic portfolios may contain components, such as a videotape, that are in an electronic format **(analog)** but perhaps not stored digitally on a computer storage medium. Digital portfolios may contain written words along with movies, still images, sounds, and interactive examples of a student's work all digitized for use by the computer, allowing pages of information and boxes of artifacts to be neatly stored on a small Zip disk, CD-ROM, or DVD. Many university students (Figure 1–3) produce interactive digital résumés that highlight their achievements and store them in a convenient format for prospective employers. More and more teachers and students are placing portfolios on secure Websites or on DVDs, both of which can be accessed using either Macintosh or Windows computers instead of Zip disks or CD-ROMs that are platform specific and may limit access to the platform on which they were made. Two different spheres of knowledge are tapped when developing a digital portfolio. These are portfolio development and multimedia production. Understanding

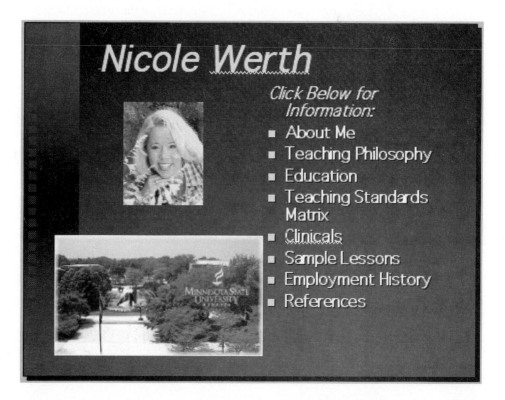

Figure 1–3
University students are using digital portfolios as electronic résumés. Some universities save copies of these as examples of student mastery of standards for accreditation.

both of these spheres will enable teachers and students alike to design, develop, and produce powerful tools that easily communicate the level of knowledge and achievement attained by the students.

Portfolio development contains several steps. The first step is the assembly of a collection of documents and artifacts (i.e., videos, images, text and text files, models, sound, and so on) that demonstrate the achievement of a specific standard. This step contains several smaller steps: the identification and understanding of the standards, the collection of documents and artifacts, and the selection of documents and artifacts that best exemplify the achievement of the standards. The second step involves thoughtful reflection on the documents and artifacts by both the student and the teacher. At this stage collaborative discussions may take place to discuss past, present, and future progress.

Several steps are involved in the multimedia development phase. First, the parameters of the portfolio must be established. There are two considerations at this point: How do we want to store and present the information, and what software and hardware are available to do this? Of course, these are closely related. Software selection need not be an issue. Hardware decisions hinge on equipment available for digitizing (e.g., scanners, digital cameras, video digitizers, and so on) and final method of storage (e.g., Zip disks, CD-ROM, DVD, Flash Drive, and so on).

The second step in the multimedia development phase consists of setting up the standards within the software package, digitizing documents and artifacts, and assembling the final product. As stated above, an important part of this phase is the evaluation and reflective commentary of the artifacts by the student. We have added portfolio exercises to the end of each chapter that are linked to one or more of the NETS·S standards.

Portfolio Programs

Software is not an issue. Specific portfolio management tools such as *The Portfolio Builder*™, the *Grady Profile*™, and *The Portfolio Assessment Kit*™ (see Figure 1–4) may be used. Wonderful portfolios have also been developed using *HyperStudio*®, *PowerPoint*® (both discussed in Chapter 10), *FileMaker Pro* (discussed in Chapter 9), and even *Microsoft Word*® (discussed in Chapter 7). Portfolio management programs are specifically designed to easily store and display student work, link the work to standards, and shed a whole new light on the terms evaluation and assessment. Some of the programs are linked to or are add-ons to other programs. For example, *The Portfolio Builder* is designed to work with *PowerPoint,* and *The Portfolio Assessment Toolkit* is designed to interface with *HyperStudio.* Linked or not, they all serve as a repository for student work. Many of the portfolio programs have several layers of information each accessed by one or more passwords for students, teachers, or administrators and can serve as a complete record of the student's time and progress in school.

For more information on developing digital portfolios go to the Digital Portfolio Module on the Companion Website www.prenhall.com/forcier

In closing this first chapter, we want to reemphasize that a computer is a tool. It is a medium between the person and the task to be performed just as a hammer is the medium between the carpenter and the nail to be driven. As the need to fasten

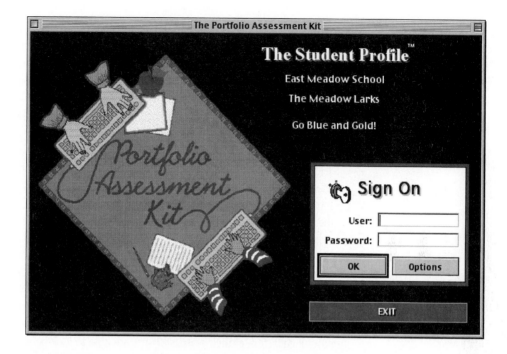

Figure 1–4

The Portfolio Assessment Kit™ works with HyperStudio™ (Courtesy of Super School Software)

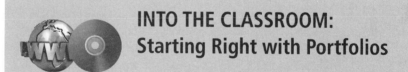

INTO THE CLASSROOM: Starting Right with Portfolios

I have been implementing standards-based electronic portfolios for three years with my fourth graders. It has been one of the most rewarding projects I have done with my students each year, and their reflections on the project, along with the benefits I have seen demonstrated in my research, make it all worthwhile. I became interested in electronic portfolios while going through graduate school, and pursued implementing them as a topic for my thesis. The procedure I used for implementation was Dr. Helen Barrett's (2000) electronic portfolio process. This process guided my research, and it still guides my process today.

The electronic portfolios my students create are based on my school district's reading and writing standards. Many elementary electronic portfolio examples today are simply digital scrapbooks due to missing the standards component. In the beginning of the process, students use a template I created for them in PowerPoint. The template contains

(Continued)

all of the basic elements of the portfolio, and students add their own work and personal touches as they go along. Each portfolio contains slides for: a cover, table of contents, purpose statement, goals, "All About Me," and three slides for each trimester of reading and writing (one for reading and two for writing). Students record a reading clip for each trimester, in addition to linking reading captions and two writing pieces with captions for each trimester. An additional component I have added over the past two years has been artwork. Students take digital camera pictures of the artwork they truly feel shows their art progress. Then, they have one slide at the end of the year that is their art reflection. Once everything is linked, and students have added their own personal touches, portfolios are burned to CDs for students to take home. PowerPoint viewer is also burned onto the CD for those students who do not have PowerPoint at home.

The benefits of using electronic portfolios are numerous. First and foremost students have captured their reading, writing, and artwork in a way that will allow them to keep it indefinitely. Having this work stored on a CD is a treasure for the students and their parents. Second, students gain increased technology skills. In this process, students become familiar with many different software applications, the digital camera, and the scanner. They are gaining skills that have lifelong implications, in addition to gaining confidence in their skills. Students become more reflective in their reading and writing. By having this purposeful collection of their work, students are able to look back on it and make accurate assessments of their abilities and areas they need to grow in. In addition to becoming more reflective about their reading and writing abilities, they become more confident in their reading and writing abilities. Using the technology is exciting for the students, which in turn creates additional enthusiasm for reading and writing.

To effectively manage electronic portfolios in your classroom, there are several important recommendations to consider. First, choose several students to be PowerPoint (or whatever software you have chosen as the medium) trainers. By doing this you have empowered the students to teach each other, and it takes a lot of the pressure off you. Give each trainer a class list of highlighted names with tasks written at the top for them to check off. Second, develop instruction sheets for how to do different aspects of the portfolio on the computer. This makes students more responsible by requiring them to use the instruction sheets after they've already learned how to do something before asking you or the trainers. Next, utilize the parent volunteers in your classroom who are willing to help with the project. Offer to train parents, and then have them work with individuals or small groups of students. By having one parent devote an entire morning or afternoon to helping with the portfolios, the entire class could complete a specific component in one day. Finally, develop a schedule for when the different aspects of the portfolio need to be done. Having a set schedule will keep you more disciplined with the process and will allow you to see what needs to be done in the future.

By sticking to your schedule, in addition to implementing the above recommendations, electronic portfolios will not be so overwhelming and time won't be such an issue. It is a challenging process, and roadblocks encountered along the way cause frustration at times.

> However, looking at the big picture, the outcome of electronic portfolios is amazing, and the positive effect it has on the students is incredible. I feel I am proof that electronic portfolios can work in an elementary classroom. Is it worth it? Absolutely.
>
> Lori Kiene
> Fourth Grade Teacher
> West Des Moines Community School District (IA)

 For more information on developing digital portfolios go to the Digital Portfolio Module on the Companion Website www.prenhall.com/forcier

something with a nail determines the choice of the hammer as the appropriate tool, the task at hand defines the proper use of the computer, or other medium. Ultimately, the task, the curriculum goal, the objectives, the instructional strategy, and the learning drive the choice of media.

SUMMARY

Teachers, administrators, school boards, and parents have grappled with the integration of computers into the classroom and the curriculum. The National Council for Accreditation of Teacher Education (NCATE) has adopted technology competencies developed by the International Society for Technology in Education (ISTE) to integrate throughout teacher preparation programs in the United States. The latest revision of the ISTE technology standards for students (NETS•S) came out in 1998, for teachers (NETS•T) in 2000, and for administrators (TSSA) in 2001. These were the results of the National Educational Technology Standards (NETS) project. Relevant ISTE/NCATE and NETS•S standards are listed at the beginning of each chapter. The complete lists of the ISTE/NCATE foundation standards, second edition (1997), the National Educational Technology Standards for Students (NETS•S), and the National Educational Technology Standards for Teachers (NETS•T) are found on this book's Companion Website.

In the twenty-first century, educational and school reform has been thrust into the public arena. Businesses have created, have funded, and are managing for-profit schools, some within the public school system. In order for schools to change, there will have to be a philosophical shift in the public's perception of education. Technology provides a turning point for that shift, because its influence pervades so much of our daily lives. Any lasting changes need to be preceded by a vision of what future learning environments will be like. The basic curriculum will change as schools focus on information and thinking skills and as the use of tools, such as computers, information storage and retrieval systems, holograms, and virtual reality simulations, becomes the norm rather than the exception. Teaching methods will change as these tools are incorporated. Instructional materials will reflect the tools being used in learning.

Rapid changes in computer technology have resulted in greatly improved and expanded applications, as well as a tremendous simplification in operation, a vastly improved user interface, and a dramatic reduction in equipment size.

Technology will provide students with access to information and the tools to produce substantial work. Computers will be linked by local and worldwide networks to teachers, parents, homes, schools, databases, electronic bulletin boards, library and information centers, and other people all over the world. The most exciting use of technology by students of the future will be the production of meaningful work. Students will write, illustrate, publish, program, and create models, movies, music, stories, poetry, art, and other products of research and learning. They will use integrated technologies involving optical disks, computers, multimedia, virtual reality, and holographic imaging. This future is now!

A new means of student assessment is the digital portfolio. It is more than simply a collection of papers and projects linked to goals and objectives. It is a well-thought-out collection of material designed to show the degree of mastery or achievement a student has attained in working toward a local or national standard. The digital portfolio is more than just a collection of student work. The student's reflection on each artifact is of utmost importance. The digital portfolio is a continually updated reflective tool that shows growth over time not only in the mastery of standards but in the ability of students to evaluate their learning.

CHAPTER EXERCISES

To complete the specified exercises on-line, go to the Chapter Exercises Module in Chapter 1 of the Companion Website.

1. Describe your personal use of any tool outside of the educational setting. Now describe how you might use the computer as a tool. Compare your two examples and demonstrate how a tool extends your human capability.
2. Why do you, as a future educator, bear a special responsibility to understand and be able to comfortably use the latest computer technology?
3. It seems that everywhere we look in education we are bombarded by a new set of standards. Why do you think that this is? Do you feel that standards are important? How do they fit into local and national priorities?
4. Review the NETS•S standards (these are for your students) in the appendix of this text. How comfortable are you knowing these and teaching them to your students? In which areas are you weak? Make a list. Review that list again at the end of the semester to see how you have progressed.
5. Review the NETS•T standards (these are for teachers) in the appendix of this text. How comfortable are you with these standards? In which areas are you weak? Make a list. Review that list again at the end of the semester to see how you have progressed.
6. Review the No Child Left Behind (NCLB) Act. How is it impacting the schools in your district? Your state's education system?
7. Research *media literacy* in the library or on the Web. List four ways that you will help the students in your future classes understand and become media literate.

8. Search the Internet to find sites related to digital or electronic portfolios. Read two current articles. Take a side, pro or con, and write a paragraph backing your position. Discuss your comments in class.
9. Design and outline a digital portfolio that you would be able to use in your job search. What particular topics would you include in this? What topics would you leave out?
10. We have had a short discussion of technology in the past, present, and future. Daydream for a while about your future classroom. How do you think that it will look? What technology would you like in it? Can you think of any technology that is not available today that you would like to have? Discuss your ideal future classroom with the class. Are there differences and similarities between your ideas and the ideas of others?

PORTFOLIO DEVELOPMENT EXERCISES

To complete this exercise on-line, go to the Portfolio Module in Chapter 1 of the Companion Website.

One of the NETS•S standards covered in this chapter was "Students use a variety of media and formats to communicate information and ideas effectively to multiple audiences" in Category 4: Technology communications tools. Begin to develop your own portfolio of lesson plans to help your students reach the NETS•S standards.

For more information on developing digital portfolios, go to the Digital Portfolio Module on the Companion Website www.prenhall.com/forcier

1. Design a lesson plan activity for elementary, middle school, or high school students encouraging them to work in teams to research one of the issues presented in this chapter (use a variety of media and formats to communicate information and ideas effectively to multiple audiences, and so on) and prepare a word-processed report. This lesson should demonstrate that your students have achieved the standard. Be sure to include a system of evaluation for your students' understanding and competence to ensure that they have met this standard.
2. Adapt the lesson plan activity you developed in exercise 1 for students to evaluate each other's work.

GLOSSARY

analog Electrical current flowing in a continuous stream. Usually depicted in a wave form with hills and valleys denoting stronger and weaker flow. Older technologies for the recording of sounds (phonographs, audiotape) and video (videotape) utilized analog technology.

binary Consisting of two parts; limited to two conditions or states of being. Computer memory is designed to store binary digits symbolized by 0s and 1s in a code. The computer circuitry is designed to manipulate information in an on/off state.

bit The single digit of a binary number, either 0 or 1; derived from the words *binary digit*.

browser A software program used to access and view sites on the World Wide Web. Common browsers are Internet Explorer and Netscape.

byte A grouping of bits (in groups of 8, 16, 32, or more); the code represents one alpha or a numeric character of data.

chip A small piece of silicon housing an integrated circuit that may contain tens of thousands of miniaturized transistors and other electronic components.

computer operator A technician trained in the operation of a large computer system who is interposed between the user and the computer.

data Vast amounts of stimuli that can be perceived in any given environment. We are constantly inundated with data in our daily lives, most of which we tend to ignore until we perceive a need.

digital Electrical current flowing in very discrete units. Usually depicted as individual packets, 0s and 1s or on/off units. Computers process only with digital data.

digital portfolio A portfolio in which all of the components have been changed into a digital format that enables all parts to be accessed using a computer. Digital portfolios may be stored on computer disks and/or CD-ROMs.

educational media Devices such as overhead projectors, video recorders, digital cameras, scanners, and computers as well as the related software. At one time called *audiovisual aids*.

electronic portfolio A portfolio in which all of the components have been changed into an electronic format. Items may be in a digital (scanned images, word-processed documents, etc.) and/or analog (videotape, audiotape) format.

end user The individual who ultimately benefits from the computer application.

graphic user interface (GUI) The on-screen use of pictorial representations (icons) of objects. The user can move a screen pointer onto an icon and click a mouse button to issue a command to the computer.

handheld computer A lightweight, battery-operated computer considerably smaller than a laptop. Many use the Palm™ operating system.

information Data selected and organized to produce meaning.

information technology The process of creating, storing, organizing, accessing, and displaying information.

integrated circuit An electronic component made up of circuit elements constructed on a single piece of silicon.

Internet A worldwide network of interconnected networks all based on the TCP/IP protocol.

laptop A portable, lightweight, battery-operated computer with an LCD screen that usually folds down onto the keyboard for ease of carrying.

media literacy The ability of an individual to encode information into and decode information stored in a form of media.

personal digital assistant (PDA) A very small, battery-operated computer, usually with limited but very specific built-in functions.

transistor A small electronic device that controls current flow and does not require a vacuum to operate.

vacuum tube A sealed electronic device designed to regulate current flow.

web-enhanced cell phones A cellular telephone able to send and receive data to and from the World Wide Web.

World Wide Web (WWW) An Internet navigation system that allows users, through a graphic browser interface, to access information organized on hypertext-linked screens called pages.

REFERENCES & SUGGESTED READINGS

Associated Press. (2002, October 12). School eliminates textbooks. *The (Mankato Minnesota) Free Press, 119*(162), 7F.

Barrett, H. C. (2000, April). Create your own electronic portfolio using off-the-shelf software to showcase your own or student work. *Leading & Learning with Technology, 27*(7), 14–21.

Collins, A. (1991, September). The role of computer technology. *Phi Delta Kappan,* 28–36.

Earle, R. (2000, April). AECT and NCATE: A partnership for quality teaching through accreditation. *TechTrends, 44*(3), 53–57.

Greene, S. (1988, September 26). Redwoods and hummingbirds. *Apple Viewpoints, 2,* 1–3.

Hill, J. (2002, October). Teaching with technology. *Presentations, 16*(10).

International Society for Technology in Education. (2000a). *National educational technology standards for students: Connecting curriculum and technology.* Eugene, OR: International Society for Technology in Education.

International Society for Technology in Education. (2000b). *National educational technology standards for teachers.* Eugene, OR: International Society for Technology in Education.

International Society for Technology in Education. (2002). *Technology standards for school administrators.* Retrieved on-line January 12, 2003 from *http://cnets.iste.org/tssa/.*

International Society for Technology in Education Accreditation Committee. (1998). *Curriculum guidelines for accreditation of educational computing and technology programs.* Eugene, OR: International Society for Technology in Education.

McLuhan, M. (1967). *The medium is the message.* New York: Bantam Books.

Milken Exchange on Educational Technology. (1999). *Will new teachers be prepared to teach in a digital age? A national survey on information technology in teacher education.* Santa Monica, CA: Milken Exchange on Education Technology.

National Commission on Excellence in Education. (1983). *A nation at risk: The imperative for educational reform.* Washington, DC: U.S. Department of Education.

National Council for the Accreditation of Teacher Education. (2002). *Professional standards for the accreditation of schools, colleges, and departments of education—2002 edition.* Washington, DC: National Council for the Accreditation of Teacher Education.

No Child Left Behind (NCLB). (2002). *The facts about . . . 21st-century technology.* Retrieved January 11, 2003 from the World Wide Web: *http://www.nclb.gov/start/facts/21centtech.html.*

Roblyer, M. D. (1992). Computers in education. In G. Bitner (Ed.), *Macmillan encyclopedia of computers.* New York: Macmillan.

Roblyer, M. D., Edwards, J., & Havriluk, M. A. (1997). *Integrating educational technology into teaching.* Upper Saddle River, NJ: Merrill/Prentice Hall.

T&L Editors (2002, September). Trend watch. *Technology and Learning, 23*(2), 8.

Tanner, R. (2000, January). Piloting portfolios: Using portfolios in pre-service teacher education. *ELT Journal, 54*(1), 20–30.

Wiebe, J. H., Taylor, H. G., & Thomas, L. G. (2000, Spring). The National Educational Technology Standards for PK–12 Students. Implications for teacher education. *Journal of Computing in Teaching Education, 16*(3), 12–17.

CHAPTER 2

Legal and Ethical Issues

1. How can the computer be modified to accommodate students with special needs?

2. What are some of the laws we have to understand in order to help diverse learners in a fair and equitable manner?

3. Do those who have home access to a computer have an unfair advantage over those who do not?

4. Do students who attend schools in affluent neighborhoods have an unfair advantage over those who do not?

5. How should we as teachers strive to promote gender equity in our classrooms? What actions must we take to affirm this goal?

6. How do the copyright laws positively affect both the copyright holder and the user of the copyrighted material?

7. How can teachers and schools limit student exposure to inappropriate sites found on the Internet?

A list of the ISTE/NCATE standards addressed in this chapter is available in the Standards Module on the Companion Website www.prenhall.com/forcier

In Chapter 2 we increase the students' understanding of NETS•S *Category 1: Basic operations and concepts* by discussing some technological adaptations to help students with disabilities utilize the computer in a meaningful way. NETS•S *Category 2: Social, ethical, and human issues* is also covered. Social contexts for computers in the classroom, including students with special needs, computer access and equity, and gender equity, we cover in detail. We also discuss copyright and intellectual property involving computers, and computer-accessed information. The discussion of students with special needs will also help understand the role that technology tools play to enhance learning and increase productivity that would fall under NETS•S standards in *Category 3: Technology productivity tools, Category 4: Technology communications tools, Category 5: Technology research tools,* and *Category 6: Technology problem-solving and decision-making tools.* This is an important chapter. It lays the groundwork for your understanding of the role of computer technology in a diverse society and sets the stage for our further discussions of the computer as an educational tool and your responsibilities concerning ethical technology use. It also raises human issues related to the fair and equitable use of this technology.

In this chapter we discuss many of the social issues pertinent to the use of computers in the classroom. Topics covered include computers as helpers for students with special needs (including disabilities, limited English proficiencies, and the talented and gifted), computer access and equity, and a discussion on gender equity.

Copyright and intellectual property along with the safe use and controlling access to the partnering for schools are discussed. This chapter lays the groundwork for ethical technology use and raises human issues related to the fair and equitable use of technology.

NETS•S Standards Addressed in This Chapter

1. Basic operations and concepts
    *   Students demonstrate a sound understanding of the nature and operation of technological systems.

2. Social, ethical, and human issues
    *   Students understand the ethical, cultural, and societal issues related to technology.
    *   Students practice responsible use of technology systems, information, and software.
    *   Students develop positive attitudes toward technology uses that support lifelong learning, collaboration, personal pursuits, and productivity.

3. Technology productivity tools
    *   Students use technology tools to enhance learning, increase productivity, and promote creativity.

4. Technology communications tools
    *   Students use a variety of media and formats to communicate information and ideas effectively to multiple audiences.

5. Technology research tools
    *   Students evaluate and select new information resources and technological innovations based on the appropriateness for specific tasks.

6. Technology problem-solving and decision-making tools
    *   Students employ technology in the development of strategies for solving problems in the real world.

SOCIAL CONTEXTS FOR COMPUTERS IN THE CLASSROOM

If you refer back to Figure 1–1, you'll realize that not only are the *what, where,* and *how* of computer usage changing but also the *who.* As the technology for computers changes, so do the people who use computers and the contexts in which they use them. No longer are building-size computers used to crunch numbers for an elite coterie of scientists and mathematicians. Now more than ever, computers are mobile, and information is accessible to many people. Adults and students in a wide range of disciplines and with vastly different levels of expertise use computers for thousands of professional, educational, and recreational applications.

Today's computer-savvy and Game-Boy-habituated learners have vastly different expectations for their educational experiences than learners of the not-too-distant past. The technoliterate MTV generation is less inclined to sit still and listen to a slow-paced lecture when stimulating, interactive educational and recreational experiences offer other multisensory options. Today's students have a high comfort level with things electronic, digital, and wired. Their level of visual literacy—a result of living in a visually rich and exciting environment—is a distinct factor in how today's students acquire and process information.

Because of their versatility and capability for individualization, computers—when they are accessible—can help teachers challenge and educate all students, including those with special needs. Let's take a look at the diversity of learners normally encountered in a typical teaching career and discuss some of the challenges presented.

Students with Special Needs

Students with special needs have often been called "at risk," because many are in danger of dropping out of school. Factors that contribute to this potential risk include "low teacher expectations, lack of motivation, academic difficulty, and lack of meaningful experiences" (Poirot & Canales, 1993–1994, p. 25). Students who are thought of as learning disabled, culturally and linguistically different, or talented and gifted are considered potentially at risk.

As the restructuring of U.S. education progresses, many paradigm shifts are occurring. One such shift is that schools are moving from students with special needs being separated from their regular classmates for instruction to educational programs and practices that have as their aim full inclusion from the child's perspective, that is, where a teacher adapts the learning environment to meet the diverse needs and backgrounds of the children being taught. Many educational theorists also seem to feel that schools will move from being organized on a grade-by-grade and course-by-course basis to being organized to accommodate developmental levels of learners. The computer has a significant role to play in both of these changes.

Students with Disabilities. The Individuals with Disabilities Education Act (IDEA) requires that any student eligible under the law for special education receive specially designed instruction. This includes adapting of content, methodology, or delivery of instruction (Special Education Regulation, 2001). In 2001, 95 percent of schools reported that they had students with learning disabilities, 67 percent had students with physical disabilities, 54 percent with hearing disabilities, and 46 percent with visual disabilities. Computers and technology help to meet the needs of these students. Many times hardware or software modifications will be needed so they may be used by a person with a disability. Currently, more than 50 million Americans have some type of disability requiring certain adaptations to hardware or software just to allow them to use computer technology (Kamp, 1999).

Assistive or adaptive technology devices are defined in The Technology-Related Assistance for Individuals with Disabilities Act as "any item, piece of equipment, or product system, whether acquired commercially or off the shelf, modified or customized, that increases, maintains, or improves functional capabilities of individuals with disabilities" (United States Congress, 1994). This technology includes special keyboards and keyboard software, touch-free switches, touch screens, scanners, monitors and printers, voice recognition and speech synthesizers, and refreshable Braille displays for the blind. Structuring a suitable learning environment for a physically challenged student requires providing the appropriate learning tools to achieve sensory and communication compensation. Research indicates that technology "can be adapted for use by disabled students and can result in higher achievement and improved self-image" (Kober, 1991, p. 17). Assistive devices of all kinds that provide visual, aural, or tactile support greatly extend the capabilities of impaired students to use the computer effectively. The computer-based Kurzweil Reading Machine scans printed documents and converts text into electronic speech. Speech synthesizers, speech recognition devices, image magnifiers, specially designed keyboards with exchangeable overlays, and a variety of switches have made the computer a tool useful to the physically impaired.

Though a good deal of attention has been paid to hardware for special education, software also plays a key role in making the computer accessible. The following list, adapted from Karen Armstrong (1995), presents software features that can be helpful to users with disabilities.

For discussion of speech recognition software, see Descy, 2000.

- *Easy-to-read screens:* Simple, legible text and menu items are represented in graphics and text.
- *Consistency:* Consistent placement of menus and objects on the screen make programs more intuitive and predictable.
- *Logical labels:* Easily understandable names in lists and menus give a reasonable sense of what will happen when they are selected.
- *Graphics:* Graphics encourage interaction and support nonreaders and beginning readers.
- *Support for inclusion:* Software that appeals to all users promotes inclusion.
- *Documentation:* Instructions are available in large print, Braille, electronic text, or recorded form.
- *Audio/visual cues:* Prompts and feedback provide important support and keep users on track.
- *Built-in access:* Alternative access methods allow users to select appropriate input devices, such as a joystick or touch screen.

A student with a learning disability often harbors feelings of inadequacy. As computers have become increasingly user friendly, they offer that student a chance to be in control and to excel. One day, while visiting a local high school, one of the authors observed a remarkable sight—"exceptional children," working as computer lab assistants, helping the "normal" students as they encountered difficulties. Those lab assistants exhibited a very positive self-concept.

Computers are patient tutors and provide simulated environments in which students with mild physical disabilities and students with learning disabilities can work. Much more information concerning the role of technology and students with disabilities can be found in *Reaching for the Sky: Policy to Support the Achievement of Students with Disabilities* (National Association of State Boards of Education, 1999).

Individual Education Plan (IEP). The Americans with Disabilities Act and Public Law 94–142 requires that each school must prepare an individual education plan (IEP) for each special needs student. Preparing this without the use of computer technology can be a time-consuming and arduous task. There are several software packages available designed to help educators with IEP preparation. *IEP Power*™ and *IEP Writer Supreme*™ are two very popular examples. *IEP Power* is a special education package that includes *Power Planner*™, a program that allows individual teachers to keep track of their daily, weekly, monthly, and yearly activities along with space for their daily lesson plans. Integrated into *IEP Power* is a second program called *IEP Maker*™. The *IEP Power* package contains all of the necessary sections needed to develop an IEP based on national guidelines right down to data collection, evaluation procedures, and transition services. It also includes space for the recording of all dates, benchmarks, lesson plans, and other information for a complete and permanent electronic record of the student's IEP.

Students with Limited English Proficiency.

The computer is a valuable tool in teaching written and spoken communication to students who are from different cultural and linguistic backgrounds than Anglo Americans. The computer's engaging visual feedback can be especially appealing to students with limited English proficiency. Graphics software allows the students to express themselves in ways reflective of their own cultures. The right software transforms the computer into a patient tutor that allows students to make mistakes and to proceed as slowly as necessary. Other software creates a microworld in which a student responds and practices newly acquired language skills. A word processor using a standard typeface or a special typeface, such as Kanji, might allow the students to express themselves in their native language and to teach their classmates a few words and expressions in that language.

Some tutorial, drill and practice, and simulation software is becoming available in non-English-language versions. The most commonly available languages are Spanish, French, and German. Some software allows users to toggle between English and a second language. Many interactive storybooks distributed on CD-ROM allow the user to select the language (English, Spanish, French, or Japanese, for example) in which they would like to read and hear the story. Spell checkers, dictionaries, and thesauruses are commonly available in languages other than English for a number of word processors.

Cooperative learning strategies appear to work well with children who are culturally or linguistically different by integrating them into small groups and then facilitating their integration into the class as a whole. The computer is a tool that lends itself well to a number of cooperative learning strategies.

Students on the Hoopa Indian Reservation spent a year constructing, in their native language , a dictionary of the plants and animals indigenous to their area (Berney & Keyes, 1990). The project proved to be a challenge for them, because their native language is an oral, not a written, language. The computer, with its graphics capability, afforded them a concrete experience.

INTO THE CLASSROOM:
ESL/Home Connection

I teach Beginning ESL (English as a Second Language) to sixth, seventh and eighth grade students in a suburban middle school near Phoenix. Most of the students are recent immigrants from Mexico while some of them are from Asia or Europe. They come with a wide variety of academic experiences but typically they have very limited English skills, some exposure to school, and little or no computer experience. Even the basic mouse movements are awkward for them at first! However, all of them are eager to learn about the computer and anxious to use it.

Due to their limited exposure and need for intensive English instruction, students primarily use the computer for word processing. I have four computers in my room available to students and usually between 15 and 20 students. Giving everyone a chance to finish their work can become a logistics problem especially when you consider that most of the students have never touched a keyboard and use only one or two fingers to type. Also, most of them do not have even basic knowledge of the computer and no understanding of computer terms in either English or their native tongue!

Due to these limitations, I use the writing process in my classroom with only their final copy done on the computer. This serves as a great incentive for them to complete their rough drafts, editing and revising so they can use the computers. They particularly love changing the style, size, and fonts in the text. They also like having a printed copy to take home to their parents.

I have developed a personal narrative unit to strengthen English literacy skills, promote computer skills, and help students make the adjustment to a new culture. In this unit, each student uses the computer to produce a book about themselves. We are using the Easy book program from Sunburst which is a simple book-making program. They have a great time making the pictures on the computer for their books. I also purchased disposable cameras and a scanner with funds from a Chase Active Learning Grant. Students take pictures of their families and friends, and scan pictures from their native countries to illustrate their stories. These books become a link between the school and the home and also a way to introduce the practical uses of technology into their homes. Finally, the goal of ESL is for the students to learn English as soon as possible, to integrate them into the American educational system and to prepare them to be successful in society. Properly utilized computer technology in the ESL curriculum contributes to the accomplishment of all these goals.

Next year, I plan to create an after school computer tutorial "club" to train a group of students who can then help the other students master the computer. This idea came about after trying to manage a class of 20, with five on the computer and everybody needing help at the same time. I also plan to make better use of our computer lab and keyboarding programs to build up their typing skills.

Suzanne Sutcliffe
English as a Second Language Teacher
Connolly Middle School
Tempe, Arizona

Students Who Are Talented and Gifted. It is important to acknowledge that even children who are recognized as talented and gifted may be at risk. Boredom, slow pace of instruction, lack of challenge, and lack of recognition of a unique learning style all may contribute to the talented and gifted children being at risk for dropping out of school or of not achieving their full potential. Enter the computer: a tool with which to experiment and test hypotheses, a tool with which to analyze information and draw conclusions, a tool with which to express oneself by drawing as well as by writing, a tool with which to explore a wide, wide world!

The computer has many times been called the ultimate individualized instruction tool. Children who are disabled and gifted represent the opposite ends of an ability continuum. A case can be built supporting computer use as a means of reaching individual students at either end of the scale. Both types of students will derive satisfaction from constructing a worthwhile product as evidence of their creativity and knowledge.

Most gifted students are inquisitive and academically uninhibited. When introduced to computer programming, they often develop a high degree of problem-solving skills and abilities. These skills stand them in good stead in other disciplines. Many talented and gifted children have difficult social adjustments to make because of their superior intellectual abilities. They are sometimes perceived by other students as uninteresting, overly academic, and having few social skills. They sometimes perceive other students as uninteresting, unchallenging, and flighty. Once again, the computer, used wisely as part of a cooperative learning strategy, can provide a positive social experience and help in the development of interpersonal skills. To build interpersonal skills, for example, these students might experiment with telecommunications software, programs that contain interactions with characters in simulations and adventures, programs about social issues, group participation and decision-making programs, and games that involve two or more players.

Computer Access and Equity

What if you gave your students an essay to write and some wrote in pencil, while others used a word processor complete with spell checker, full dictionary, thesaurus, and grammar checker? You would, of course, expect the products to be different regardless of the individual student's skills and aptitudes. Why? Because of the tools used. The essays prepared in pencil would probably have some erasures. The essays prepared on the computer, with full control of the elements of the font, may present the best visual appearance. Not only will they appear the best but they should also be free of typing and spelling errors. They also will probably make the best use of words. Why couldn't the students writing with pencils use a dictionary and thesaurus? They could, of course. Doing so, however, would add a considerable amount of time and effort beyond that spent by the students who used the computers. The conclusion here is that the computer, with its support for easy editing, revision, and text presentation, is a significant tool in the writing process. The student writing an essay on a computer is at a distinct advantage. If you consider all of the various types of computer software through which the computer can extend the user's capability, you see that the use of this tool has a significant impact. Equal access to that tool is then a serious concern. We currently have a class of "haves" and a class of "have-nots," those with access to computers and those without.

There are schools in affluent neighborhoods or with staff possessing grant-writing expertise that are well equipped with computers. They have a reasonably high ratio of computers to students. The computers are located in individual classrooms, in a library media center, and in open computer labs available before, during, and after school hours. Students can search for information, practice skills, learn concepts, and create their own products.

However, because of a scarcity of resources, apathy toward technology, or lack of leadership, other schools have an inadequate number of computers and a poor selection of software. Students at these schools are deprived of the richness of the resources found elsewhere. Although some affluent schools also have lackluster computer-based learning programs, students from these schools usually enjoy supportive, well-educated families that supplement school-based training with home computers. Federal surveys suggest that whites are about three times as likely to have computers at home as are African Americans or Hispanics; affluent students are nearly four times as likely as poor students.

According to *U.S. News and World Report* ("Digital Divide Hooey," 2000), the 1999 Commerce Department survey, *Falling Through the Net,* found that among American families earning between $15,000 and $35,000, 33 percent of whites owned computers but only 19 percent of African Americans did. In 2000, 45 percent of whites were on-line compared to 35 percent of African Americans. However, the percentage of African Americans increased almost 50 percent from the prior year. African American families increased spending on personal computers at a rate 14 times faster than white families. In reviewing an October 2000 Pew study, *USA Today* ("Blacks Post Net Gains," 2000) states that "the Internet's racial divide is closing" (p. 10).

One of the most common reasons given for purchasing a home computer is to assist in the education of children. A recent contact with a leading educational software publisher revealed that the volume of its sales to the home market was significantly greater than that to schools. Unfortunately, some home computers turn into simple game machines, with very little software to help children learn. Students with access to a home computer having a word processor and other productivity software constitute an elite group, one with a distinct advantage that more than two-thirds of the student population does not enjoy. This variability of access should influence a teacher's expectation when it comes to the quality of product prepared by the students.

Differences in achievement for students with and without access to home computers exist. Allen and Mountain (1992) reported that, in their study of inner-city, African American children with access to computers and an on-line service, one of the primary factors in increased test scores appeared to be whether the children perceived themselves as "haves" or "have-nots." A study by Nichols (1992) suggested that higher achievement scores for students with access to home computers might be the result of those children having an increased desire to succeed.

Regardless of the reason—higher self-esteem, higher motivation, or simply more powerful tools with which to work—students with computers tend to achieve higher outcomes.

As stated above, computers and technology help to meet the needs of students with disabilities. Unfortunately, special hardware (for example, screen readers, closed-caption television, and special keyboards) for students with disabilities were found in only 47 percent of schools with high minority enrollment as opposed to 61 percent in schools with low enrollment (National Center for Educational Statistics, 2002a).

Fortunately, a survey by the National Center for Educational Statistics (2002c) found that in the fall of 2001, 99 percent of public schools in the United States had Internet access. Having Internet access in schools is not enough though. Students have to have access. In 2001, schools with the highest poverty and minority enrollment had the lowest percent of instructional rooms (classrooms, library/media centers, computer and other labs, and other rooms used for instructional purposes) connected to the Internet (79 percent and 81 percent, respectively), whereas schools with the lowest levels of poverty and minority enrollment had the highest percent of instructional rooms connected (90 percent in each case) (National Center for Educational Statistics, 2002c). If we are going to have all of our citizens thrive in this technological society, we must increase access to computers and technology in schools with high poverty and minority enrollments. Increased access should help drive down the gap between "haves" and "have-nots."

How can access be improved? Teachers in schools with inadequate computer resources should demand access to such an important educational tool. They should make the administration, the school board, and community groups aware of the need. Don't overlook grants and private funding. Many national retail chains (Target, Kmart, Wal-Mart, for example) and local industries and organizations are all places to look for help. Teachers in schools with reasonable computer resources should work toward making the computers available, with an acceptable measure of security and supervision, outside of normal school hours to students, parents, and community groups.

The many uses of the computer empower students to express themselves and use new tools to achieve their goals.

Gender Equity

Gender equity should be a continuing cause of concern to educators. Computer use suffers from an inherited gender bias that holds that math and science are not "feminine things." Although there are efforts to remedy this bias and progress is being made, it is difficult to overcome the fallacy that women cannot excel in math and science. This bias has its roots in the seventeenth century, when inventions in science and technology were made not by aristocrats but in the monastic environment of the universities, which were under the control of the male-dominated political and religious forces of the time. The elite created an aura of a quasi-priesthood of science and technology and erected barriers to keep others, primarily women, out (Noble, 1992). From that point until the mid-twentieth century, women were basically told that math and science were not for them.

It is interesting to note here that the person generally recognized as the first computer programmer was a woman, Ada Lovelace (Augusta Ada Byron, Countess of Lovelace), daughter of Lord Byron!

Research shows the equal participation of boys and girls in computer literacy and application activities in the elementary and middle-level grades. Girls and boys appear to be equally enthusiastic when it comes to using the computer. As students move into high school, gender differences and, in many cases, unfair stereotypes exert themselves. Girls continue to refine word processing skills and other business (read "clerical") skills, whereas boys overwhelmingly populate the computer science classes. High school girls tend to develop negative attitudes regarding computers (Kirk, 1992). Luckily, this is changing because of the widespread use of the Internet. According to a Pew report, gender parity was reached in Internet usage in 1999 (Pew Research Center, 2000). Perhaps this will increase the comfort level in females and carry over to other computer applications as well.

Teachers sometimes demonstrate gender bias by giving the more difficult computer class assignments to the boys, who, therefore, receive more personal attention and time from the teacher. According to Koch (1994), teachers ask boys technical questions and are more likely to answer a boy's questions, but they take over and complete a task for a girl. This kind of teacher behavior fosters learned helplessness rather than self-sufficiency in girls.

In a typical school computer lab, computers are available on a first-come, first-served basis. With more students than computers, the more aggressive students usually get them. Many boys spend countless hours playing video games as preadolescents and gravitate toward the use of computers.

Software itself can contribute to gender inequity. For example, research shows that clip art libraries severely underrepresent women and ethnic minorities, and they reinforce gender stereotypes about sex roles and work (Dyrud, 1996). Additionally, recreational software tends to be loud, flashy, violent, and based on competitive win/lose situations. Even educational software has at times exhibited some of these characteristics. Females tend not to be drawn to this type of software and, therefore, spend less time at the computer as an enjoyable diversion.

Parental encouragement is another factor influencing gender bias. Parents often envision their sons in scientific or technical careers and encourage them to take computer science classes and attend computer camps. Parents are more likely to buy computers for use by their sons than by their daughters. Boys get the message that spending time at a computer is a worthwhile activity.

How should we as teachers strive to promote gender equity in our classrooms? What actions must we take to affirm this goal? We should go out of our way to praise girls' accomplishments on the computer. We must be sure to include them in any special computer-based projects. We can encourage equal access to computers by instituting sign-ups, rotation schedules, and other democratic systems. We should include girls' names in computer examples we give. We must buy and use gender-equitable software and avoid programs that aren't. We should encourage girls to consider careers involving computer use beyond standard clerical applications. We must provide more female role models by inviting women who are computer scientists or who make extensive use of the computer in their professions to speak to our classes. We must continually examine our own behavior and guard against any subtle, even unintentional, actions we might take that would in any way diminish girls' interest or discourage them from interacting with the computer in a meaningful way. More than 200,000 technology-related jobs go unfilled in the United States every year. We cannot afford to let anyone, black or red or brown or white, female or male, rich or poor, be shut out from reaching their full potential because of our unintentional actions.

INTO THE CLASSROOM:
Geek Is Chic—Integrating Technology into the Lives of Girls

Girls and Technology—can the two be successfully integrated? There is a significant body of research that validates what girls in coeducational schools experience on a daily basis, that with regard to technology, girls lag behind boys in use, understanding, and interest on many levels. A growing number of studies indicate that girls are not involved in technology at the level needed to advance the critical thinking skills that are highly valued in the areas of math, science, and technology careers. Classroom teachers have the power to reverse this trend, if they take into consideration the research recommendations that girls prefer collaborative, rather than isolated, use of technology in education.

How can you, as a future teacher, encourage and support girls in the use of technology within everyday learning experiences? The key is to group girls together, in collaborative, project-based exercises that utilize whatever technology resources are available at your school. We have found that with the wealth of the many project-based resources available on the Internet, that it is not necessary to create innovative projects from scratch. Begin by letting the girls discuss their perceptions of technology. Partner your girls with girls from another school. Let the girls design and control their own projects. Their enthusiasm and inspiration, under your leadership as their teacher, will provide the foundation they need to find that 'Geek is Chic!'

Since we began our 'Geek is Chic' project, our girls have assumed responsibility for their own learning. They have learned to approach their work as a design team in much the same way a team in the corporate world works—they brainstorm, share, discuss, implement, evaluate, and refine, all traits that are key to successful careers in the math, sciences, and technology fields. As a result of this collaboration, they are now much more confident users of technology. Feeling empowered through a sense of ownership about the technology has been a major key to the success of our project.

One of the key recommendations from an American Association of University Women study is that *computation should be integrated across the curriculum, into such subject areas as art, music and literature as well as engineering and science . . . subjects that already interest girls, as well promoting critical thinking and lifelong learning.* This recommendation also gives both educators and girls the opportunity to use the technology as designers, rather than being mere consumers. The report also recommends the *creation and support of computing clubs and summer school classes for girls, mentoring programs, science fairs and programs that encourage girls to see themselves as capable of careers in technology.*

Even though cultural biases and inequities cannot be changed overnight, you, as a classroom teacher, can affect positive change, one girl at a time. Even if the girls decide that a career involving technology is not for them, you will at least have given them the experience they need to make an informed decision. Our model for changing girls' perceptions of, and involvement with, technology might be just what you need to encourage your girls to realize that 'Geek is Chic!'

Robyn Treyvaud (Australia)
Curriculum & PYP Coordinator
Junior School, Wesley College
Prahran, Melbourne, Victoria

Lori Rounds (USA)
Director of Technology
The Bullis School
Bethesda, Maryland

OBLIGATIONS AND EXPECTATIONS IN A COMPUTER LITERATE SOCIETY

Computers have permeated every aspect of our society as we start the twenty-first century. As with all new technologies, we have responsibilities when it comes to using them. Computer technology allows us to do things that we could not easily do before. It is now easy to record some special music onto our computer and send it to our friends. We can copy almost anything on the Internet or in our pocket, and even copy our favorite movie all with just the touch of a few keys and a few mouse clicks. Computer technology is so different from the older print and recording forms. It allows so much to be done by so many that many times regulations and laws can't seem to keep up. Computer technology and the Internet have brought about some of the biggest changes in our ideas about copyright and intellectual property. They have also vastly changed our expectations regarding computer literacy.

Copyright and Intellectual Property

Copyright is a way of protecting intellectual property. **Intellectual property** is something conceived in the mind of an individual and made available to other individuals. This textbook is intellectual property and so is the syllabus for the course you are taking as well as the computer software you may use. The ownership of intellectual property is defined and protected by copyright law. The first copyright law was passed in the U.S. Congress in 1790.

Quite simply, **copyright** is designed to protect the financial interests of the creators, producers, and distributors of original works of art and information. Without copyright laws there would be little incentive to create or distribute information and works of art. This may sound like a one-sided situation. But it is not if we stop to think about it. Would Microsoft have developed the Windows operating system or Microsoft Office®, or would Apple have developed AppleWorks® (or would someone have written your favorite book, movie, song, music video, or developed your favorite video game) if there were no financial incentives? Companies and individuals that develop intellectual property win by having their efforts rewarded financially, and we win by having vast amounts of top-notch products available for our use. Copyright is a win/win situation! Upholding copyright laws enriches everyone involved! We must strive to set a good example in all that we do. It is important that we uphold copyright laws in our professional and private lives and that we instill this respect and appreciation for intellectual property and copyright in our students.

Remember, we as teachers and parents are role models. Saying one thing and doing another will just reinforce the benefits of doing another to our students and our own children. It is not only illegal but it is also unethical to use or distribute software in ways other than outlined in copyright law. Let's hope that our students will learn as much about upholding copyright law by observing what we do in our classrooms as by listening to what we say. Copyright laws *and their interpretations* are always changing. As we write this, the Supreme Court is about to rule on the legality of changes in the copyright law Congress passed in 1999. Part of your professional responsibility is to keep up with the laws that pertain to teaching, learning, and your professional area of expertise. Congress has amended the copyright laws with regard to the fair use of copyrighted computer software. We may do the following:

- Install one copy of the software onto our computer hard drive.
- Adapt software to another language as long as it is not available in that language.
- Add features to the software that will help us to better use it.
- Make one archival or backup copy of the software. If the software is copy-protected, we may use utility software to unlock and copy it.

We may not do the following without the permission of the copyright owner:

- Put single-user software on a network.
- Make multiple copies of software for ourselves.
- Make multiple copies of software to give away, loan, lease, sell, or transmit to others.
- Sell our adaptation of the software.

In addition to copyrighted software, you will probably come into contact with two other types of software. **Freeware** is software that may be copied and distributed free of charge. The author still holds the copyright but has simply given everyone permission to copy and use it. The author of **shareware** has given permission for anyone to try it out and to distribute it. The program's opening screen often lists the conditions for its use usually including a payment made to the author if you continue to use the software. Shareware is usually priced between $10 and $50. There are many sites on the Internet that contain huge archives of freeware and shareware for you to download, install, and enjoy. Check these sites often and take advantage of free e-mail newsletters from many of them. Cnet.com and zdnet.com are two sites that have links to huge freeware and shareware collections and also have free newsletters containing information on new, favorite, and helpful programs. You may be able to find a program that would be a great help to you or your students at a fraction of the cost of the commercial software equivalent (or—it may even be free).

Plagiarism or the representation of someone else's work as one's own has been made simple and quicker with the help of technology. It is now much easier to copy words, paragraphs, and even complete documents. We all know how easy it is to cut and paste. With the help of the Internet, it is now possible to cut and paste our way around the world. How do we, as teachers, combat this? It is not easy. There are sites on the Internet that help you track down articles from phrases or paragraphs but sometimes it may be as simple to just type a phrase into several search engines and take a fast look at the hits. Unfortunately, there is no easy and sure answer.

Protecting Your Students, Your School, and Yourself; Acceptable Use Policies. Teachers should educate their students in appropriate use of their school's network and the Internet. They should also monitor student usage because some parts of the Internet contain material not suitable for minors. Many school districts have developed **acceptable use policies (AUPs)** outlining proper Internet use and student responsibilities and require permission forms signed by both parent and student before allowing student access to the Internet. *All* schools using the Internet should have acceptable use policies just as they should have selection policies for library materials. An acceptable use policy for an instructional setting might be thought of as similar to the laboratory safety contract that a science teacher might require. It would include a statement of the responsible behaviors expected of students, with particular attention to potentially unsafe or inappropriate actions, and a set of measured consequences. Acceptable use forms should be signed by the instructor, student, and parent or guardian before the student is allowed on-line. Parental notification demonstrates that the parents are aware of the instructor's intent and reasonable supervision in order to ensure the educationally productive use of classroom resources.

 To view a sample AUP go to the Supplemental Information Module in Chapter 2 of the Companion Website at http://www.prenhall.com/forcier

Controlling Access to the Internet. It is not very difficult to find or just stumble upon inappropriate materials on the Internet. Under the Children's Internet Protection Act (CIPA) (Public Law 106–554), the validity of which is currently being tested in the courts, no school may receive the E-rate discount to help them pay for Internet access unless the school certifies that it is enforcing a policy of Internet use that includes the use of some sort of blocking or filtering technology (Universal Service Administrative Company, 2002). In 2001, 96 percent of schools with Internet access had in place various procedures and/or technologies to control student access to inappropriate material. Of this number, 98 percent of schools used these procedures or technologies on all Internet-connected computers used by students. These procedures and technologies include monitoring of student use by teachers or staff members (91 percent), blocking or filtering software (87 percent), written contract co-signed by parent (80 percent), written contract signed by student (75 percent), using computer monitoring software (46 percent), honor codes (44 percent), and using only private school intranets (26 percent) (National Center for Educational Statistics, 2002b).

One of the concerns frequently expressed by many teachers, school administrators, school boards, and parents is that of the potential for students to access

Internet materials that are inappropriate for minors. These materials might be either intentionally or inadvertently located via one of the search engines and may include expressions or descriptions of violence, ethnic hatred, or pornography. As stated previously, it is advisable for the classroom teacher, school building, and school district to have workable acceptable use policies agreed to in writing prior to student use of the Internet. However, even with these in place, many educators are looking to a **web filter,** or blocking program (for example, *Net Nanny*™ or *Cyber Patrol*™), to screen out undesirable content. Filter programs are somewhat effective in looking for key descriptive terms that may reside at Internet locations and thus block student access. However, they may also block an educationally valid search term that possesses meanings other than those appropriate for students of a specific age or ability. None of the blocking programs is perfect and all allow some "undesirable" sites to pass through unblocked. Schools may also be opening themselves to lawsuits if they rely solely on filter programs for protection and these sites pass through unblocked. Whether it is appropriate to use Internet filtering programs has created much controversy in individual classrooms right up through state legislatures. Perhaps the best policy, as with most educational functions, is to provide consistent expectations for student behavior, combined with diligent teacher supervision of student activities during the course of any Internet-based activity.

INTO THE CLASSROOM:
Rules of the Road

We require student and parental signature on the DoDEA Student Computer and Internet Access Agreement at the time a student registers. This general acceptable use agreement sets forth expectations for the student's use of computer resources at school.

We have 'rules of the road' on the information superhighway that simplify these expectations in words that are easier for students to remember. Essentially, I view computers and the Internet as instructional resources (like the reference books). Students are not to play games, 'chat,' download without permission, or subscribe to any on-line 'offers'. Students use gaggle.net for free e-mail pertaining to schoolwork, so they are not allowed to access their personal e-mail on school computers.

Audio files are distracting to other users, so we mute the sound on the computers in the library.

Students have individual accounts on our local area network (LAN); in case of violations, their privileges can be suspended. Our Intranet features a "virtual library" page from which students access selected World Wide Web subject directories and search engines as well as recommended sites pertaining to the curriculum. I keep and regularly update a copy on my personal web site so that students can access the page from home as well.

Janet Murray
Information Specialist
Yokosuka Middle School
Department of Defense Dependents Schools
Yokosuka, Japan
janetm@surfline.ne.jp

SUMMARY

Students with special needs, who are sometimes thought of as learning disabled, culturally and linguistically different, or talented and gifted, are often at risk of dropping out of school. As the restructuring of U.S. education progresses, educational programs and practices will have as their aim full inclusion from the child's perspective, and schools will be organized to accommodate the developmental levels of learners. Structuring a suitable learning environment for a physically challenged student requires providing the appropriate learning tools to achieve sensory and communication compensation. A student with a learning disability often harbors feelings of inadequacy. As computers have become increasingly user friendly, they offer that student a chance to be in control and to excel. Computers are patient tutors and provide simulated environments in which students with mild physical disabilities and learning disabilities can work.

The computer is a valuable tool in teaching written and spoken communication to students who are culturally and linguistically different. Graphics software allows the students to express themselves in ways reflective of their own culture. Other software creates a microworld in which a student responds and practices newly acquired language skills. A word processor might allow students to express themselves in their native language.

Boredom, slow pace of instruction, and lack of challenge may contribute to the talented and gifted child being at risk for dropping out of school. The computer can be used as a tool to test hypotheses, to analyze information and draw conclusions, to express oneself by drawing and writing, and to communicate with others around the world. Talented and gifted children often have difficult social adjustments to make because of their superior intellectual abilities. The computer, used wisely as part of a cooperative learning strategy, can provide a positive social experience and can help in the development of interpersonal skills.

Students using computers are at a distinct advantage because they are using a tool that can extend their capabilities. Some schools are well equipped, with a high ratio of computers to students readily available, and others are not. Whites are about three times as likely to have computers at home than African Americans and Hispanics; affluent students are nearly four times more likely than poorer students. Students with access to a home computer having a word processor and other productivity software constitute an elite group with a distinct advantage that more than two-thirds of the student population does not enjoy.

As students move into high school, boys overwhelmingly populate the computer science classes. Parents are more likely to buy computers for their sons than for their daughters and encourage boys to take computer science classes and attend computer camps. Teachers must actively seek out software without gender biases and continually guard against any subtle actions that would in any way diminish girls or discourage them from interacting with the computer in a meaningful way.

Copyright laws are designed to protect the rights and financial interests of the person or people who develop works considered to be intellectual property. Without copyright laws, many incentives would not exist and development of new and improved products and ideas would slow considerably. It is in everyone's best interest to respect the copyright laws.

CHAPTER EXERCISES

To complete the specified exercises on-line, go to the Chapter Exercises Module in Chapter 2 of the Companion Website.

1. Do an on-line bibliographic search in the library on the topic "Computer Access: In School and at Home." Select only articles written in the past four years. Using a word processor, write a report of at least two double-spaced pages on the issues. Cite references and include a bibliography.

2. Search the Internet to find information on the topic "Computers and Gender Bias: Cause and Effect." Find four Web pages on the subject posted in the past four years. Using a word processor, write a report of at least two double-spaced pages on the issues. Cite references and include a bibliography.

3. Examine vendor catalogs and locate three programs, in at least two different subject areas, that use a language in addition to English.

4. Locate available graphics software or a word processing program. Make three different 8 1/2-by-11-inch signs to be placed in the computer lab reminding students of copyright laws.

5. Locate several on-line sources of freeware and software. Can you list any that would be of use to you in your teaching?

6. As our society moves rapidly from an industrial society to an information society, what are the implications of information technology for schooling?

7. What are some of the ways that you will insure equity for your students when you prepare lessons?

8. Obtain an Acceptable Use Policy from a nearby school district or from the Web. Do you feel that it meets all of the requirements you think are important? What would you add or delete?

9. Research Internet filtering software in the library or on the Web. Write a short paper in which you discuss the pros and cons of Internet filtering. Are you in favor of it or opposed to it? Why? Discuss what you found in class.

10. Research copyright law with respect to education. List and discuss four ways that teachers might unintentionally violate the copyright law.

PORTFOLIO DEVELOPMENT EXERCISES

To complete this exercise on-line, go to the Digital Portfolio Module in Chapter 2 of the Companion Website.

One of the NETS•S standards covered in this chapter was "Students understand the ethical, cultural, and societal issues related to technology" under *Category 2: Social, ethical, and human issues.* Begin to develop your own portfolio of lesson plans that demonstrates your ability to have your students reach the NETS•S standards.

For more information on developing digital portfolios, go to the Digital Portfolio Module in the Companion Website www.prenhall.com/forcier

1. Design a lesson plan activity for elementary, middle school, or high school students encouraging them to work in teams to research one of the issues presented in this chapter (computer access and equity, gender equity, intellectual property, equity laws dealing with education, and so on) and have them prepare a presentation for the other students in their classroom. This lesson should demonstrate that your students have achieved the standard. Be sure to include a system of evaluation for your students' understanding and competence to ensure that they have met this standard.

2. Adapt the lesson plan activity you developed in exercise 1 for students to evaluate each others' work.

GLOSSARY

acceptable use policies (AUPs) Outline proper Internet use and student responsibilities and require permission forms signed by both parent and student before allowing student access to the Internet.

copyright Laws designed to protect the financial interests of the creators, producers, and distributors of original works of art and information.

freeware Software that may be copied and distributed free of charge.

intellectual property Something conceived in the mind of an individual and made available to other individuals.

shareware Software distributed free of charge with conditions that usually include a payment made to the authors if software continues to be used after a trial period.

web filter Blocking program that screens out undesirable content but may also block an educationally valid search term that possesses meanings other than those appropriate for students of a specific age or ability.

REFERENCES & SUGGESTED READINGS

Allen, A. A., & Mountain, L. (1992, November). When inner city black children go online at home. *The Computing Teacher, 20*(3), 35–37.

Armstrong, K. (1995, October). Special software for special kids. *Technology & Learning, 16*(2), 56–61.

Berney, T., & Keyes, J. (1990). *Computer writing skills for limited English proficiency students.* Brooklyn, NY: Report to the New York City Board of Education.

Blacks post net gains. (April 17, 2000). *U.S. News and World Report, 128*(15), 45.

Brown, J. M. (1997, March). Technology and ethics. *Learning & Leading with Technology, 24*(6), 38–41.

Descy, D. (2000, April). "Good morning, HAL-9000". . . "Good morning, Don". . . A primer on speech recognition software. *TechTrends, 44*(3), 4–6.

Digital divide hooey. (April 17, 2000). *U.S. News and World Report, 128*(15), 45.

Drumm, J. E. (1999, April). Teaching information skills to disadvantaged children. *Computers in Libraries, 19*(4), 48–51.

Dyrud, M. (1996, November). *An exploration of gender bias in computer clip art.* Paper presented at the Association for Business Communication Annual Conference, Chicago, IL.

Grogan, M. (1999, October). Equity/equality issues of gender, race, and class. *Educational Administration Quarterly, 35*(4), 518–536.

Hartshorn, K. (2000, November). Girls take charge of technology. *Leading and Learning with Technology, 23*(3), 18–20.

Kamp, S. (1999). How does 'fair use' apply to software being used in the schools? *Technology and Learning, 5*(1), 58.

Kirk, D. (1992, April). Gender issues in information technology as found in schools: Authentic/synthetic/fantastic. *Educational Technology, 32*(4), 28–35.

Klauk, R. R. (1999, December). *Does the use of Internet filtering software in elementary schools work as intended?* Unpublished masters alternate plan paper, Minnesota State University, Mankato.

Kober, N. (1991). *What we know about mathematics teaching and learning.* Washington, DC: Council for Educational Development and Research.

Koch, M. (1994, November). Opening up technology to both genders. *Educational Digest, 60*(3), 18–22.

National Association of State Boards. (1999). *Reaching for the sky: Policy to support the achievement of students with disabilities.*

National Center for Educational Statistics. (2002a). *Internet access in U.S. public schools and classrooms: 1994–2001 Special hardware and software for students with disabilities.* Retrieved February 15, 2003 from the World Wide Web at *http://nces.ed.gov/pubs2002/internet/6.asp.*

National Center for Educational Statistics. (2002b). *Internet access in U.S. public schools and classrooms: 1994–2001 Technologies and procedures to prevent student access to inappropriate material on the Internet.* Retrieved February 15, 2003 from the World Wide Web at *http://nces.ed.gov/pubs2002/internet/8.asp.*

National Center for Educational Statistics. (2002c). *Internet access in U.S. public schools and classrooms: 1994–2001 School access.* Retrieved February 15, 2003 from the World Wide Web at *http://nces.ed.gov/pubs2002/internet/3.asp.*

Nichols, L. M. (1992, August). Influence of student computer-ownership and in-home use on achievement in an elementary school computer programming curriculum. *Journal of Educational Computing Research, 8*(4), 407–421.

Noble, D. E. (1992). *A world without women: The Christian culture of modern science*. New York: Knopf.

Pew Research Center. (2000, May). *Tracking online life: How women use the Internet to cultivate relationships with family and friends*. Retrieved March 23, 2003 from the World Wide Web at *http://www.pewinternet.org/reports/toc.asp*.

Poirot, J. L., & Canales, J. (1993–1994, December/January). Technology and the at-risk—An overview. *The Computing Teacher, 21* (4), 25–26, 55.

Simpson, C. (1999, September–October). Managing copyright in schools. *Knowledge Quest, 28* (1), 18–22.

Special Education Regulation. (2001). Cited in *Internet access in U.S. public schools and classrooms: 1994–2001*. Retrieved March 3, 2003 on the World Wide Web at *http://nces.ed.gov/pubs2002/internet/6.asp*.

Sutherland, S. (2000, March). Accessing technology: How special education can assist. *TechTrends, 44* (2), 29–30.

Timm, J. T. (1999, Summer). Selecting computer programs and interactive multimedia for culturally diverse students: Promising practices. *Multicultural Education, 6* (4), 30–31.

United States Congress. (1994). *Technology-related assistance for individuals with disabilities act of 1988 as amended in 1994*. Retrieved February 21, 2003 from the World Wide Web at *http://www.resna.org/taproject/library/laws/techact94.htm*.

Universal Service Administrative Company. (2002). *Children's internet protection act*. Retrieved February 21, 2003 from the World Wide Web at *http://www.sl.universalservice.org/reference/CIPA.asp*.

Webb, B. J. (2000, March/April). Planning and organizing—Assistive technology resources in your school. *Teaching Exceptional Children, 32* (4), 50.

CHAPTER 3

Learning About the Computer

1. What are the primary processes involved in a computer system?

2. What typical hardware exists to facilitate entering data?

3. What is a CPU?

4. What are the different types of memory and how do they differ?

5. What typical hardware exists to facilitate extracting information?

6. How has the user interface evolved and what is its impact on you as a user?

7. What is networking's impact on schools?

This chapter covers much information that is needed to understand the computer and to help your students meet the standards found in four NETS•S categories. NETS•S *Category 1: Basic operations and concepts* is dealt with by covering basic terminology used in discussing and describing computers and computer peripherals. Basic knowledge of computer hardware is needed to become proficient in the use of computer technology. NETS•S *Category 2: Social, ethical, and human issues,* and NETS•S *Category 4: Technology communications tools* will come into play as you learn more about the parts of the computer and appreciate how it and its peripherals allow them to address issues through faster, easier, and more efficient means. NETS•S *Category 5: Technology research tools* is addressed by information found in this chapter that should help in the selection of computer resources based on their appropriateness for specific tasks. The information here is necessary to truly understand the computer, its parts, and their uses.

With new or updated computer equipment entering the marketplace constantly, a discussion of hardware can never be truly current. As this is being written, a new product is undoubtedly entering the market; however, this chapter will give you a good basic understanding of computer hardware and establish a firm foundation as you continue to learn about technology and computers during your entire teaching career.

The shift in computer paradigms identified in Chapter 1 becomes apparent as we trace the development of the technology and in particular the development of computer hardware. Now the mobile user employing a personal computer or handheld is able to interconnect with a network of other users in order to search a labyrinth of databases to access valuable information. These connections may be through wires, through glass fiber, or, more and more, through thin air. Location is no longer a limiting factor.

A list of the ISTE/NCATE standards addressed in this chapter is available in the Standards Module on the Companion Website www.prenhall.com/forcier

NETS•S Standards Addressed in This Chapter

1. Basic operations and concepts
   - Students demonstrate a sound understanding of the nature and operation of technology systems.
   - Students are proficient in the use of technology.

2. Social, ethical, and human issues
   - Students develop positive attitudes toward technology uses that support lifelong learning, collaboration, personal pursuits, and productivity.

4. Technology communications tools
   - Students use a variety of media and formats to communicate information and ideas effectively to multiple audiences.

5. Technology research tools
   - Students use technology resources for solving problems and making informed decisions.

WHAT IS A COMPUTER?

An understanding of the computer as a tool requires an awareness of its component parts and an appreciation of what each part may contribute as we attempt to use the computer to solve the problems we may encounter. A user must be able to put data into a system, manipulate those data, and retrieve information in an appropriate manner. The user does this by employing a variety of hardware, software, and firmware. Tangible objects such as a monitor, a keyboard, a mouse, a joystick, a printer, or a disk drive are examples of **hardware.** Not all tangible objects are encompassed by this term, however. For instance, floppy disks or CD-Rs, which are tangible objects, are generally termed "media" and are considered consumable supplies. Recording a computer program on a floppy or CD changes the terminology of the disk to **software.** More precisely, the actual recorded program itself on the medium is the software, but you can see that at some point it is impossible to separate the two. A third term, **firmware,** denotes software that is stored permanently in chips usually located on add-on computer cards or printer circuit boards. To unravel the confusion related to equipment specification, let's examine Figure 3–1 that illustrates the three processes of input, operation, and output involved in a computer system.

The *input* is the process of entering data into the computer system. The *operation* is the process of manipulating the data in a predetermined manner by the computer itself or, more precisely, by the **central processing unit (CPU)** using instructions defined in the program. The *output* is the process of retrieving the information once

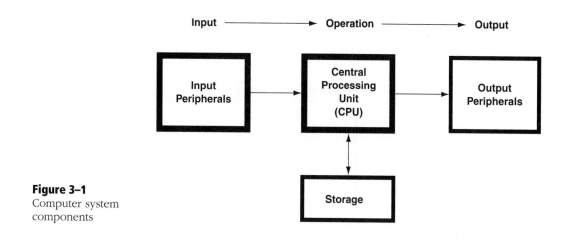

Figure 3–1
Computer system
components

the CPU has acted upon it. All hardware other than the computer itself is referred to as peripheral equipment.

Input peripherals such as a keyboard and a mouse allow the user to enter data into the computer system. **Output peripherals** such as a monitor and a printer allow the user to retrieve information from the computer system.

WHAT IS HARDWARE?

Hardware is a term commonly used to designate the equipment components of a computer system. To unravel the confusion related to equipment specification, this chapter is organized according to the three processes of input, operation, and output involved in a computer system (see Figure 3–1). We will examine the hardware and some software related to each. We will also discuss a fourth process, the storage of information.

Before we discuss the actual peripherals, let's take a moment to examine ways to connect peripherals to the computer CPU. Communication, or the ability to transmit information to and from the computer, must occur between the input peripherals and the CPU as well as between the CPU and the output peripherals. This communication is sometimes referred to as an interface. It is essentially composed of two parts, one built into the peripheral device and the other either software added to the computer or a firmware card that plugs into one of its expansion slots. A cable or wireless device links the computer and the peripheral. Figure 3–2 illustrates the relationship of the various parts. An **extension** is a small program that is added to the operating system that allows the application software to interact with the operating system. A device **driver** is a small program that is added to the operating system that allows the operating system to interact with certain hardware peripherals (e.g., a printer). Peripheral devices depend on adequate connections or interfaces to the computer to function well. The speed of data transfer, usually measured in millions of bits per second (Mbps), is an important characteristic of the

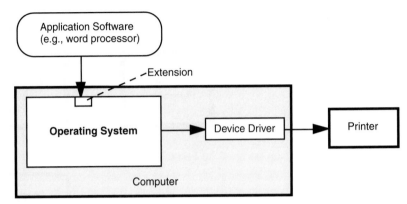

Figure 3–2
Communication
between components

connections between peripheral devices and the computer. The older *serial* (one data stream at a time) or *parallel* (multiple data streams at a time) interfaces have been replaced by the **Universal Serial Bus (USB)** standard developed by an industry-wide consortium. USB is a high-performance cross-platform (Windows/Macintosh) technology, yet is simple and user friendly. USB technology can transfer data at a far faster rate than the older serial or parallel connections. Peripheral devices are simple to connect. A device driver is installed in the computer. The cable (which has distinctively different connectors at each end, depending on the type of connection) is then plugged into the peripheral and the computer. USB connections are **hot-swappable,** meaning that peripherals can be plugged or unplugged from the system without shutting down and restarting the computer. USB can support up to 127 simultaneous devices such as keyboards, mice, trackballs, digital cameras, printers, and storage devices.

Digital video and other forms of media have increased the need to transfer vast amounts of data into and out of the CPU. To do this in a time-saving manner, a new standard for connectivity called **FireWire** was developed. FireWire 400, also known as IEEE 1394 or iLink, is faster than USB, hot-swappable, and also platform independent. It allows for the simultaneous attachment of up to 63 peripherals at distances up to 14 feet away. As with USB, many FireWire peripherals don't need a power cord since they can get their power directly from the computer. Hewlett-Packard, Intel, Lucent, Microsoft, NEC, and Phillips jointly developed an even higher speed connection called USB 2.0, released in April 2000. Apple Computer introduced FireWire 800 in February 2003 that has a transfer speed of up to 800 Megabits per second (hence the name) and a theoretical future transfer speed of up to 3,200 Mbps! By the time you read this, there may be an even newer interface. Figure 3–3 offers a comparison of data transfer speeds.

Input Devices

Let's review some hardware components whose function is to enter data into the computer through tactile, audio, video, or electronic means.

Figure 3–3
Interface connection
speeds

```
Serial              =        .6 MBps
Parallel            =       3.0 MBps
USB                 =      12.0 MBps
FireWire 400        =     400.0 MBps
USB 2.0             =     480.0 MBps
FireWire 800        =     800.0 MBps
```

The **keyboard** is the primary device through which data are entered into a personal computer system by generating a digital code that can be entered into the computer's memory and be understood by the CPU. We all know that each keyboard contains at least two key configurations, uppercase and lowercase, that can be accessed by using the shift key. Most computer keyboards, however, also contain a third, fourth, or even fifth configuration of keys that can be accessed by pressing combinations of alternative keys simultaneously with the alpha-numeric key. The *AlphaSmart* is an inexpensive portable keyboard powered by rechargeable batteries and capable of storing up to 100 pages of text in various files or folders, which can then be downloaded to a computer.

The **mouse** is a small, handheld input device that a user moves on a flat surface such as a desk. Software stored inside the computer moves the cursor on the screen, replicating the motion of the mouse. The software constantly monitors the position of the cursor on the screen. Pressing a button on the mouse results in one of several actions, depending on the program being used.

The **trackpad,** usually found on laptop computers, is a pressure-sensitive pad. By pressing a finger to the pad, the user moves a pointer on the screen.

Printed bar codes similar to the **UPC** (Universal Product Code) found on many products make data entry extremely fast and accurate. The codes are read by devices that sense the sequence of thick and thin lines and their spacing. Two commonly used types of **bar code readers** are the handheld wands and the stationary readers similar to those commonly employed at grocery checkout counters. The bar code readers generate light, which reflects from the bar code in a light and dark pattern. The reader, sensing the pattern, generates the appropriate matching digital code, thus eliminating the need for time-consuming keyboard entry, with its inherent typing errors.

A school library's automated circulation system is based on a bar code applied to each student's identification card, with appropriate bar codes placed on book spines or card pockets. A bar code reader reads information into a computer and in seconds the checkout procedure is completed.

Graphics tablets similar to that depicted in Figure 3–4 are input devices that allow the user to create or trace figures or drawings of any kind. A student can draw a picture with a stylus provided on the surface of the tablet and see it replicated on the monitor screen. The stylus allows the user far greater control than the mouse in drawing intricate designs. The accompanying software translates the stylus's position

Figure 3–4
Graphics tablet

and displays it as a point on the monitor screen. The series of points are the representation of a straight or curved line segment making up a total picture. You can also fill in solid areas of color, as well as enlarge or reduce the drawing. Again, using the software, the user can select certain shapes, shadings, and line widths or "paintbrush" effects. An art teacher might choose to have students use this device to execute lessons in perspective, line, or contour drawing. With its inherent ability to trace existing material, the graphics tablet is also an excellent device to facilitate the production of maps for a social studies lesson. Keyboards, mice, track pads, bar code readers and graphics tablets may be common to the CPU by wires or wirelessly, using radio waves or infrared energy.

Speech recognition devices have been available for a few years to interface with personal computers. Some current applications are part of the operating system and allow words to be spoken into a microphone that conveys the command to the computer. Several voice recognition software packages have entered the market that will allow a computer to enter spoken words into a word processing program. At present speech recognition software can match spoken word to printed word with about 95 percent accuracy. Voice entry has the advantage of eliminating the need to learn keyboarding skills. It offers speed, ease of use, and the potential for voice recognition security. Voice recognition software will help many physically disabled individuals gain access to a computer who can't access them now. There are a few excellent, yet inexpensive speech recognition products such as IBM's *Via Voice* available for both the Windows and Macintosh platforms. *Dragon Naturally Speaking* is another one worth considering.

Let's briefly consider photographic and video input devices. These devices greatly facilitate the creation of graphic images in the computer. Still-image **digital cameras,**

Figure 3–5

A digital camera, the
Canon PowerShot
S50 (Courtesy of
Canon, Inc.)

similar to the one shown in Figure 3–5, have become very popular and more affordable. Most models are easy to use and store a large number of digital images on
removable media such as the small postage-stamp-size cards called *CompactFlash,
Multimedia, Secure Digital,* or *Memory Stick.* The media is sometimes labeled 8×,
12× or even 40× to indicate the transfer rate for the information from the camera's
chip to the memory device. The higher the rate, the shorter the interval required between pictures taken. When the camera is connected to a computer directly or the
memory card is placed in a card reader, the images may be downloaded to the computer. They may be manipulated in a variety of ways such as cropping, removing
red-eye, adjusting color, brightness, etc., using appropriate software provided by the
camera or computer manufacturer or by the outstanding program (in our opinion)
Photoshop Elements™ and stored as graphic files. Other fine programs are *Apple
iPhoto*™ and *Microsoft Picture It*™. They are great tools for incorporating photographic images into presentations, newsletters, and pamphlets. Many digital cameras
(such as the one shown in Figure 3–5) can also record short digital video clips as
well as sound. The **resolution** of input devices such as a digital camera is measured
in **pixels** (*PIC*ture *EL*ements). A pixel is a single dot or point in a graphic image.
The more pixels in a given area, the higher the resolution or clarity of an image. Most
digital cameras use a charge-coupled device (CCD) to capture an image. The CCD
changes light falling on it into electric energy. The greater the number of pixels on
the CCD, the higher the image resolution and the larger you can print your photos.
This resolution is expressed in **megapixels** (millions of pixels). It is generally accepted that a 2-megapixel camera is sufficient for printing uncropped 4-by-6-inch

photos or displaying web or screen images. A 3-megapixel camera is better for 5-by-7-inch prints. And a 4-megapixel camera is required for 8-by-10-inch prints or for cropping and enlarging of prints. 5-, 6-, and 7-megapixel cameras are now common. Two methods are used to zoom in on the scene being photographed. The optical zoom capability (using a zoom lens like a regular film camera) actually enlarges the image reaching the camera, whereas the digital zoom only enlarges the pixels already captured by the camera, thereby degrading the image resolution. This form of enlargement is better done in the computer. As with film cameras, lens quality and camera body construction play a role in pricing.

Digital video cameras along with computer-based video editing systems are making an impact on schools as teachers and students alike become comfortable with the technology. They look and feel like conventional analog video cameras but don't require the student or teacher to learn to use software to convert the analog video signals to digital signals used by a computer. Many computers now have FireWire or USB 2.0 connections and come loaded with video editing software, which makes it possible for very young students with little training to produce professional looking edited movies. *iMovie*™ from Apple Computer was the first simple digital video editing software. It is distributed free on most Macintosh computers. Similar video editing software such as *Windows Movie Maker*® (also free), *VideoStudio 6.0*®, and *Pinnacle Systems Studio DV*® are also available for Windows machines. Other popular video editing software are *Avid Cinema*™ and *Final Cut Express*™. Many schools have now put movie making into their curriculums. The Public Broadcasting System (PBS) is developing partnerships with schools in several areas of the country to broadcast video produced by students with digital equipment. Your local public access cable channel might even welcome video productions produced by you or your students.

Software and video boards are available that allow computer screens to be recorded on videotape to serve as titles, credits, animated graphics, or instructional text screens. A variety of wipes and dissolves that allow one image to merge into another lends sophistication to the recording.

Scanners (Figure 3–6), somewhat resembling small photocopiers, digitize photographs, line drawings, and printed text by reading light reflected from the surface of the object. Some scanners allow the scanning of negatives and color slides by transmitting light through them. The scanner's resolution refers to the number of dots per inch (dpi) that a scanner is able to capture. This number is typically expressed by two numbers (1,200 by 2,400, for example). The first number represents the number of dots across the width of the scanning area and the second number represents the number of dots down the length. The important number to remember is the smaller number. This is the limit that the scanner can achieve without using **interpolation,** a process in which the software creates pixels without actually capturing greater detail. The scanner is accompanied by software that allows you to exercise some degree of control over the scanned image's brightness, contrast, resolution, and image size. It is often possible for the user to vary the image's size by **cropping** (adjusting only the outside dimensions) or **scaling** (proportionally enlarging or reducing the entire image) and adjusting brightness and contrast. Flatbed scanners, depending on the model, accept originals with dimensions up to 11-by-14

Figure 3–6
An optical scanner
(Courtesy of Hewlett
Packard)

inches. **Optical character recognition (OCR)** software allows the scanned text to be used in a regular word processing program. Recent software releases have come a long way toward improving the accuracy of the text translation but there is still some improvement needed.

Output Devices

Output devices are all the hardware items that display information from the computer through audio, video, print, or electronic means. Video monitors and printers are the most common output devices.

The color **video monitor** accepts a computer's digital video signal directly and is capable of displaying a picture of much higher resolution than a television receiver displays; therefore, it is the standard for computer applications. Although one or two interconnected large-screen (25 inches or larger) video monitors may suffice when presenting information to a relatively small group of viewers, they are not ideal for large-group presentations.

Video projectors such as the one shown in Figure 3–7 are capable of displaying a large (10-foot diagonal or larger) projected image. In a school setting, portable projectors are often housed in a library media center and circulated from there. The brightness of the screen image relates to the projector's output measured in **lumens.** The projected image's lower level of brightness and the presence of ambient room light striking the screen often demand a darkened room to maximize the impact of the projected image.

Printers.   The early computer printers, called **daisy-wheel printers,** were slow and noisy typewriter-like devices. They employed a three-inch diameter disk that had letters arranged in a circular fashion like spokes on a wheel that were struck by a hammer to print a letter. Then, for many years, the most popular type of printer in schools was the **dot matrix printer** that prints by pins striking a ribbon and creating an

Figure 3–7
A video projector
(Courtesy of
InFocus)

impression on regular bond paper. These printers still persist in applications where multiple part carbon or carbonless forms are generated.

The low-cost **ink-jet printer** also prints on regular bond paper or letterhead as well as on photo-finish paper and is currently the most popular printer purchased for the home and for the school. Rather than pins striking an inked ribbon, the ink-jet's print head squirts ink on the paper (Figure 3–8). An ink-jet printer has two main components, the *printhead* and the *ink tank*. In the lower-end printers commonly found in schools, these two components are usually combined in what is known as the *ink cartridge*. In the high-end printers commonly used in graphics shops, due to the need for a larger ink supply, ink is pumped from stationary tanks to the printhead that traverses across the page. By either case, any electric current is applied to a plate causing it to vibrate. This vibration causes dots of quick-drying ink to squirt through precisely controlled nozzles onto the paper. The size of the ink drop can be varied by varying the amount of electricity to the plate and hence the vibration.

Remembering that most print heads are an integral part of the ink cartridge, refilling ink cartridges several times is probably not a good idea since eventually the print head should be replaced. Printers with a resolution of 1200 dots per inch (dpi) or greater are sometimes referred to as photo quality. Ink-jet printers can achieve a resolution of 2400 × 1200 dpi or greater and are much quieter than dot matrix printers in their operation. With their low cost, ease of maintenance, high resolution, and full color capability, it's no wonder that they have become so popular for many school, home, and office applications. Multifunction ink-jet printers combining printing, scanning, copying, and faxing, sometimes called "all-in-one" printers, are becoming popular as the choice for home or home office.

Laser printers use a laser beam to create an image on a photosensitive drum surface. The image is transferred by means of a carbon toner to produce letter-quality (approaching typeset quality) printing of text and graphics onto plain bond or letterhead paper at a very high resolution, exceeding 1,200 **dots per inch (dpi).** This technology is very similar to the one employed by photocopiers. Laser printers have become a popular choice for a number of school applications. They are commonly found in school offices and on networks where several computers can share their use.

A laser printer receives information from a computer and stores it temporarily in its internal memory. It transfers this information as a code that governs the operation of a laser that strikes a photosensitive drum, as illustrated in Figure 3–9, setting up electrical charges on its surface. The drum rotates past a carbon particle toner

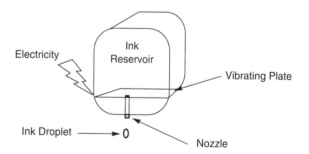

Figure 3–8
How an ink-jet
printer works

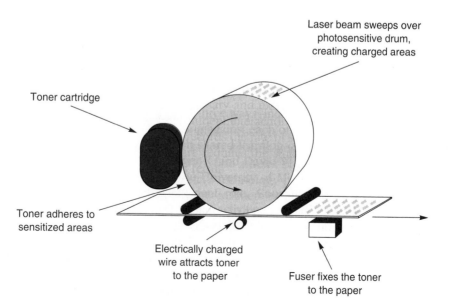

Figure 3–9
How a laser printer
works

reservoir, where toner is attracted to the charged areas. A sheet of paper is pressed against this toner-bearing drum and the toner transfers to the paper. Before exiting the printer, the paper passes through a thermal fuser section, which hardens and fixes the toner on the paper.

There are several questions to think about when you purchase a printer. Understanding its primary use will help you to answer the following questions. Do you need black-and-white or color? What is its resolution (dpi)? How many pages can it print per minute? Would a multifunction printer save money in the long run? Will the printer accept your digital camera's memory card so you can print photos directly from the card? How expensive are the ink/toner cartridges? (Manufacturers make most of their profit on the ink and toner rather than on the printer.) We should caution you, however, to always buy brand-name ink cartridges from a reputable dealer. Over $2 billion in counterfeit ink cartridges are sold each year to unsuspecting individuals. These cartridges can spray ink, leak, clog print mechanisms, void your warranty, and cause permanent damage to your printer.

Modems.   The telephone or cable **modem** (MOdulator-DEModulator) is both an input device and an output device. It translates digital computer information into analog signals of varying frequency that can be transmitted over telephone or cable lines and analog signals into a digital form that can be processed by a computer. The relatively inexpensive modem is a vital link allowing computers to exchange information. Computer modems are now commonly available in a transmission speed of 56 **Kbps** (56,000 **bps** or bits per second). Modems that operate over cable or specialized phone lines are far faster yet. **Cable modems,** using existing cable television wiring, or **digital subscriber lines (DSL)** from your phone company are up to 50 times faster than modems using ordinary telephone lines. Proponents of these technologies state that speeds of up to 8 **Mbps** (8,000,000 bps) are theoretically possible with DLS and 30 Mbps (30,000,000 bps) with a cable modem! Figure 3–10 reviews some of the choices currently available. In reality, however, speeds are considerably slower than that.

With telefacsimile (fax) machines so commonplace in businesses and schools, most modems include software that allow them to behave as **fax-modems.** It allows a computer to communicate with another computer or with a fax machine. Fax machines send and receive information in a type of graphic format so that pages of text are transmitted as images. Faxes received by fax-modems are stored in the computer as graphic documents unless software is used to convert them into text files that can be edited.

Central Processing Unit

The central processing unit (CPU) is the heart of the computer system through which all instructions and information flow. This term is a throwback to large mainframe jargon, when the CPU was in fact a separate piece of equipment. The CPU is now often referred to as the microprocessor. An important consideration of computer CPUs is how fast they can access and carry out instructions and process data. This is known as **clock speed** or the number of electronic cycles per second that a CPU will process. The more electronic cycles, the faster the CPU carries out instructions.

Technology	Speed	Comments
Dial-up modem	56 Kbps	Most common Uses analog phone lines Longest response and download times
DSL	128–768 Kbps	Slower farther from phone company switch Not available everywhere
Cable TV modem	1–7 Mbps	Fastest connection Constant connection More users = slower service

Figure 3–10
Typical modem
speeds

Clock speed is measured in millions of cycles (megahertz or MHz) or billions of cycles (gigahertz or GHz) per second. Speeds exceeding 3.0 GHz are now quite common. Clock speed is not the sole determiner of CPU performance, however. The speed at which data can be transferred from memory to the CPU is also an important factor.

Some new computers have two or more processor chips and are known as multiprocessors. This not only makes the computer faster but also allows it to run several programs more smoothly and efficiently at the same time.

Internal Memory

Computer manufacturers store instructions that govern the fundamental operations of the computer in a nonvolatile memory called **ROM** (read-only memory). Integrated circuits contain the ROM, which consists of instructions that, once encoded by the manufacturer, cannot be erased, written to, or modified in any way by the user. ROM is called "nonvolatile" because it stays on the chip even when the power is turned off. Since the user has no control over the instructions in the ROM, it is often taken for granted. It is, however, responsible for *booting* the computer at startup and providing important behind-the-scenes control of the computer.

The **volatile memory** is internal memory available and accessible to the user. When you load a prepared program from a magnetic disk or optical disc, type a letter using a word processor, enter information into a database management program, or write an original program, you are in fact entering instructions or data and placing them in the computer's volatile memory called random-access memory, or **RAM.** Most computers now use a type of RAM called *DDRRAM* (Double Data Rate RAM) that transmits data on both halves of the CPU's clock cycle, effectively doubling the flow of data between the memory and the CPU. RAM is called volatile memory because it requires a constant source of power to maintain itself. Should power fail for even a brief moment, the contents of RAM are lost forever. This is one reason why it is very important to save your work onto the computer's hard disk at least every few minutes. We could write chapters on all of the horror stories we have heard from students about the papers, projects, and assignments that have been lost because of a momentary loss of power or because of a computer that froze and needed to be rebooted again. As careful as we try to be, we have also lost work. No one is immune! Users who are concerned about power outages or interruption usually connect their computer to a backup or uninterruptible power supply **(UPS).**

In most instances, your work is stored in RAM until it is saved to a disk. RAM is really only a temporary holding area, where the ideas are manipulated and the data organized before being passed on and stored more permanently on the hard drive or disk. In the case of RAM, bigger is indeed better. The more RAM available, the larger and more sophisticated the application program that can be run on the computer, the more applications can be open at one time, and the larger the file that can be processed. Graphics and digital video files, for instance, can consume a very large amount of RAM. The amount of RAM is measured by counting the potential bytes of information. A byte is usually the amount of memory required to represent one alphabetic or numeric character. The amount of RAM may be expressed in units of 1,000 bytes, represented by the symbol **K,** for **kilobytes,** units of 1 million by the symbol **MB,** for **megabytes,** or in units of 1 billion bytes by the symbol **GB,** for **gigabytes.** Computers today are sold with millions or even billions of bytes of RAM. The computer that we are using to write this chapter has 768 MB of RAM expandable to 70 GB!

Mass Storage

Auxiliary storage of vast numbers of programs and data is often very important. Most often, removable media such as a magnetic disk or optical disc, housed in a piece of equipment located in the computer or sometimes separate from the computer cabinet itself, are employed. Information such as programs can be copied into or read by the computer (input), and files can usually be saved (output) to this hardware to be later retrieved from it.

Magnetic Storage Devices. The primary type of mass storage in the 1980s and early 1990s was the **floppy disk,** a small wafer of flexible polyester film coated with an emulsion having magnetic properties similar to audio or videotape. It was encased in a 5 1/4-inch square, flexible protective plastic jacket, hence it was called a *floppy* disk. The 3 1/2-inch **microdiskette** format—with its smaller size, improved protection against dirt and physical damage, and far greater storage capacity—replaced the 5 1/4-inch floppy disk. Though encased in rigid material, it was still referred to as a "floppy."

Another common form of mass memory is the **hard disk.** It is composed of one or more rigid platters coated with a magnetic emulsion similar to that used on a floppy disk. The hard disk is a sealed unit that is usually enclosed in the computer's case and is then referred to as an internal hard disk or drive. An external hard disk is enclosed in its own separate case and connected by cable to the computer.

The reasonably priced **flash drive, pen drive,** or **thumb drive** is a secure and convenient data storage device in an ultra-small package. It's about the size of your thumb and one end of it plugs directly in to a USB port on your computer. Holding upwards of 2 gigabytes of storage in a solid-state (no moving parts) memory system, it is a useful medium to transport data to and from school.

Hard disks usually offer gigabytes (1,000 megabytes) of storage. This amount of memory allows users to place many programs permanently on the hard disk drive.

It is important to remember to save important documents in more than one location, perhaps on a hard disk and a Zip disk. Disks are a magnetic medium composed of a piece of plastic or metal coated with a metal oxide. Disks can wear and fail with age or when stored in less than ideal conditions. When this happens you may not be able to retrieve a document stored on them. The authors of this text store the book chapters on their own desktop computer hard drives, laptop computer hard drives, a Zip disk, and exchange chapters between themselves on CD-Rs. Remember though, if your disk fails and it contains documents that you need, don't just throw it away. There are many utility programs available specifically designed to recover crashed or damaged files or files that have been accidentally erased. It is a good idea to have a copy of a utility program such as *Norton Utilities*® in your school computer lab or media center for just this purpose!

The disk drive's function is to save data to and retrieve data from the floppy disk or CD-R. It does this by engaging the disk and rotating it at high speed on a motor-driven spindle while the magnetic read-write head scans the surface, sensing or creating magnetic domains (Figure 3–11). This aspect is, in fact, similar to audiotape recording and playback. When a song is played from a tape, it is not removed from the tape. Likewise, when a program is read from a disk, it is only copied into RAM and not removed from the disk. The actual process of searching for and loading a program, however, is analogous to playing an audio CD rather than playing an audiotape. The computer disk and the audio CD are random-access devices with multiple access points. Many different files can be stored on the same disk. Each file has a unique identifier stored in a disk directory or catalog track. When selecting a song to play from an audio CD, you can punch in a code number that will select the beginning of a particular song as the CD is spinning. When you instruct the computer to load a particular file from a disk, the spindle rotates the disk while the read-write head scans the surface, looking for the beginning of the file you selected, which it then loads into RAM. Combining the two factors of spinning the disk at high speed and quickly moving the read-write head in and out across its surface results in rapid random access to any information on the disk.

It is necessary to prepare a magnetic disk to receive data. This **formatting,** or **initializing,** process allows you to save your programs later onto the disk. In

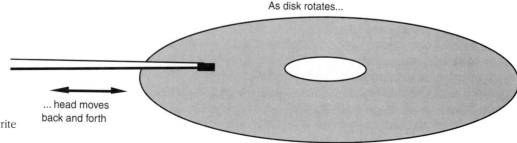

Figure 3–11
Disk read-write access

As disk rotates...

... head moves back and forth

preparing a disk, the computer lays out an indexed map on the disk so it will know where to write the programs and files to be saved. It may be important to format the disk for your particular computer. Programs on magnetic disks are indexed by track and sector number. When the disk is formatted, a directory is created and concentric circles called **tracks** are laid out on the surface of the disk (Figure 3–12). These are the major divisions of the disk. Each circular track is divided into units called **sectors.** Each sector is capable of storing a certain number of bytes of information. Newer operating systems allow much greater storage density than did previous ones.

This format directory, or computer-created map, on the disk can be compared to a road map. You can find a city on a map by looking up its horizontal and vertical location coordinates in the map index. The index may also tell you the population of that city. The disk map, or directory, tells the computer where to find a specific file and its memory size.

As disks are used over time, new files are added and old files are erased. Eventually, this causes newly saved files to be scattered, or **fragmented,** in segments at various points of the disk. This fragmentation erodes disk performance and slows down the retrieval of files. Running defragmentation utility software periodically cleans up this storage issue and improves disk performance. That copy of *Norton Utilities* we mentioned earlier will do this for you also.

Optical Storage Devices.   Because of the technology used to record and read CD-Audio, Photo-CD, CD-ROM, CD-R, CD-RW, DVD-ROM, and DVD-Video, they are grouped under the term **optical storage devices.** All of these discs are produced using a laser beam to encode and read information stored in tracks on their surface. The laser beam burns pits into the surface of the disc. Another laser bounces light off the surface and the pits to read the information on the disc. We use the term *optical* since a laser beam is really a beam of light. Technological developments in laser disc optical storage have greatly facilitated the development of multimedia. Due to the vast amount of information present in multimedia programs, this technology has demanded a great deal of **external memory** storage. Traditional floppy disks were inadequate but optical disc technology provided the answer. (You may have noticed a change of spelling in this paragraph. At the present time, magnetic storage medium is spelled disk—with a "k." An optical storage medium is generally spelled disc—with a "c.")

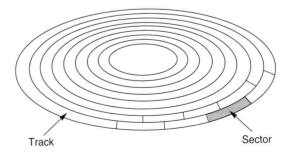

Figure 3–12
Tracks and sectors
established by
formatting

Track   Sector

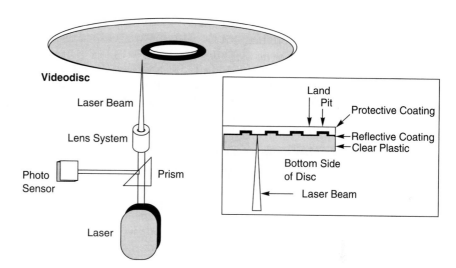

Figure 3–13
Optical disc system

As shown in Figure 3–13, a laser beam reads a precise series of tiny depressions (called pits) and smooth reflective areas (called lands) on the bottom surface of an optical disc. The lands reflect the laser beam to a photo sensor and the pits diffract the light beam away from the sensor. This creates a series of 'on,' 'off' pulses thereby producing a digital signal. The optical disc reader or player decodes the data into the original information that can be displayed on a video screen or printed as hard copy.

CD-Audio. The *CD-audio* (compact disc-audio) digital format, introduced in 1983, has achieved phenomenal success, with millions of players installed all over the world. In only a few years it made record players obsolete. It has supplied the economy of scale and research and development funds that have contributed to the development of CD-ROM and other compact disc formats. MP-3 and SACD are popular current audio formats.

Photo-CD. Eastman Kodak Company developed and marketed this format making it is possible to drop your photographic film at just about any photo-finishing outlet and pick up your photographs in a digital format on a **Photo-CD.** Played back in most CD-ROM or DVD drives, the images can be viewed on a monitor, projected onto a screen, or downloaded into your computer for editing and creative manipulation.

CD-ROM. This pervasive medium, the compact disc read-only memory (CD-ROM) was introduced in 1985, two years after the introduction of the CD-audio. This digital format disc measures only 4 3/4 inches but can contain approximately 650 megabytes of data, the equivalent of approximately 300,000 typewritten pages of text. Even as far back as 1998, approximately 90 percent of computers manufactured included an internal CD-ROM drive. Although the medium began as a read-only technology, CD-Recordable (CD-R) and CD-Rewriteable (CD-RW) are two recording formats now readily available. The very inexpensive (25¢ or less) CD-Rs are recordable only once and usually store up to 80 minutes of audio or 700 MB of data. CD-RWs are four to six times more expensive, store up to 74 minutes of audio and 650 MB of data, but are recordable more than once. Some users feel that CD-Rs are less error prone and more dependable. To add to the complexity of this optical storage issue, you might note that there are CD-R and CD+R as well as CD-RW and CD+RW formats and that they are not compatible with one another. Drives that can record CD-ROMS and/or DVDs (below) are often called **burners** and the process of recording is called burning. Most new computers sold today include either a CD-R, CD-RW, DVD-R, or a combination drive that can record all three formats. So pervasive has this new technology become that some computers no longer include floppy disk drives.

DVDs. Digital Versatile Disc (DVD), also known as Digital Video Disc, is one of the most exciting incarnations of the digital disc medium. DVD players have gained phenomenal acceptance in the home. DVD movie rentals have become the norm. DVD players and recorders are now a very popular option on many personal computers. As with CD-ROMs (above) there are many competing and incompatible formats: DVD-R, DVD+R, DVD-R/RW, DVD+R/RW, and DVD-RAM, to name a few, so it is best to check on compatibility when purchasing a unit. A DVD can be played on either platform's (Windows or Macintosh) operating system. It physically resembles the CD-ROM but, by employing new compression technology, stores much more data (4.7 GB using older red-laser technology and up to 35 GB using the new blue-laser technology) than the CD-ROM. As well as storing vast amounts of data, a DVD can present a feature film containing high-quality video and multiple tracks of surround sound audio channels and 32 tracks of subtitle channels. Due to the DVD's large storage capacity, a film can include a number of different takes of the same scene and multiple endings from which the viewer can choose with the navigation control provided. It is easy to understand why in many areas, video rental stores now rent mostly DVDs and few, if any, videotapes.

The optical disc technologies have gained widespread acceptance as media for classroom instruction. Once a price/performance breakthrough occurs in large video screen, flat screen, and video projection, optical disc technologies will become universally accepted. The film camera is fast becoming an endangered species as digital still camera and DVD technology is improving and becoming more affordable. Figure 3–14 reviews storage capacities of some common media.

Figure 3–14
Overview of external storage device capabilities

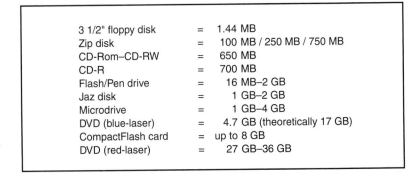

3 1/2" floppy disk	=	1.44 MB
Zip disk	=	100 MB / 250 MB / 750 MB
CD-Rom–CD-RW	=	650 MB
CD-R	=	700 MB
Flash/Pen drive	=	16 MB–2 GB
Jaz disk	=	1 GB–2 GB
Microdrive	=	1 GB–4 GB
DVD (blue-laser)	=	4.7 GB (theoretically 17 GB)
CompactFlash card	=	up to 8 GB
DVD (red-laser)	=	27 GB–36 GB

USER INTERFACE

The **user interface** can be thought of as the interaction between human and machine. It is receiving a good deal of attention in the design of new **operating systems.** An operating system is a set of programming instructions that sit between the user and the computer. The operating system interprets your actions and executes the desired procedures. It also projects the position of the mouse on the screen as you move it on your desktop. Early interfaces progressed from mechanical (throwing switches) to text based (typing command words). Microsoft's MS-DOS (Microsoft-Disk Operating System) used a text-based command line interface that gave the user a great deal of control over the functions of the computer, but it was complex, requiring the memorization of numerous command words.

Apple Computer revolutionized the desktop computer market when it introduced the Macintosh in 1984. It capitalized on research done by Xerox Corporation in the 1970s and was the first commercially successful computer to substitute a **graphical user interface (GUI)** for the text-based command line interface. The computers that run Microsoft Windows and Macintosh computers that you now use all employ GUIs that use icons, pointers, desktops, menus, and windows. You just have to move the mouse around, point, and click to make things happen. OS X (Ten), based on the UNIX operating system, is the most recent Macintosh operating system. Since 1984, graphics have become much more important to the manner in which humans interact with computers. Microsoft introduced a graphic interface for IBM and compatible systems called Windows 1.0 in 1985 that ran once the MS-DOS operating system was loaded. It has followed that with Windows 3.0, Windows 95, Windows NT, Windows 98, Windows 2000, Windows XP (Home and Professional, Windows XP Tablet PC Edition, and its current derivative). The Linux operating system can be configured to control IBM compatible computers, Macintoshes, and most other CPUs. Operating systems can be large, complex programs that may take up significant amounts of hard disk space. Presently, 75 percent of school computers and 90 percent of computers worldwide use a Windows operating system.

All major computer operating systems are substituting the use of **icons,** or pictorial representations, for complex verbal commands. Instead of typing a command to retrieve a file from external memory, you might simply move a screen arrow to point to the icon of a file folder and click the mouse button to open the folder. The file can be opened immediately by pointing to it and double-clicking the mouse button. Should you decide later that the file is no longer needed, you can drag its icon to an icon of a trash can or recycle bin, thus "throwing away" or "recycling" the file. Here the screen action replicates kinesthetic behavior associated with everyday occurrences in the work environment.

In examining Figure 3–15, it is easy to see that folder icons look very much like manila file folders used in a filing cabinet. Software publishers design their own unique icons to represent their software and the files or documents created by their software. Program and document icons can be dragged to folder icons in order to store them in that folder. Folders may even be placed inside other folders.

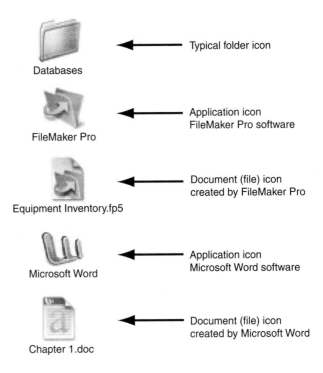

Figure 3–15
Various types of
icons

Just as the GUI and pen-based systems have revolutionized the use of the computer, the next generation user interface may take us into brand new territory. The next interface may revolve around voice entry, allowing the user to speak command words to the computer. A great deal of research and development is occurring in this field. The new interface may be able to recognize many different voices and, depending on the voice recognized, would allow or deny certain operations or access to certain files. It's fun to contemplate! Interface becoming popular is the pen-based interface where the user simply writes on the screen and software converts it into alphabetic or numeric characters. The research and development in improving the user interface is focused on making use of the computer as natural and as easy as possible so that the hardware use becomes transparent to the purpose at hand. Rather than being overly conscious of the hardware and concerned with how to perform a computer task, the user should be allowed to concentrate on the content and nature of the problem being addressed.

HANDHELD COMPUTER TECHNOLOGY

We cannot end this section without a few words about small handheld computers. Sometimes mistakenly called PDAs (personal digital assistants), palmtops (after the popular Palm® models), or personal PCs, handheld computers are appearing in schools around the country. Due to the availability of software specifically designed for K–12 schools, increased functionality, and lower costs, many teachers are incorporating them into their classes. These devices use one of two operating systems: Palm OS with about 75 percent of the market and WindowsCE/Pocket PC with most of the rest. Palm OS handhelds are ideal for schools because of their ease of use and school software availability. Windows CE is harder to use, crashes more easily, and does not have the school-based software base Palm OS has. Most handhelds contain an address book, note pad, date book, and to-do list and also may come with specially designed versions of Word, Excel, and PowerPoint. Free Web browsing and e-mail software is also available. Handheld computers can be connected to a computer with wires, infrared, and/or wireless technology. A fast Web search for software will find much free and low-cost educational software available for these compact and expensive helpers.

NETWORKING

A cluster of interconnected computers and peripheral devices sharing information is called a **network.** Networks are constructed in order to maximize the use of software, hardware, and the exchange of information. Software made available on a network can be accessed by a number of different machines, providing that the appropriate license fee has been paid to the software publisher.

Networks, though they are sometimes thought of as local facilities, in reality span the globe. Effective long-distance communications are in fact moving us toward the promised *global village.* As teachers are becoming more comfortable with telecommunications, they are exploring the concept of *global classrooms.* These are composed of computers in classrooms around the world interconnected for the purpose of sharing information, ideas, interests, collaborative projects, and questions. Children and young adults in global classrooms are indeed in the process of becoming citizens of the world.

Networking offers several important advantages to schools. A network permits resource sharing—that is, the sharing of software and peripheral equipment. Buying network licenses is considerably less expensive than purchasing multiple copies of individual software packages. Without a network, one peripheral device (such as a printer or a scanner) can serve only one computer. A network allows many computers to access connected peripheral devices regardless of where they are physically located.

A network also promotes resource management. Individual users do not have to have every program or file on a disk because those resources can reside on a central network server. Many school networks employ student data management software that provides security and recordkeeping functions. Finally, and most important, a network facilitates information exchange and student collaboration. Students can read files created by a teacher, exchange files among themselves and a teacher, communicate with others by e-mail, or, with the proper software, work simultaneously and interactively on a project. When the network is composed of devices that are housed in close proximity to one another such as in one building or on a campus, the network is referred to as a **local area network,** or **LAN.** A network that spans greater distances or covers a wide geographical area is called a **wide area network,** or **WAN.**

Wireless Communications Hardware

Wireless communications is taking the country by storm. In the mid to late 1990s the telephone industry led the way with cellular and satellite telephones. This revolution paved the way for wireless Internet services and wireless networks now appearing in schools, homes, airports, and even coffee shops. Apple Computer and Lucent Technologies were the first manufacturers to introduce consumer wireless computer networking with their *AirPort*™ feature available on Apple's *iMac*™ desktop and *iBook*™ laptop in 1999. *AirPort* can be accessed by Windows-based computers as well. The major computer manufacturers followed soon after. These wireless systems, transmitting data at up to 54 Mbs, include a base station that can transmit and receive data over airwaves thus eliminating the need to wire computers and peripherals together. Most wireless networks use one of the IEEE 802.11 family of standards (802.11, 802.11a, 802.11b, and 802.11g). You may have heard the term **Wi-Fi,** which is short for Wireless Fidelity, a generic term for any device that uses one of the IEEE 802.11 standards. Wi-Fi devices are appearing all over allowing wireless access in hotels, shops, coffee shops, and even on the street. IEEE 802.11 devices are also sometimes called *wireless Ethernet.* HomeRF is a wireless standard developed for home use and Bluetooth is a short-range standard that is primarily used to replace cables that connect devices such as a printer or handheld computer to a desktop computer. A summary of these standards is presented in Figure 3–16.

Wireless networking offers all of the advantages of regular networking and one additional one—cost. There is no need to map out and run wires between the various pieces of equipment throughout the building. Wiring may be particularly difficult and costly in older school buildings. Many schools are purchasing mobile

Figure 3–16
Common wireless
standards

Bluetooth (computer to peripherals)	=	1 MBps (30 feet)
HomeRF (computer to peripherals)	=	2 MBps (150 feet)
802.11b (Wi-Fi)	=	11 MBps (300 feet)
802.11a (Wi-Fi 5)	=	54 MBps (10–20 feet)
802.11g (current standard)	=	54 MBps (500+ feet)
802.11i (under development at publication time)		
802.16 (WiMax)	=	70 MBps (31 miles)

Figure 3–17
Mobile wireless
computer carts are
popular in many
schools (Courtesy of
Apple Computer,
Inc.)

carts (Figure 3–17) that hold a number of wireless laptops and a wireless receiving hub or access point. These carts are rolled into the classroom, the wireless hub is plugged into the school's network or a telephone line, and the students are able to use their wireless laptops without having to worry about wires to connect them to the network. Mobile wireless computer carts bring the learning right into the classroom. Space is freed up because a separate computer lab is not needed and cost can be reduced because costly wiring is not needed throughout a classroom/computer lab. Students are also freed up to work in comfortable groups as they carry their wireless laptop to special areas of the room and perhaps to the media center if it is within range or it has its own wireless access point. Computer educators see this as the wave of the future (or really, the wave of the present!). Unlike **infrared wireless** connections that rely on direct line of sight transmission, present radio frequency wireless hardware can send and receive signals up to 300 feet, even through walls, floors, and ceilings.

INTO THE CLASSROOM:
A Wireless Classroom

We've used our wireless laptop lab to complete many lessons. However, one stands out above the rest—our biome project. As a fourth-grade teacher, one skill that needs to be covered in science is creating a food chain, along with expository paragraph writing in language arts, and exploring different regions in social studies. We combined these benchmarks by having our students work in groups to research different regions and biomes.

Each group picked a region to research. Within that region, they found a biome, the plants and animals in that biome, and created a slide show depicting the food chain for that biome. Each food chain was different, because the plants and animals were specific to the chosen biome. Finding good pictures of some animals proved challenging, but each group managed to find exactly what they were looking for on the Internet.

Groups worked in the wireless laptop lab collecting information and graphics to be used in their slide show. The wireless laptops added the mobility to our lesson that we needed. The students could gather in any configuration needed to work on their projects. Also, keeping their information in a folder on the networked drive enable the students to have easy access to their "saved" work. Each day students simply took up where they left off the day before by opening their folder on the networked drive and adding new information to their folder. Once enough information was collected, they were ready to compile this information into a PowerPoint slide show.

The students saved their finished slide shows in two different formats: (1) presentation format and (2) Web page format. The reason we did this was because not all computers have the Microsoft PowerPoint program. Saving the slide show under a Web page format would enable the slide show to be opened with any computer that had access to the Internet. Because the slide shows were also saved on the networked drive, they were easily accessed in all classrooms. Even so, we saved the shows to disks as well to be sure to have access to them no matter where we were for the presentation.

Completed projects were presented to the class and neighboring classes. The students also created a poster-sized food chain, using a word processing program to be displayed outside our classroom. This project was completed in approximately two weeks and the students were so excited about their work that they brought in disks to copy their slide show onto to show family members.

Vicki Ersek
Fourth-Grade Teacher
Albany Upper Elementary School (Louisiana)

SUMMARY

This chapter contains an overview of the computer and computer peripherals. We viewed the computer as a system of components for input, operation, and output. We discussed several input peripherals whose function it is to enter data into the computer and make accessing of computer software easier for the user. We discussed common computer input peripherals, as the mouse and trackpad, and also others such as digital cameras and scanners. Output peripherals display information from the computer through audio, video, print, and electronic means.

The older parallel or serial connections are being replaced by the powerful, cross-platform FireWire or USB. External storage devices such as CD-ROMs and DVDs were explained. We also discussed software components of the computer used for its operation such as the disk operating system.

Networking is the interconnecting of computer stations with input and output devices to facilitate sharing of information and equipment and to reduce the number and cost of peripherals. We talked about wireless telecommunications and discussed wireless computing in schools.

You will come in contact with most of the items we discussed. They are all very common; in fact, many of you own most of these right now.

CHAPTER EXERCISES

To complete the specified exercises on-line, go to the Chapter Exercises Module in Chapter 3 of the Companion Website.

1. Review a copy of a recent *PCWorld, MacWorld,* or other computer magazine. What are some of the newer computer technologies or programs that they are talking about? How would these advances fit into an educational environment?

2. Research the newest offerings that Windows (PC) and Macintosh manufacture. What pros and cons do you see with each operating system?

3. Describe the difference between RAM and ROM. How much RAM does a modern computer have?

4. We can store data on an internal hard drive, a 3.5-inch floppy, a Zip disk, and a CD-ROM. What are the pros and cons of each storage medium? How large are the internal hard drives on the computers in your school? How large are typical hard drives on the new models?

5. On which of the storage devices in number 4 do you store your classwork and homework? Why have you chosen this storage medium? Do you back up your work? Is this a good idea? Why or why not?

6. Check some prices and features for the latest printers. Choose one for a lab in the school in which you may teach. Write a short note to the principal indicating your choice and giving reasons why you chose this particular printer.

7. Research the latest models of digital cameras. Which model would you purchase for home use and which would you purchase for your classroom? Write a short note to the principal indicating your choice and giving reasons why you chose this particular model of digital camera.

8. Discuss the pros and cons of a wired and a wireless classroom. Research some schools in your area. Are they wired or wireless? Why do you think this is the case?

9. Research the different computer models on the market. Which model would you purchase for home use and which would you purchase for your classroom? If these are different models, why did you make this choice? Write a short note to the principal indicating your choice and giving reasons why you chose this particular model of computer.

10. Call a local school library media specialist or computer coordinator. Ask them if you could tour a school computer lab and discuss the type of network it has. Report your results to the class.

PORTFOLIO DEVELOPMENT EXERCISES

 To complete this exercise on-line, go to the Digital Portfolio Module in Chapter 3 of the Companion Website.

One of the NETS•S standards covered in this chapter was "Students demonstrate a sound understanding of the nature and operation of technology systems" under *Category 1: Basic operations and concepts.* Begin to develop your own portfolio of lesson plans that demonstrates your ability to have your students reach the NETS•S standards.

1. Design a lesson plan activity for elementary, middle school, or high school students in which they design a computer lab. They should be able to give reasons why they decided on the number of computers, the computer operating system, and whether the lab would be wired or wireless. This lesson should demonstrate that your students have achieved the standard. Be sure to include a system of evaluation for your students' understanding and competence to ensure that they have met this standard.

2. Adapt the lesson plan activity you developed in exercise 1 for students to evaluate each other's work.

GLOSSARY

bar code reader A device that translates the sequence of spaced thick and thin lines to the computer, enabling it to identify an object.

bps A measure of data transmission speed between computers in *bits per second.*

burner A term used to describe a drive that records data onto optical discs such as a CD or a DVD. A CD-R is a CD drive that can write data onto the disc. A CD-RW drive can write and rewrite data onto special CD discs that can record data over again on the same disc.

cable modem A peripheral device that connects a computer to a television cable system. Speeds of up to 30 Mbps are possible.

central processing unit (CPU) The point (a chip) in the computer where all parts of the system are linked together and where the calculations and manipulation of data take place (may be referred to as a microprocessor).

clock speed The number of electronic pulses per second that a CPU will process. The more electronic pulses, the faster the computer carries out instructions. Modern clock speeds are between 800 MHz and 2.5 GHz.

cropping Controlling the size of an image without affecting the size of any of its components. Cropping an image smaller than the original eliminates some of the content.

daisy-wheel printer An impact printer that has letters and numbers set at the tips of a spoke on a rimless wheel.

digital camera A device that captures and stores still images in a digital format.

digital subscriber line (DSL) A service available from some phone companies for fast Internet access. Speeds of up to 8 Mbps are possible.

digital video camera A device that captures and stores moving images in a digital format.

dot matrix printer An impact printer that uses a series of electrically hammered pins to create characters composed of a pattern of dots.

dots per inch (dpi) The number of discrete elements produced by a printer. Used to describe the resolution of the printer. Printer output normally ranges from 300 dpi to 2,400 dpi.

driver A small program added to the operating system that allows the operating system to control certain hardware peripherals (e.g., a printer).

extension A small program added to the operating system that allows the application software to interact with the operating system.

external memory The auxiliary storage of programs and data, often on a removable medium such as magnetic disk or tape, housed in a piece of equipment usually separate from the computer cabinet.

fax-modem A device that allows a computer to communicate by phone lines with a facsimile (fax) machine or with another modem-equipped computer.

FireWire A very high-speed connection between peripherals and the computer that allows for the transfer of large amounts of data such as digitized video. (Also called IEEE 1394 or i.LINK.)

firmware Software that is permanently stored on a computer chip.

flash drive An ultra-small, pocket-sized device capable of storing up to 2 GB.

floppy disk An external storage medium made of flexible polyester film with magnetic properties, similar to audiotape. The term is now applied to the newer microdiskette.

formatting Preparing a blank disk to receive information.

fragmented The dispersal of files stored on disk into segments scattered at various points on the disk.

GB or **gigabyte** One thousand megabytes, or one billion bytes, used as a reference to memory storage capacity.

graphical user interface (GUI) The on-screen use of pictorial representations (icons) of objects. The user can move a screen pointer onto an icon and click a mouse button to issue a command to the computer. Besides icons and pointers, basic GUI components include desktops, menus, and windows.

graphics tablet A flat input device on which the user writes. This is changed to digital input for use by the computer.

hard disk An external storage medium consisting of a rigid platter coated with a magnetic emulsion and not removable from the disk drive; three to five times larger than a floppy disk, it has far greater memory storage capacity.

hardware Tangible computer parts such as a keyboard, mouse, disk drive, and printer.

hot-swappable The ability to plug or unplug peripherals from the computer system without having to shut down and restart the computer.

icon A pictorial representation of an object.

infrared wireless A system of connections that relies on direct line of sight transmission.

initializing See *formatting.*

ink-jet printer A printer that uses a series of electronically controlled nozzles to create characters composed of a pattern of dots squirted onto the paper.

input peripherals Equipment whose function is to enter data into the computer.

interpolation A process in which the scanner software makes up pixels without actually capturing greater detail from the scanned image.

K or **kilobyte** One thousand bytes (actually 1,024 in computer terms); used as a reference to memory capacity.

Kbps A measure of a modem's data transmission speed between computers in thousands of bits per second. Common rates are 56 Kbps and faster.

keyboard The primary input device for the computer; it generates a digital code that can be understood by the microprocessor.

laser printer A printer that uses a laser beam to create an image on a photosensitive drum and transfers this by means of carbon toner to paper.

local area network (LAN) A network composed of devices located in close proximity to one another.

lumens A measure of a video projector's output affecting the brightness of the screen image.

MB or **megabyte** One thousand kilobytes or one million bytes, used as a reference to memory capacity.

Mbps A measure of a modem's data transmission speed between computers in millions of bits per second.

megapixel One million pixels. Used to describe the resolution of digital cameras, video monitors, and scanners.

microdiskette A 3 1/2-inch format that houses a magnetic disk in a rigid plastic protective case.

modem A device that translates digital computer information into analog signals that can be transmitted over telephone lines and analog signals into a digital form that can be processed by a computer.

mouse A handheld device connected to the input port of a computer, which, if moved up, down, left, or right on a flat surface, moves a pointer on the screen that selects functions or options.

network The interconnection of computers to allow multiple users to access software and to exchange information.

operating system An operating system enables the central processing unit (CPU) to control and communicate with internal and external devices. Windows versions are common on IBM compatibles and a version of OS X is popular on the Macintosh.

optical character recognition (OCR) Software that allows scanners to digitize text so that it can be used and manipulated as regular text in a word processor.

optical storage device Storage peripherals that are written to and accessed by laser light beams such as CD-ROMs and DVD's.

output peripherals Equipment that displays information from the computer.

pen drive See *flash drive.*

Photo-CD Eastman Kodak Company developed this technology, which allows up to 100 color slides or negatives to be scanned onto an optical disc. Played back in a Photo-CD player or in most CD-ROM drives, the images can be viewed on a monitor or projected onto a screen.

pixel Abbreviation for *picture element*. One pixel is a single point in a graphic image. More pixels in the same area mean a sharper image in a digital photograph, screen display, or printer output.

RAM Random-access memory; volatile internal memory that is erased if power to the computer system is interrupted.

resolution The sharpness of an image. Used to describe output from graphic images, monitors, and printers.

ROM Read-only memory; constant memory contained in an integrated circuit or chip that cannot be modified by the user.

scaling Controlling the size of an image and, in direct proportion, all of its components. Scaling an image reduces or enlarges all of its elements.

scanner An input peripheral that digitizes photos, line drawings, and text by reflecting light off their surface.

sector A segment of a track as determined by the disk operating system.

software Information and directions to control the computer. A computer program preserved on a recording medium (e.g., floppy disk, CD-ROM) often accompanied by written documentation.

speech recognition devices A software program with accompanying microphone that changes the spoken word into text but can be used in a word processing program.

thumb drive See *flash drive*.

track The path followed by a disk drive read-write head, on which data are recorded to or read from a disk.

trackpad A pressure-sensitive pad on which a user presses a finger in order to move a pointer on the screen.

Universal Serial Bus (USB) A powerful, cross-platform communication standard developed to link the computer to external devices.

UPC Universal Product Code; a sequence of thick and thin lines on consumer products spaced to identify a specific item, read by an optical bar code reader.

UPS An uninterruptible power supply is a device that provides emergency power from batteries in the event of an AC power failure.

user interface The interaction between human and machine.

video monitor A television set that has been manufactured to accept a video signal directly and is capable of displaying a picture of much higher resolution than a standard television receiver.

video projector A device that accepts a video signal and projects an image onto a screen.

volatile memory Internal memory that is available and accessible to the user and requires a constant source of power to maintain itself; also called RAM.

wide area network (WAN) A network that spans great distances or covers a wide geographic area. Wide area networks often interconnect LANs. The Internet is an example of a wide area network.

Wi-Fi (Wireless Fidelity) A generic term for any device that uses one of the IEEE 802.11 wireless transmission standards.

REFERENCES & SUGGESTED READINGS

Axelson, M. (1996, September). Networking 101. *Electronic Learning, 16*(1), 52–55.

Dennison, R. F. (2000, May). Don't use a hammer: Appropriate educational uses based upon the characteristics of network tools. *TechTrends, 44*(4), 26–29.

Descy, D. (2000, April). "Good morning, HAL-9000" . . . "Good morning, Don" . . . A primer on speech recognition software. *TechTrends, 44*(3), 4–6.

Fraundorf, M. C. (1997, April). Distributed computers and labs: The best of both worlds. *Learning and Leading with Technology, 24*(7), 50–53.

Fritz, M. (2000, March). DVD dream. *Presentations,* 38–45.

Joss, M. (2001). Now playing in schools: Digital video. *Technology & Learning, 22*(3), 17–19.

Pownell, D., & Bailey, G. D. (2000, May). The next small thing. *Learning and Leading with Technology, 27*(8), 47–49.

Randall, N. (2000, April 18). Setting up a webcam. *PC Magazine,* 138–140.

Saba, F. (1999, January). The death of distance and the rise of the network society. *Distance Education Report, 3*(1), 1–2.

Varvel, V. E., & Thurston, C. (2002, Summer). Perceptions of a wireless network. *Journal of Research on Technology in Education 34*(4), 487–502.

Learning and Instruction

1. What are the basic tenets of behaviorism?

2. What are the basic tenets of constructivism?

3. How can the computer support each perspective?

4. How is information acquired?

5. What is the relationship between concrete and abstract experiences?

6. How can the presentation of the message be enhanced using computer software?

7. How can we use cooperative learning in the classroom?

8. What are the benefits of using authentic assessment in the classroom?

9. What role can rubrics play in classroom assessment?

10. What are the types of intelligences described by Gardner and how might these help you when teaching your students?

11. What should be considered in the evaluation and selection of software?

We cover parts of two NETS•S Categories in Chapter 4. NETS•S *Category 2: Social, ethical, and human issues* is touched on as we discuss the role of the computer in instruction and learning. Explanations of the behaviorist and constructivist perspectives of learning are covered as we move from theory to application. We include here an important discussion on ethical uses of information centered on a discussion of copyright and intellectual property. Appropriateness and effectiveness of software and criteria that may be used for the evaluation of software are also discussed here. In many cases, using poorly designed software is worse than using no software at all. We discuss places to find educationally sound software and ways to find written software evaluations. These topics also hinge on the standards under *Category 3: Technology productivity tools* along with information and instruments for evaluating educational software. It is important that you, as your students' teacher, be a living example of appropriate and ethical use of software and any technology that is used in the classroom and your students' personal lives.

This chapter establishes the groundwork for looking at the computer's role in instruction and examines its role in student learning. Recognizing that there are several theories of learning, that classroom practice is often based on one or more of these theories in combination, and that this text does not purport to be an instructional theory textbook, we review behaviorist and constructivist theories of learning and instruction that are covered in greater depth in courses dealing with pedagogy. The intent here is to demonstrate that the computer can be a practical tool used in concert with multiple teaching strategies that have a solid theoretical basis.

Much learning in the classroom is teacher directed and is based on behaviorist theories that purport that learning takes place in small incremental steps. We present an introduction to this theory and describe ways that computers are used in this approach. Acknowledging that there is a growing interest in constructivist theories of learning, this chapter also presents an overview of a moderate constructivist perspective so that the use of the computer as a productivity tool can be better understood in that environment. The thoughtful application of the computer can make students more productive in the construction of their knowledge through problem solving.

Many of the problems faced by educators could be solved with the assistance of a computer. If the computer is to be an effective tool in increasing productivity, fundamental questions to be answered by the teacher include the following: "When do I use a computer? Will using a computer save time? Will it allow me to perform tasks that might otherwise be beyond my skills? Can I get better, more complete, and more accurate information by using a computer or will it only complicate my life?"

Using computers in education depends on the effective use of software that can increase productivity. As computer users, we need to be thoroughly familiar with the process of problem solving. Most of us will never choose to become computer programmers, but as educators we need to be good users of computer programs, and we need to acquire skills to develop problem-solving specifications.

Looking beyond our own needs as educators, problem-solving proficiency is an essential skill that we must help our students develop. According to **constructivism,** students interact with the real-life experiences that surround them, and they construct mental structures that provide an understanding of their environment. If students are to build these mental structures, they must refine the skills needed to solve the problems they will encounter, whether they are working individually or in cooperative learning groups.

Not all people's thinking patterns and learning styles are alike, although many different cognitive processes and intelligences are valid and should be valued. This chapter gives an overview of perception and communication in order to emphasize the importance of analyzing our student population and matching instructional materials to student needs.

NETS•S Standards Addressed in This Chapter

2. Social, ethical, and human issues
   - Students understand the ethical, cultural, and societal issues related to technology.
   - Students develop positive attitudes toward technology uses that support lifelong learning, collaboration, personal pursuits, and productivity.

3. Technology productivity tools
   - Students use technology tools to enhance learning, increase productivity, and promote creativity.
   - Students use productivity tools to collaborate in constructing technology-enhanced models, prepare publications, and produce other creative works.

PERSPECTIVES ON TEACHING AND LEARNING

Every learning environment has an implied method of information presentation. Learning activities are based on a belief of how students best learn. Of the many philosophical doctrines, two stand out rather clearly as examples related to software development, selection, and use: the behaviorist perspective and the constructivist perspective.

Behaviorism uses a teacher-directed approach that is based on theories developed by B. F. Skinner, Robert Gagné, Richard Atkinson, Lee Cronbach, and David Ausubel. Behaviorists view the teacher as the manipulator of the environment that is experienced by the learner. B. F. Skinner, well known for his work in behavior modification through operant conditioning, was a proponent of programmed instruction. Skinnerian-style lessons use carefully planned steps of stimulus-response pairing and reinforcement to reach a goal. The lessons and their accompanying drills are administered in small, incremental steps to minimize the likelihood of incorrect responses. The techniques used reflect a belief that, by tightly structuring the environment, the behavior of the organism (the student) can be shaped to achieve desired changes (learning). **Linear** programmed instruction is an example of this concept of education, where the accumulation of knowledge is preparing the student for predicted future needs. Traditional classroom instruction has included strong components of this behaviorist theory, which is referred to at times as objectivist. The teacher, with the prescribed textbook, is the source of information. Behavioral objectives are identified, lessons are planned, instruction is delivered, guided practice is provided, retention and transfer of learning activities are encouraged, and testing the information taught is the standard means of assessment.

In direct contrast to the behaviorist viewpoint is the perspective espoused by constructivists, who view education as inseparable from ordinary life. Constructivists base their model on work by Jerome Bruner, Seymour Papert, Jean Piaget, and Lev Vygotosky. Through developmental exploration and play, students assume control of educational activities by making choices related to individual interests. The students discover rules and concepts during the course of interactions in an environment that encourages the use of problem-solving strategies, which in turn are developed while learning how to think. The teacher learns along with the students and becomes a guide, a facilitator, and a supportive partner in this educational process. Education is considered a guided tour of preparatory experiences in which students practice making decisions by simulating real-world situations. The teacher becomes the facilitator of education by selecting the experiences that offer the appropriate practice to the students. In this way students construct their own knowledge and gain skills that will be needed in a future environment, which may be quite different from the present one. If reduced to a single overriding distinction, it could be said that constructivism encourages the learner to pose a problem and then solve it, whereas according to behaviorism, the role of the teacher or other external source is to pose the problem to be solved. It should, therefore, be noted that the teaching of problem-solving strategies is important in both perspectives.

Software may reflect one or both of these approaches and may make assumptions about the teaching/learning style that will be used in the classroom. Different techniques are selected to achieve educational goals in relation to different philosophical perspectives. Teachers must learn to identify the instructional approaches embodied in particular software if they are to effectively harness the power of the computer in their classrooms.

The Behaviorist Perspective on Learning

Robert Gagné (Gagné, Briggs, & Wager, 1992, pp. 54–66) lists types of intellectual skills in a linear scheme, ranging from simple discriminations to complex problem-solving processes. This approach is predicated on the belief that the acquisition of knowledge at any stage depends on what has been learned at an earlier one. Thus, a learner must master the lower-level abilities before tackling the higher orders.

Elements of a Good Lesson.   A great deal of research has gone into identifying the components of a good learning situation. Gagné views learning theory as technology— that is, there is a set of rules that can be followed in the design of instructional events. His point of view draws on many theories of outstanding psychologists and resulted in the formulation of the following instructional events as elements of a good lesson (Gagné, Briggs, & Wager, 1992, p. 190):

1. Gaining attention: Stimulation to gain attention to ensure the reception of stimuli.
2. Informing learner of the objective: Informing learners of the learning objective to establish appropriate expectancies.
3. Stimulating recall of prerequisite learning: Reminding learners of previously learned content for retrieval from long-term memory.
4. Presenting the stimulus material: Clear and distinctive presentation of material to ensure selective perception.
5. Providing learning guidance: Guidance of learning by suitable semantic encoding.
6. Eliciting the performance: Eliciting performance involving response generation.
7. Providing feedback about performance correctness: Informing students about correctness of responses.
8. Assessing the performance: Following the opportunity for additional responses, inform the learner of mastery and give further directions.
9. Enhancing retention and transfer: Arranging variety of practice to aid future retrieval and transfer of learning.

Wedman (1986) found it quite revealing to examine the elements of a good lesson as they relate to the instructional functions provided by computer-assisted instruction (CAI) software. By describing common ways in which software provides each of the instructional events, he offers a method of analyzing a program's strengths and weaknesses relative to the elements in a good lesson as described by Gagné, Briggs, and Wager. Wedman then examines the teacher's role in complementing the instruction provided by the software to provide a complete instructional unit. The chart presented in Figure 4–1 displays the CAI software and teacher techniques related to each instructional event.

A diagram of these events as they might occur in a computerized lesson using the program *Odell Down Under*® (The Learning Company, Inc.) is provided in Figure 4–2. This example, set in Australia's Great Barrier Reef, is a worthy successor to the award-winning *Odell Lake* and uses all the instructional events described by Gagné, Briggs, and Wager.

Figure 4–3 is an example of the high-quality graphics used to gain attention. Animation is also present on the computer screen. Some software, of course, uses only some of the instructional events. In such cases, the teacher must provide the missing events for the lesson.

Human Factors.   A great deal of attention has been given to individual responses during interactions with computers. These effects are critical to the effectiveness of a program, because they influence the learning events of a good lesson. Early writings by Gagné and Briggs (1974, p. 11) recognized eight human factors affecting the learning event. These factors, identified as external stimulus factors and internal cognitive factors, are listed in Figure 4–4.

The three external stimulus factors are contiguity (time relationship between stimulus and response), repetition (frequency and rate of exposure to a stimulus), and reinforcement (follow-up to the reception of a stimulus). The three internal cognitive factors are factual information (from memory or external sources), intellectual skills (ability to manipulate information), and cognitive strategies (ability to process or interpret into meaningful information). Added to these are the internal affective factors of inhibition (reluctance to react to a stimulus) and anxiety (a tension often stemming from a lack of confidence).

These factors relate to a theory of how information is stored in and retrieved from short-term and long-term memory. Gagné and Briggs believe that information that is sensed is held in the auditory, visual, or tactile register for only a second before it is disregarded or sent to short-term memory. There it is encoded for about one-half minute before storage in long-term memory. Because of the short periods involved, a stimulus must be limited to one idea, and there must be enough time to process and store the information without interference or overload. Meaningful repetition is believed to contribute to control of the processes and, in turn, to learning. The effectiveness of a lesson depends on the internal responses to a stimulus, the senses used, and the ease of use of the computer so as to minimize distractions during computer-assisted learning.

Behaviorists favor software designed for drill and practice or tutorial instruction. Popular titles of this type of software on the market today include *Math Blaster*® *6–8; Math Munchers Deluxe*®; *Word Munchers Deluxe*®; *Read, Write & Type;* and *Mavis Beacon Teaches Typing*®.

The Constructivist Perspective on Learning

Cognitive psychologists as early as Whitehead (1929) have insisted that learning is an active and highly individualized process. They clearly point out that learners must actively construct new knowledge based on their own individual experiences and

Events of Instruction	CAI Techniques	Teacher Techniques
1. Gaining attention	• Graphics • Sound • Games	• Demonstrate relevance of content • Present high-involvement problems • Use related, highly attractive media • Assign groups to use software
2. Informing learner of objectives	• Pretest • Textual statement of objectives • Graphic illustration of objectives • Brief interactive demonstration	• Pretest • Tell the learner what is expected • Demonstrate use of the content
3. Stimulating recall of prerequisites	• Pretest for prerequisites • Textual review of prerequisites • Graphic display of prerequisites	• Test prerequisite content • Review prerequisite content and vocabulary
4. Presenting stimuli	• Textual display of new content • Graphic display of new content • Learner control over presentation sequence and display rate • Reference to non-CAI material	• Use other media to present new content
5. Providing guidance	• Attention focusing devices (e.g., animation, sound, pointers) • Help screens • Examples and illustrations	• Organize peer tutoring • Cross-reference difficult content to examples and remediation in other materials
6. Eliciting performance	• Questions on new content • Applications of new content to solve problems or control situation (e.g., flight simulator)	• Ask questions • Create performance tasks where the learner applies the new content (e.g., lab experiment)
7. Providing feedback	• Display score or correct answer • Help screens for incorrect answers • Additional information or examples	• Provide answer keys • Provide reference materials coordinated with correct answers • Provide outcome guides coordinated with performance tasks (e.g., lab experiment check sheet)
8. Assessing performance	• Test questions • Limited response time (for memory-level questions) • Recordkeeping	• Give paper-and-pencil tests • Conduct performance tests • Use computers for context-rich testing
9. Enhancing retention and transfer	• Repeating content not mastered • Applying new content to a different, but related situation	• Provide alternative instructional materials for content not mastered • Create situations (not involving a computer) where students must apply new content

Figure 4–1

CAI and teacher techniques related to events of instruction (Wedman, 1986. Courtesy of *The Computing Teacher*)

Gaining attention

> A reef is shown with fish swimming around and music playing.

Stating the objective

> The student is informed that the object is to discover the relationship between fish, which to eat, which to avoid, and which ones will clean off parasites.

Stimulating recall of prerequisite learnings

> The student is reminded to use all of the information presented in the picture and to make choices. The student can interrupt the program at any time to review information about the various reef dwellers.

Presenting the stimulus material

> When the student has chosen a fish and read the given information, the computer generates a picture of the reef with the chosen fish shown in some situation.

Eliciting the performance

> The student is asked to control the fish's behavior by moving the mouse, clicking when appropriate, or pressing the spacebar.

Assessing the performance

> The computer indicates whether the chosen behavior was correct, incorrect, or indifferent.

Providing feedback about the performance

> The action in the given reef situation is carried out demonstrating the behavior chosen by the student.

Enhancing retention and transfer

> Another situation is presented to the student based on past performance.

Figure 4–2
Elements of a good science lesson demonstrated in *Odell Down Under,* a simulation of a predator/prey model

understandings. This constructivist model of learning is based on the concept that knowledge is produced by the individual learner rather than processed from information received from an external source. The student becomes the producer rather than the consumer of information. The teacher becomes the guide and facilitator of learning rather than the director of instruction. Goals are still set, but the learner is given significant freedom in how to attain them. Assessment is still performed, but benchmarks are established and the teacher employs authentic measures such as evaluating a product or examining a portfolio.

A foundation for some of the current constructivists' beliefs can be found in the work of Jean Piaget. He is best known for proposing four stages of development in a child's cognitive abilities: (1) from birth to about age two, the sensorimotor stage (when children begin to explore their environment and to differentiate themselves from the world around them); (2) from age two to about seven, the preoperational

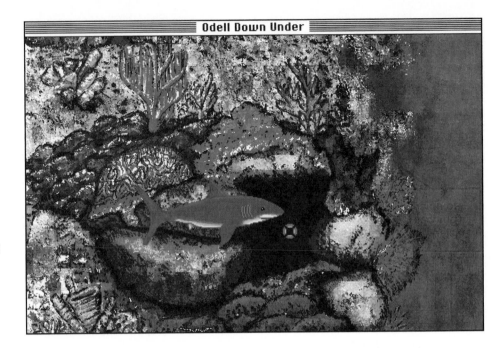

Figure 4–3
A screen from *Odell Down Under* (Courtesy of TLC Properties Inc., a subsidiary of The Learning Company, Inc.)

External Stimulus Factors

- Contiguity
- Repetition
- Reinforcement

Internal Cognitive Factors

- Factual information
- Intellectual skills
- Cognitive strategies

Internal Affective Factors

- Inhibition
- Anxiety

Figure 4–4
Eight human factors affecting the learning event

stage (when language and intuitive thought develop); (3) from age seven to about 12, the **concrete** operational stage (when classifying and ordering of items and inductive reasoning develop); and (4) from about age 12 on, the stage of formal operations (when more **abstract** and formal thought, control of variables, and proportionality can be managed). Piaget attributed these stages to a naturally occurring process of maturation and the appropriate exposure to experiences that encourage development.

The idea that children learn without being taught is central to this learning theory. Long before children enter school, they have mastered the complexities of language and speech enough to understand and communicate with those around them. They have gained a sense of intuitive body geometry that enables them to move around in space, and they have learned enough logic and rhetoric to convey their desires to parents and peers. Children learn all these things effectively without formal teachers and a curriculum, and without explicit external rewards or punishments. They learn by simply interacting with their environment, relating what is new to what they know from past experience.

For example, a very young child can build a cognitive structure or a concept of "dogness": dogs look, feel, sound, and smell a certain way. Whenever a dog is encountered, the child attempts to make sense of the experience by calling on a previously formed cognitive structure of "dog." Piaget calls this assimilation. But a new dog may be different from the one met before. As new elements are encountered (a curly tail instead of a straight one; long, shaggy hair instead of short hair; and so on), the cognitive structure for "dog" must be modified and enlarged to encompass the new information, a process Piaget called accommodation.

If we think of learners in Piagetian terms, as the active builders of their own cognitive structures, we should consider the kinds of experiences and material our culture provides for use in this building process and examine the potential contribution of the computer.

Figure 4–5 summarizes the predominant differences between the behaviorist and constructivist perspectives. They should be viewed as points on a continuum, not as absolutes. Though the trend in the United States is toward constructivism, most classrooms exhibit some characteristics of both.

Behaviorist	Constructivist
Teacher-centered	Learner-centered
Teacher as expert	Teacher as member of learning community
Teacher as dispenser of information	Teacher as coach, mentor, and facilitator
Learning as a solitary activity	Learning as a social, collaborative endeavor
Assessment primarily through testing	Assessment interwoven with teaching
Emphasis on "covering" the material	Emphasis on discovering and constructing knowledge
Emphasis on short-term memorization	Emphasis on application and understanding
Strict adherence to fixed curriculum	Pursuit of student questions highly valued

Figure 4–5
Comparison of behaviorist and constructivist perspectives

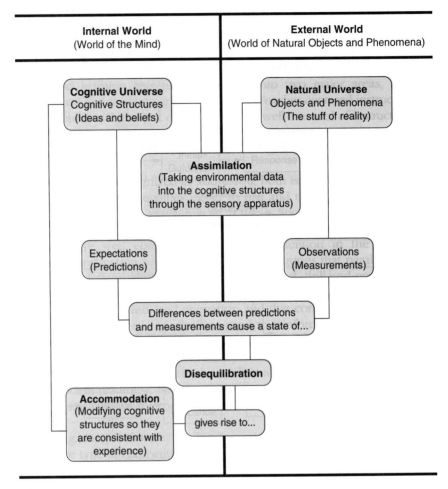

Figure 4–6
A constructivist
learning model
(Reprinted with per-
mission from School
Science and
Mathematics.)

Saunders (1992) illustrated the constructivist perspective with the model shown in Figure 4–6. He states, "Constructivism can be defined as that philosophical position which holds that any so-called reality is, in the most immediate and concrete sense, the mental construction of those who believe they have discovered and investigated it." The conflict between expectations (what we think will happen) and observations (measures of what actually happens) causes disequilibration. The problem is resolved through accommodation, or learning—the process of reconciling new information with previously held ideas and beliefs. Explained this way, it becomes clear that constructivism is a philosophy in which problem solving is a central element.

From a constructivist perspective, learners must be provided with a rich environment of sensory experiences, to which they will respond in a problem-solving fashion in order to build understandings. The computer, through its use of text, sound, graphics, animation, and multimedia, is ideally suited to present such a rich environment. In a constructivist classroom, technology is encountered that will enable the student the opportunity to experiment with it, construct individually and in groups, and reconstruct models and simulations that aid them as they build their own ideas and beliefs. Many of the computer applications that we discuss in this text will be useful tools for your students to help them construct their own knowledge. We stated in the beginning that computers are simply a tool to help people perform tasks easily and more efficiently. Students who have ownership in a product take care as they construct their own knowledge. This sometimes poses a dilemma for teachers who have been successful in their schooling using the older behaviorist approach. Many may feel that they are losing control of learning rather than understanding that they are co-controlling learning now with their students.

Constructivists favor software designed to pose problems and construct scenarios designed to make students active participants in their learning. Popular titles of this type of software on the market today include *Hot Dog Stand*®, *SimCity2000*®, *Where in the World Is Carmen Sandiego?*®, *Inspiration*®, and the ever-popular *Oregon Trail*®.

The shifting paradigms described in Chapter 1 describe a transition from a centralized environment to a personalized one, with the user in command of the computer, and to an interpersonal one, where users interact with one another. There is a distinct move from the computer operator to the end user interacting directly with the computer and to a networked community of users interconnected electronically. Finally, we have moved away from a fascination with huge amounts of stored data to a concern for the value of the information and the development of knowledge. Every one of these paradigm shifts parallels the shift in philosophical foundations of education toward a more constructivist approach emphasizing problem solving.

Compared with behaviorist approaches to instruction, in which "covering the material" is emphasized, constructivist approaches to instruction focus on students "discovering the material." When students are actively engaged with other students and teachers in the process of learning through the completion of authentic tasks, they need both problem-solving tools and problem-solving skills to assist them.

COOPERATIVE LEARNING

All learning takes place in one of three ways: individually or students working alone, competitively or students working against each other, and cooperatively or students working together to accomplish shared learning goals. While all three should be a part of a child's education, Roger R. and David W. Johnson, co-directors of the Cooperative Learning Center at the University of Minnesota, recommend that the cooperative mode play the dominant role. Cooperative learning—or collaborative learning, as it is sometimes called—activities tend to promote the development of communications skills, higher-order thinking skills, positive self-esteem, social awareness, improved motivation, and a greater tolerance of individual differences (Johnson & Johnson, 1994).

A productive environment must be created by carefully grouping students and monitoring the behavior of groups to prevent students from "slacking off" and riding the coattails of more able partners and to prevent higher-ability students from lowering their own effort and achievement because of a feeling of being used by others. True collaboration must provide for structured sharing in creation and decision making, resulting in a negotiated product. Teachers must prepare students for collaborative computer activities by issuing specific directions relating to each group member's role and expected interaction with others and the computer. Individual and group assessment must be considered. Individual student journals or portfolios may be used, along with an evaluation of the product produced by the group. Individual assessment tends to keep the individual student on task, while product assessment fosters peer tutoring and a feeling of responsibility to the group.

Cooperative learning prepares the student for the world of work, where some measure of collaboration is found in nearly every job situation. Research indicates that cooperative learning supports task-oriented behavior and improved peer relations. It provides social skill benefits, with achievement benefits for low-achievers and no penalty on high-achievers (Schlechter, 1990). Thus, cooperative learning, correctly implemented, is one way teachers can effectively stretch scarce computer resources.

Technology can serve an important role in cooperative learning environments. The teamwork needed to plan and produce a technology-enhanced lesson or project allows students with diverse skills, backgrounds, and abilities to work together as a team and be successful in their individual roles. Most schools do not have enough computers or equipment to allow for individual work on projects so cooperative learning, with all of its benefits, is an excellent way to change a computer-poor situation into a learning-rich one.

ASSESSMENT

It is important to assess student learning accurately if we are to truly measure progress. Many teachers do not feel that traditional paper-and-pencil testing and measurement accurately reflect the amount of student learning actually taking place. One of the ways that is being used more and more to increase the accuracy of the measurement of student learning is **authentic assessment** or **performance-based assessment.** Authentic assessment refers to assessment tasks that resemble real-world situations. Authentic assessment does not encourage passive testing or rote learning but rather focuses on the student being able to integrate learning to overcome a real-world problem. Authentic assessment encourages students to use higher-order thinking skills to solve problems by utilizing *performance samples* such as open response questions, short investigation of problems, performance assessment, portfolios, and self-assessment. Authentic assessment allows students to not only understand information but also helps them develop this understanding in real-world skills that are much easier to transfer to the outside world. Assessments usually reflect learning over time and enable instructors to better evaluate performance and achievement in a way not available with standard paper-and-pencil examinations. Project development can be documented that also shows learning over time.

Project-based learning is an authentic assessment model for teaching in which projects are used to assess student learning. Students involved in this model actively construct their own knowledge, complete meaningful tasks, create realistic projects, and/or solve real-world projects. Checklists, rating scales, rubrics, and portfolios are all authentic assessment methods of evaluating student learning.

Checklists are simple ways of observing and categorizing behaviors in a bimodal (observed/not observed) manner. **Ratings scales** on the other hand are more complex, where each observation is placed on a scale, usually of numerical values that measure the degree to which a student completes a task.

Another way to score authentic assessment projects is through the use of a **rubric.** A rubric is a scoring matrix that differentiates the quality of learning using a graduated scale of exemplar behaviors. These benchmarks assist teachers by providing objective guidelines to evaluate student performance on a task. The behaviors may be correlated with qualitative or quantitative scores. Rubrics are used to place student achievement at a point on a scale that enables the student to see what is needed to achieve mastery. Many times rubrics are distributed beforehand to help students plan and measure their learning.

Well-constructed rubrics:

- Present learners with explicit guidelines concerning the expectations of their teacher,
- Supply a model for the learners to impart emphasis, focus, and detail to refine their capabilities,
- Present learners with a sequential progression of behaviors that guide them to a higher level of knowledge,
- Allow learners to pattern their own education to meet the expectations of their teacher,
- Enable the teacher to accurately assess learning on a predetermined scale.

Below is a partial rubric that might be used to evaluate a Web page.

Authority:
- *Level 1:* No author or e-mail contact is listed.
- *Level 2:* No author is listed but an e-mail address is given.
- *Level 3:* An author is listed but there is no way to find out about their credentials.
- *Level 4:* An author is listed along with their credentials that are appropriate for the material on the page.

Dating:
- *Level 1:* There is no way to tell when the Web page was produced or updated.
- *Level 2:* Information on the page was updated within the past two years but still seems to be relevant.
- *Level 3:* Information on the page was updated within the past year and seems to be up-to-date.
- *Level 4:* Information on the page was updated within the last three months and reflects up-to-date knowledge on the subject.

Bias:
- *Level 1:* The information on the page discusses only one point view with generalizations and seemingly unprovable assumptions.
- *Level 2:* The information on the page discusses only one point of view with little reference to known authorities in the field.
- *Level 3:* The information on the page discusses only one point of view with references to known authorities in the field.
- *Level 4:* The information on the page seems fair and balanced.

Purpose:
- *Level 1:* It is difficult to understand the purpose of the Web page.
- *Level 2:* The Web page seems to have a purpose but contains information that does not seem relevant to it.
- *Level 3:* The purpose is somewhat clear though it contains some distracting elements.
- *Level 4:* It is easy to define the purpose of the Web page.

Portfolios are also used as a measure of authentic assessment. We discussed portfolios in Chapter 1.

It is easy to see how technology can aid the teacher and the student in an authentic assessment environment. The student can match goals, outcomes, and standards with work accomplished using databases and electronic portfolios. Teachers can use technology in many of the same ways matching students, progress, and projects in databases, spreadsheets, and electronic storage systems.

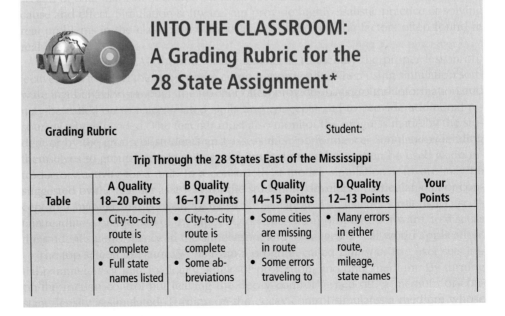

INTO THE CLASSROOM:
A Grading Rubric for the
28 State Assignment*

Grading Rubric					Student:
Trip Through the 28 States East of the Mississippi					
Table	**A Quality 18–20 Points**	**B Quality 16–17 Points**	**C Quality 14–15 Points**	**D Quality 12–13 Points**	**Your Points**
	• City-to-city route is complete • Full state names listed	• City-to-city route is complete • Some abbreviations	• Some cities are missing in route • Some errors traveling to	• Many errors in either route, mileage, state names	

	A Quality 9–10 Points	B Quality 8 Points	C Quality 7 Points	D Quality 6 Points	
	• Miles are completely accurate • Columns are left aligned except for mileage (centered)	used in state names • Miles are completely accurate • Columns are aligned properly	contiguous states • Miles are complete & accurate • Some mis-alignment in columns	• Table is incomplete, misaligned, etc.	
Map	**A Quality 9–10 Points**	**B Quality 8 Points**	**C Quality 7 Points**	**D Quality 6 Points**	**Your Points**
	• All states are labeled with the correct abbreviation • Title • Used a ruler • Route is clearly marked • Mississippi River follows the correct route & is labeled • No spelling errors • No more than 5 distinctly different colors were used • Outlining/ shading • Map is free of erasures & smudges • Writing is clear & legible	• Title • Used a ruler • Two or less errors in labeling states and/ or spelling • Route is clearly marked • Mississippi River follows the correct route & is labeled • Used more than 5 colors or colors weren't distinctly different • A few conti-guous states same color • Very few erasures or smudges • No outlining or shades, if present it is messy • Very little of the writing is illegible	• Title messy or incom-plete • Some ruler • More than three errors in labeling states or spelling • Route is marked but may have some confusions • Mississippi River isn't clearly marked • Used more than 5 colors or colors were not distinct or different • Contiguous states same color • Coloring is missing or incomplete • Smudges or erasures	• Final product messy or incomplete • Smudges on product are distracting • Erasures are messy • Words are illegible or incorrect • Carto-graphic rules have been ignored • Route isn't complete or is difficult to follow • Mississippi River path is confusing or missing	

(Continued)

Chart	A Quality 14–15 Points	B Quality 12–13 Points	C Quality 11 Points	D Quality 9–10 Points	Your Points
Cover Sheet	**A Quality 5 Points**	**B Quality 4 Points**	**C Quality 3 Points**	**D Quality 2 Points**	**Your Points**
	• All required information is included • Border is neatly printed • Paper is free of erasures & smudges • No spelling errors • Writing is clear & legible	• All required information included • Border may be some-what messy • Very few smudges, erasures • No spelling errors • Writing is crooked, somewhat unclear, or illegible	• Some information missing • No border • Some smudges or erasures that detract • 1–2 spelling errors • Writing is crooked, unclear, or illegible	• Numerous smudges or erasures • Incomplete • Numerous errors • Writing is crooked, unclear, or illegible	
Total Points					50

Paula Conley
Skyway Elementary School
Coeur d'Alene, Idaho
*THIS RUBRIC WAS USED TO GRADE STUDENTS FOR THE
INTO THE CLASSROOM FOUND IN CHAPTER 1.

INSTRUCTION AND LEARNING

Just as problem-solving strategies vary among individuals, so do types of intelligence, perception, and motivation. Good teachers always try to individualize their instruction, even when dealing with 30 students in a classroom. They attempt to know each student as an individual; to recognize strengths and weaknesses; and to identify, accommodate, and respect different types of intelligence and different learning styles. The computer is becoming an invaluable tool aiding the teacher in each of these ways. Good teachers also understand the role of perception and motivation in learning, and how computer software can increase both faculties. Understanding students as individuals allows teachers to make intelligent and informed decisions when choosing software for their classrooms.

Types of Intelligence

Howard Gardner proposes that there are at least eight intelligences: linguistic, logical-mathematical, spatial, musical, bodily-kinesthetic, interpersonal, intrapersonal, and naturalist (Pennar, 1996). Your students may exhibit one type of intelligence in particular or may have several strengths. Gardner defines intelligence as "a set of skills of problem solving—enabling the individual to resolve genuine problems or difficulties that he or she encounters and when appropriate, to create an effective product; it also entails the potential for finding or creating problems, thereby laying the groundwork for the acquisition of new knowledge" (Gardner, 1983, pp. 60–61). Gardner believes that intelligence defines not only how people acquire information but also how they process this acquired information. Although many people tend to think of intelligence more narrowly, it is important to recognize and support individual aptitudes by ensuring that all students have resources to help cultivate their full range of talents and intelligences. Unfortunately, today's schools usually address only two of Gardner's intelligences: linguistic and logical-mathematical (Ross & Olsen, 1995). Reflecting on these intelligences and seeking to create a computer environment supportive of all students, Eichleay and Kilroy (1993–1994) suggest types of software appropriate to each intelligence.

Not all students will react alike to the same piece of software. A study of Figure 4–7, adapted from Eichleay and Kilroy (1993–1994, p. 39), and modified by Forcier in 1998, will suggest ways in which a variety of software can be applied to meet the needs of different learners. More information on expanding Gardner's theory into effective classroom practice can be found in Campbell, Campbell, and Dickinson (1999), listed in the reference section of this chapter.

Perception

What we know about the world we have experienced through our senses. Free of any physical impairments, we usually gain information through all five senses. Infants are intrigued by the wondrous variety of sounds and sights and smells to which they are exposed, and they seek to explore every sensory stimulus. As we mature, our visual and aural senses assume an overwhelming importance in the acquisition of knowledge. Indeed, a great deal of the information we possess as adults has been acquired through the sense of sight.

Perception is relative, not absolute. Sensory stimuli are accepted by the learner and given meaning based primarily on past experiences. Thus, sensory experiences result in perceptions. Because perceptions, in turn, are organized into understandings, the quality of the visual and aural stimuli embodied in software assumes great importance.

Intelligence	Type of Software
Linguistic	Word processors, word games, software with speech output, crossword puzzle generators, books on CD-ROM.
Logical-mathematical	Spreadsheets, databases, problem-solving software, computer programming, logo, strategy game formats.
Spatial	Graphic production, three-dimensional modeling, mazes and puzzles, logo, maps, charts, and diagrams, multimedia.
Musical	Song creation, music concepts/skills, story and song combinations, recording music, singing, or rhymes with a microphone.
Bodily-kinesthetic	Alternative input devices, keyboarding/word processing, science and math with manipulatives and probes, programs where the user can move objects on the screen.
Interpersonal	Telecommunications, interactions with characters in simulations and adventures, programs about social issues, group participation/decision-making programs, two or more player games.
Intrapersonal	Tutorial, self-paced games played against the computer, self-awareness/ self-improvement building programs.
Naturalist	Spreadsheets, databases, image capture software.

Figure 4–7
Multiple intelligences and software types [Adapted with permission from "Hot Tips for Inclusion with Technology" by K. Eichleay and C. Kilroy, December/January, 1993–1994, *The Computing Teacher, 21*(4), pp. 38–40. Modified by Forcier in 1998.]

As an infant, the concept of "fiveness" might be acquired by handling five items (units), gradually seeing them represented by five fingers (digits), and then processing the meaning as the numeral 5 (symbol). Once a child has been exposed to a variety of concrete experiences, pictorial and then verbal experiences are an effective and much more efficient way of building understandings. These more abstract expressions of ideas must have a concrete basis. Examining well-designed software, we find that computer graphics, visuals, and certainly multimedia serve as more concrete referents to meaning than do written words. Because visuals resemble the items they represent, they offer the viewer concrete clues to meaning. To enhance the perception of visual information in software, research by Guba et al. (1964) and others has shown that, in good graphic design, distracting elements must be kept to a minimum. This point is particularly important, because the learner is constantly bombarded by a multitude of sensory inputs. Software must be designed to limit distraction and guide the learner's attention to the essential information. Visual and aural cues should give order to the message, and difficult concepts should be broken down into easily digested steps providing concrete reference points familiar to the learner.

FROM THEORY TO APPLICATION

Good practice should be based on an understanding of sound theory. As we study theories of learning, reflect on our experiences, and examine our own motivations—as well as those of our students—we should seek to develop a knowledge base and a skill level that will enhance our application of computers to the classroom. This knowledge and skill will guide us through many decisions related to curriculum, teaching and learning strategies with the computer, equipment purchases, and computer software selection.

Appropriateness of Software

Because the learning theory on which software design is based dictates the role of the computer, the role of the teacher, and the role of the student, recognizing these elements is an important first step toward making good use of the computer in the classroom. Instructional objectives will be met only if the software and the intent of the lesson are closely related.

To understand why the computer lesson must be consistent with the kinds of learning students have come to expect, consider the following example. Imagine that we have prepared a lesson plan calling for practice on the subtraction of whole numbers less than 100. Surveying a curriculum resource guide for software to use, we find a program that presents a subtraction algorithm. This software on subtraction is designed for discovery learning. That is, when a student misses the answer, the software branches back to work that should have been mastered earlier and presents a different problem. However, if our classroom method prior to this lesson has been directive, replete with examples, some students would be frustrated by the computer lesson, because it fails to give them the information they expect. Clearly, in this case, our students would be better served by software built around a more linear approach.

Effectiveness of Software

In assessing the effectiveness of software, keep in mind that the internal responses to a stimulus correspond very closely with the events of a good lesson. The student is alerted or motivated, perhaps by curiosity, to interact with the program. The objective of the program sets an expectancy for performance that interests the student. The student must be able to retrieve prerequisite information that provides meaning to the activity. The stimulus of new information must be perceived selectively over time, or through repetition, from processing to memory. Feedback in the form of favorable reinforcement should bolster self-worth. The information should have relevance to the student's environment for generalization and transfer of learning to occur. If the progression of these responses is not smooth, the chain of events is interrupted, and the lesson is less effective.

Teachers must appeal to multiple senses to gain students' attention and keep them interested. As with other classroom activities, a variety of events is more effective than one or two continuously repeated actions. Variety can be achieved by offering, for example, interaction through the tactile response of typing on the keyboard; using different sounds, bright colors, and interesting graphics; and introducing new topics to challenge reasoning. In addition, students should interact at the appropriate level to avoid frustration or boredom.

When evaluating software, remember that the process of interacting with the computer must be simple, so students can concentrate on the content of the program. Elements that contribute to ease of use center on a simple means of input and a simple presentation of output. To simplify input, a mouse click, single-key command, and single-key selection of activities from a menu of options limit typing errors and speed up program execution. Error-free programs (no bugs) and error-trapped designs (in which mistakes are correctable or not accepted at all) prevent frustration with stalled or prematurely terminated lessons.

Clarity in eliciting responses from the student also avoids confusion when interpreting what or how to respond. Output can be simplified, for example, by limiting the field of perception by presenting simple, uncluttered displays one page at a time; double-spacing text for readability; grouping ideas for easy understanding; formatting the screen to focus on one point; and highlighting major points by effectively using color, animation, and sound. Most of these features are encountered frequently in films, slides, textbooks, and other instructional materials.

Based on an understanding of learning theories and an awareness of factors dealing with intelligence, perception, and motivation, it is possible to postulate the following guidelines for effective software:

- Software must stimulate a high degree of interest in the learner.
- Software must contribute to developmental learning and, thereby, increase the permanence of that learning.
- Software must be based in concrete experience to enhance understanding.
- Software must make optimum use of the visual and, where appropriate, the aural sensory channels to strengthen the reality of the experience.

SOFTWARE EVALUATION

Keep in mind that the fundamental reason for using computer software is to enhance teaching and learning. The fundamental reason for software evaluation is to determine whether it fits your educational goals. D'Ignazio (1992) states:

> Technology has the potential to dramatically improve the performance of teachers and students, and enrich the learning environment. However, in order to produce these outcomes, technology must be used to support the "best practices" for teaching and learning.
>
> Technology must be used by teachers to create a classroom that encourages:
> - Heightened student attention, engagement, and enthusiasm for learning
> - Inspired teaching
> - Students taking responsibility for their learning and for coaching fellow students

- Student authoring, publishing, and presentations
- Cooperative learning
- Problem solving, critical thinking, questioning, and analysis
- Collaborative inquiry, research, and investigation. (pp. 54–55)

When evaluating software, keep some kind of permanent record that describes the product and lists its features and potential applications. Enter the information from the evaluation into the school's electronic resource guide to media available in the school or into the public access catalog of the school library's automated system if the software is purchased.

Some of the criteria for evaluation are general to all software, whereas some of the evaluative criteria are specific to types of software: drill and practice, tutorial, simulation, or tool. The following sections consider the evaluation process, first according to general criteria, and then according to criteria related to software type.

INTO THE CLASSROOM:
Software Evaluation

We, as educators, are faced with a vast array of educational software. Some of it is excellent and some of it is worthless. It is not enough that we purchase software based on brightly colored advertisements in our professional publications or the words of vendors at a conference or even based on how many awards the software has received. We must spend time with the software: using it, dissecting it, and evaluating it. We must find out for ourselves if it matches our needs, our students' needs, our goals and objectives, and the time and technology that we have available.

It is important that we evaluate software in a systematic way. There are many evaluation forms available. They can be found in textbooks, professional periodicals, and on the Internet. I have used several. Following is an example of a typical evaluation form that I have found useful.

Title of software: Kid Works 2
Publisher: Davidson and Associates, Inc.
Subject area: Language arts and fine arts
Specific topics: Writing, spelling, speaking, and drawing
Grade levels: Kindergarten, first grade

(Continued)

Objectives: Students can exercise their creativity and improve their language skills with this program.

Prerequisite skills: Students need to know how to use the keyboard and the mouse.

Teacher options: I could not find any.

Nature of program: Tutorial, art, and "story writer"

OPINIONS

Feedback strengths: After students type in their stories, they can click an icon and have the computer read them out loud. They can hear what they wrote.

Feedback weaknesses: The program reads misspelled words, and students may not know that they misspelled a word.

Self-paced: Yes

Graphics/sound quality: This program has great graphics and sound. There are pictures that represent many different nouns, verbs, and adjectives, and the pictures are all identified in writing underneath, so the program is very conducive to learning. There are sounds for all of the different icons that you push, which adds to student involvement and enjoyment. The program can also read out loud what students type.

Nonsexist: Yes. There doesn't seem to be anything in this program that would be considered sexist.

Reflects racial/ethnic diversity: Marginal. This program lacks cultural diversity. Although there are some African American people in the pictures, most of the people are Caucasian. There are no other ethnic groups represented.

Appropriate for ESL students: This is a great program for ESL students. The different pictures are labeled so when they look at a picture of a dog, for example, they can read the word "dog" displayed underneath it. Also, the program can read the words out loud to the student so the student can hear the word as he or she learns to read and speak basic English nouns, verbs, and adjectives.

Appropriate for students with special learning needs: Yes. Students use this program at their own pace. There are also no right or wrong answers in this program, so it will not discourage slow students.

Recommendation: This seems to be a wonderful program. I highly recommend it. It will fit the present needs of my class.

Brief description of the program: When you open the program, there are icons for a Story Writer, Story Illustrator, Story Player, and Icon Maker. Students can write stories, illustrate them, and have the computer play them back. When students are writing their stories, they can click on icons for nouns, verbs, or adjectives. Under these icons, there are labeled pictures for many different words that students can put in their stories. Students can also write their own words and have the computer replace them with pictures or read them out loud. In the Story Illustrator, there is a great program for drawing pictures. Students can use paint buckets, pencils, and several other tools to create their own pictures. There are many different colors of crayons for them to use. There are also patterns and stamps and whole pictures that they can color themselves. In the Story Player it is assumed that students can get the computer to play their stories back to them, although, for some reason, I could not get this to work. In the Icon Maker, students can make their own labeled pictures and then use them as they use the other labeled pictures in the Story Writer portion of the program.

Erica Krajnik
Second-Grade Teacher
Annapolis Elementary School
Annapolis, Maryland

General Criteria

Familiarize yourself with the total software package. Read the instructions to the teacher and to the user. Look over the manuals, if available. Pay attention to the organization and layout of the written material.

Run the program following the written or on-screen directions to determine whether the program leads you through the material in a well-organized fashion. Notice whether the program lets you correct mistakes or whether it traps data entry errors. Can you exit the program at any point without difficulty? Are there any dead ends or blind alleys? Is the information accurate, free from stereotyping, and unbiased? Are the displays well organized and easy to understand?

After you are familiar with the intent of the program, use the following guidelines to determine the soundness of the software. The actual worth of the program is determined by the school's curriculum needs. A program can be very good technically but may not develop the needed goals, or it may be of fair technical quality but very good in terms of its approach to subject and content.

Many programs can be used in a variety of settings. Individual interaction focused on gathering information for a group promotes cooperation and teamwork, enhancing the development of problem-solving techniques. Group interaction, whether as an entire class or as a small group of students in a lab setting, can encourage communication and sharing, which leads to a broader range of ideas. Team interaction can occur in either a cooperative or competitive situation. When reviewing software, consider the possible settings in which the program may be used.

Many factors are viewed differently depending on the classification of the software as drill and practice, tutorial, simulation, or as a construction tool for word processing and creating databases. The following general guidelines will help to measure the soundness of a program and to gather information about a piece of software in the drill and practice, tutorial, and simulation formats. After examining these guidelines and considering the information presented in a later section of this chapter, you could develop an evaluation instrument specifically designed for your school or classroom.

General Evaluation Guidelines for Educational Software

1. Documentation
   a. Is a manual included?
   b. Are the instructions clear and easy to read?
   c. Are goals and objectives clearly stated?
   d. Are suggested lesson plans or activities included?
   e. Are other resource materials included?
2. Ease of use
   a. Is minimum knowledge needed to run the program?
   b. Are potential errors trapped?
   c. Is text easily readable on the monitor screen?
   d. Can the user skip on-screen directions?
   e. Can the student use the program without teacher intervention?
3. Content
   a. Is the content appropriate to the curriculum?
   b. Is the content accurate?
   c. Is the content free of age, gender, and ethnic bias or discrimination?
   d. Is the presentation of the information interesting and does it encourage a high degree of student involvement?
   e. Is the content free of grammar and punctuation errors?
   f. In a simulation, is the content realistic?
4. Performance
   a. Does the program reach its stated goal?
   b. Is the goal worthwhile?
   c. Does the program follow sound educational techniques?
   d. Does the program make proper and effective use of graphics and sound?
   e. Does the program present appropriate reinforcement for correct replies?
   f. Does the program handle incorrect responses appropriately?
5. Versatility
   a. Can the program be used in a variety of ways?
   b. Can the user control the rate of presentation?
   c. Can the user control the sequence of the lesson?
   d. Can the user control the level of difficulty?
   e. Can the user review previous information?
   f. Can the user enter and exit at various points?
   g. In a tutorial, is the user tested and placed at the proper entry level?
   h. In a tutorial, is there effective remedial branching in the instruction?
   i. In a simulation, can the instructor change random and control factors?
6. Data collection
   a. Is the program's data collection and management system easy to use?
   b. Can student data be summarized in tables and charts?
   c. Is the student's privacy and data security ensured?

Evaluating the Use of Graphics and Sound.   As we contemplate general characteristics in the evaluation of educational software, we must look beyond text as the carrier of the message. The computer as a tool for instruction and learning must first gain a student's attention and then hold that interest to satisfy a curiosity. Our students are all from the MTV™ and beyond generation. Addressing the student's interest by using the computer's capabilities of graphics and sound yields the optimum presentation of the software's message in a drill and practice, tutorial, or simulation format. The use of graphics and sound has become so ubiquitous in educational software that it deserves special consideration in the evaluation process.

Sound can enhance the learning experience by adding a degree of realism and by holding the user's attention. It can be used as a reward or reinforcement. Sound can help to highlight key concepts. Music and speech synthesis are important factors in some software. Conversely, sound can be distracting in a classroom or in a room full of computers. The ability to turn sound on or off is desirable. If sound is important to the concept being presented, the user should be able to direct it to an external connection rather than to the computer's built-in speaker, to permit the use of headphones.

Learning theorists stress the importance of graphic representation as a means of simplifying complex interactions of verbal and nonverbal communication. A picture contributes an image to be stored in memory for later retrieval. This function is critical to learning.

Graphics included in computer-assisted instruction have the same impact on the student. In a review of visual research, Francis Dwyer (1978) concluded that a moderate amount of realism in a visual results in the maximum amount of learning. Too little realism may not offer enough visual clues, and too much may distract the viewer. Graphics in software are often used to focus student attention. Studies have shown, however, that visual stimuli used to attract attention may not be the most effective in sustaining attention (Dwyer, 1978). High-resolution computer graphics offering a moderate degree of realism have the potential to maximize learning. Graphics must support the ideas being communicated without detracting from the instructional objective of the activity. Some very poor programs have been marketed that pair graphic symbols with unrelated text or that animate a concept improperly, making the lesson needlessly confusing. These program flaws must be detected in the evaluation process.

The graphic design of text must be considered in combination with visual presentation. Screen layout and design are important in maintaining student attention and interest. The screen should not be overcrowded and should present only one major idea at a time. Animation extends the descriptive impact of the concept being communicated by showing the logical sequence of development.

In reviewing basic math materials found in products of three large commercial software publishers, Francis Fisher (1982) found examples of terrible graphics design, inappropriate use of sound, and other misapplications of computer technology. Although significant improvements have been made since Fisher's initial research, his findings are still applicable as an element of evaluation.

The program in Figure 4–8 responds to a wrong answer with a confusing screen display. What response is the question "How many are there?" supposed to elicit? The number of empty circles? The number of filled circles? The total number of circles? Is it likely that students who cannot add 7 and 2 in the first place will be able to figure out the intended connection between empty circles and the first number in

Figure 4–8
Example of a
confusing screen
display

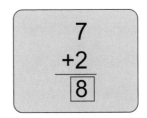

Figure 4–9
Example of poor
allocation of screen
area

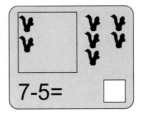

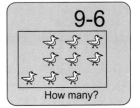

the problem and filled circles and the second number? Such students can and probably will get the answer faster by counting on their fingers than by puzzling over these complicated, poorly organized instructions.

Figure 4–9 illustrates poor use of the screen area. In the screen to the left, five squirrels have left the box. The two remaining squirrels are located directly above the number 7. The answer box (in which the user is supposed to enter 2) is placed under the five squirrels. The potential confusion here is caused by a designer working against the advantages of the medium. Instead of using the screen space to illustrate the subtraction process plainly in terms of numbers and related squirrel symbols, the designer created a visual juxtaposition of actual minuend with the subtrahend symbolized by the two squirrels and the minuend symbolized by the five squirrels with the intended answer. The screen to the right also has a poorly placed, misleading question that appears to be asking how many are in the box. In evaluating software, be alert for such misuses of graphics capability.

An Evaluation Instrument for Educational Software

Having familiarized ourselves with general criteria and guidelines for the evaluation of educational software, we must attempt to develop a process for its evaluation. An effective instrument is at the heart of a successful process. Just as one set of curricular materials is not expected to meet all the needs of all students, one type of software cannot be expected to address all needs. One "standard" list of criteria will not measure all the necessary elements of good educational software in the areas of drill and practice, tutorial, and simulation. A reliable list includes the set of characteristics that make up the events of a good lesson in a particular learning situation. A "best fit" happens when the teacher skillfully matches instructional needs with elements in a software program.

An evaluation instrument must provide for the recording of descriptive information about the software being evaluated as well as a listing of performance criteria. Once the software is described, it must be examined and rated against performance criteria. Reflecting on the general evaluation guidelines previously presented, a criterion section could be developed that would examine some common traits as well as allow for the specific characteristics of drill and practice, tutorial, and simulation software to be analyzed.

There is no single correct way to evaluate educational software. An instrument could be developed that would include only broad guidelines and allow the evaluator considerable leeway in interpreting and applying them. However, an instrument might have a long list of specifics and a complex scoring system, leaving little to the judgment of the evaluator. Think of an evaluation instrument as a communication device that describes and assesses the value of a given software item. It must convey an accurate impression of the software and be easy and convenient to use. A cumbersome evaluation instrument is more trouble than it is worth to potential evaluators and, therefore, will be of little use. A sample form is presented in Figure 4–10. During your study of databases in this course, you may wish to design your own evaluation on a file manager such as AppleWorks or FileMaker Pro®. You will undoubtedly appreciate the inherent advantages of file managers when applied to the task of designing forms and storing the data for later review.

SOFTWARE SELECTION

Software that may be effective in one setting may not be useful in another, even if it covers the same concepts. It is important to have a process for determining the quality and content of materials with respect to the needs of the student.

Evaluation is used to assess the quality of the software product. Selection takes evaluation a step further by matching the quality and cost of the software to the specific needs of your school. This can be accomplished in several ways. In the case of an inexpensive or highly specific stand-alone program, the individual making the evaluation may complete the process by recommending purchase. When a more substantial purchase is contemplated or the software under consideration may be applicable in a variety of settings, the collective wisdom, experience, and training of a team of educators may be valuable in order to better analyze collected evaluations and arrive at a decision regarding selection. Individual teacher requests should certainly play a role in shaping a software collection, but requests should be measured against current software availability in the collection. Notice should be given to teachers in all subject areas, but the areas of greatest need and use (based on an understanding of a particular school user community) should be emphasized. Decisions will always take into account costs and budgets, software currently in the collection, equipment that is presently available or that needs to be purchased, the number of machines and the number of students per machine, and the computer literacy of the staff. The important issue in each case should be the "best fit" between the needs of students and teachers and the features of the software.

DESCRIPTION

Program Title: _____ OS Requirement: _____

Vendor Name & Address: _____ Program Cost: _____

Content Area: (e.g., Math) _____ Topic: (e.g., Decimals) _____

Grade Level: _____ Supplementary Material Included: _____

Brief Description: _____

_____

_____

EVALUATION

Use the following checklist to refresh your memory regarding important aspects of educational software. Read the entire list first, then check the appropriate items after examining the software. Use the *Summary Evaluation* section to record your impressions of the software.

General Criteria Applicable to All Categories

____ 1. Content is accurate.

____ 2. Content is appropriate to educational goals.

____ 3. Instructions are clear.

____ 4. Program is easy to use.

____ 5. Format is interactive.

____ 6. High level of interest is maintained.

____ 7. User establishes the pace.

____ 8. Progresses in levels of difficulty.

____ 9. Reinforces/rewards user appropriately.

____ 10. Teacher able to modify the content.

____ 11. Keeps record of student progress.

____ 12. No age, gender, or ethnic discrimination.

____ 13. Sound can be controlled.

____ 14. Computer is used effectively.

____ 15. Has suggested off-computer activities.

____ 16. Support materials are effective.

Additional Criteria Specific to Tutorial Programs

____ 1. Variety in presentation

____ 2. Logical, sequential concept development

____ 3. Positive reinforcement

____ 4. Limits frequency of incorrect responses

Additional Criteria Specific to Simulations

____ 1. Clear directions

____ 2. Realistic situation for role playing

____ 3. Results predicated upon user input

____ 4. Promotes problem solving

Summary Evaluation (E = Excellent, VG = Very Good, G = Good, F = Fair, P = Poor)

Appropriateness	E	VG	G	F	P
Performance	E	VG	G	F	P
Documentation	E	VG	G	F	P
Ease of Use	E	VG	G	F	P
Overall Rating	E	VG	G	F	P

Figure 4–10

A sample software evaluation form

Comments: _____

_____

Recommend for purchase? _____

Evaluator's Name: _____ Date: _____

Teachers have the final word on instructional use and must use the characteristics of a good learning situation as the criteria to measure the value of the software package. Because district needs and student characteristics vary, professional judgment on what elements are present or missing in relation to an instructional situation is the only feasible standard for evaluation. This judgment also determines what elements need to be supplied in the learning environment or what adaptations need to be made to the software.

Collection development is often the responsibility of the school library media specialist. This person must promote the collection's effective use by teachers and students. This can be done by circulating or posting memos featuring particular software, especially new acquisitions, and short presentations at group, team, department, and school faculty meetings. Bibliographies pertinent to specific topics or events might be posted. One-on-one consulting to meet an individual's need is, perhaps, the most effective way of ensuring good use of the collection.

SUMMARY

According to behaviorist theory, the teacher is the manipulator of an environment that is experienced by the learner. The techniques used reflect a belief that, by tightly structuring the environment, the student's behavior can be shaped to achieve learning. According to constructivist theory, education is inseparable from ordinary life. Learning is an active and highly individualized process in which learners must construct new knowledge based on their own individual experiences and understandings. Knowledge is produced by the individual learner rather than processed from information received from an external source.

We have moved away from a fascination with huge amounts of stored data to a concern for the value of the information and the development of knowledge. This paradigm shift parallels the shifts in the philosophical foundations of education toward a constructivist approach emphasizing problem solving. Cooperative learning fits nicely into this context. To maximize the constructivist learning experience, students need problem-solving tools and problem-solving skills. Authentic assessment techniques enable the teacher and the learner to better emphasize the learning taking place. The use of rubrics for both the learner and the teacher and portfolios enable the student and teacher to measure learning that has taken place.

Just as problem-solving strategies vary among individuals, so too do types of intelligence and perception. Understanding students as individuals allows teachers to make sound and informed decisions when choosing software for their classrooms. A variety of software can be applied to meet the learning needs of individuals with different types of intelligence and learning styles.

Sensory stimuli are accepted by the learner and given meaning based primarily on past experiences. As perceptions are organized into understanding, the quality of the concrete, visual, and aural stimuli embodied in the software assume significant importance. The more abstract expressions of ideas must have a concrete basis. Examining well-designed software, we find that computer graphics, visuals, and certainly multimedia serve as concrete referents to meaning. Attention remains focused on well-designed software in large measure because of the continuity of thought promoted when text is coupled with graphics and at times with sound. Motivation is further heightened when the learner is asked to respond to the program overtly. Communication is enhanced when fields of experience overlap.

It is possible to postulate the following guidelines for effective software: (1) software must stimulate a high degree of interest in the learner; (2) software must contribute to developmental learning and, thereby, increase the permanence of that learning; (3) software must be based in concrete experience to enhance understanding; (4) software must make optimum use of the visual and, where appropriate, the aural sensory channels to strengthen the reality of the experience.

As we study theories of learning, reflect on our experiences, and examine our own motivations—as well as those of our students—we should seek to develop a knowledge base and a skill level that will enhance our application of computers to the classroom.

The software selection process consists of finding sources, product information, and reviews; evaluating the product; and then selecting the product for adoption in a given setting.

An instrument to evaluate software must facilitate the recording of both descriptive and evaluative information. It is a communication device that describes and assesses a given software item. It must convey an accurate impression of the software and be easy and convenient to use.

CHAPTER EXERCISES

To complete the specified exercises on-line, go to the Chapter Exercises Module in Chapter 4 of the Companion Website.

1. Select one piece of software in a curriculum area that is of special interest to you and analyze it in light of Gagné's events of instruction as elements of a good lesson.
2. Design a lesson that you might teach in your class. Do this twice. The first time use a behaviorist approach and the second time use a constructivist approach. Discuss the pros and cons of each approach with reference to your lesson. Which approach would you rather use? Why?
3. Discuss authentic assessment. Do you think that this is a step forward or a step backward for our educational system? Explain. How would you use it in your classroom?
4. Review the sample evaluation forms at the Companion Website. Develop your own form for the evaluation of software in the area of drill and practice, tutorial, and simulation.
5. Run a program and evaluate it using the form you designed. Comment on the process of reviewing. Was it frustrating or rewarding? How long did it

take you to evaluate the program thoroughly? Would you make any changes in your form now that you have used it?

6. Design a lesson for your classroom in which cooperative learning is stressed. What benefits and hazards might you encounter if you use this lesson with your students? How would you include students with special needs in this lesson?

7. Develop a rubric that would help you and the students evaluate how they did on the lesson you designed in exercise 6.

8. Although there are ideal ways to evaluate and acquire software, what constraints do you believe exist in a school situation that might interfere with performing an evaluation in an optimum way?

9. Determine the evaluation system used by two different magazines or journals that publish software reviews. In each case, who does the reviewing? Is the review based on student use of the program? Describe strengths and shortcomings of both magazines' reviewing systems.

10. Obtain a software catalog from "Learning Services" (1-800-877-3278 or www.learningservicesinc.com). Review their list of the "Top 25 Educator's Choices." Are you surprised with the software in this list? Which software in the list do you feel that you should learn more about? Review the "Top 10" list for your content area.

PORTFOLIO DEVELOPMENT EXERCISES

To complete this exercise on-line, go to the Digital Portfolio Module in Chapter 4 of the Companion Website.

One of the NETS•S standards covered in this chapter was "Students practice responsible use of technology systems, information, and software" under *Category 2: Social, ethical, and human issues.* Begin to develop your own portfolio of lesson plans that demonstrates your ability to have your students reach the NETS•S standards.

For more information on developing digital portfolios, go to Digital Portfolio Module on the Companion Website www.prenhall. com/forcier

1. Design a lesson plan activity for elementary, middle school, or high school students in which they design a software evaluation form that can be used in your class. This form must include objective (cost, platform, publisher, date, and so on) and subjective (overall impression, value in curriculum, and so on) information. Have other students use this evaluation form to evaluate several software packages. This lesson should demonstrate that your students have achieved the standard. Be sure to include a system of evaluation for your students' understanding and competence to ensure that they have met this standard.

2. Adapt the lesson plan activity you developed in exercise 1 for students to evaluate each others' work.

GLOSSARY

abstract Symbolizing an object, event, or occurrence that can be observed by the learner.
authentic assessment Consists of assessment tasks that resemble real-world situations.
behaviorism A theory of learning that perceives the teacher as the manipulator of an environment that is experienced by the learner.
checklists Simple ways of observing and categorizing behaviors in a bimodal (observed/not observed) manner.
concrete Actual, direct, purposeful happenings involving the learner as a participant.
constructivism A theory of learning that holds that students interact with the real-life experiences that surround them and construct mental structures that provide an understanding of their environment.
linear Proceeding in a step-by-step, sequential manner.
performance-based assessment See *authentic assessment*.
project-based learning An authentic assessment model for teaching in which projects are used to assess student learning.
ratings scales Complex measures where each observation is placed on a scale, usually of numerical values, that measures the degree to which a student completes a task.
rubric A scoring matrix that differentiates the quality of learning using a graduated scale of exemplar behaviors.

REFERENCES & SUGGESTED READINGS

Boettcher, J. (2000, August). Designing for learning: What is meaningful learning? *Syllabus, 14*(1), 54–57.
Bruner, J. (1966). *Studies in cognitive growth.* New York: John Wiley & Sons.
Campbell, L., Campbell, B., & Dickinson, D. (1999). *Teaching and learning through multiple intelligences,* 2nd ed. Boston: Allyn & Bacon.
D'Ignazio, F. (1992, August/September). Are you getting your money's worth? *The Computing Teacher,* 54–55.
Dwyer, F. M. (1978). *Strategies for improving visual learning.* State College, PA: Learning Services, pp. 33, 156.
Eichleay, K., & Kilroy, C. (1993–1994, December/January). Hot tips for inclusion with technology. *The Computing Teacher, 21*(4), 38–40.
Fisher, F. D. (1982, Summer). Computer assisted education: What's not happening. *Journal of Computer-Based Instruction, 9*(1), 19–27.
Gagné, R., & Briggs, L. (1974). *Principles of instructional design.* New York: Holt, Rinehart and Winston.
Gagné, R., Briggs, L., & Wager, W. (1992). *Principles of instructional design.* Fort Worth, TX: Harcourt Brace Jovanovich.
Gardner, H. (1983). *Frames of mind.* New York: Basic Books.
Gardner, H. (1993). *Multiple intelligences: The theory in practice.* New York: Basic Books.
Guba, E., Wolf, W., DeGroot, S., Kneneyer, M., VanAtta, R., & Light, L. (1964, Winter). Eye movements and TV-viewing in children. *AV Communications Review, 12,* 386–401.
Information Technology in Childhood Education Annual. (1999). The state of children's software evaluation: Yesterday, today, and in the twenty-first century, 220–221.
Johnson, D. W., & Johnson, R. T. (1994). *Learning together and alone. Cooperative, competitive, and individualistic learning,* 4th ed. Edina, MN: Interaction Book Company.

Merrill, M. D. (2002). First principles of instruction. *Educational Technology Research and Development, 50*(3), 43–59.

Papert, S. (1991). *Constructionism: Research reports and essays, 1985–1991.* Norwood, NJ: Ablex Publishing.

Pennar, K. (1996, September 16). How many smarts do you have? *Business Week,* 104–107.

Piaget, J. (1954). *The construction of reality in the child.* New York: Basic Books.

Randolph, T., Scolari, J., & Bedient, D. (2000, February). Too few computers and too many kids: What can I do? *Learning & Leading with Technology, 27*(5), 28–30.

Ross, A., & Olsen, K. (1995). *A vision of the middle school through integrated thematic instruction.* Kent, WA: Books for Educators.

Saunders, W. L. (1992, March). Constructivist perspective: Implications and teaching strategies for science. *School Science and Mathematics, 92*(3), 136–141.

Schlechter, T. (1990). The relative dystructional efficiency of small group computer-based telecommunications for instruction. *Journal of Computer-Based Instruction 6*(3), 329–41.

Skinner, B. F. (1974). *About behaviorism.* New York: Knopf.

Sprague, D., & Dede, C. (1999, September). Constructivism in the classroom. If I teach this way, am I doing my job? *Learning and Leading with Technology, 27*(1), 6–9, 16–17.

Wedman, J. F. (1986, November). Making software more useful. *The Computing Teacher, 13*(3) 11–14.

Whitehead, A. N. (1929). *The aims of education.* New York: Macmillan.

CHAPTER 5

Computer Applications in Education

1. What are some functional categories of computer applications in education?

2. How do the categories in school management relate to tasks you might commonly perform as a teacher, school library media specialist, or administrator?

3. What is computer literacy and what is its future?

4. How does the application of the computer to instruction and learning relate to teacher- or student-centered strategies?

5. What is a typical tutorial lesson format and how can the computer be used in such a lesson?

6. What is a typical drill-and-practice lesson format and how can the computer be used in such a lesson?

7. What is a typical simulation lesson format and how can the computer be used in such a lesson?

8. What are the roles of the student and the teacher in the three strategies?

9. What constitutes multimedia and what does it have to offer the learner?

10. What does computer-managed instruction offer you as a teacher?

11. How can the computer enhance your capability as a teacher to design teaching materials?

12. How can the computer be used as an information tool by the student?

13. How is the computer an action research tool?

Chapter 5 contains information relevant to a number of NETS•S standard categories. *Category 1: Basic operations and concepts* is well covered as we describe the many uses that the computer tool is put to in the modern school system. We shall see that it affects all aspects of education. *Category 2: Social, ethical and human issues* is enforced as technology systems are described leading the students to increase their appreciation of the role of the computer in education. Chapter 5 again returns to two NETS•S categories discussed previously in the book. *Category 5: Technology research tools* is covered in the discussion of computers in education in general and action research in particular. Many different computer applications used in education are discussed in this chapter. *Category 6: Technology problem-solving and decision-making tools* is discussed throughout the chapter as we consider many of the ways computers are used in schools from budgets to inventories, from teac[...] and student records to library circulation. The section on instruction and learning covers bot[...]

areas as we discuss the different classifications of computer-assisted and computer-managed instruction. This chapter presents a broad overview of computer applications to help you develop a better understanding of the role computers play in society, especially with respect to education. You will develop a better understanding of the various types of computer software available, along with some of the advantages and disadvantages of each. This discussion will aid you in the appropriate selection of software to meet your educational objectives.

The title of this book is *The Computer as an Educational Tool: Productivity and Problem Solving*. As discussed previously, too often the term *productivity* has been used with a limited vision. But the deeper understanding we seek demonstrates its applicability not only to word processors, graphics, spreadsheets, and database use but also to computer-assisted instruction, computer-enhanced learning, and administrative applications. If we believe that education is in the business of fostering student learning, computer applications that help students to learn, teachers to teach, and administrators to manage efficiently and effectively should be seen as productivity tools.

Changes are occurring in education, as well as in technology, with school restructuring suggesting a different way of looking at and measuring teacher effectiveness. Pupil learning gains are being included in discussions of productivity. Tutorial instruction, drill and practice, and simulation, all time-tested teaching strategies, are being joined by multimedia instruction and learning. Integrated student records and student portfolios track the progress of students as they gain and construct new knowledge. If computer software implements these strategies in an effective and efficient manner, should not this software be seen as a teacher productivity tool?

This chapter demonstrates that computers are practical tools used by students and teachers in concert with various teaching and learning strategies. Therefore, this chapter presents an overview and classification of computer applications in education so that we may gain an improved perspective of the breadth of applications and better understand their relationships. The classification proposed is hierarchical, with divisions made according to function. Classification schemes, no matter how well reasoned, are, by nature, arbitrary. Some applications may not fit neatly in the pigeonholes of the structure but may cross boundaries and overlap, much as the subjects we teach our students cross boundaries and overlap. Thus, this chapter recognizes the importance of multidisciplinary curriculum integration.

COMPUTERS IN EDUCATION

Any classification is an attempt to group like items together in order to study them, noting their similarities and their differences. Early software classifications described **computer-assisted instruction (CAI)** and **computer-managed instruction (CMI).** They, by themselves, are no longer adequate. The software classification model proposed in Figure 5–1 emphasizes function. It places primary emphasis on how software is used.

In this model, the functional use of computers in education has been divided into three categories: management, instruction and learning, and action research. The *management* category includes school and classroom applications in budgeting, accounting, recordkeeping, printed and electronic communication, and information retrieval. The category of *instruction and learning* has been subdivided into *teacher-centered instruction*, which includes software functions interacting directly with stu-

A list of the ISTE/NCATE standards addressed in this chapter is available in the Standards Module on the Companion Website www.prenhall.com/forcier

NETS•S Standards Addressed in This Chapter

1. Basic operations and concepts
   - Students demonstrate a sound understanding of the nature and operation of technology systems.

2. Social, ethical, and human issues
   - Students develop positive attitudes toward technology uses that support lifelong learning, collaboration, personal pursuits, and productivity.

5. Technology research tools
   - Students use technology tools to process data and report results.
   - Students evaluate and select new information resources and technological innovations based on the appropriateness for specific tasks.

6. Technology problem-solving and decision-making tools
   - Students use technology resources for solving problems and making informed decisions.
   - Students employ technology in the development of strategies for solving problems in the real world.

dents under the teacher's control in the design, development, and delivery of instruction, and *student-centered learning,* which includes recognizing functions that are related to the student involved in constructive activities, which leads to learning. Categories are further subdivided to recognize common computer applications. The *action research* category includes applications in data storage and statistical analysis and must be recognized for the contribution it makes to teaching and learning by placing the teacher in the role of researcher, often examining some aspect of classroom practice. Software classification permits the identification and comparisons of like programs. Organization schemes other than the one proposed in this chapter are, of course, possible and should be encouraged if they will facilitate the study of software and its application. The development and use of classification methods to identify software will facilitate the task of teachers, who ultimately decide which material to use in the classroom. It will promote a better understanding of software selection, evaluation, and collection management. Classification methods can also promote better communication between teachers and publishers. Teachers can more clearly explain their needs to publishers, and publishers can better describe their available products. The software classification must reflect accepted theories and practices in education.

The primary emphasis in this text is on the instruction and learning category and then on the management category, although the category of action research is h covered as well. The elements of teacher-centered instruction are addressed thoroughly. Learning theories and the continued evaluation of new technologies are increasingly placing strong emphasis on the growth and development of student-centered learning.

INSTRUCTION AND LEARNING

Since we consider the category of instruction and learning to be the most important, we begin the examination of the model proposed in Figure 5–1 with this category. It is separated into *teacher-centered instruction*—dealing with those functions that directly include the student in either an individual or a group setting and that take into account teacher planning, preparation, and delivery of instruction—and *student-centered learning*—including the functions that deal with the student involved in constructive activities that lead to learning.

Teacher-Centered Instruction

As seen in Figure 5–2, teacher-centered instruction includes the areas of computer literacy, computer-assisted instruction, computer-managed instruction, and design of teaching materials. Computer literacy acquaints the student with the computer and its functional use. The presentation of information through CAI, under the control of the teacher, and the management of the student's performance and interaction with that information through CMI, though viewed separately for the purpose of functional examination, sometimes overlap. As a design tool, the computer has become widely used by teachers to create hard copy, as well as projected, instructional materials. Many of these functions are covered in more detail in other chapters.

Computer Literacy as an Element of Teacher-Centered Instruction. The subject of **computer literacy** focuses on the computer as the object of instruction. This topic is not to be confused with computer science instruction, which studies hardware, operating systems, and computer languages. In computer literacy, a scope and sequence of curriculum goals is usually developed within a school district that specifies what is to be learned about the use of the computer and about its role in society. Computer literacy is not easy to define. It often examines the history of computing, computer awareness, and the functional use of computers, as well as the broader role of the computer as it relates to societal issues, such as computer access, gender relationships, software copyright, rights of privacy, data security, and information ownership. Many times computer literacy is divided into three broad areas: *basic computer skills,* such as keyboarding, using various input and output devices, and other basic skills; *computers in society,* discussing uses and misuses of computers as well as the impact of computers on society; and *basic applications skills,* such as word processing, databases, and spreadsheets. Some of these issues were already introduced; others are addressed in later chapters. We are using the ISTE/NCATE Foundation Standards and NETS•S as the basis for our definition of computer literacy.

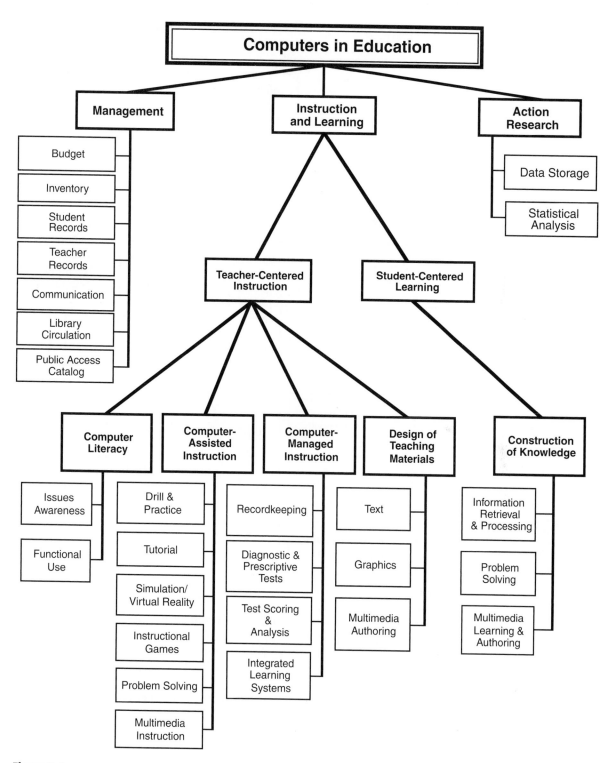

Figure 5–1
Classification of computers in education

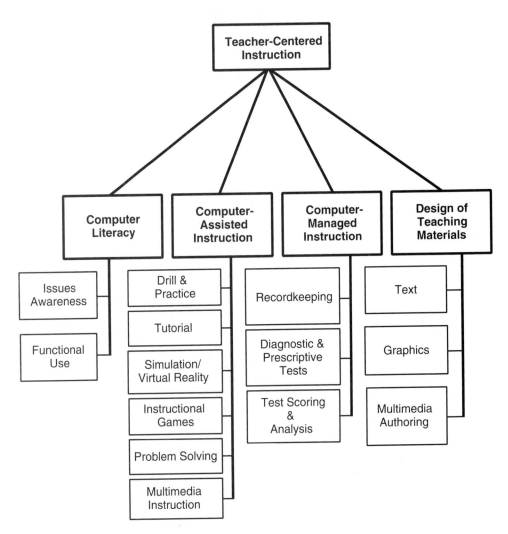

Figure 5–2
The computer in
teacher-centered
instruction

Some educators argue that, as computers become commonplace items in homes and schools, the need for computer literacy will be diminished in the curriculum. Some believe that although teaching scope and sequence of skills may no longer be necessary, computer-related issues will still need to be discussed.

Computer-Assisted Instruction as an Element of Teacher-Centered Instruction.
Computer-assisted instruction is a term applied to a teaching/learning situation that involves the direct instructional interaction between computer and student. In this teacher-centered approach, the teacher, ultimately having responsibility for all instruction in the classroom, sets up the learning environment through careful selection and analysis of the instruction material; ensures that each student has the necessary entry-level knowledge, skills, and attitude to engage in a particular activity; monitors the

learning activities, adjusting them according to the students' needs; and follows up with activities designed to promote retention and transfer of learning.

Regardless of the underlying philosophy in the classroom, *tutorial instruction, drill and practice, simulation, gaming,* and *problem solving* are time-tested instructional strategies. They are strategies that behaviorists can apply in a teacher-centered instructional situation and that constructivists can apply in a student-centered learning environment. Depending on how they are used, they are strategies that can gain attention, stimulate recall of prior learning, and present new information in ways that approximate real-life situations at a more concrete level than most media used in the classroom.

They are strategies that address the right or the left hemisphere of the brain. They can be tailored to support activities favored by students with concrete-sequential, concrete-random, abstract-sequential, or abstract-random preferred styles, and they can be appealing to students with diverse strengths and intelligences. Teachers who understand the individual needs of their students will tailor their strategies and the computer applications to meet those needs. Al Mizell (1997) at Nova Southeastern University states forcefully,

> I don't believe enough attention is focused on the value of using computers where they are strongest; e.g., as patient tutors, competent analysts, master presenters of stimulus material, and evaluators of consequences of various decisions made by the student. In other words, they are more valuable for higher level thinking and processing skills than when they are used as electronic page turners. (p. 4)

Tutorial Applications. A **tutorial** program exposes the student to material that is believed not to have been previously taught or learned. A tutorial program often includes a placement test to ensure student readiness and sometimes a pretest on specific objectives to validate the placement test. The computer usually assesses a student's prior learning; determines readiness for the material; and presents material for student observation, note taking, and other interaction. New material is commonly provided in small increments, replete with instructional guidance and appropriate feedback to encourage correct student response.

Tutorial instruction often follows a linear programmed instruction model mainly because it is difficult, time consuming, and, therefore, expensive to write **branching** programs that attempt to remediate incorrect responses. Both linear and branching formats present information and questions that lead toward an identified goal. Linear programs present information in a sequential manner and do not attempt to remediate errors. Tutorials often include initial guidance in the form of prompts to encourage the student to answer correctly, especially at the outset of the lesson.

The diagram in Figure 5–3 illustrates a representation of a linear format often used in tutorial programs. Some programs employ modest branching techniques to provide alternative paths, or branches, for remediation or acceleration. Tutorials must record student responses and allow for teacher analysis of the student's progress to determine whether a goal has been met.

Tutorial programs are often used to help students who have been absent from class. They may also be effective when assigned as independent study to students exhibiting difficulty with specific skills and concepts.

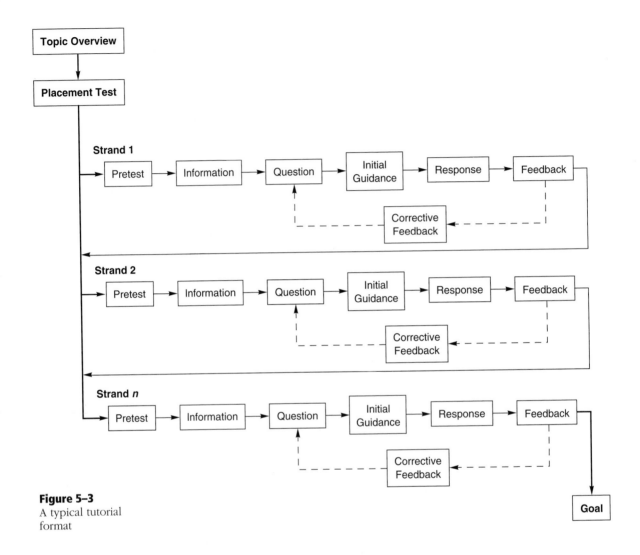

Figure 5–3
A typical tutorial
format

In a behaviorist model, the teacher identifies the proper lesson objectives, selects the appropriate computer program, maintains a reasonably comfortable environment free from unnecessary distractions, and, where needed, provides additional resources and encouragement to the student. The teacher must also monitor the progress made by the student by interpreting data collected by the computer program and must be prepared to intervene if necessary. In a constructivist model, the teacher might suggest tutorial software as a way for the student to acquire a particular skill or concept once its value is recognized. The teacher's role is to ascertain readiness on the part of the student, to select the appropriate software, to assess the student's performance as the newly acquired skill or concept is applied to a meaningful task, and to determine whether further practice is required. Working directly at a computer on a tutorial program can provide interest and motivation, if the teacher keeps in mind that it is only one alternative among various strategies to teach specific skills or concepts. Two major complaints leveled at tutorial software are that much of it deals with trivial information and it is not well written. The educational quality of the program must be ascertained and, to maintain its effectiveness, the strategy should not be overused. Many have used tutorial programs that accompany a new piece of software such as Microsoft Word. Mavis Beacon Teaches Typing! and the Super Tutor math series are wonderful examples of tutorial software.

Drill-and-Practice Applications. **Drill and practice** is a time-honored technique.

It is used by teachers to reinforce instruction by providing the repetition necessary to move acquired skills and concepts into long-term memory. It assumes that the material covered has been previously taught. In the past, teachers used flash cards, worksheets, board games, and verbal drills to achieve results. Computer programs present an additional and, if used well, more powerful alternative.

Criticism leveled in the past at drill-and-practice software was really aimed at poorly designed software that was boring, that treated all users the same regardless of ability, and that employed undesirable feedback. Teachers tell of students deliberately giving incorrect responses in order to see flashy animated graphics on the screen. The reward offered by that software for making correct responses was the presentation of another boring problem. The diagram in Figure 5–4 illustrates a typical format used in drill-and-practice programs.

Whenever this technique is used, the assumption is made that the topic has already been introduced to the student and that some prior instruction has taken place. In a behaviorist model, the teacher's role, in addition to determining the appropriate lesson objective and delivering the initial instruction, is to select the appropriate software, monitor the student's progress through the material, and assess the student's performance. In a constructivist model, a teacher may suggest drill-and-practice software as a way for the student to refine a particular skill or concept once its value is recognized. The teacher's role, in addition to determining that the student understands and accepts an agreed-on goal, is to ascertain that initial information has been acted on by the student, select the appropriate software, and assess the student's performance as the skill or concept is applied to a meaningful task.

The student must interact with the computer by responding to screen prompts and by providing appropriate keyboard or other input. The student should request teacher or peer assistance if necessary and examine the results of the activity. The computer presents material for student interaction, provides appropriate feedback to student responses, and usually records the rate of success, often displayed as a score or percentage. Effective software requires the student to respond based on deductions and inferences, as well as recall.

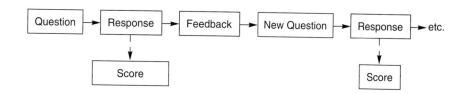

Figure 5–4
A typical drill-and-practice format

INTO THE CLASSROOM:
Drill-and-Practice Gaming Fun

Many students choose to spend considerable time on the computer performing drill-and-practice writing lessons in a game format. They get immediate feedback on anything they do. It makes learning exciting for them.

Becky Benjamin
Seventh Grade Language Arts Teacher
Carrollton Junior High
Carrollton, Georgia

Figure 5–5 illustrates screens from an older popular drill-and-practice program called *Number Munchers*®. In the top half of the illustration, the number muncher is seen in the second row of the second column. The user guides the character to those boxes that contain numbers that are multiples of 9. Beware of the Troggle, though, who eats number munchers. The entertaining video game format encourages users to spend extended time at the keyboard, practicing skills they have acquired.

A number of factors influence the effectiveness of drill-and-practice software. The teacher must know the program well enough to determine the accuracy of the content and the match between the presentation of the material and an individual student's learning style. If the software is to be used in a group setting, should intrinsic gaming strategies be used or can external gaming strategies be used by the teacher? Students must find the material and its presentation interesting enough to be willing to become mentally and emotionally involved. The program's use of basic graphic design, as well as a variety of stimuli such as color, sound, and animation, in both its presentation and feedback screens greatly enhances its effectiveness.

Simulation/Virtual Reality. **Simulation** is another time-honored teaching strategy used to reinforce instruction by the teacher. It can also function effectively in a student-centered environment by providing a climate for discovery learning to take place or for newly acquired skills and concepts to be tested. A simulation can present a sample of a real situation and can offer genuine practice at solving real problems unhampered by danger, distance, time, or cost factors. Simulations require decisions to be made by the student. In the past, teachers used board games, drama, and role-playing to implement the simulation technique. The computer is a useful tool to manage this technique. A sophisticated simulation can present the facts and rules of a situation in a highly realistic manner without the limiting factors of time, distance, safety, and cost and then can adjust these factors to respond to interaction by the student. High levels of cognitive skill are involved in the synthesis of facts, rules, and concepts in solving problems. Simulation permits this synthesis to take place within the classroom.

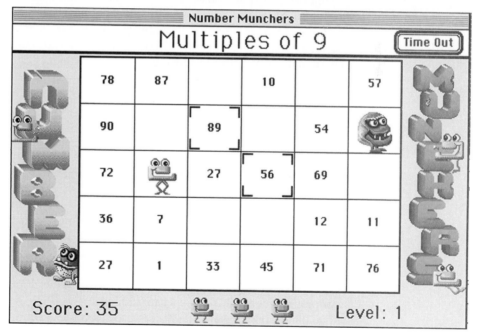

Figure 5–5
Screens from
Number Munchers
(© 2004 Riverdeep
Interactive Learning
Limited, and its
licensors)

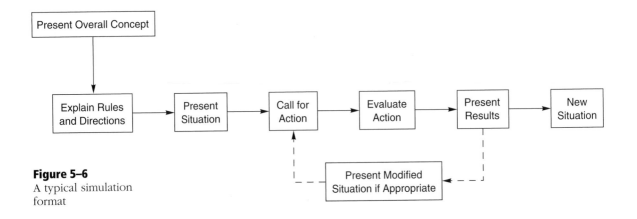

Figure 5–6
A typical simulation format

Consider, for example, the teacher who wants to teach the concept of free elections in a representative democracy. Figure 5–6 suggests a common flow of events in a typical simulation.

A classroom simulation might call for the creation of class offices, including development of a nomination process, establishment of platforms, identification of a polling place, preparation of secret and secure ballots, and agreement on term of office for the successful candidates. This simulation has been conducted for years without a computer. A computer program, however, can increase the sophistication of the simulation and can extend it into a broader context. For instance, it could introduce a number of historical variables that might influence decisions made in the running of a presidential election campaign. In this case, the program could store a wealth of data that can be called on as needed and cross-referenced to demonstrate cause and effect. Simulation software can provide highly realistic practice at solving real problems in the classroom without many of the limiting factors often found in real life.

As in any use of CAI, the role of the teacher is to identify the proper lesson objectives and to select the appropriate computer program. When using simulation software in a behaviorist model, the teacher often provides background information and may be called on to teach related skills and concepts and to provide additional resources where needed. The teacher must also monitor the progress made by the student or by the group of students and assess their performance. Simulations lending themselves to group use promote social interaction and can often be used as an introductory activity for a unit. In a constructivist model, simulation software may be suggested by the teacher as a way for the student to develop a particular skill or concept in a manner that is close to a real-life situation. The teacher's role is to ascertain readiness on the part of the student, to select the appropriate software, to discuss the student's performance in the simulation, and to suggest a real-world application.

The top screen in Figure 5–7 is from a program called *Ballistic*. The user sets initial parameters of initial velocity, angle of projection, and drag medium. By turning on the friction control but leaving the decay control turned off, a medium of constant density is simulated. Turning on the decay control simulates a medium whose

INTO THE CLASSROOM:
Software Simulations

I use SimEarth™ on the one computer I have in my classroom along with an LCD panel on an overhead projector. The first team of students designs their environment to maximize population expansion; the second to maximize plant life; the third to maximize sustainable growth; and the fourth to factor in natural disasters. Each team presents to the whole class. Ensuing discussion examines consequences of each choice.

Jim Long
Marine and Environmental Science Teacher
North Salem High School
Salem, Oregon

density decreases with altitude. Once launched, the projectile leaves a trace in the display window. By varying the parameters of initial velocity, angle of projection, air friction as the drag medium, and altitude-related decay, the user can compare the results of these combined factors as traces in the display window.

The bottom screen in Figure 5–7 is from a program called *Potential*. Users choose from four one-dimensional potential wells or create their own. The illustration represents a triangular well: A ball travels downward along the left slope, reaches bottom, rolls a certain distance upward on the right slope, then reverses its direction. This is repeated with diminishing distances until all energy is spent. A damping effect can be employed to observe the effect of various dissipating conditions. Kinetic and potential energies are continually displayed in a column at the right of the screen. Velocity or acceleration can be plotted for each path of the ball.

Both of these examples are intrinsic simulation models that create an artificial environment for the user to explore. In these microworlds, elements of the environment operate according to a regular set of rules. The student manipulates things to learn what their characteristics are within the artificial environment.

In *Oregon Trail*, an award-winning program now available with sophisticated graphics on CD-ROM as *Oregon Trail* 5th Edition EEV,® the user is placed in the position of traveling the 2,000-mile Oregon Trail from Independence, Missouri, to Oregon's Willamette Valley. Having declared an occupation and thereby receiving an allocation of available funds, the user begins preparing for the journey by carefully purchasing supplies.

The screen of Figure 5–8 is a typical one seen as the program progresses. A log, or diary, of the journey appears below the map. Four buttons are arranged at the bottom of the screen, presenting the user with options. The guide button reveals pertinent information about the geography of the region in a separate window. The user is

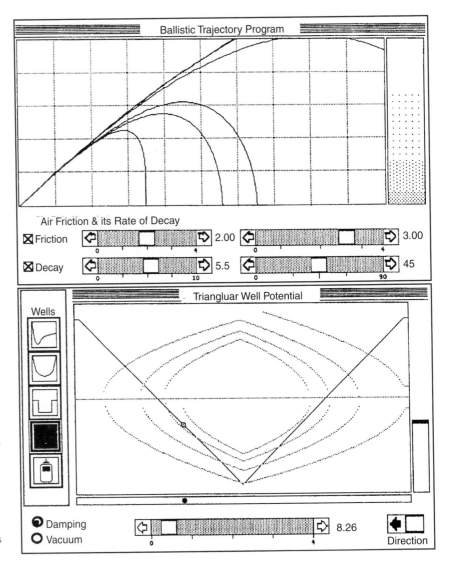

Figure 5–7
Physics simulation
series (Developed by
Blas Cabrera,
Stanford University
and published by
Intellimation, Santa
Barbara, CA)
(Reprinted with
permission from Blas
Cabrera)

encouraged to keep a diary. The health status of the party can be revealed by pressing
the appropriate button. As the journey progresses, the user can change the pace of
travel and adjust the rationing of food. "Hunt" calls forth an arcade-type game, allowing the user to collect food. At each stop along the way, the user can see who's around
and choose to talk to one or more people, often revealing clues or historical facts.

A Wagon Score is displayed only if the user successfully crosses the trail. A value
is placed on the people and supplies that complete the journey. Some occupations
receive a smaller allocation of funds than others; some have a more difficult time
successfully completing the trip. A mathematical weight is, therefore, assigned depending on the user's chosen occupation.

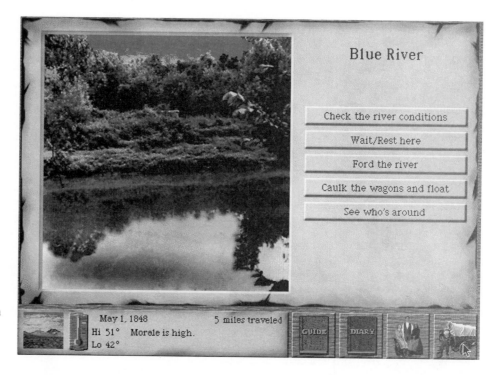

Figure 5–8
Traveling the Oregon Trail (Reprinted with permission of Riverdeep, Inc.)

The program has a management option protected by a password that allows the teacher to clear the List of Legends, adjust the simulation speed and hunting time, and determine network use, if any. A new network version of the program allows a number of users to interact simultaneously with one another on their journey.

The award-winning Carmen Sandiego series of programs (Where in the USA . . . , Where in the World . . . , Where in Europe . . . , and so forth) is the all-time, best-selling software in grades K–12. The premise of each program is that, as a detective, you must pick up the trail of one of Carmen's villainous gang members and, following geographic (or historic) clues, deduce the identity of the villain, follow the trail, and ultimately apprehend the culprit (see Figure 5–9).

The program has been so popular for a number of years that it spawned a television program and Carmen Sandiego clubs all over the country. The program simulates actions that might be taken in the real world and requires the user, often working cooperatively with others, to make decisions based on facts gathered. Each program provides an appropriate reference book, such as Fodor's *USA*. The computer's role usually is to create a realistic environment and present material for student interaction, to provide appropriate feedback to student responses, and, based on decisions made by students, to modify the environment and present new material, allowing the students to witness the results of their decisions.

Students might be asked to trace their travels in the simulation on a map and list the countries through which they travel. Students could be named as "ambassadors" representing each country. They would research the country they represent and

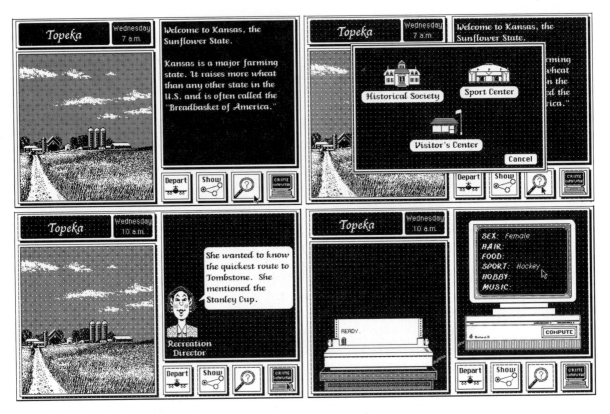

Figure 5–9
Four Scenes from *Where in the USA Is Carmen Sandiego?* (Reprinted with permission of Riverdeep, Inc.)

present brief reports or hold a mock United Nations meeting and discuss issues of importance to them.

Virtual reality (VR) is a computer-based technology that creates an illusion of reality. Participants interact with, and in fact are immersed in, an artificial environment to the degree that it appears real; it is highly interactive, multisensorial, and vivid enough for the participants almost to think it is reality. Virtual reality, according to Furness (Miller, 1992, p. 14), is "just like you're walking into another world, and you're perceiving it as if it becomes reality itself."

Instructional Games. **Gaming** can be found in all computer-assisted instruction categories. The technique includes a set of rules and a clear contest. Students or groups of students may compete against each other or against the computer or another fixed standard. **Instructional games** may be combined with any number of formats, such as drill and practice, simulations, or problem solving. Most computer games are highly competitive, either with another player or with the computer, and many introduce the elements of speed or time. In most cases they involve some type of fantasy atmosphere. They are usually highly motivational and engage the learner in a situation or

Figure 5–10
Logical Journey of
the Zoombinis
Deluxe. The
Zoombinis must
choose the right
pizza toppings so
they can continue
along the road
(Reprinted with
permission of
Riverdeep, Inc.)

situations where the learner is competing for a high score, a prize of some sort, a specific outcome, or a "personal best" effort. Good examples of this type of software include *Dragon in a Wagon, Stickybear Word Scramble®*, and *Super Solvers: Gizmos & Gadgets.*

It is possible to first choose one of several levels, such as beginner or mastery level categories, at which to play the game. A popular program in this category is *Logical Journey of the Zoombinis Deluxe®* (Figure 5–10). In this highly entertaining and interactive program, students use pattern recognition and logic to overcome 12 challenges in getting the Zoombinis to their new homeland. There are four levels of difficulty for students in grades 3 through 8. It is designed based on the National Council of Teachers of Mathematics standards 1 through 4. The program contains at least three elements that should be looked for in an instructional game: several levels of mastery, standards or objectives based, and lack of violence or aggressive behavior.

Games can be fun and motivating and many times students are not aware of the learning that is taking place. Some software catalogs have a special section for instructional games under a heading such as "Edutainment."

Problem Solving. When using **problem-solving software,** students use previously mastered skills to solve a challenging problem. This type of software places emphasis on critical thinking, analysis, logic, and reasoning. Students are usually either presented with a problem or have to identify the problem from a given set of data, then state a hypothesis, plan strategies, and follow a set of procedures to achieve the final goal or outcome. Students may learn some content as they exercise their higher-order thinking skills.

There are many examples of problem-solving software, even though this category, as with all of our other categories, blend in with each other. *Logical Journey of the Zoombinis Deluxe, Where in the USA Is Carmen Sandiego?* and *Oregon Trail* have all been described previously in other categories, but they also fit neatly into this category. We usually think that problem-solving software is designed for older children. This is not necessarily true. Problem-solving software has been developed for children of all age levels. *Playtime for Babies* was developed for children ages 9 through 24 months. It contains 11 activities including a read-along where the child's face and voice can be added. *Arthur's® Kindergarten* along with *Arthur's 1st Grade* and *Arthur's 2nd Grade* cover preK through second grade and include a variety of problem-solving and critical thinking activities. *Sesame Street Music Maker®* is designed for ages three and above. It contains eight activities dealing with musical instruments from around the world and actually allows children to compose their own music. *Yoda's Challenge™ Activity* contains six missions, each with four levels of difficulty incorporating critical thinking, geometry, music, map reading, and other skills. We should emphasize that all of these programs may be easily used or adapted for use by students with special needs in higher grades. Other popular problem-solving titles include *Clearwater Detectives, Turtle Math,* and *Widget Workshop™*.

Problem-solving software may be used in a behaviorist-centered classroom but is most often found in one with constructivist leaning. In a constructivist environment students would be given little direct training in problem solving; instead, they would be presented with a highly motivating problem and the opportunity and encouragement to solve it on their own or in a group. Constructivists believe that this method of solving problems helps students in a number of ways.

1. Students actually see how information can be used to solve problems in real-life situations.
2. Students find that discovering answers themselves is highly motivating.
3. Properly designed problem-solving software, being both motivational and interesting, will aid students in acquiring and applying content information and research and study skills.

A summary of the teacher, student, and computer roles in computer-assisted instruction is presented for your review in Figure 5–11.

Software to Aid in Problem Solving. We have mentioned how the application software used by the authors helped solve the problem of presenting a manuscript to the publisher containing proper spelling, punctuation, and grammar. It was the tool used to solve a very specific problem: that of producing a reasonably polished manuscript. Just as this software helped the authors with writing, other software is designed to help people through the problem-solving process.

Think back to some of your own problem-solving experiences. Did you try to picture the problem in your mind or jot some things down on paper to try to organize your thinking, to find relationships, and to come up with a solution (or solutions)?

	Teacher	Computer	Student
Tutorial	Determines objectives Selects materials appropriate to students Monitors progress Assesses student performance	Presents original material Assesses progress Displays feedback Provides guidance May assess performance Records performance Tests for objectives	Interacts with computer Responds to feedback Controls pace of presentation Examines results
Drill & Practice	Determines objectives Selects materials appropriate to students Teaches original skills or concepts Monitors progress Assesses student performance	Presents material in form of problems or questions Displays feedback May assess performance May record performance	Interacts with computer Responds appropriately Examines results
Simulation	Determines objectives Selects materials appropriate to students Teaches related skills Often prompts students to discover concepts May take active role in a group Assesses student performance	Presents a situation Elicits student response Modifies situation May assess performance Demonstrates result of student action	Reacts to situation Refers to external resources if needed Confers with others as needed Makes choices based on information
Instructional Games	Determines objectives Selects materials appropriate to students Sets limits Monitors progress Assesses student performance	Presents situations and material Competes with student Displays feedback Records performance	Interacts with computer Learns rules Devises strategies Competes with computer Increases skills
Problem Solving	Determines objectives Selects materials appropriate to students Assigns problems Monitors and assists progress Assesses student performance	Presents problem Displays feedback May manipulate data May assess performance	Defines the problem Interacts with computer Sets up solution Manipulates one or more variables Uses trial and error Increases skills

Figure 5–11
Role comparisons in CAI

Organizing, diagramming, picturing on paper or on a blackboard are particularly helpful when trying to explain information, problems, or relationships to others. Movie directors use storyboards that picture each scene's actors, set, and camera angle. Chemists use models to help explain difficult chemical reactions. Leonardo da Vinci filled books with diagrams and sketches. This process is called visualization. "A picture is worth a thousand words," so they say. It is true and we can help our students save time, energy, and words if we can help them visualize ideas, relationships, and concepts. Many students use the popular Inspiration software (Figure 5–12) to help organize and visualize those relationships and concepts. You have learned in other education courses that visual learning is a powerful tool in the students' cognitive arsenal.

INTO THE CLASSROOM:
Kidspiration Learning Experiences

Kidspiration® (grades K–5) and *Inspiration*® (grades 3–adult) are digital semantic mapping tools used for graphically expressing ideas. I have found Inspiration and Kidspiration to be excellent vehicles for engaging students in active learning while integrating technology into the curriculum. Using these tools increase my students' comfort level with working in an electronic environment while utilizing critical thinking skills.

This software allows students to organize their ideas in a visual way. Visual maps, also known as graphic organizers, concept maps, and mind maps, can be used for brainstorming, comparing and contrasting, and identifying misconceptions. Both Inspiration and Kidspiration allow the user to show relationships and to present information in linear and nonlinear formats.

Kidspiration and Inspiration not only help students brainstorm and visualize their thinking, but also appeal to students' different learning styles and lend themselves to inquiry-based learning and are a natural component in a Web-based learning environment.

Kidspiration was used in the following example to design an appealing, interactive learning experience that would engage students. In this "Cinderella Around the World" activity, students are instructed to answer questions using either words or symbols from the program's symbol palette (seen on left). (Students can also import graphics, play sounds, fill in text, and select fonts and effects.) At the end of this unit, concept maps can be printed out and compared so that students will have a visual representation of the essential question of the unit, that is, how setting and culture affects the elements of a fairy tale.

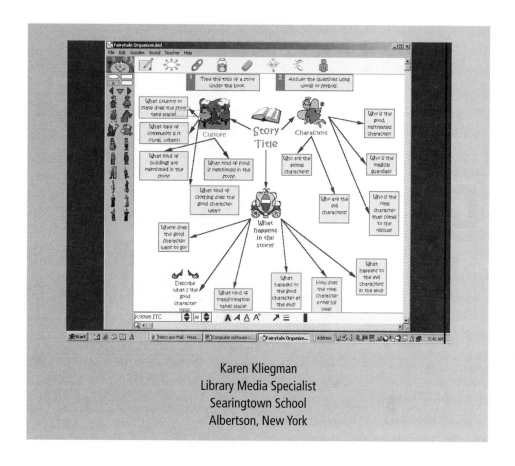

Karen Kliegman
Library Media Specialist
Searingtown School
Albertson, New York

Computer software can help you visualize a problem. It is easy to make concept maps, webs, and flowcharts using any one of the many drawing programs found in most school computer laboratories. Just as a carpenter might pick a specialized hammer (e.g., framing or tack) to solve the problem of nailing a specific type of nail into a specific medium, we may choose specialized software designed to help us with our problem of making a concept map, web, or flowchart. *Inspiration* for grades 6 to adult and *Kidspiration* for grades K through 5 are examples of specialized software designed to aid in this visualization. They are an easy-to-use, powerful tool that lets the user create pictures of ideas, relationships, and concepts. They allow the user to design, create, and modify concept maps, webs, time lines, outlines, and other graphical organizers at the stroke of a key, the click of the mouse and/or the drag of an icon. Ideas can be placed on the screen, expanded, rearranged, and organized with ease. Students can quickly grasp visual relationships as these ideas are spread out on the screen or printed on paper. This visualization aids in clarifying thinking, understanding concepts, developing organizational skills, and increasing retention.

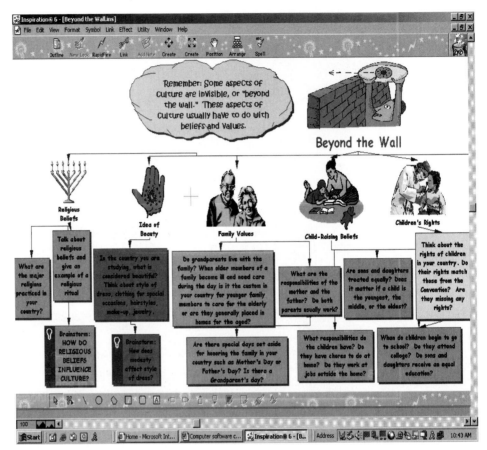

Figure 5–12
A fifth-grade Cultural Research Organizer made with *Inspiration*® (Courtesy of Karen Kliegman)

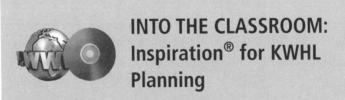

INTO THE CLASSROOM: Inspiration® for KWHL Planning

During the past few years, I have used Inspiration with my kindergarten students to help them develop, investigate, and explore their ideas. Inspiration can be used for a variety of classroom techniques that allow students to explore their ideas visually using graphical organizers. One activity I found especially beneficial—and the students found quite engaging—was using Inspiration for KWHL planning.

A KWHL chart is a graphical organizer used to gather and illustrate information on any topic: What we **KNOW,** What we **WANT** to know, **HOW** to find out, and, later, What we've **LEARNED.** I have used KWHL charts to brainstorm with my students before we start just about any unit.

Using Inspiration for KWHL charts is a great way to integrate technology into an everyday classroom activity. With my computer connected to a big screen television, I open up a new Inspiration document and introduce the topic. Last February, it was Valentine's Day. Prompted by my question—"What do we KNOW about Valentine's Day?"—the students brainstorm and share ideas while I record them into the graphical organizer using Inspiration's Rapid-Fire™ feature. We then move on to the W and the H parts of the graphical organizer.

When we're done, I print the chart out and post it in a prominent place in the classroom. We refer to the diagram frequently and keep track of our progress in the "What have we learned" category, a great way to help young students begin to develop critical thinking and research skills.

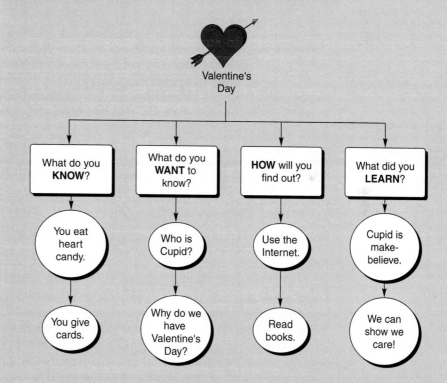

Using Inspiration with my kindergartners has been fun and engaging. It has also made it easy for me to bring technology into everyday classroom activities with very young students. Using KWHL charts, along with other types of graphical organizers, has helped even the youngest students organize their thoughts, develop critical thinking skills, and even monitor their own learning.

Donna Hall
Kindergarten Teacher
Pinellas County Schools
Pinellas, Florida

Both *Inspiration* and *Kidspiration* present a diagram view that is the visual representation of thoughts, ideas, and concepts; and an outline view that presents the same information in a standard outline form. They both also contain a catalog of over 500 objects, boxes, balloons, and symbols to add interest and drama to the diagram view.

Figure 5–13 is a simple concept map that shows relationships in the development of early civilizations. In it we visually portray the relationship between agriculture and animal husbandry and the dynamics leading the growth of populations and the development of cities.

Compare this visual version of the information with the outline version of the same information in Figure 5–14. Note that both the diagram and the outline contain the same relative information but the graphical representation on the concept map seems to show relationships in a clearer manner.

A web is a second type of visual representation showing how different pieces of information relate to each other. There is usually a core concept or main idea in the center with relationships radiating out from the core concept like the spokes of a wheel. Webs are often used to diagram relationships between characters, conflicts, themes, and settings in books and plays. Johnna Solting Horton, a high school media specialist in Minnesota, created Figure 5–15, a web revolving around the play *Romeo and Juliet*. She began with one of the templates included with *Inspiration*. Students viewing this could see at a glance several relationships within the play.

Now compare Figure 5–15 with the outline version of the same information presented in Figure 5–16. Do you find it much harder to visualize relationships?

A preview copy of Inspiration and Kidspiration software can be downloaded free from their site http://inspiration.com

Curriculum Applications of Problem Solving. Rather than attempt to address all of the problem-solving applications (should we call them opportunities?) across the entire curriculum, let's concentrate on information technology, since it is the focus of this book. The term *information technology* was defined in the first paragraph of Chapter 1 as the application of a tool to solve problems related to information to be created, received, stored, manipulated, or disseminated. As teachers in an information-rich society we must strive to encourage students to develop their information skills and to realize that information is power.

Figure 5–17 may be helpful as a lesson-planning tool to develop problem-solving skills in your students. Identifying available resources describes the "Given," and specifying the performance indicators establishes the "To Find." The analysis phase is completed. Specifying the need to create, record, access, analyze, and synthesize information suggests "Procedure" to solve the problem and completes the synthesis phase of problem solving. The examination of the one or more component parts to the procedure will reveal the information skills that need to be learned by the students. The content dealt with becomes the vehicle for the acquisition of the problem-solving skills.

Multimedia Instruction. Few, if any, pieces of software are "pure" drill and practice, tutorial, simulation, instructional game, or problem solving. Some are predominantly one type but embody elements of other approaches. **Multimedia instruction,** more than any other category of software, blurs these lines of distinction. It is also closely related to **multimedia learning.** Refer to Figure 5–1, and notice that multimedia

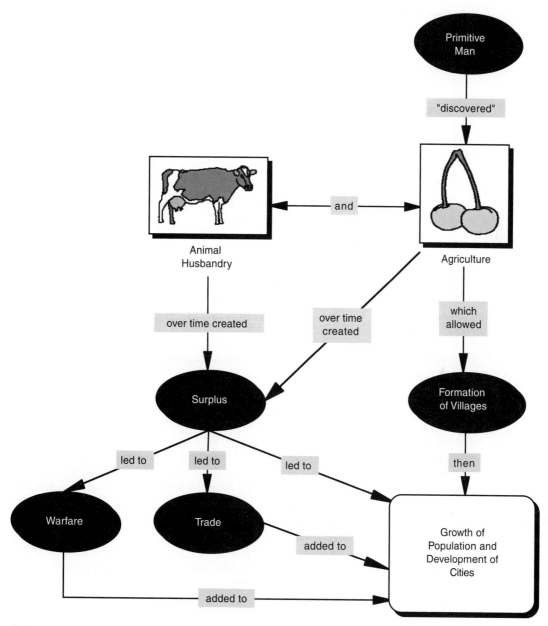

Figure 5–13

Concept map showing relationships between animal husbandry, agriculture, population growth, and city development (Courtesy of Inspiration Software, Inc.)

Figure 5–14
Outline showing relationships between animal husbandry, agriculture, population growth, and city development (Courtesy of Inspiration Software, Inc.)

Primitive Man

A. Agriculture

    1. Led to the formation of villages to tend stationary crops

    2. Surpluses created as agricultural skills increased

B. Animal Husbandry

    1. Surpluses created as animal husbandry skills increased

C. Surpluses led to

    1. Warfare to protect and annex land

    2. Trade to secure other products and export surplus

    3. Growth of populations and development of cities

---

learning is a subcategory of construction of knowledge under the category of student-centered learning.

Multimedia programs are often used to control the presentation of video information from external sources, such as videotape or DVD, as well as graphic, audio, or textual information from CD-ROM. Although the majority of these programs are designed for individual instruction, they may be adapted for group use by the instructor. Typically, audio and video material (still frames, sounds, or moving images with sound) is presented to the viewer accompanied by computer-generated text in a true multimedia fashion. The instructional designer uses the computer to select the video segment and present it on the screen, often interspersed with computer-generated question frames. Depending on the response to the question, the designer can program the computer to repeat the segment, present another one in a remediation mode, or move on to new information.

Multimedia instruction in CAI format is blossoming rapidly in business and industry as an effective and efficient training tool. It is receiving a good deal of attention at the college and university level and is making some inroads in K–12 education as better software becomes commercially available and as teachers develop increasing confidence and skill in designing their own lessons. In an information tool format, multimedia allows students to create their own visuals and incorporate them into their products or to create their own navigation through existing resources. Because of the breadth of classroom applications possible with this technology, multimedia, hypermedia, and virtual reality are discussed in greater detail in Chapter 10.

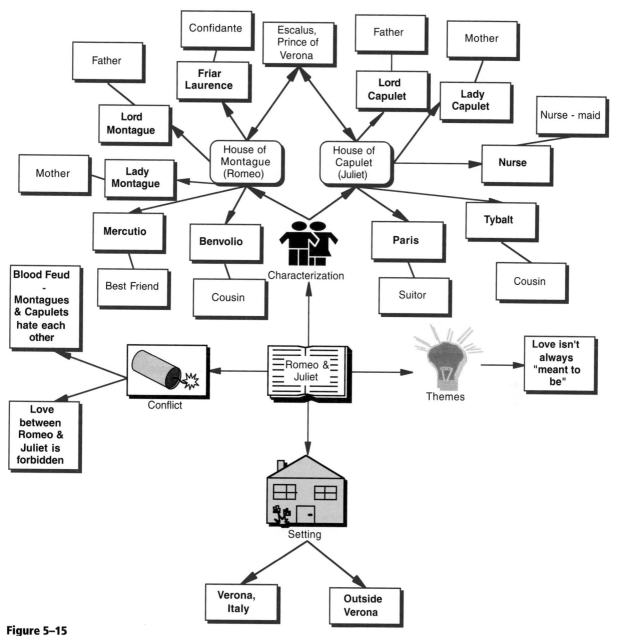

Figure 5–15

Web diagram of *Romeo and Juliet* showing relationships between characters, conflicts, themes, and settings

Romeo & Juliet
    I. Setting
        A. Verona, Italy
        B. Outside Verona
    II. Characterization
        A. House of Montague
            1. Friar Laurence
                a. Confidante
            2. Lord Montague
                a. Father
            3. Escalus, Prince of Verona
                a. House of Capulet
                    1. Lord Capulet
                        a. Father
                    2. Lady Capulet
                        a. Mother
                    3. Nurse
                        a. Nurse - maid
                    4. Tybalt
                        a. Cousin
                    5. Paris
                        a. Suitor
            4. Lady Montague
                a. Mother
            5. Mercutio
                a. Best Friend
            6. Benvolio
                a. Cousin
    III. Conflict
        A. Blood Feud -
            Montagues & Capulets hate each other
        B. Love between Romeo & Juliet is forbidden
    IV. Themes
        A. Love isn't always "meant to be"

Figure 5–16
Web outline of
Romeo and Juliet
showing
relationships
between characters,
conflicts, themes,
and settings

Students with Special Needs. When properly used, the software categories we have examined occupy a unique place in the curriculum. Software from each of the categories can be found or adapted for students with special needs. In many cases computers are ideally suited for this task, augmenting, but not replacing, teachers and support personnel. An interesting study of at-risk high school students by Swan and

Unit of Study: _____

Performance Indicators: _____

_____

_____

_____

Resources Available: _____

_____

_____

Information Needs:

• Creating   (writings, drawings, maps, charts, etc.)

_____

_____

_____

• Recording   (facts, opinions, and impressions for future reference)

_____

_____

_____

• Accessing   (from student- or teacher-created reports and data files, from bound
references, from electronic encyclopedias and atlases, etc.)

_____

_____

_____

• Analyzing   (comparing and contrasting text, numerical, and picture data in order to
form conclusions)

_____

_____

_____

• Synthesizing   (reflecting on available data to create new information)

_____

_____

_____

Figure 5–17
Problem solving in
information
technology

Mitrani (1993) found that there were *more* teacher–student interactions in classrooms where computer-based applications were used than in traditional classrooms. They also found that these interactions were *more* individualized and student centered. Computers can be good teachers and companions for students with special needs, ready to repeat information in a wide variety of ways, patiently waiting for input, and even correcting or channeling input for best results. *Write:OutLoud*® from Don Johnson is an award-winning, talking word processing program that also contains a talking spell checker. *Co:Write*®, another award-winner from Don Johnson, is a user-friendly, word-prediction program that works in conjunction with any word processor. It predicts the completion of partial words that are input, thereby reducing the number of keystrokes needed. Proper use of graphics and sounds can motivate and reinforce students with special needs to further achieve school and personal goals. As stated previously, any of the software programs designed for younger children may be used or modified for use with older students with special needs.

Many different types of special needs devices may be added to a computer to increase the ability of students who have poor coordination or are physically challenged to access and use computers and computer software. These may include such features as a modified keyboard, enlarged monitor, spoken text, and voice recognition.

Curriculum Integration. A danger in examining discrete elements and in categorizing software or computer applications is that we neglect the whole as we examine the separate parts. Much software available today spans more than one category. Tutorial software may well have drill-and-practice components. Simulation software may well introduce new concepts and repeat previously learned material. Classification schemes can become counterproductive if they interfere with an understanding of the potential application of software.

The somewhat arbitrary classification of curriculum during the past decades, especially at the secondary school level, into specific subject matter areas is now breaking down in favor of the integration of disciplines to foster rich learning environments. As we consider computer applications, then, we should keep in mind the concept of integration. The following excerpt by David Thornburg (1991) in his book *Education, Technology, and Paradigms of Change for the Twenty-First Century* is an excellent example of classroom application of the computer in an integrated curriculum:

> Suppose you are a teacher who is exploring California for social studies. One way to do this is to present the students with material right from the textbook. This familiar approach takes a fascinating topic and makes it boring. It causes some students to say, "Who cares?"
>
> On the other hand, in the same period of time, a teacher who really cares about the subject may try a different approach. After exploring California's location on the planet and talking about the geologic upheavals that created some of the spectacular landscape, the students might be encouraged to imagine themselves as members of an ancient tribe of Indians, the Ohlones, for example. Student research on this tribe would allow them to think about the rich civilization these Indians had when the pyramids were being built in Egypt.

As the students learned more about these ancient people, they could learn how to identify animals from their tracks. For this task, students could use *Animal Trackers,* a program from Sunburst Communications that provides clues from which the students must identify a particular animal. Because this program supports databases for grass-lands, desert and wooded areas, it can be used all over the country. Each clue provides information of a different sort—habitat, nesting, food, and footprints. After working with this program for a while, students will have learned a lot about native American animals, as well as honing their higher-order thinking skills. This activity provides an opportunity for science to become integrated with social studies.

As the year proceeds, the students might see a new animal through Indian eyes—the strange creatures with two heads and four legs (the Spanish explorers on horse-back). At this point some students might want to retain the Indian perspective and others might want to join forces with Portola or Father Junipero Serra as the colonization of California took place.

Later on in the course, the teacher might show the film *Dream West,* showing the life of Fremont as he explored the West and paved the way for the United States to expand its boundaries. At this point, students could use the *Oregon Trail* simulation from MECC to see how well they might fare on their own journey across the country. (pp. 22–23)

Computer-Managed Instruction as an Element of Teacher-Centered Instruction. Although computer-assisted instruction, especially tutorial software, sometimes includes some management and recordkeeping function, its emphasis is on the presentation of information or instruction. Computer-managed instruction, however, stresses the management of student performance in a direct, on-line approach, with the student working directly at the computer or in an off-line approach away from the computer. This category includes programs for *keeping student records,* for *diagnostic and prescriptive tests,* for *analyzing test scores,* and for *integrated learning systems.*

Most teachers believe in the concept of individualized instruction. With great effort, many succeed. Individualized instruction is not to be confused with independent study. With individualized instruction, a teacher knows all students well on the basis of their personal, cultural, experiential, and academic background; scholastic ability; and learning style. Knowing the students in this manner, the teacher is capable of providing for diversity in the classroom. Given current typical student–teacher ratios, the mainstreaming of students with special needs into the regular classroom and the attendant, legally mandated IEPs, the recordkeeping involved in individualizing instruction is a monumental task. It is, however, a task well suited to the computer. Student progress can finally be tracked effectively and efficiently.

Integrated Learning Systems (ILS). Perhaps the pinnacle of computer-assisted instruction is the **integrated learning system (ILS).** A classification system by its very nature is arbitrary. We have chosen to place ILS under computer-managed instruction because of its exhaustive management design. It is really a total learning package spanning both computer-assisted instruction and computer-managed instruction categories. ILS are very powerful and very expensive. They usually require their own computer (a file server) to house all of the student software (drill and practice, tutorial, simulation, instructional games, problem solving, and so on) along with software required to individualize instruction, track student progress, store records, and print a variety of reports. Students and teachers gain access to the file server through a network of microcomputers. When a student logs into the file server, the server downloads particular assignments and coursework to the student's computer. It then tracks student progress, tests, and remediates as necessary. Individualized instruction is the major selling point for ILS. Teachers are able to access student progress notes and tailor the ILS accordingly. Most ILS contain the entire scope and sequence for a given topic or content area and usually encompass several grade levels of work.

Design of Teaching Materials as an Element of Teacher-Centered Instruction. Many teachers have relied heavily on commercially prepared teaching materials in the form of bulletin boards, overhead transparency masters, printed masters for worksheets, and other handouts. At times this has resulted in an accommodation between the teacher's perceived needs and the materials available that are designed by a third party. This reliance on commercial materials could, at times, be attributed to teachers' lack of confidence in their own creative ability, as well as to the time demands for producing original materials. Teachers are learning that the computer can significantly increase their ability and dramatically decrease production time demands. Much of the information, illustrations, and exercises in this text will help you do just that!

Text. The computer is ideally suited to creating display materials, and users are presented with a wide variety of software from which to choose. A word processor can be used to prepare practice exercises for the student to complete in school or at home. By selecting a large type size, this same program can prepare an overhead transparency master. Color can be used to highlight keywords by separating the components of the transparency into two masters and printing them in different colors. Special attention might be paid to programs that facilitate the easy integration of graphics and sound with text.

Graphics. Many individuals do not have a high degree of confidence in their artistic drawing ability. Graphics programs level the playing field. They facilitate the creation of respectable illustrations and often bolster the self-esteem of self-prescribed nonartists. Programs such as Freehand™, Illustrator®, CorelDRAW®, AppleWorks, Kid Pix™, PC Paint™, and Print Shop® facilitate the creation of bulletin board and display graphics and text. PowerPoint allows the creation and projection of a series of images containing text, graphics, sound, and video. Programs such as AppleWorks, Delta-Graph, Excel®, and Microsoft Works® generate line graphs, bar graphs, and pie charts from numeric data.

Multimedia Authoring. You have noticed in Figure 5–1 that multimedia applications appear as subcategories under teacher-centered instruction, as well as under student-centered learning. Much multimedia software is not procured from commercial sources but created locally by teachers and students. When creating lessons in the multimedia format, the teacher controls audio and video information, as well as text from internal and external sources. Sophisticated yet easy-to-use software such as ToolBook®, mPOWER®, and HyperStudio turn the teacher into a multimedia author.

Programs are available that allow computer screens to be recorded on videotape to serve as titles, credits, animated graphics, and instructional text screens. A variety of scene transitions that allow one image to fade or to merge into another lends sophistication to the recording. Desktop presentation software permits the projection of computer screens by a video projector. Software that supports the design of teaching materials serves as an extension of the creative teacher. Although these materials can be created in other ways, the computer makes it easy and quick, thereby stimulating teachers to maximize their creative efforts.

Student-Centered Learning

Student-centered learning is an approach that views the computer as an information tool for the student to use to create, access, retrieve, manipulate, and transmit information. One or more students can approach a computer on an as-needed basis in a classroom, school library, or computer lab environment.

When you examine this portion of our classification scheme dealing with student-centered learning, know that many facets referred to under teacher-centered instruction may apply in varying degree to this section as well. The effort here, however, is to focus attention on the student as the user, creator, and disseminator of information and as the builder of knowledge.

Construction of Knowledge. As can be seen in Figure 5–18, student-centered learning encourages students to view the computer as a tool similar to a pencil, brush, or calculator in order to solve a problem. The techniques embodied in student-centered learning are found in subsequent chapters dealing with the computer as a word

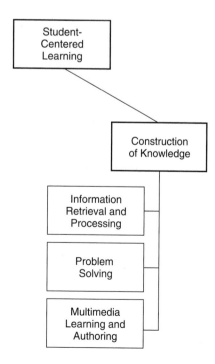

Figure 5–18
The computer in student-centered learning

processing, spreadsheet, database, graphics, or Internet tool. The computer is not only a productivity tool for the teacher but also a tool that enhances the productivity of the student.

The word processor allows the student to express ideas and, with the teacher's guidance, refine the quality of that expression with a reasonable amount of effort in a short period of time. Inquiry strategies can be mapped, content outlines prepared, and detailed reports written. Simple skill-building exercises can become pleasurable. Classroom and school newspapers can be published with word processors and desktop publishing software. Students of all ages can become authors and their books placed in the school library for others to read.

We live in an environment where visual images are constantly bombarding our sense of sight. The advertising industry has made a science of using graphics. Computers have emerged as devices to manipulate visual images and to create forms of video animation. Having recognized the power of visuals to communicate ideas and to persuade viewers, this industry remains at the forefront of computer graphics applications.

Paint and draw programs allow students not only artistic expression but also a powerful nonverbal way to communicate an idea as they prepare signs relating to a cocurricular activity, maps for a social studies project, posters promoting a candidate in a school election, and banners proclaiming significant events. They allow students to explore the spatial relationships of an idea. Graphing programs allow students to examine abstract numeric relationships in a concrete manner.

Information Retrieval and Processing. Telecomputing on the Internet, research on the World Wide Web, database searching, and spreadsheet forecasting allow a student to investigate information in depth. By developing powerful search strategies, a student can find answers to perplexing questions, connect related facts, and derive new information. By sorting information, a student can examine precedence and develop a better understanding of linear relationships or hierarchical order. By altering variables in a problem, a student can explore cause-and-effect relationships and forecast results of a decision. The computer is indeed a tool that amplifies a person's ability to build knowledge.

Problem Solving. The use of the computer as a problem-solving tool is a major focus of this book. Problem-solving strategies revolve around having a certain background knowledge, understanding the material at hand, knowing what is expected, developing a solution strategy, and reflecting on its effectiveness. Both linear and nonlinear strategies are considered. The computer can provide background knowledge and act as a tool to explore solution strategies. It can organize and manipulate information, allowing the user to test tentative solutions before adopting the most appropriate one.

Multimedia Learning and Authoring. Multimedia learning gives the student control of powerful tools in the exploration and creation of information. Multimedia tools allow a student to compose a complex message that might include computer-generated sound, graphics, and animation, along with sound and visual forms stored in another medium, such as videotape, DVD, and CD-ROM, or downloaded from a source on the Internet. Multimedia allows the student to explore communication through multiple senses and become the creator, the artist, and the storyteller as vivid mental images are painted. Students learn to access and organize information; display text, graphics, audio, and video information; and present the products as evidence of knowledge they have constructed.

MANAGEMENT

The chart presented as Figure 5–19 suggests that there are several areas in the realm of school and classroom management that are well suited to computer applications. In each area, the computer can be used as a tool to save the user some time, improve the accuracy of information, and allow the user to efficiently handle large amounts of data.

Budget

Budgets must often be built by teachers, department heads, and other administrators to deal with instructional materials, field trip costs, student club activities, personnel, and departmental needs. In preparing a budget, school administrators and teachers depend on records of historical information as a basis for the projection of future needs. It is necessary to understand past practices, allocations, and expenditures. It is equally important to be able to project ahead in areas of school and program enrollment, staffing needs, curriculum changes, and inflation. Computer-based

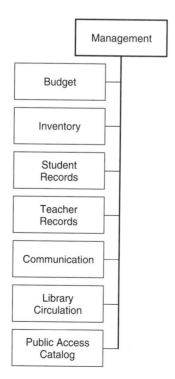

Figure 5–19
The computer in
school and classroom
management

file managers and **spreadsheets** are particularly useful tools to accomplish tasks relating to budget preparation and management. On the one hand, they provide the user with current, accurate records in a timely fashion, and, on the other hand, they provide the ability to reflect changes dynamically as the user manipulates variables to look at projections. Spreadsheets have earned their well-deserved reputation as being "what if . . . " tools. They immediately reflect the results when the user asks, "What if this amount were changed? What impact would this have?"

Inventory

School personnel are accountable for a wide variety of items, ranging from food and janitorial supplies to textbooks, curriculum materials, and instructional equipment. A computer-based file manager can record use, track inventory levels, record the location of items and their condition easily and accurately, and make information available at a moment's notice.

Student Records

A school is required to keep many records concerning students. Many of these are ideally suited for electronic storage. Health and immunization records begin in the primary grades. Information about home and parents or guardians is recorded. Attendance is closely followed. Grades are calculated and stored; then grade reports are generated from these electronic grade books. Individual education programs (IEPs) are tracked, and students' growth in ability and performance levels is monitored. Student portfolios may contain numerous artifacts or samples of student work that can be easily stored, organized, and retrieved electronically. Participation in athletics, music programs, programs for the talented and gifted, and extracurricular activities are noted. Well-designed, computer-based systems are efficient and yield more potentially useful information by creating more complete profiles of the students. Integrated student record packages are being used by more and more school districts in the United States and abroad. These packages allow all aspects of a child's education to be stored and accessed through a common interface. They can provide an instantaneous review of specific records regarding a student by teachers, administrators, and special service personnel. Teachers may input and review grades, attendance, and comments right from their desks. Nurses may input and review immunization and medical records from their offices. Guidance counselors may look up attendance and tardy records during a discussion with a parent or student. Administrators may review multiply grouped statistical data that describes student populations to quickly discern past and current trends and projections of future trends.

With the growing trend toward outcome-based education and authentic assessment, the need for software to keep track of, store, and display student achievement has increased. A number of student portfolio development packages have been developed to meet this need. Some of these are stand-alone programs and others are add-on programs for such programs as PowerPoint and HyperStudio. Many of these packages link student work to school, district, and national goals and objectives and standards. Specific software examples are discussed in Chapter 4.

Teacher Records

Teachers manage information on students, but they also need to manage their own information: syllabi, lesson plans, test banks, evaluation notes, worksheet masters, handouts, and so forth. They can record their participation in professional growth activities that may generate district credit toward advancement. As teachers develop their continuing professional development plans, they may want to use a word processor to keep a reflective teaching journal or use database managers as electronic résumés to store audio or visual artifacts in their own electronic professional teaching portfolios. Many of these activities can now be managed electronically using software described in Chapter 4.

Communication

Parental involvement can increase student achievement and improve the parents' relationship with the school. Written and electronic communication is greatly facilitated by the computer and tends to increase the amount of correspondence between school and home. A **desktop presentation** program allows teachers and administrators to enhance their presentations to students, as well as to parents, school board and community groups, by projecting text, graphics, sound, and video on a screen. Modems and district-wide networks allow schools throughout a district to communicate by exchanging memos, notices of important events, attendance, and other data. Teachers can access lesson plans stored on electronic bulletin boards, Websites, or the school or district server. Most schools have home pages, where students and parents can check class assignments, view class and school information, and use e-mail to ask classmates or school-provided tutors questions on homework assignments.

Library Circulation

Manual library circulation systems have existed for a long time in schools and public libraries. A manual system, though acceptable for recording the checkout and return of books and other materials, is time consuming and provides little additional information of benefit to the user. A computerized automated circulation system can record the checkout and return of materials and can generate lists of the library's holdings, record borrowers' transactions quickly and efficiently, generate lists of overdue materials, provide inventory control to a level that was never before possible, and calculate use statistics.

Public Access Catalog

Just as an automated library circulation system can enhance the distribution of materials, an on-line **public access catalog (PAC)** of a library media center's materials collection can greatly improve access to information. Such a system should allow a user to browse the collection electronically and to perform author, title, subject, and keyword searches.

ACTION RESEARCH

The functional application of the computer to classroom action research, as addressed in Figure 5–20, includes data storage and statistical analysis. Once again the computer is seen as a tool. It is a tool that supports **action research,** placing the teacher in the role of the researcher, often examining some aspect of classroom practice. "Action Research is a fancy way of saying let's study what's happening at our school and decide how to make it a better place" (Calhoun, 1994).

Many researchers divide action research into three forms: the teacher researcher, collaborative research, and school-wide action research. The first form, teacher researcher, has for its focus classroom teachers trying to solve a problem in their classrooms. The results of this investigation may or may not go beyond the teacher's individual classroom. Many teachers run small studies to make their classrooms run smoother or to discover ways to increase student learning. The second form, collaborative research, usually involves the teacher and other school personnel and is focused on changes in several classrooms, grade levels, or departments. The third form, school-wide action research, focuses on improvement throughout the school. Many members of the school, from individual teachers through the school leadership and even external groups, may take part in this form of action research (Calhoun, 1993). We are sure that you will be doing action research once you get into the classroom and want to find out why something is happening or how you can improve something. Action research is a wonderful opportunity for you to make a difference. There are many Internet sites that will help get you started.

The state of Oregon has required for several years that student teachers demonstrate their ability to impact pupil learning as a requirement for initial teacher licensing. Faculty at Western Oregon University developed a work sample methodology to address that requirement. A number of teacher preparation programs including Western Kentucky University, California State University at Long Beach, Eastern Michigan University, University of Northern Iowa, and the University of Tennessee at Knoxville have adopted this methodology as part of their programs. Work samples are required by the teacher licensing agencies in Louisiana (beginning license) and Oregon (beginning and continuing licenses).

Simply described, the methodology requires student teachers to gather appropriate data to describe their learning environments as fully as possible and to prepare

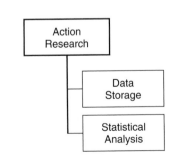

Figure 5–20
The computer in
action research

a sample of their work. Community, school setting, grade level, class size, gender ratio, number of exceptional students [talented and gifted youngsters, children with learning disabilities, those for whom IEPs have been written, those with limited English proficiency (LEP), at-risk youth, and so on], and available classroom resources all are described as the context in which instruction and learning take place. A two- to five-week unit of instruction is then designed. Unit goals and objectives are developed based on statewide curriculum goals and district specific goals. A pretest based on the unit's objectives is developed and administered to the class. Appropriate scoring guides are written for the test items and a **quartile analysis** performed. Lesson plans are written. Following the two- to five-week period of instruction, a posttest is administered. The student teacher is required to compare the test results, analyze the level of learning outcomes, reflect on the instruction given within the described context, and draw conclusions. The personal computer behaves as a number cruncher, providing for the storage and analysis of relevant data in the work sample. Pupil names and pretest scores may be entered in a spreadsheet and sorted in descending order of scores. The teacher may separate the resulting list into four groups and have the spreadsheet calculate the average score for each quartile. Later, individual posttest scores are entered. Once again the spreadsheet can calculate the average score for the previously established quartiles and can calculate the change in quartile averages as well as in individual scores and present the information in graph form based on the data. Reflecting on the demands and support of the teaching context, the teacher can then rate the level of progress toward desired learning outcomes and the equity in the level of progress across the four quartiles.

Data Storage

As in the example on work sample methodology, data storage integrates with other functions dealing with the management of information. Stored data accumulated from various sources can be accessed in the future to examine correlations on SAT scores, GPA, and individual student performance. With the help of a personal computer and appropriate software, teachers and researchers probing a specific topic can analyze data collected on their sample populations and gleaned from student records. Although this certainly could have been done before the advent of the personal computer, now it can be done more easily and cost effectively.

Statistical Analysis

The availability of statistics programs on personal computers allows teachers to analyze data and draw conclusions. This ready access especially encourages the growth of action research at the K–12 level. Numbers entered into spreadsheets can yield simple to complex analyses. Even a simple grade book designed on a spreadsheet can reveal mean, range, and standard deviation of scores. As teachers move toward new product-oriented, criterion-based methods of assessment, they are also attempting to understand and compare student performance through new and different means.

SUMMARY

This chapter examined a framework for software in three major categories: school management, instruction and learning, and educational research.

Instruction and learning was further divided into two major areas, teacher-centered instruction and student-centered learning. Teacher-centered instruction examined the computer as the object of instruction, as well as a tool of instruction and the management of instruction. It was subdivided into the categories of computer literacy, computer-assisted instruction, computer-managed instruction, and design of teaching materials.

Computer literacy was recognized as addressing both issue awareness and functional use. As the computer becomes easier to use and more commonplace, less time and effort will be needed to teach how to use it. Societal issues related to the computer such as access, copyright, rights of privacy, data security, and information ownership may well continue to command attention in the classroom. Computer-assisted instruction was subdivided into categories that parallel learning theory. Computer software might take the form of tutorial, drill and practice, simulation, instructional games, problem solving, or interactive multimedia software that combines text, graphics, sound, and animation and that controls live-action video sequences. Drill and practice is a technique used to reinforce previous instruction and newly introduced concepts by providing the repetition necessary to move skills and concepts acquired into long-term memory. A tutorial software program is designed to introduce new information to the student and often includes a placement test to ensure student readiness. Simulation software supports the problem-solving learning that all students must experience to connect concepts into major clusters of knowledge.

Instructional gaming software reinforces previous learning using graphics, sounds, and some type of competition format. Problem-solving software introduces students to situations in which they must use new or previously learned information and concepts to state hypotheses, plan strategies, and follow some set of procedures to achieve the final goal or outcome.

Multimedia instruction uses more than one way of conveying information in a multisensory manner.

The distinguishing characteristics that separate the different categories of computer-assisted instruction are beginning to blur, because strategies are being combined to achieve a wider range of objectives.

Computer-managed instruction was discussed as a category of software that helps the teacher track students' progress. If this time-consuming work can be done more efficiently with the aid of the computer, then the teacher will have more time to help students. This alone can make for a more effective learning environment.

The use of computer technology can aid teachers in the design, development, and creation of teaching materials. A vast array of tools are available to the creative teacher to design and produce materials that communicate effectively.

In student-centered learning the computer is a tool for the student to use to create, access, retrieve, manipulate, and transmit information in order to solve a problem. Understanding the concept of the computer as an information tool relies on accepting the fact that the computer is a productivity tool for the student and teacher alike.

School management was divided by data processing and information retrieval functions into seven functional categories: budget, inventory, student records, teacher records, communication, library circulation, and public access catalog.

Classroom action research includes functions relating to information gathering and processing. The teacher and researcher may examine student performance data in new and revealing ways.

As we consider computer applications, we should keep in mind the concept of curriculum integration.

CHAPTER EXERCISES

To complete the specified exercises on-line, go to the Chapter Exercises Module in Chapter 5 of the Companion Website.

1. Create a mock budget for a student activity club in an area of personal interest. List income and expenditures. How could a computer assist you in managing this budget?

2. Identify as many tasks as you can that are included in a school lunch program. Which of these tasks might be facilitated by a computer? Which would not?

3. Describe what we mean by each of these three categories of educational software: school management, instruction and learning, and educational research. Explain how each may be used in the school environment.

4. What is your definition of *computer literacy?* Does it differ from ours? If so, in what ways?

5. Using a subject and a grade level that you may be teaching in, think of a problem or subject that you could use webbing or concept mapping to explain. Diagram this on a sheet of paper. Now do the same using *Inspiration* or *Kidspiration*. If a copy of *Inspiration* or *Kidspiration* is not available to you, download a trial copy from inspiration.com and use it to make the same web or map.

6. Find a school in your area that uses computers in their school for management. Talk to one of the teachers there about what they and others in the school think of it. Report your findings to the class.

7. In the library or on the Web, find articles or information discussing and outlining a school or district's technology plan. Does this school or district give a technology test to new teachers before they are hired? Report your findings to the class.

8. In a small group, discuss the role of computers in all aspects of education. Make a list of three reasons how computers can make a teacher's life easier and more interesting, three reasons why school computers can benefit the administration and parents, and three reasons that may slow down the

utilization of computers by teachers and the administration. Discuss your answers with the class.

9. Think of a problem that you may encounter in your teaching for which you could apply action research to find a solution. Design a small action research study that will help you find the solution.

10. Is there a "best" format (e.g., drill and practice, tutorial, and so on) for educational software? Explain your answer.

PORTFOLIO DEVELOPMENT EXERCISES

To complete these exercises on-line, go to the Digital Portfolio Module in Chapter 5 of the Companion Website.

One of the NETS•S standards covered in this chapter was "Students evaluate and select new information resources and technological innovations based on the appropriateness for specific tasks" under *Category 5: Technology research tools.* Begin to develop your own portfolio of lesson plans that demonstrates your ability to have your students reach the NETS•S standards.

For more information on developing digital portfolios go to Digital Portfolio Module on the Companion Website www.prenhall.com/forcier

1. Design a lesson plan activity for elementary, middle school, or high school students in which they study a career or occupation of an individual or group that you will be studying or someone who is appropriate for your subject area. Using this career or occupation, have students list particular tasks that are performed by members of this occupation and list technology that is available to make workers' tasks in this industry easier. These technologies need not currently be used in the occupation. This lesson should demonstrate that your students have achieved the standard. Be sure to include a system of evaluation for your students' understanding and competence to ensure that they have met this standard.

2. Adapt the lesson plan activity you developed in exercise 1 for students to evaluate each others' work.

GLOSSARY

action research The teacher as researcher investigates a problem, usually arising from some classroom practice. Results are applicable only to the setting in which the research was conducted.

branching A design of some programs that uses techniques to provide multiple alternative paths, or branches, for remediation or acceleration.

computer-assisted instruction (CAI) The direct instructional interaction between computer and student designed to produce the transmission of information.

computer literacy The study of the development and functional use of the computer, as well as related societal issues.

computer-managed instruction (CMI) Use of the computer as a diagnostic, prescriptive, and organizational tool to gather, store, manipulate, analyze, and report information relative to the student and the curriculum.

desktop presentation The display of screens (images or text) of information stored in a computer. The display device is often a video projector or flat panel overhead-projection device.

drill and practice A category of computer software that uses the teaching strategy to reinforce instruction by providing repetition necessary to move acquired skills and concepts into long-term memory. Problems are presented and feedback is provided for the student's response.

file manager Software that is designed to create and to manage data files. According to current usage, this term is synonymous with database manager.

gaming A strategy that can be incorporated into all instructional software categories. Includes the elements of a set of rules and competition against others or against a standard.

instructional games A category of software that is highly competitive, is intriguing, may include elements of speed or time, and often involves some type of fantasy atmosphere. The learner is usually competing for a high score, a specific outcome, or a "personal best" effort.

integrated learning system (ILS) A hardware and software package designed to present and manage the scope and sequence of one or several content areas. These content areas may encompass several years of instruction. A file server and series of networked computer workstations are usually required.

multimedia instruction The technique of accessing and displaying textual, graphic, audio, and video information stored in electronic, magnetic, or optical form under the control of a computer to meet objectives specified by the teacher by conveying information in a multisensory manner.

multimedia learning The technique of accessing, organizing, and displaying textual, graphic, audio, and video information stored in electronic, magnetic, or optical form under the control of a computer to meet student needs by conveying information in a multisensory manner.

problem-solving software A category of software that presents students with a problem for which they must state the hypothesis, plan strategies, and follow some set of procedures to achieve a final goal or outcome.

public access catalog (PAC) A computer-based system that provides users access to a library's holdings.

quartile analysis The ranking of performance measures from high to low and the separation of the measures into four groups to study performance by high, medium, and low achievers.

simulation A category of computer software that uses a teaching strategy based on role-playing within structured environments. It provides an environment for discovery learning to take place and for newly acquired skills and concepts to be tested.

spreadsheet Software that accepts data in a matrix of columns and rows, with their intersections called cells. One cell can relate to any other cell or ranges of cells on the matrix by formula. Often used with numeric data to forecast results of decisions.

tutorial A category of computer software that uses the teaching strategy in which the student's level of knowledge is first determined before new information is introduced along with learning guidance. The computer usually assesses a student's prior learning, determines readiness for the material, and presents material for student observation, note taking, and other interaction.

virtual reality (VR) A computer-generated simulated environment with which a user can interact.

REFERENCES & SUGGESTED READINGS

Calhoun, E. (1993). Action research: Three approaches. *Educational Leadership, 51*(2), 62–65.

Calhoun, E. F. (1994). *How to use action research in the self-renewing school*. Alexandria, VA: Association for Supervision and Curriculum Development.

Ertmer, P. A., Addison, P., Lane, M., Ross, E., & Woods, D. (1999, Fall). Examining teachers' beliefs about the role of technology in the elementary classroom. *Journal of Research on Computing in Education, 32* (1), 54–97.

Hill, W. F. (1977). *Learning: A survey of psychological interpretations*. New York: Harper & Row, 214–216.

International Society for Technology in Education. (2000). *National educational standards for teachers*. Eugene, OR: International Society for Technology in Education.

Miller, C. (1992, November). Online Interviews; Dr. Thomas A Furness, III, Virtual Reality Pioneer. *Online, 16* (6) 14–27.

Mizell, A. (1997, July). Unpublished review, Nova Southeastern University, Miami, FL.

Sosenke, F. (2000, May). World tour. *Learning & Leading with Technology, 27* (5), 32–35.

Swan, K. & Mitrani, M. (1993, Fall). The changing nature of teaching and learning in computer-based classrooms. *Journal of Research on Computing in Education, 26* (1), 40–54.

Thornburg, D. (1991). *Education, technology, and paradigms of change for the twenty-first century*. San Carlos, CA: Starsong Publications.

Part
2
Classroom Applications as Learning Tools

Learning with Graphics Tools

1. Discuss the usefulness of two electronic input devices in the creation of graphics.

2. What are some tools you might use for creating computer graphics?

3. What are bit-mapped graphics?

4. What are vector, or object-oriented, graphics?

5. What is clip art and how can it be used?

6. What is a practical application of computer graphics that you might use as a teacher in designing instructional materials for your classroom?

7. What are some basic rules to follow when designing overhead transparencies on the computer?

8. What are some of the tools that you can use to capture images and graphics?

9. What are some tools you might find useful for displaying computer-generated graphics?

The adage "a picture is worth a thousand words" is an appropriate beginning to any basic discussion about **graphics.** Teachers appreciate the value of this statement because pictorial representations have always been an important means for communicating ideas and concepts to students quickly and accurately. Our earliest ancestors used graphics on the walls of caves or rock outcroppings in Europe, Africa, and Asia, as did Native Americans on skins and bones to record great hunts and other events. Egyptians and Central and South American Indians carved events and rituals on their temples and pyramids. And every schoolroom in the country has a map, poster, bulletin board, or other graphic display to brighten the room and educate the students.

Many different graphics tools have been used in instructional situations. The chalkboard, drawings, flowcharts, diagrams, print of different sizes, underlining, and arrows are common tools for enhancing the communication of ideas to students. Video recorders, overhead projectors, photographs, posters, maps, textbooks, and television have also added different dimensions to our capabilities in using visuals to affect the learning experience. Each tool expands the user's ability to refine the presentation of ideas and to emphasize key parts through motion, color, size, and blank space. The computer is a visual tool that can present many of these capabilities interactively, adding even more power to graphic communication. Schools have recognized the uniqueness of visual literacy, and many include visual literacy skills training as part of their curriculum.

Just as music and language have discrete systems of notation, visuals have a complex code system composed of color, texture, size, medium, realism, and so on. These codes combine to make visuals powerful tools. Teachers have recognized that students are surrounded and constantly bombarded by visual stimuli and, often as part of a visual literacy skills curriculum, have attempted to teach them effective **decoding** skills in order to derive accurate meaning from these stimuli. Computer-generated graphics also provide students with the opportunity to learn powerful **encoding** skills as they analyze the symbols they choose in order to communicate effectively.

Still images can stimulate interest and assist the understanding of verbal materials. Line drawings, easily prepared in a computer graphics program, can sometimes simplify a complex visual reality. Projected on a screen, these graphics can reach a large group through conventional delivery methods such as an overhead transparency or through the electronic projection process called desktop presentations.

Information found in this chapter highlights three NETS•S standards categories. Information dealing with standards listed under *Category 1: Basic operations and concepts* is found throughout the chapter, especially in the sections dealing with input and output devices and graphic types. This is also true of standards listed under *Category 3: Technology productivity tools*. Computer graphics and graphic programs are just one of the communications tools used to satisfy the standards listed under *Category 4: Technology communications tools*. Many other communications tools are discussed throughout the text. Pay particular attention to how one teacher used moviemaking to help his students communicate information and feeling to each other and their community. It describes one of the many ways that technology communicates on both an intellectual and an emotional level to really touch the hearts and minds of people of all cultures and all ages.

A list of the ISTE/NCATE standards addressed in this chapter is available in the Standards Module on the Companion Website www.prenhall.com/forcier

NETS•S Standards Addressed in This Chapter

1. Basic operations and concepts
   - Students demonstrate a sound understanding of the nature and operation of technology systems.
   - Students are proficient in the use of technology.

3. Technology productivity tools
   - Students use technology tools to enhance learning, increase productivity, and promote creativity.
   - Students use productivity tools to collaborate in constructing technology-enhanced models, prepare publications, and produce other creative works.

4. Technology communications tools
   - Students use telecommunications to collaborate, publish, and interact with peers, experts, and other audiences.
   - Students use a variety of media and formats to communicate information and ideas effectively to multiple audiences.

TOOLS FOR CREATING GRAPHICS

Drawing and painting computer programs have been used by teachers and students alike for decades for three general purposes: (1) to *create* graphics to use for a variety of purposes; (2) to *change* graphics that have been obtained from other sources such as previously created graphics, clip art, scanned images, and images captured by digital cameras; and (3) to *convert* images from one file format to another to make them accessible to other software programs and the World Wide Web. Adobe Illustrator®, PC Paint, CorelDRAW, Kid Pix, Kid Works Deluxe, Painter™, Canvas™, Photoshop Elements™, and other graphics programs are available for Windows and Macintosh to facilitate the creation of worksheets, newsletters, bulletin boards, and other displays of graphics and text. Although these materials can be created in other ways, the computer along with digital cameras and scanners makes it easier and less time consuming and thereby stimulates teachers to reach out and maximize their creative efforts.

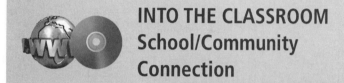

INTO THE CLASSROOM
School/Community
Connection

I work in San Fernando High School in North Los Angeles. Many people would write our school off as a lost cause. We have more than 4,000 students in a school designed to hold 1,700 . . . 83 percent score below grade level . . . and many are also struggling with English as a second language. Technology? Only 4 percent of the students have access to any technology at home! We do have a great resource though: our students! My fellow teacher, Veronica Marek, and I decided to use desktop movie production to magnify our student's excitement and passion for learning, hopefully to take them to heights we could only dream of achieving!

Veronica and I decided to have the students take a personal look at immigration and the American dream. We decided rather than talk at great lengths about Ellis Island and the vast waves of European immigrants as many texts do, we would instead focus on real-world, touch-me immigration: the real and personal stories of the student's families, their friends and themselves.

We had the students gather family photos and documents to design and produce a living, breathing history . . . their history. This assignment preserved their family history and also opened meaningful, personal dialogues between students and parents. Students learned real-world lessons about their families and their heritage. They discovered where they crossed the border and considered their goals and expectations.

(Continued)

Making desktop movies let my students know that they, their families, and their stories are important. They are important to me, important to the school and important to the community. Videotaping parents and grandparents connected meaningful education to the home. At home and at school and in our student's minds, thinking, writing, and research were all given real-world meaning. With careful planning, actually putting the video, documents, and photographs together on our iMac DV's using the built-in iMovie software was a breeze. The ease with which it was accomplished made the technology practically transparent to the project. They and their projects were one. Going the extra mile to get it "just right" was exciting and fun.

The school and community learning connection did not stop at production time. When it came time to share their movies . . . their lives . . . students asked me to arrange a special evening presentation for the community. The students acted as ushers and even catered the event. Parents and grandparents filled the audience. The video stories were shown with pride and a huge sense of accomplishment . . . and by the end of the evening you could not find a dry eye in the house.

Marco Torres
Social Studies Teacher
Director, San Fernando Education Technology Team
San Fernando High School
San Fernando, California

GRAPHICS TYPES AND GRAPHICS PROGRAMS

There are two basic types of graphics created by the computer: bit-mapped and vector (or object-oriented). **Bit-mapped graphics** rely on direct changes to each dot or pixel that makes up an image. Paint programs are used to create and change bit-mapped graphics. **Vector,** or **object-oriented, graphics** rely on mathematical equations to define the image. Drawing programs are used to create vector, or object-oriented, graphics. Each type of graphic has its own advantages and disadvantages.

Bit-Mapped Graphics. For bit-mapped graphics, the computer-generated image is composed of bits, or screen picture elements called pixels. Pretend your monitor screen is a map or grid 600-pixels high by 800-pixels wide. Pixels can be turned on (to appear black or colored) or off (to appear white or clear). Many programs that incorporate the name "paint" in their titles produce bit-mapped graphics. This led to the practice of calling bit-mapped programs *paint programs*. Programs such as PC Paint, Kid Pix (Figures 6–1 and 6–2) and Kid Works Deluxe often are the user's first introduction to computer graphics. These are very functional programs with a very simple interface that is easily understood by young children. They, as all paint programs, have definite limitations though.

Figure 6–1
Screenshot from Kid Pix in which little reading is required; when the top left icon (pencil) is clicked, pencil thicknesses appear on the lower bar (Reprinted with permission from Riverdeep, Inc.)

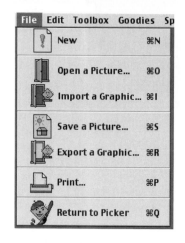

Figure 6–2
Kid Pix menus are also designed for the non-reader (Reprinted with permission of Riverdeep, Inc.)

A simplified bit-mapped drawing of the side view of a child's wagon created in a paint program is presented in Figure 6–3, with a dot pattern applied to the body and a solid pattern applied to the wheels.

Figure 6–4 shows that same wagon with a section of the drawing enlarged. Horizontal and vertical lines are smooth, but notice the jagged edges of the circle (wheel)

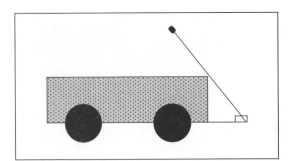

Figure 6–3
Wagon in bit-
mapped graphics

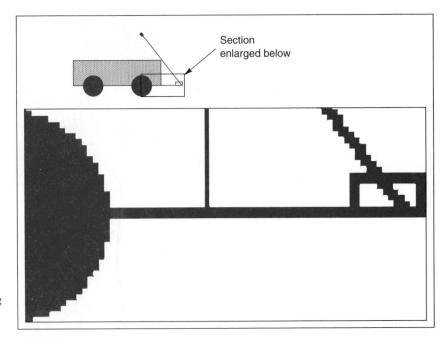

Figure 6–4
Enlargement showing
the low resolution of
bit-mapped graphics

and diagonal line (handle shaft). The square shape of the pixel becomes apparent. One of the inherent drawbacks of bit-mapped graphics is that the size of the pixel limits the sharpness, or resolution, of the drawing, regardless of the resolution of the monitor or printer used to display the graphic.

Normally, bit-maps are created at a resolution of 72 dots per inch (dpi). One pixel is 1/72 of an inch. Phosphor dots on a video tube are much smaller and many are required to make up a pixel. Laser printers and common ink-jet printers frequently found in schools are capable of printing at 1,200 or more dpi. Unfortunately, bit-mapped images cannot take advantage of either the higher screen display or higher printing resolution.

Once a bit-mapped image or lettering is created, it is very difficult to change. In order to modify an existing image in a paint program, the user must turn pixels on

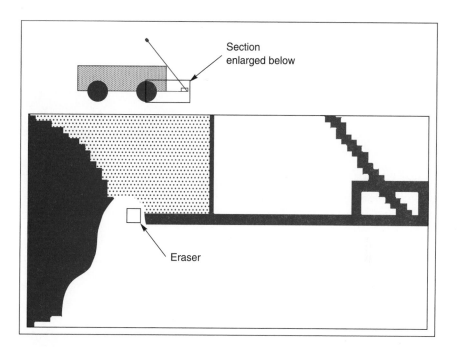

Figure 6–5
Erasing bits

and off individually or erase large segments, as shown in Figure 6–5. Notice that the eraser (the white square) is turning bits off; that is, it is turning black or colored pixels white against a white background, virtually making them disappear. Once text is inserted into a "paint" document, typing errors cannot be easily corrected, nor can typefaces, sizes, or styles be changed. Whenever text is inserted, the text itself also becomes a bit-mapped graphic. Think of it as a picture of the words. Once text is fixed in position, it cannot be edited. Pixels composing the letters can be erased like any other graphic element, thereby allowing entire letters and words to be erased. Paint programs allow for some changes in position of the images after they have been created. Unfortunately it is more along the lines of cutting the image out of a magazine page and pasting it into another position.

Vector, or Object-Oriented, Graphics (Drawing Programs). The other type of computer graphic is called a **vector,** or **object-oriented, graphic.** This computer-generated image, instead of being composed of bits or screen pixels that are turned on and off, is determined by mathematical formulas that create discrete objects of a certain size and position. Adobe Illustrator, Canvas, and most programs that incorporate the label "draw" in their titles such as CorelDRAW produce object-oriented graphics. This has led to the practice of calling object-oriented programs draw programs. Integrated software packages such as AppleWorks and Microsoft Works include a draw program or module.

In Figure 6–6, the front wheel has been moved away from the rest of the drawing. Each picture element is a separate object and can be changed independently. It can be enlarged, reduced, moved, or have its pattern changed. Creating an image in

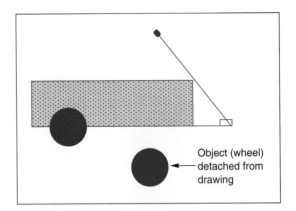

Figure 6–6
Wagon in vector, or
object-oriented,
graphics

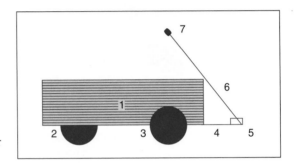

Figure 6–7
Objects making up
the drawing in vector
graphics

a draw program is conceptually very different from creating one in a paint program. Rather than drawing freehand with a pencil or paintbrush, the user of a draw program creates objects of different shapes (e.g., lines, circles, rectangles, and polygons), adjusts line thickness, applies patterns to the objects, then organizes them into new, more complex objects.

Once objects are created in draw programs, their shape, size, and position can be changed. Two or more objects may be linked or grouped together to form a new object. Text inserted in a drawing remains an editable text object. Typing mistakes can be easily corrected, and typefaces, sizes, and styles can be changed at any time. Being a discrete object, text may also be repositioned at will.

Count the objects making up the wagon in Figure 6–7. There are seven objects: (1) the shaded body of the wagon, (2) the rear wheel, (3) the front wheel, (4) the steering plate, (5) the handle tongue, (6) the handle shaft, and (7) the handle. Because the drawing is composed of independent objects, they may overlap or be layered on top of one another. Notice that, unlike in Figure 6–6, the rear wheel is placed underneath the body of the wagon in Figure 6–7 and that the shading of the body has been changed to a striped pattern. Some graphics programs include both bit-mapped and draw layers so that the user can take advantage of what each approach has to offer.

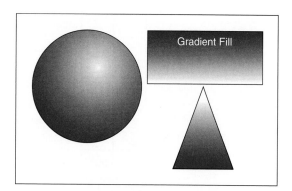

Figure 6–8
Sample use of
gradient fill

Many draw programs allow the use of **gradient fill** patterns similar to those shown in Figure 6–8 that begin with a certain density of pattern or opacity at a determined point and gradually fade to a less-dense pattern or increase to a denser one. Gradient fills can create the appearance of a third dimension on an object and are a dramatic background for text.

The Tools of Paint and Draw Programs

Figure 6–9 illustrates tools that are common to a number of paint and draw programs. As noted previously, high-end graphics programs such as Painter (Figure 6–9) incorporate both paint and draw modes and have many more tools enabling precision control of graphics.

If a paint or a draw program is truly to become a productivity tool, the user must become comfortable with the individual program and adept at using it. The following lists and descriptions help to introduce you to these tools.

Paint tools are those that create bit-mapped images in paint programs.
  marquee selection tool Selects a rectangular area, including any white background present.
  lasso selection tool Selects an irregular shape without any extraneous background.
  magic wand Selects adjacent pixels of the same color.
  paintbrush Paints strokes of various sizes and shapes.
  pencil Paints fine lines in a freehand manner. One of the first tools people learn to use in a paint program.
  paint bucket Used to fill an enclosed shape with color, pattern, or gradient.
  spray can Used to create a spray-painted effect.
  eraser Erases part of an image, pixel by pixel.

Draw tools are those that create objects in draw programs.
  pointer Selects, moves, and resizes objects.
  arc tool Draws an arc curving between two points.
  polygon tool Draws closed shapes made up of straight lines and angles.

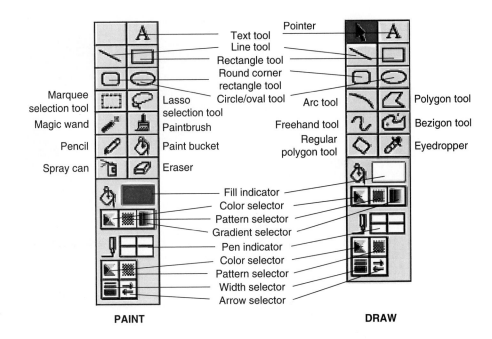

Figure 6–9
Tools commonly
found in paint and
draw programs

freehand tool Draws irregular lines in the manner similar to a pencil.
bezigon tool Draws shapes, with the user selecting specific points. The tool
draws smooth curves through those points.
regular polygon tool Draws polygons of equal sides.
eyedropper Picks up colors, patterns, and gradients from any object drawn and
adjusts the proper selection tool. The result appears in the Fill indicator.

**Some tools are used by both paint and draw programs, though they behave
somewhat differently in each.**
text tool Inserts text on the screen in a selected font.
line tool Creates straight lines.
rectangle tool Creates rectangles and squares.
round corner rectangle Creates rectangles and squares with round corners.
circle/oval tool Creates ovals and circles.
color, pattern, and gradient fill selectors Allow user to select specific color,
pattern, or gradient to fill a shape or an object.
color, pattern, width, and arrow pen selectors Allow user to select specific color,
pattern, width, and arrow style for the pen.
fill and pen indicators Display the specific fill and pen characteristics that have
been selected.

In addition to using paint and draw programs, we often have need to modify photographic images. We perhaps have to crop the image, or adjust the brightness or
contrast, or perhaps the color hue or saturation, or perhaps we simply wish to remove "red-eye" from a photo. Of the many programs available, Adobe Photoshop
Elements, as shown in Figure 6–10, is a reasonably priced, easy-to-use, and yet very

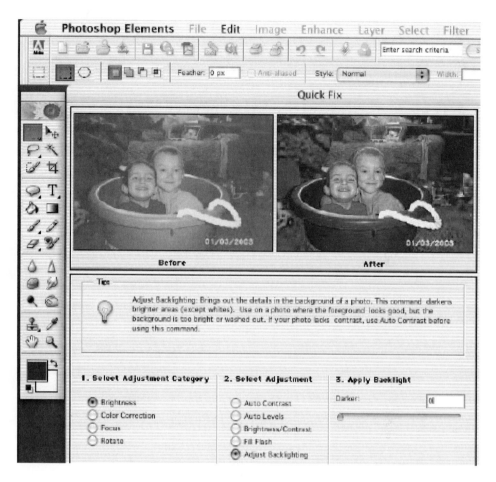

Figure 6–10
Photoshop elements
(Courtesy of Adobe®
Systems Inc.)

powerful choice. It has a reduced feature set of the high-end and expensive program, Adobe Photoshop. Photoshop Elements allows us to perform all the tasks mentioned above and more. We can blend multiple images into panoramic views, compress photos for e-mail attachments, create animations and slideshows, apply frames and drop shadows to our photos, and save printing costs by printing multiple photos in different sizes on the same page.

CLIP ART

For many years, graphic artists subscribed to services that provided them with printed drawings and images. The artists clipped out any illustration that suited their needs and incorporated it into their own original work. This is outdated technology. With the transition to computer graphics, **clip art** files on disk and through the World Wide Web are now readily available.

Clip art is a great time saver for all and an exceptional resource for those of modest or limited artistic skills and talents. Examine the various illustrations found in

Figure 6–11
Samples of clip art
(Courtesy of
Hermera
Technologies Inc.)

Figure 6–11. Some files are line drawings, some are detailed illustrations, and others are photographs. Notice the lettering textured with African violets. Among the many sources of clip art, the award-winning *The Big Box of Art* by Hermera Technologies (available for both Windows and Macintosh) is an impressive and reasonably priced standout. It contains approximately a quarter million illustrations and comes on over 20 CDs. Along with a printed volume of images, it includes a search engine that lets you search by graphic type as well as by topic and displays thumbnails of each illustration indicating which CD to insert once you've chosen your graphic. The textured lettering is accomplished by using the included software, *PhotoFonts*.

Another huge source of graphics is the Internet. A quick search will find thousands of images in many different file types to download to your computer.

Copyright

Purchasing a clip art disk or CD-ROM entitles users to copy images or parts of images to use in their own drawings usually with some restrictions. Be sure to review the copyright statements on the clip art package you use to find out what they are. Some packages allow the purchaser to use the clip art for educational or private home use only. Other packages allow the user to use the clip art for business. Still other packages have no restrictions. It is wise to purchase clip art for school through a source that also sells educational software. These vendors place clip art disks and CD-ROMs in their catalog knowing that they will be used in a school environment.

Ownership of clip art and images found on the World Wide Web is sometimes difficult to ascertain. Even though the Internet was to be a medium for the free exchange of information, it is no more. Remember that the act of placing something on the Web automatically copyrights it. Therefore, you should think of everything (graphics and text) on the Web as copyrighted. Luckily, there are many sites containing huge archives of clip art and images that are available to use copyright free. Be careful of some sites though. We have found such things as the Nike and Coca-Cola trademarks on some sites. Advertising logos and trademarks are always owned by the company and should never be used without permission. If there is any question, it is a good idea not to use any of the graphics or images found on the site.

With the availability of high-quality, inexpensive scanners, more and more students and teachers are using graphics and pictures in their newsletters, reports, and Web pages. Remember, unless you took the photograph yourself, you probably don't own the copyright. For instance, many people do not realize that unless they specifically bought the rights to their own wedding pictures, they cannot copy them. The copyright for their own wedding pictures is held by the original photographer. Check the copyright notice written in or on the source of the material. Some material can be copied for noncommercial, educational use.

FILE FORMATS

Once you create a graphics document, you must choose a file format to save the file in order to share the document with others or to open the document in a specific graphics application. Though all these formats can store graphics information, each was designed for a reason. Some are specific to applications while others were designed for sharing among applications.

Graphics files tend to be very large, therefore, each file format employs a compression technique. One technique examines repeated data patterns and replaces them with a code that describes the pattern and the number of its repetitions. This technique is called *lossless compression* since, though the file is smaller, no information is lost. This type works well with drawings. The other technique, *lossy compression,* discards information it judges unnecessary, thereby losing some information. It re-creates as much of it as possible when the file is opened. The resulting file is much smaller than with a file format employing lossless compression.

Color photographs are prime candidates for lossy compression. Any tonal gradations can be identified by the two extremes and intermediate values discarded to be re-created mathematically when the file is opened. Though there are many graphics file formats, the following represent the most common ones used today.

BMP This bit-map type is the native file format for Windows OS and employs a lossless compression technique suitable for drawings and very simple color im-ages. Its file extension is .BMP.

GIF The Graphics Interchange Format was developed for fast transfer of files over the Internet and is still one of the dominant file types used on Web pages. It's best used for vector drawings with a small number of colors. Though it uses a lossless compression technique, it limits color depth to 8 bits of color data for up to 256 colors but can support multiple images in the same file, allowing for the appearance of animation. Its file extension is .GIF.

JPEG The Joint Photographic Experts Group format supports a full color range and, using lossy compression, allows the user to choose compression ratios and can achieve very high rates of compression. Unfortunately, at the high compression rates, fine details can be lost and *artifacts* (missing or unwanted pixels created in the conversion process) can become quite visible. It's best used for the efficient storage of photographs. Its file extension is .JPG.

TIFF The Tagged Image File Format, using lossy compression, is easily recognized by Adobe Photoshop™ users. Though its files tend to be the largest, it is commonly used to store photographs from digital cameras and complex high-resolution images. Its usual file extension is .TIF, though .TIFF may be used.

EPS Encapsulated PostScript is typically used in page layout programs using the PostScript language. Its files contain both graphics and text. When an EPS file is imported into one of the popular graphics programs, its raster images become paint objects and its vector objects are maintained. Text remains text objects. Its file extension is .EPS.

Before leaving the topic of graphics file formats, we should comment on video file formats. Each video file format works with one or more software codec (compressor/decompressor). The codec compresses the data when it is being saved and decompresses it when the video is being played. The common video file formats are MPEG (Moving Picture Experts Group), A-VI (Audio-Video Interleaved), WMV (Windows Media Video), MOV (Movie), and QuickTime.

MPEG (using the MPEG-2 codec) is often used for DVDs. It produces reasonable screen resolution with CD-quality audio. Its file extension is .MPG.

AVI files are larger but offer a greater selection of codecs. Though it has limited resolution and cannot support streaming video, its biggest advantage is that almost any Windows computer can play this format. Its file extension is .AVI.

WMV achieves a small file size by using a lossy compression but usually with some loss of quality. Its file extension is .WMV or .ASF.

QuickTime, an International Organization for Standardization (ISO) format, is the most versatile video file format supporting the greatest number of codecs and various kinds of data. Its file extension is .QT or .MOV. QuickTime and MPEG are usually the formats of choice for streaming video over the Web.

DESIGN OF INSTRUCTIONAL MATERIALS

In designing any communication, whether it be oral, written, or graphic, the sender of the message must know the anticipated audience that is to receive it and design the communication appropriately. The user must know what will capture the audience's attention and get the information across clearly and convincingly. Many times graphics do just that. Graphics, when properly used, support key points, draw the reader's attention and add interest to a presentation. Improperly used graphics may be irritating and distracting.

Line drawings are the most common type of graphics created on the computer. When considering line illustrations, a few simple rules apply:

- Present one topic or main idea per illustration.
- Use thick (bold) lines.
- Keep the use of text to a minimum and use a bold style.

Today, most people make overhead transparencies using either the office copy machine or an ink-jet or laser printer. Specially treated clear plastic sheets are used depending on which process (copy machine, ink-jet or laser printer) will be used. After designing the transparency on a computer, it is either printed directly onto the special plastic transparency sheet or printed on paper and copied onto a special sheet fed into the office copier.

Designing transparencies in computer graphics is a fairly straightforward task. Using any "Paint" or "Draw" program, create the image you want to project and print it. Using *PowerPoint*™ as a graphics tool, you could create the entire image to be projected as the finished transparency and save it as a master slide. Print the slide and you have a transparency master. Whether you are projecting an image from your computer or from an overhead projector, if you wish to design a series of images that, when used sequentially, build in an additive nature to a final concept, open the master slide. Decide what elements of the image should be presented first, delete the rest, and save the result as slide #1. Subsequent steps require you to open the master slide, delete unwanted elements, and save the results as a new slide #2, etc.

 These transparency design guidelines may also be found at the Companion Website http://www. prenhall.com/forcier

In examining the process just described, it is apparent that the user, once having acquired a certain degree of skill and comfort level with a computer graphics program, can use it as a tool that extends abilities in a low-tech environment. Other examples include banners that can be created on continuous-form computer paper by programs such as *Print Shop*.

Some programs take an original (either scanned into the computer or created in a paint program) and allow the user to enlarge it to huge dimensions. The image is printed in segments on four to 16 (or more) standard 8 1/2-by-11-inch sheets of paper that are tiled, or assembled, into the finished product. The example in Figure 6–12 shows an image printed on 16 sheets of paper. The sheets are assembled and fastened to each other to form a poster approximately 34 inches by 44 inches. Graphics programs such as these enhance the creative ability of students and teachers and facilitate visual communication.

Thanksgiving

Figure 6–12
Sample of a tiled
graphic

OTHER GRAPHICS PROGRAMS

As we have said throughout the text, computers and computer software are tools to be used to help you and your students to be more efficient in your work. Software programs that are particularly helpful and engaging are those devoted to simple graphics and desktop publishing. There are many of these programs on the market today. We have already discussed award-winning *Kid Pix,* a versatile program for students in grades K–8 and *Kid Works Deluxe,* which can be found on the accompanying CD-ROM and is for PreK through fourth grade students. Both allow students to express themselves by writing stories using pre-created and user-created backgrounds and pictures, and *Kid Works Deluxe* adds sounds as well. The handy *Month by Month* software package that goes along with *Kid Works Deluxe,* and also found on the accompanying CD-ROM, adds utility by giving the teacher pre-designed cross-curricular theme-based projects to use with his or her students. Another program in the same vein is *Paint, Write & Play*™ (Figure 6–13) designed for students in grades K–2.

Graphics Utilities

There are many programs that fit into the graphics utility category from *The Print Shop* and *Publish It!* to *Quark XPress*™ and *PageMaker.* The most common program in this group found in schools is one of the versions of *The Print Shop* (The Print Shop, The Print Shop Deluxe™, The Print Shop Premier®, The Print Shop 10, etc.). Figure 6–14 illustrates options available to students in grades 3 through 12 (and of course teachers) as they use Print Shop to create banners, calendars, certificates,

Figure 6–13
The art studio in the program Paint, Write & Play
(Reprinted with permission from Riverdeep, Inc.)

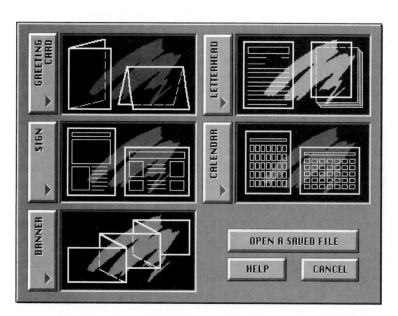

Figure 6–14
A Print Shop® deluxe menu
(Reprinted with permission from Riverdeep, Inc.)

bookmarks, newsletters, student activity sheets, and much more. Users can also design their own Websites with this program. Each project is made by following a series of assistant-like steps.

The Print Shop Deluxe contains more than 1,500 graphics and photos on two CD-ROMs, 30 scalable typefaces, 2,000 quotes and verses, a spell checker, and a thesaurus. School versions include a comprehensive teacher's guide containing lesson plans and projects for students in grades 1 through 12. There is a special Print Shop Website containing more than 25,000 additional images, a design center, a chat group, and more.

As an example, let's go through the steps for making a banner using The Print Shop Deluxe. When we click on the Banner button on the main menu, a box (Figure 6–15 left) appears asking us to choose the banner orientation. When we click on the button for the orientation we want to use (we choose horizontal), a box appears (Figure 6–15 right) for us to choose the background graphic. We choose School Jumble. We can view each option on the banner displayed at the top of this box.

We click OK and another box appears for us to select how the words will be placed on the banner (Figure 6–16 left). We choose School Jumble 5, click OK, and the banner appears on our computer screen (Figure 6–16 right) along with a tool menu to customize our creation. A double-click on the gray area in the center allows us to add words to our banner.

A Banner Text box appears (Figure 6–17 left) where we type in our text and choose the font attributes. A final click on the OK button brings us back to the screen revealing our completed banner (Figure 6–17 right). We can now print our banner or save it to a disk. We can use the Tools menu to change the banner, and simply double-clicking on the banner text will send us back to the Banner Text box for revisions. This is a very colorful banner that will add interest and color to the classroom. Note that this banner requires nine sheets of paper to print out completely.

We have seen how easy it is to make a banner with one of these programs. It is just as easy to make any of the other projects. Previously written text and graphics

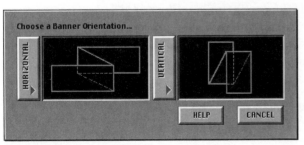
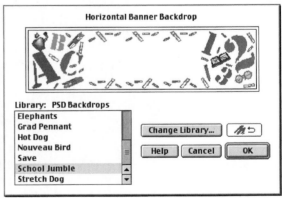

Figure 6–15
The Print Shop banner orientation menu (left) and backdrop menu (right)
(Reprinted with permission of Riverdeep, Inc.)

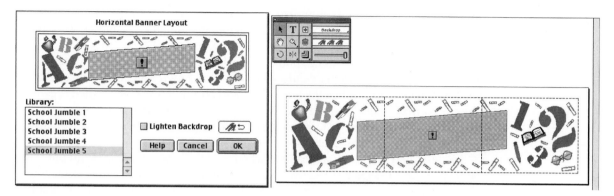

Figure 6–16
The Print Shop layout menu (left) and computer screen (right)
(Reprinted with permission from Riverdeep, Inc.)

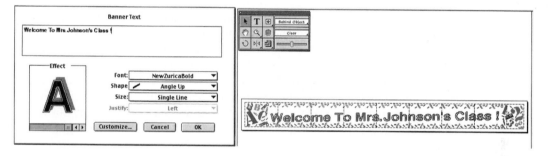

Figure 6–17
The Print Shop banner text box (left) and banner screen display (right)
(Reprinted with permission from Riverdeep, Inc.)

(from clip art to digital photographs) can be imported into many of the projects. Productivity tools, such as *The Print Shop,* really do make time-consuming and difficult projects very easy. These tools save time and energy and increase teacher and student efficiency. Technology should be transparent. It should ease difficult tasks. Productivity tools focus on the end product of learning and not on the technology needed to achieve the end product.

SUMMARY

Some graphics programs facilitate the creation of graphics for bulletin boards and other displays. Some generate drawings; others automatically generate line graphs, bar graphs, and pie charts from numeric data. Although these materials can be created in other ways, the computer makes it easy and less time consuming, thereby stimulating teachers to maximize their creative efforts.

In bit-mapped graphics, the computer-generated image is composed of bits, or screen picture elements called pixels, that are turned on and bits that are off. One of the inherent drawbacks of bit-mapped graphics is that the size of the pixel limits the sharpness, or resolution, of the drawing, regardless of the resolution of the monitor or printer used to display the graphic.

In vector, or object-oriented, graphics, each picture element is a separate object and can be changed independently. The user of a draw program creates objects of different shapes, adjusts line thickness, applies patterns to the objects, then organizes them into new, more complex objects. Text inserted in a drawing remains an editable and movable object. Clip art is available as files in paint or draw formats on disk for use in computer graphics programs.

In designing any communication, whether it be oral, written, or graphic, the sender of the message must know the anticipated audience that is to receive it and design the communication appropriately in order to capture attention and get information across clearly and convincingly.

Signs, posters, maps, and banners can be easily created; so can overhead transparency masters. There are six basic design rules to keep in mind when creating overhead transparencies.

The first step in designing transparency masters in computer graphics requires the user to create the entire drawing and save the document. The second step involves deciding what elements of the total drawing should be presented first. All other elements are deleted from the drawing and the file is saved under a different name. The third and subsequent steps require the user to open the original complete document, delete unwanted elements, and save the results as a new file with a different name.

Presentation software makes it possible to index slides, view thumbnail representations in a slide sorter format, and prescribe their subsequent viewing in a specific sequence.

CHAPTER EXERCISES

To complete the specified exercises on-line, go to the Chapter Exercises Module in Chapter 6 of the Companion Website.

1. Discuss the usefulness of two electronic input devices in the creation of graphics.
2. What two computer output devices are essential in a classroom setting? What other device would be useful? Discuss how this other device would be particularly useful to display graphic images.
3. Using a paint program, create a cover page for a report. How does the graphic you created heighten the reader's interest in the report?
4. Write a brief report on a topic of current national interest and use a graphic captured from a scanner to illustrate your report.
5. Using the draw component of an integrated package or a stand-alone draw program, create a set of informational or directional signs for a school lunchroom.
6. Using the same program, create a set of bookmarks that might be placed in a school library to promote books worth reading.

7. Using a paint program, draw the outline map of your state. Add the major cities and other significant geographical features such as rivers and mountains. Print the results as a base cell and two overlays. Explain why you divided the elements the way you did.

8. Using a computer, design a transparency with two overlays. Use one of the methods mentioned in the text to produce a transparency from this. What did you find was the most difficult part of this assignment?

9. Review the copyright notice on disk or CD-ROM clip art. Is it legal to use in a classroom environment? In what instances would it be illegal to use?

10. Search for Websites containing educational clip art. Find two or three good sites. Share these sites with your class and instructor.

PORTFOLIO DEVELOPMENT EXERCISES

To complete this exercise on-line, go to the Digital Portfolio Module in Chapter 6 of the Companion Website.

One of the NETS•S standards covered in this chapter was "Students use technology tools to enhance learning, increase productivity, and promote creativity" under *Category 3: Technology productivity tools*. Begin to develop your own portfolio of lesson plans that demonstrates your ability to have your students reach the NETS•S standards.

For more information on developing digital portfolios go to Digital Portfolio Module on the Companion Website www.prenhall.com/forcier

1. Design a lesson plan activity for elementary, middle school, or high school students in which they use a graphics program to produce an outdoor scene. Some examples may include farm, lake, desert, or mountain scenes. Each scene should contain several objects (people, buildings, modes of transportation, vegetation, etc.) along with background, sky, and so on. Try to combine several tools found in the graphics programs. The number that you use should depend on the grade level. Younger students may only use simple tools (background, shapes, etc.). Older students will be required to use more sophisticated tools (patterns, drawing and painting tools). This lesson should demonstrate that your students have achieved the standard. Be sure to include a system of evaluation for your students' understanding and competence to ensure that they have met this standard.

2. Adapt the lesson plan activity you developed in exercise 1 for students to evaluate each others' work.

GLOSSARY

bit-mapped graphics Computer-generated images composed of bits, or screen pixels, that are turned on (black or colored) and bits that are turned off (white or clear).

clip art Prepared files of black-and-white or color line drawings and halftone images available on disk in the draw or paint format for use in computer graphics programs that are intended to be incorporated into the user's own original work.

decoding The process of giving meaning to data being communicated.

encoding The process of selecting symbols and other elements to communicate desired information.

gradient fill A pattern that begins with a certain opacity or density of pattern at a determined point and gradually fades to one that is less dense or increases to one that is more dense.

graphics Nonphotographic, two-dimensional representations of an object or event.

object-oriented graphics Computer-generated images determined by formulas that create discrete objects of a certain size and position.

scaling Controlling the size of an image and, in direct proportion, all of its components. Scaling an image reduces or enlarges all of its elements.

vector, or **object-oriented, graphics** See *object-oriented graphics.*

REFERENCES & SUGGESTED READINGS

Benedetto, S. (2000, August). DVD Video: A primer for educators. *Syllabus, 14* (1), 46–49.

Bradley, H. (2000, June). Designer documents: 40 ways to make documents look good. *Australian PC User, 12* (6), 67.

Buchler, B. (1999, April). The museum in our classroom and the mastodon in our backyard. *Learning & Leading with Technology, 26* (7), 32–35.

Burmark, L. (2002). *Visual literacy: Learn to see, see to learn.* Association for Supervision and Curriculum Development.

Daniels, L. (1999, Spring). Introducing technology in the classroom: PowerPoint as a first step. *Journal of Computing in Higher Education, 10* (2), 42–56.

Hodges, B. (1999, September). Electronic books: Presentation software makes writing more fun. *Learning and Leading with Technology, 27* (1), 18–21.

Kelly, R. (1999, September). Getting everybody involved: Cooperative PowerPoint creations benefit inclusion students. *Learning and Leading with Technology, 27* (1), 10–14.

McInerney, P. (2000, May). Worth 1,000 words. *Learning & Leading with Technology, 27* (8), 10–15.

Reissman, R., & Gil, E. (2000, February). Technology takes on fairy tales and folktales. *Learning & Leading with Technology, 27* (5), 18–21.

Setters, P. (1999–2000, December/January). Communicate with pictures: Using still and video photography in science. *Learning & Leading with Technology, 27* (4), 36–39.

Utay, C., & Utay, J. (1999, April). Blast off!: A technology-supported, project-based learning model for success. *Learning & Leading with Technology, 26* (7), 18–21.

CHAPTER 7

Learning with Word Processor Tools

1. What is a word processor?

2. What are some common features of word processors?

3. What are some editing functions found in word processors?

4. Why is lettering important and what are some guidelines for its effective use?

5. How might the word processor be a productivity tool for you as a teacher or an administrator?

6. How is the word processor a productivity tool for the student at different grade levels?

 A list of the ISTE/NCATE standards addressed in this chapter is available in the Standards Module on the Companion Website www.prenhall.com/forcier

Chapter 7 deals with word processing as well as word processing applications for teaching and learning. NETS•S *Category 1: Basic operations and concepts* is covered throughout the chapter especially in the section dealing with input and output devices. Basic word processing operations, as well as some very sophisticated ones, are covered in this chapter. Word processing is one of the first tools that students discover to help them meet the standards listed under NETS•S *Category 3: Technology productivity tools.* Information, techniques, and concepts found in this chapter will help students more fully use word processing as they publish and communicate with individuals and meet one standard listed under NETS•S *Category 4: Technology communications tools.* Word processing applications are undoubtedly one of the most important groups of software applications that you and your students will use throughout your and their lives. It is imperative that you understand the uses and capabilities of this software and are able to pass along this knowledge to your students. As you read the chapter, take some extra time to review and really get to know the word processing software you and your students use. You will be glad you did, because modern word processing applications are no longer simply typing programs but rather have the ability to format, spell and grammar check, and even change case and punctuation on the fly as you type. Word processing applications are some of the most advanced technology communications tools with which you will ever come in contact.

NETS•S Standards Addressed in This Chapter

1. Basic operations and concepts
   - Students demonstrate a sound understanding of the nature and operation of technology systems.
   - Students are proficient in the use of technology.

3. Technology productivity tools
   - Students use technology tools to enhance learning, increase productivity, and promote creativity.
   - Students use productivity tools to collaborate in constructing technology-enhanced models, prepare publications, and produce other creative works.

4. Technology communications tools
   - Students use a variety of media and formats to communicate information and ideas effectively to multiple audiences.

Remember our metaphor that a tool is a medium for completing some work more efficiently and extending the user's ability. We either create a tool or select one from a variety of existing tools and apply it to the task at hand to solve a problem (for example, we use a screwdriver to fasten something, a sewing machine to assemble clothing, an automobile to transport us swiftly and comfortably, and a word processor to record our thoughts in a quick, flexible manner). Accepting this definition of a tool allows us to see its intervention between the user and the information to be created, received, stored, manipulated, or disseminated. The student who locates and downloads information from the Internet, uses a database to search for additional information, then uses a word processor to write a report and a graphics program to draw a map for inclusion in the report is using the computer as a tool to enhance efficiency and effectiveness in response to the problem at hand.

It's time, once again, to check our own perceptions and to ask ourselves the question "What is technology?" Technicians carry screwdrivers around in their pockets and tinker with hardware, such as a computer. Technologists, however, understand how to use that hardware (the computer in this case) and related software as problem-solving tools. The tools or equipment, the computer, the VCR, the camcorder, the ubiquitous overhead projector, all are the "things" of technology. To be most successful as a teacher, these "things" of technology have to become almost transparent. We don't want to call attention to them but rather, as technologists, focus our efforts on the problems we are trying to solve, the objective we are attempting to reach.

The factory model compared productivity with efficiency, defined it as producing a tangible product, and was often linked to the notion of accomplishing menial, repetitive tasks. A more productive worker built more widgets than a less productive one. All too often, the term *productivity tool* has been used with the limited factory model vision. The constructivist perspective demands a broader understanding. In schools, the term *productivity tool* has been easily understood and readily applied to word processors, graphics, spreadsheets, and databases. A deeper understanding would apply it to learning with computers and would also compare productivity with effectiveness. Rather than limiting our view to developing a product often associated with the performance of clerical or manual tasks, we have begun to see productivity as using tools (such as computers) to maximize or extend our innate capabilities in order to surmount challenges and solve problems. Productive learners might learn more but they also learn better. Productive writers and artists are not only prolific but, using our definition, have a greater impact on their readers, viewers, and listeners.

Is the computer a productivity tool for the secretary? Absolutely! It enhances the performance of repetitive clerical tasks. But it is also a productivity tool for the administrator to make projections, find information, and communicate effectively. It is a productivity tool for the teacher who selects appropriate hardware or software and adapts it to the instructional, management, or research task at hand. A computer is a productivity tool whenever it is used to assist individuals in solving problems. Students are increasing their productivity by developing sophisticated skills in the creation, access, manipulation, and transmission of information in order to respond to an assignment or solve a problem. We are witnessing the evolution of some time-tested teaching and learning strategies and philosophies as they change to account for new tools and innovations. The computer is a tool that can give students a wider variety of educational experiences than has ever before been offered.

One of the first reasons you probably used a computer as a tool was to write reports and term papers. You have no doubt found the word processor to be a trusted friend. You may have even marveled at the development of word processors over time, especially over the past few years. This friend doesn't simply place your words on paper anymore; it also automatically corrects spelling and grammar and may even place everything in the format that you preset. You could almost say that, to some extent, it is proofing and retyping your paper for you. Just as it has undoubtedly helped you as a student, you will find that the word processor is indispensable to you as a classroom teacher.

Classroom teachers are not the only educators who can make use of word processors. Just about everyone in the school uses them. Special educators can use word processors to maintain individual student correspondence files that are continually updated. They can build a student's IEP and later recall the IEP to update it easily. Library media specialists can also use word processors to maintain bibliographies of the available print and nonprint materials. Principals and administrative office staff can use word processors in many of their tasks, because they maintain the ongoing records and reports for the school. Some documents must be updated every year, yet only parts of each form are actually changed. A document kept on the computer can be amended at any time and reprinted when needed without having to reconstruct it in its entirety.

Word processing has also become a powerful tool in the hands of students. We have seen that the use of word processing improves students' attitudes toward writing by making them want to write more and making them feel better about their writing using a larger vocabulary, because they find it easy to correct spelling.

WORD PROCESSORS

The term **word processor** is used to denote a whole category of software whose primary purpose is to facilitate written communication. As indicated in Figure 7–1, word processing is a systematic organization of procedures and equipment to display information efficiently in a written form and to preserve it electronically. Though it is possible to purchase stand-alone hardware "appliances" called word processors that only do word processing, this section focuses on computer software available to assist in the creation of written material.

Word processing programs usually consist of two basic, interacting parts—a text editor to manipulate text and a print formatter to deliver the text file to the printer. Depending on the individual software, several additional parts such as a spell checker, a dictionary, a thesaurus, and a grammar checker are also present. The **text editor** is the most visible part of the program and is the one that allows the user to manipulate text on a screen display. It is used during the text entry phase as you add, change, and delete text, as well as locate words and phrases and embed the format commands needed to control the print formatter. From the text editor, you can insert the commands to determine the print font, margins, line spacing, and so on. The editor also contains the means to save, merge, copy, and insert text from one file to another. All modern word processors display the text on the screen the exact way that it will appear on the printed page. This display is often referred to as **WYSIWYG (what you see is what you get**—pronounced "wizzy wig"). The **print formatter** works behind the scenes to deliver the text file to the printer and ensure that it is printed correctly on paper.

There are several good word processors from which to choose. Selecting the one that is best for you depends on your computer system and on your individual needs. The two most popular word processing programs are Microsoft Word for Windows and Macintosh (usually found as part of the Microsoft Office suite) and AppleWorks for the Macintosh. Either program is a good choice, because they have most of the same features. There are also several word processing programs for younger students such as Read, Write & Type for grades 1 and 2 and Student Writing Center for grades 4 through 12. Students with special needs may benefit from Write:OutLoud, a talking word processor and speller, and Co:Writer, a word prediction program that decreases the number of keystrokes needed to complete each word.

 For a copy of a word processor evaluation form, go to the Supplemental Information Module in Chapter 7 on the Companion Website www.prenhall.com/forcier

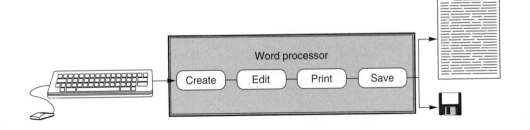

Figure 7–1
Word processing

WORD PROCESSOR FEATURES

Following is a brief list of the features found in word processing programs.

column formatting In addition to specifying top, bottom, and side margins, many word processors allow the user to format a page in more than one column.

dictionary This feature provides word definition and syllabication, as well as allowing the user to confirm spelling.

footer Similar to a header, a footer is a brief message that may include text or a date, time, or page display that is automatically added to the bottom of each page and can usually be suppressed on a title page.

footnotes Some programs allow the user to mark words in the text to be referenced automatically as footnotes at the bottom of the page or as endnotes at the end of the document.

formatting Document layout and margins can be applied. Bullets and numbering can be automatically applied to lists; drop caps can begin paragraphs; customized indents and spacing as well as special control over page breaks can be applied to a paragraph; and borders and shading can be applied to sections of text.

glossary Often-used words and phrases such as a return address or the closing of a letter can be created and stored in a glossary to be called up at any time by a simple keyboard command.

grammar checking A grammar checker attempts to identify wordiness, awkward constructions, singular/plural agreement, and the use of passive voice, among other things. Some word processors allow the user to customize the grammar checker by selecting writing styles such as casual, formal, or technical.

header A header is a brief message that may include text or a date, time, or page display that is automatically added to the top of each page and can usually be suppressed on a title page.

hyphenation Because **word wrap** can leave lines of varying lengths, thereby creating a ragged right margin, some word processors allow the user to turn on a hyphenation feature that will generate a hyphen at the most appropriate syllable break in a word at the end of a line.

index The creation of an index can be greatly facilitated by a feature that allows a user to mark words that are then automatically copied, along with a page reference, to an index at the end of the document.

insert Page breaks, page numbers, date and time stamps, auto-text (e.g., mailing instructions, salutations, closings, signature), special symbols and characters (C, ', ©, etc.), pictures, movies, and hyperlinks can be inserted into your document.

mail merge An almost indispensable feature—when sending form letters that appear to be personalized with appropriate names, addresses, and even specific content—is the ability to merge data from one file to another at the proper place in the document.

orphan/widow control **Orphans** are single lines of text that occur at the bottoms of pages. **Widows** are single lines of text that occur at the tops of pages. Some word processors will not allow these to occur but, instead, will force the appropriate page break so that at least two lines of text appear together.

outlining Some of the more powerful word processors have integrated outliners built into them, allowing the user to create an outline of the document and to expand or collapse various levels.

pagination Once a user sets the page length of the document by prescribing top and bottom margins on a specified size of paper, this feature allows a word processor to generate page breaks, indicate them on the screen automatically, number pages, and renumber them when editing is performed.

preview document All worthwhile word processors allow the user to see the document on the screen as it will look when printed and closely approach a WYSIWYG (what you see is what you get) state.

save as Word processors save the documents created in their native format (e.g., Microsoft Word version "x" saves a document as a Word version "x" file). Most word processors can also save documents in several other file formats. Saving them as a file in a very basic *Text* format allows the documents to be readily transported between word processors. If you want your document to look a bit better, you might want to save it in *Rich Text Format* (*RTF*), which is a *Text* format that also keeps a number of the formatting attributes of the original file. Many word processors also allow users to save files as *HTML* documents for the web. Before leaving this topic, we must mention another way to save documents. A program called Adobe Acrobat® saves a document in a *PDF* format (*Portable Document Format*) so it looks like an exact copy of the original document (text, graphics, and all). You must purchase Adobe Acrobat if you want to save documents in this format but Adobe Acrobat Reader®, the program needed to read PDF documents, is free. You should download a copy to your computer if you don't already have it. It is probably possible for you to go to the Website for your college or university and download applications and other PDF documents needed at your school. A word to the wise: Get Acrobat Reader and learn how to use it. When you are looking for a job, the employer might just tell you to go to their site and download the application.

sort Lists may be sorted alphabetically in ascending or descending order.

spell checking Unlike a dictionary, a spell checker does not display definitions but, rather, compares all words found in the document against its master list. Any word not matching is called to the user's attention and, if possible, a replacement word is suggested. Most allow the user to add frequently used unusual words (proper nouns, acronyms, etc.) to a custom list. We have added the words Forcier and Descy to ours.

style sheet A style is a set of format characteristics (left aligned, 10 point, Times, .5 inch first line indent, for example) that can be applied to text. A style sheet is a collection of styles used in a document. Choosing a style for text about to be entered is a timesaving device.

table of contents A feature that facilitates the creation of a table by allowing a user to mark words that are then automatically copied to a table of contents at the beginning of the document.

thesaurus This feature soon becomes a writer's favorite tool. A selected word is compared with a list in the thesaurus and a number of synonyms are suggested to avoid undue repetitions or to adjust a subtle nuance in the writing.

Once you have determined your word processing needs in general, consider the major features that will affect your usage and will minimize the problems you may encounter. If you intend to use a word processor to create a document at home and then wish to print it at school, you will need word processing programs that are able to save and open the same file in a manner that preserves the document's format.

WORD PROCESSOR FUNCTIONS

Word processors are commonly available either as individual programs or as integrated software suites, such as Microsoft Office and AppleWorks, which may also contain a spreadsheet, a file manager, and graphics and telecommunications components.

Editing Functions. A representative sample of editing functions is presented in Figure 7–2. The user can navigate through the document, adding, deleting, finding, replacing, inserting, and moving information at will.

Operating in the Macintosh or Windows environments, many editing features are invoked through pull-down menus and most have keyboard shortcuts or double-key presses so that the program can distinguish a command from a text entry. A double-key press simply means that the user holds down a designated key such as the Command or Alt key and presses a second key. Most word processing programs use similar keyboard shortcuts. Holding down the command key and pressing the "x" key cuts highlighted text, command key and "c" key copies highlighted text into the computer's memory, and command key and "v" key pastes the saved text in both Microsoft Word (Figure 7–3) and AppleWorks. Learn to use key commands. They will speed up your word processing.

In addition to the editing commands, there is a set of commands to determine the format of the printed output. These print commands, of course, are not printed out as text; they are the embedded control commands giving instructions to the printer being used. They allow the user to describe paper size; margins; character typeface, size, and style; right, left, center, or full line justification; and more.

Another way to speed up your word processing is to use the toolbars that come with each word processing program. Most programs automatically display one or two of these. You can display or hide any that you want. The Microsoft Word program that we used has 19 different toolbars we could display. We used two, one called Formatting toolbar and one called Word for Macintosh toolbar (Figure 7–4). All 19 can be turned on and off in the Toolbars option menu found in the View menu.

Create a new document	• Select New in the File menu.
Open an existing document	• Select Open in the File menu and choose the document in the dialog window.
Insert text	• Click the mouse where you want to add text and begin typing. Typing spreads apart the existing text to accommodate the new entry. The new material may be as little as a single letter or many paragraphs long.
Word wrap	• After setting the line length for your document, a word that is too long to fit at the end of a line is automatically moved to the following line. Hyphenation can be turned on or off.
Delete text	• With the mouse, highlight the text to be deleted and press the delete key.
Replace text	• With the mouse, highlight the text to be replaced and begin typing. Placing the cursor immediately following a text character and pressing the delete or backspace key erases the character to its immediate left, one character at a time. The remaining text is then automatically rearranged properly, with word wrap and page breaks taken into account.
Move text	• 1. With the mouse, highlight the text to be moved. 2. Select Cut from the Edit menu to remove the text. (If you wish to duplicate the text, select Copy instead.) 3. The item is now stored in temporary memory. With the mouse, move the cursor to the point where you want the text to appear and select Paste from the Edit menu.
Find/Replace text	• Select Find from the Edit menu. In the dialog box, type the word or phrase you wish to find and click on Find Next. The cursor will move through the document until it finds your request. • Select Replace from the Edit menu. In the dialog box, type the word or phrase you wish to replace. Type the replacement in the appropriate area and click on Find Next. The cursor will move through the document until it finds your request. You can either replace the item or skip over it by clicking Find Next again.
Undo an edit	• Select Undo from the Edit menu. This command will undo the very last or several of the last keystrokes that you typed. This can be a lifesaver if you hit the wrong keys and something strange happens to the text.
Save your document	• Select Save from the File menu. The first time only that you save a new document you will be asked to name it. It's a good idea to save a document every few minutes. • If you wish to save a different copy of your document, select Save As and give your document a different name.

Figure 7–2

Some word processor editing functions

Figure 7–3
Some keyboard shortcuts in Word® (Reprinted with permission from Microsoft, Inc.)

Figure 7–4
In top-to-bottom order: the menubar, formatting toolbar, and Word for Macintosh toolbar in Microsoft Word (Reprinted with permission from Microsoft, Inc.)

WORD PROCESSOR TEMPLATES

Many word processing programs now contain templates (sometimes called Stationery, Assistants, or Wizards) that take much of the work out of setting up these tasks. Microsoft Office (which includes Word) presents a Project Gallery, as shown in Figure 7-5, meant to simplify the creation of various documents.

Figure 7–6 shows the Letter Wizard available to users of Microsoft Word. Notice the tabs at the top. A number of choices can be made in each tab and a preview of the document is shown. Because Microsoft Word is marketed toward the business environment, many of the Wizards are designed for that audience. It is possible to download some education Wizards and templates from the Microsoft Website.

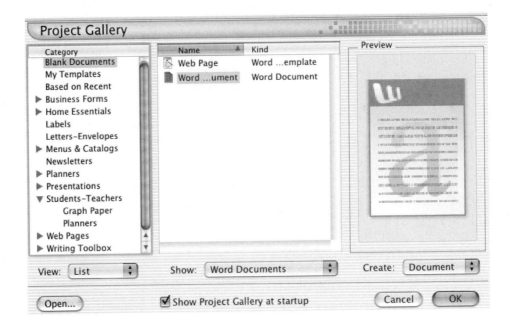

Figure 7–5
Microsoft Word
Project Gallery

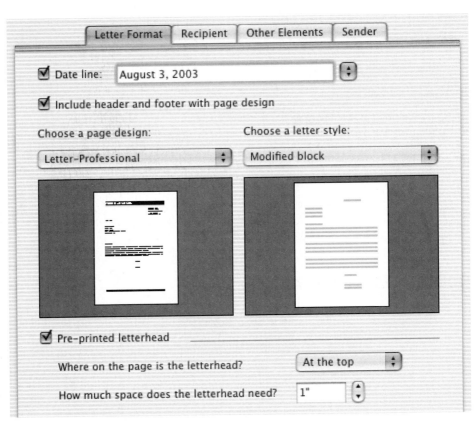

Figure 7–6
Microsoft Word Letter
Wizard

LETTERING

Word processing has added a new graphic dimension to communicating in print. It's not only what you say and how you say it but also how it looks on the page. Word processing has placed at our disposal the ability to affect the appearance of the printed word easily yet markedly. Reflecting on the adage "a picture is worth a thousand words," word processing adds somewhat of a "picture" quality to the text medium and requires us to attend to some terms and some guidelines concerning the appearance of text.

Font

The collection of characteristics applied to a **typeface** in a particular size and style is called a **font.** Sample fonts are illustrated in Figure 7–7. Through common usage the term *font* has unfortunately become synonymous with typeface.

Size

The height of a letter, expressed in points (1 point equals 1/72 of an inch), is the **size.** The left side of Figure 7–8 illustrates a progression from 9-point to 24-point type. Different typefaces vary in letter width and thickness of line, sometimes giving the appearance of a variation in size.

Figure 7–7
Sample fonts
(combination of
typeface, size, and
style)

Bookman in 14-point bold
Geneva in 12-point italic
Palatino in 18-point plain text

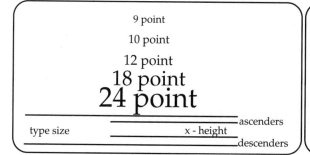

Figure 7–8
Sample point sizes on the left and sample styles on the right

Style

Style refers to the appearance of a particular typeface as visual modifications are applied, as illustrated in the right side of Figure 7–8.

Typeface

A **typeface** is the design of the letter and the name given to the design. New designs are constantly emerging and are usually copyrighted by the creator. Typefaces affect the feeling imparted by the message, as well as its content. Some have harsh, angular lines, whereas others have soft curves. Some are narrow and condensed; others are round or broad. Some use thick lines and convey a heavy or dark impression to a text, whereas others use thin lines, resulting in a light text. Others are designed for special purposes, such as holidays, flyers, or greeting cards. Serif typefaces such as those illustrated in Figure 7–9 have fine lines that finish the major strokes of the letters. These serve as decorative yet functional connectors that appear to join adjacent letters, thereby helping the reader to perceive groups of letters as words. Therefore, serif typefaces enhance the speed and ease with which text can be read. This textbook is printed in a serif typeface.

Notice that even in plain text some typefaces are darker than others. Also notice that some typefaces occupy more line length in the same point size because of the rounder shape of their letters. The rounder shape of the lowercase letters in Bookman in Figure 7–9 makes this most apparent.

Times	An analysis of factors that influence
Palatino	An analysis of factors that influe
Bookman	An analysis of factors that inf

Figure 7–9
A sample of serif typefaces

Avant Garde	An analysis of factors that influen
Geneva	An analysis of factors that influenc
Chicago	An analysis of factors that influe

Figure 7–10
Samples of sans serif typefaces shown in 18-point plain text

Brush Script:	*An analysis of factors that influence typeface selection*
UMBRA:	AN ANALYSIS OF FACTORS THAT INFLUENCE TYPEFACE SELECTION
Snowcap:	An analysis of factors that influence typeface selection

Figure 7–11
Samples of ornate typefaces shown in 18-point plain text

Palatino (proportional)
An analysis of factors that influence typeface selection must incl
Courier (monospaced)
An analysis of factors that influence typeface

Figure 7–12
Proportional and monospaced typefaces

Sans serif typefaces, such as those illustrated in Figure 7–10, usually should not be used in body text. Their clean lines and lack of connectors make them somewhat difficult and tiring to read in body text. Sans serif typefaces should be used primarily in a bold style and large size as headlines and titles. Also notice that different typefaces have thicker or bolder lines, thereby making a stronger statement.

Ornate typefaces, such as those illustrated in Figure 7–11, are certainly attention getting and effective if used sparingly. They are as much graphic as they are text. The message embodied in the ornate design should support the written words.

Every text example shown thus far has been a **proportional-spaced** typeface. That is to say, its design attempts to achieve **optical spacing** by allowing the surface area of the space between each letter to be roughly the same. The distance will, therefore, vary between each letter, depending on its shape. **Monospaced** typefaces, such as Courier or Monaco, are sometimes referred to as having **mechanical spacing.** Their design allows each letter to be equally distant from the next, regardless of the letter shape. As you examine Figure 7–12, which illustrates the difference between the two types of spacing, pay particular attention to the letters i and l and their adjacent letters.

Lettering Guidelines

- Select a suitable typeface to enhance readability and the expression of your words.
- Use sans serif typefaces in a large size for headlines or titles. Used sparingly, they have a simplicity that commands attention. Large amounts in body text are difficult to read.
- Use serif typefaces for body text. The decorations on the letters help to guide the reader's eye movement from one letter to the next, thereby helping the reader to perceive words rather than letters.
- Use ornate text sparingly for special visual effects.
- Avoid mixing typefaces within the same document except for a distinct purpose. Rarely should you mix more than two typefaces in the same document.
- Select a letter size appropriate to the message and its intended impact. Consider that not all output is intended for 8 1/2-by-11-inch paper. Consider the optimum viewing distance and the medium (e.g., a minimum of 18-point size should be used for overhead transparencies and 24-point or larger for presentation slide shows).
- Allow ample leading (space) between lines of text so that ascenders and descenders do not touch.
- Use style (plain, bold, italic, outline, shadow, underline) for emphasis.
- Allow plenty of white space around a block of text. A block of text takes up space, so be sure to consider it in your overall design.

These lettering guidelines may also be found at the Companion Website http://www.prenhall.com/forcier

WORD PROCESSOR APPLICATIONS

As stated in the introduction to this chapter, teachers want help in alleviating the paperwork demands made on them. They want help in accomplishing activities that do not involve students directly and are quite often done outside of actual class time. If the time required to perform these tasks could be decreased, teachers would have more time to devote to working with students.

Administrative Applications

Teachers create some written classroom material that changes very little from one year to the next. An exercise sheet or another resource material such as a game or puzzle used once in a unit plan may be used the following year with only slight modification. Material, once designed, can be easily modified to serve a similar purpose in another unit of study. By using a word processor, the teacher could develop a few standard templates and then make appropriate changes as needed.

In addition to the preparation of instructional materials, consider the writing that is expected of a teacher. Ask yourself how a teacher might save time and effort and still accomplish the writing tasks effectively. One example of these writing tasks

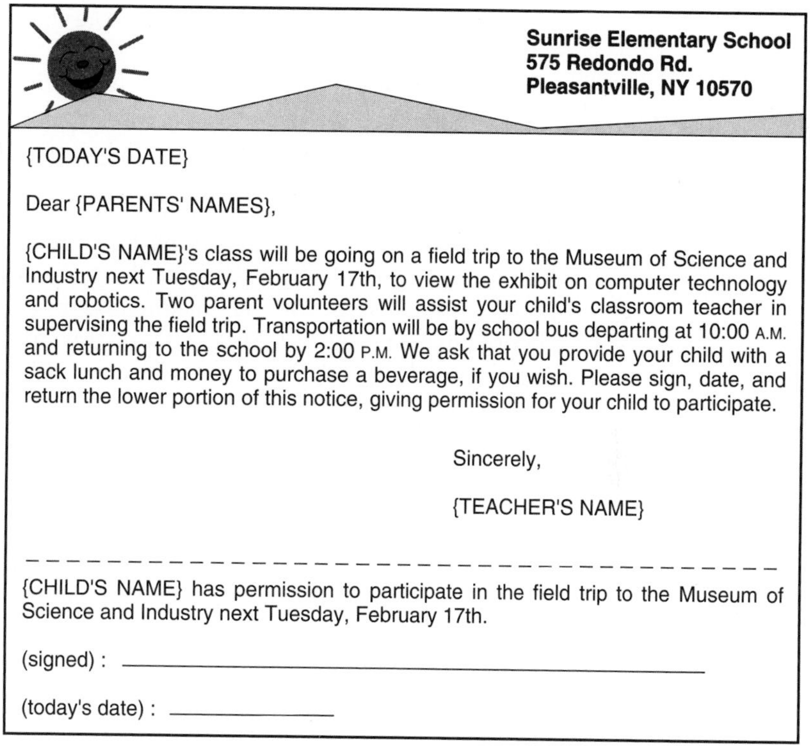

Sunrise Elementary School
575 Redondo Rd.
Pleasantville, NY 10570

{TODAY'S DATE}

Dear {PARENTS' NAMES},

{CHILD'S NAME}'s class will be going on a field trip to the Museum of Science and Industry next Tuesday, February 17th, to view the exhibit on computer technology and robotics. Two parent volunteers will assist your child's classroom teacher in supervising the field trip. Transportation will be by school bus departing at 10:00 A.M. and returning to the school by 2:00 P.M. We ask that you provide your child with a sack lunch and money to purchase a beverage, if you wish. Please sign, date, and return the lower portion of this notice, giving permission for your child to participate.

Sincerely,

{TEACHER'S NAME}

– –

{CHILD'S NAME} has permission to participate in the field trip to the Museum of Science and Industry next Tuesday, February 17th.

(signed) : _____

(today's date) : _____

Figure 7–13
Sample personalized
form letter

might be asking parents to allow their child to participate in a school-sponsored field trip. The task might be accomplished by sending home an impersonal request form and asking the parents to fill in the name of their child and sign the form. Using a word processor and merging information from a data file, this process can be personalized, as shown in Figure 7–13. Labels in curly brackets, { }, indicate an item to be inserted from the data file. In addition to appearing as a personal communication to the parents, the form letter could be used as a **template** for any other field trip permission form, with a minimum of retyping. **Boilerplate** is a term that comes from the legal profession and signifies material that can be used repeatedly without modification. The term **stationery** is sometimes used as a replacement for template.

Teaching Applications

We often think of a word processor as a tool that enhances an individual's personal productivity, and indeed it is. Collaborative writing, however, is a technique that allows more than one student to engage in a writing activity together. The technique often calls for students to agree on an outline and then to divide the writing tasks among themselves. The written documents are then merged together, and the students edit each other's work and rewrite the composition. If the writing is done in a computer lab, students can brainstorm a story idea and then begin drafting the story on their own computers. After 15 to 20 minutes, students can exchange places and continue writing where the previous student ended. New software allows students sitting at computers on a network to write and to edit each other's documents in real time.

For many years teachers have promoted the teaching of writing as a process of drafting, revising, editing, and publishing. Teachers need to guide students' composition and provide necessary feedback for revision. The word processor supports writing instruction by making the writing process less tedious, thereby encouraging a far more positive attitude toward writing and motivating students to experiment with language. A study (Raef, 1996) of elementary school students identified as having weak writing skills indicated that the students' motivation to write increased with the use of word processing. Figures 7–17 through 7–26 depict lesson activities to illustrate how a word processor might be used as a tool by students to explore creative writing—to write reports, compositions, and poetry. These examples can be modified to serve in a variety of subject areas and grade levels. Word processing objectives, writing objectives, and subject matter objectives often dovetail. If students are to capitalize on the power of the word processor as a tool and use it with confidence, they must develop an understanding of its application and a reasonably high level of skill in its use. Using this tool, they will enhance their written communication as they acquire and construct knowledge in various content areas.

Word Processing Lessons

Commercially published "Big Books" are in a large format that lend themselves to being read and displayed in front of a group of students. They usually contain one story; some have repetition on each page, as illustrated in Figure 7–14.

The example in Figure 7–15 shows a continuous story, with each child responsible for writing and illustrating one page. Books created by children can range over a wide variety of topics and can integrate a number of subject matter disciplines.

Consider the following ideas:

- Write about endangered animals: an illustration and facts about the animals that would require some research.
- Use alliteration with names from your hometown or state to foster recognition of place names, cities, towns, rivers, and so on: "Suzy Smith from Seaside sings in the shower" or "Terrific Terry from Troutdale travels along the Trask River."
- Report on a classroom activity: "What I learned about raising quail chicks in school."
- Read a story such as "Alexander and the Magic Pebble" and respond to it: "If I had a magic pebble, I would . . ."
- Engage in wonderful word problems. Write and illustrate math word problems. Place answers to the student-written problems on the last page.

Billie, Billie, what do you see?
I see a white bunny rabbit looking at me.

Suggested Lesson: Children use "Big Books" in primary grades to acquire simple language skills. Following the pattern of a "Big Book," children could dictate one page of a story to the teacher or to a parent volunteer who would enter it into a word processor file leaving space for an illustration. In this particular example, children were asked to name an animal and a color along with their name in a rhyme.

Children would be encouraged to draw a picture illustrating their words. Drawn on a simple graphics paint program, the image could then be inserted into the word processor file. If it were drawn by hand on paper, the drawing could be scanned into an electronic form and then this image inserted into the word processor file.

Stories could be bound and placed in the school library media center to be read by others.

Figure 7–14
"Big Book" sample page

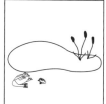
Frog and toad swam in the pond.

Later they rode bikes.

"Would you like to come to my house for dinner?" said frog.

"Sure,. . .," etc.

Figure 7–15
"Big Book" authored by students

The lessons illustrated in Figures 7–16 through 7–23 are summarized in the following table.

Lesson	Topic
Figure 7–16	Developing the main idea in a paragraph and writing a topic sentence.
Figure 7–17	Composition, creative expression, and use of graphics to illustrate writing.
Figure 7–18	Poetry rhyme and meter.
Figure 7–19	Collaborative creative expression and writing style.
Figure 7–20	Developing a gender-neutral style.
Figure 7–21	Use of modifiers to affect meaning.
Figure 7–22	A whole-class exercise on expressive style.
Figure 7–23	Developing a chronological order.

He had told all hands that they ought to see to their equipment; once they got on the trail, opportunities for repair work might be scarce. The Spettle brothers, for example, had no equipment at all, unless you called one pistol with a broken hammer equipment. Newt had scarcely more; his saddle was an old one and he had no slicker and only one blanket for a bedroll. The Irishmen had nothing except what they had been loaned.

"Lonesome Dove"
Larry McMurtry

Suggested Lesson: Using a word processor, the teacher types a selection from a popular novel, eliminating the first topic sentence and running two or more paragraphs together, then saves it as a word processing file.

Class discussion reviews topic sentences and getting the main idea of a paragraph. Students are assigned to load the teacher's file, create a topic sentence, and separate the paragraphs. They then print out their modified file.

Discussion follows in which the teacher indicates the correct paragraph breaks and students listen to each other's topic sentences discussing their merits. The teacher then reads the original selection from the book.

Figure 7–16
Topic sentence

Mrs. Prosser's Classroom News
May 21, 2001

School Built on Site of Indian Village

Mr. Gerald Girod showed his collection of arrowheads to Mrs. Prosser's fifth-grade class. He grew up here in Chicopee Falls and started his collection when he was a young boy. He found his first arrowheads in what is now the school playground years before the school was built. He found some small arrowheads that he thinks were used to hunt birds.

Mr. Girod also showed some broken pieces of pottery that he found down on the river bank. The pottery shards, the arrowheads, and pictures of what the playground area looked like before the school was built will be placed in the display case in the school library.

Suggested Lesson: The teacher serves as guide and advisor as students publish a class newspaper. They discuss events of the past week and decide which to report. They focus attention on the importance of the headline and take turns writing the stories. They edit each other's stories for content, spelling, grammar, and creative expression.

An extension of this activity could have the teacher encourage students to interview local business and civic leaders, examine local occupations, or record stories told by old-timers in the community.

Student photographs and drawings could be scanned and inserted in the document. Modest page layout software could eventually replace the word processor and give the publication a more sophisticated look as the students gain skills and experience.

Figure 7–17
Classroom newsletter

'Twixt optimist and pessimist

_____

The optimist sees the doughnut;
    The pessimist sees the hole.

        The pedigree of honey
        Does not concern the bee;
        A clover, anytime, to him

_____

                Dogs in the country have fun.

                _____

                But in the city this species
                Is dragged around on leashes.

Suggested Lesson: Using a word processor, the teacher types selections from several poems eliminating one line from each poem, then saves the document as a word processor file.

   Class discussion reviews rhyme and meter. Students are assigned to load the teacher's file and create the missing line. Each student then prints a copy of the completed poems.

   Discussion follows in which the students listen to each other's poems and discuss their merits. The teacher then reads the original selection.

Figure 7–18
Poem

What would the Oregon country be like, she wondered as she gazed at her child burning with fever. Would this interminable trek ever end? Would they find the answer to their prayers? Would she, Abner, and their children ever see the green valleys and rushing streams about which they had heard?

The parching heat and blowing dust make every mile seem like 10. The slow creaking of the wagon wheels and plodding of the oxen add to the monotony. The scout says there's a river an hour away where we will make camp for tonight. The thought of water and some rest lift my spirits and give me the energy to keep going.

Suggested Lesson: Students agree on a story outline. Using a word processor, they develop some ideas as they write paragraphs into a file. Students merge their separate files into one document.

This example shows two students' files merged together. Each student then takes a copy of the document and rewrites the entire segment in such a way as the paragraphs take on a coherence and unity of expression.

Students print their own file when they are finished and exchange papers to compare writing styles. Students are then given the opportunity to modify their own document.

Figure 7–19
Collaborative
exercise

A student approached Mrs. Alderson after class with a request for help. She said that she was confused between the terms *latitude* and *longitude*. She couldn't remember which was which.

Mrs. Alderson responded with a comparison of the similarity in the words *latitude* and *altitude* pointing out their North–South or "up–down" and height relationship. She concluded by suggesting that latitude be thought of as a ladder that she would climb up and down and pointing out the alliteration, *l*adder and *l*atitude.

Suggested Lesson: The purpose of the lesson is to rewrite sentences eliminating the gender specific pronouns "he" and "she" when they do not refer to an identifiable person in the story.

Using a word processor, the teacher prepares a paragraph using several pronouns and saves the document as a word processor file.

Class discussion reviews pronouns and antecedents. Students are assigned to load the teacher's file and to rewrite the paragraph replacing gender specific pronouns where appropriate. Students print the modified file. Discussion would follow in which the modified paragraphs were examined.

Figure 7–20
Gender-neutral style

It was a * and * night. The moon was * hidden behind a * cloud and a * wind was blowing from the North. It was a night when imaginations could * run * .

 * , Jim and Gwenda heard an * sound coming from just outside their campground. They wondered if their * sister, Margaia, had heard it too. They heard it again. This time it seemed * .

Suggested Lesson: Using a word processor, the teacher prepares a file consisting of a selection with missing modifiers replaced by asterisks. After reading the selection, students replace the asterisks with one or more adjectives or adverbs. Students underline the modifiers that they inserted, rename the file, and save it to a diskette or to a folder assigned to them on a hard disk or file server.

A follow-up activity could have students load each other's files and substitute other modifiers for all underlined words in order to change the mood or meaning of the selection. A discussion should follow on how modifiers can alter the meaning of a story.

As a further creative writing activity, students could be asked to complete their story.

Figure 7–21
Modifiers

I predict for America, not despair but rather great hope. I believe that anything is possible if people want it badly enough.

I see America, not in the setting sun of a black night of despair ahead of us, I see America in the crimson light of a rising sun fresh from the burning, creative hand of God. I see great days ahead, great days possible to men and women of will and vision . . . .

—Carl Sandburg

Suggested Lesson: The teacher finds a quotation that illustrates expressive language. Using a word processor, the teacher paraphrases the quotation in a direct style and, after spacing down the page, enters the quotation. Using a large monitor or an overhead display panel, the teacher shows the first section to the class.

After reading the first section, students rewrite the selection using a more expressive style. They may then read their selection aloud or display it for the class to read. The teacher then displays the original quotation and leads the class in analyzing the style.

A follow-up activity could have students load each other's files and edit each other's work in an attempt to influence the mood of the selection.

Figure 7–22
Whole-class writing exercise

The state of Oregon was founded.

John Jacob Astor established a flourishing fur trade.

Andrew Jackson became president.

Wagons completed the first journey over the Oregon Trail.

The Oregon Territory was created.

The Civil War ended.

The first missionaries arrived in the Willamette Valley.

Lewis and Clark reached what is present-day Astoria, Oregon.

Suggested Lessons: Using a word processor, the teacher prepares a file consisting of a series of historical events in a scrambled chronological order.

Students read the statements on the computer screen. Using the cut-and-paste function of the word processor, students arrange them in the correct chronological order and print the file. Using reference tools in the classroom and in the library, students verify the correctness of their printout.

A follow-up activity might have students assign dates to each event and identify names of important people and places related to the events where appropriate.

A slight variation of this activity might mix local, state, national, and world events in the file prepared by the teacher. Another variation might mix events from social studies, science, and the arts in order to foster cross-curriculum integration.

Figure 7–23
Chronological order

DESKTOP PUBLISHING

The most fully featured extension of the word processing program is the desktop publishing program. The term **desktop publishing** implies the ability to create so-phisticated printed documents. Programs in this category contain the most extensive set of commands and include advanced page layout capabilities. These programs may require an investment of time or training to take full advantage of their many features, as well as continual use to maintain skill level. They contain all of the nec-essary functions for work on full reports, newsletters, brochures, and documents that include **text-wrapped graphics** such as shown in Figure 7–24.

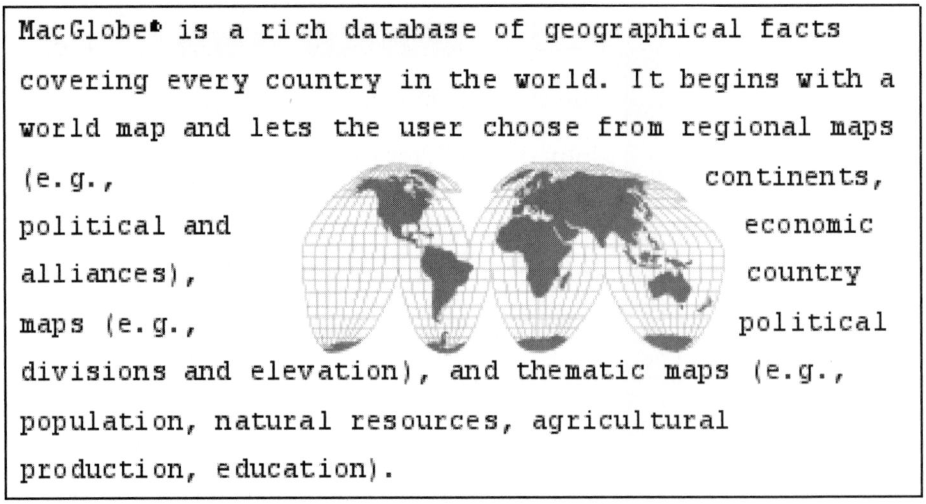

MacGlobe® is a rich database of geographical facts covering every country in the world. It begins with a world map and lets the user choose from regional maps (e.g., continents, political and economic alliances), country maps (e.g., political divisions and elevation), and thematic maps (e.g., population, natural resources, agricultural production, education).

Figure 7–24
Text-wrapped graphic

In addition to the features mentioned for standard word processors, desktop publishing programs include the ability to create a master page layout or design that is repeated on every page, to format variable-width columns, to use drop caps at the beginning of paragraphs, to import and format graphics, and to wrap lines of text around graphics' irregular edges. Many of these features are being introduced into regular word processing programs as well.

Desktop publishing really takes advantage of the power of the printed page. Embodying all of the features of less-powerful word processing programs, it adds to the writer's expressive ability by improving the visual presentation of text and visuals by controlling their juxtaposition. By careful control of the white space on the page, the writer controls the overall appearance of the document and gives added impact to the intended message. A few of the tools used to organize the appearance of text are presented in Figure 7–25. This illustration is presented in what is called a "greeked" fashion. You are not expected to read any text but rather to look at blocks of text as objects.

Headlines grab attention and encourage the viewer to become a reader of the article. To be effective, headlines should be concise and delineated from the body of the text by use of the same or contrasting typeface in a larger size and different style. Boxes can separate parts of a document. They are usually used to isolate specific information, sometimes called sidebars. Horizontal lines or rules can also separate parts of a document. Margins create a white space surrounding the text, which affects a document's feel. Wider margins result in a lighter document. The width of the space between columns, called the gutter, also contributes to the feel of the document. Columns may be of different widths, often with artwork extending across one or more columns. Figure 7–26 is an effort by the authors to compile the most common desktop publishing organization tools into a chart to which you might wish to refer from time to time.

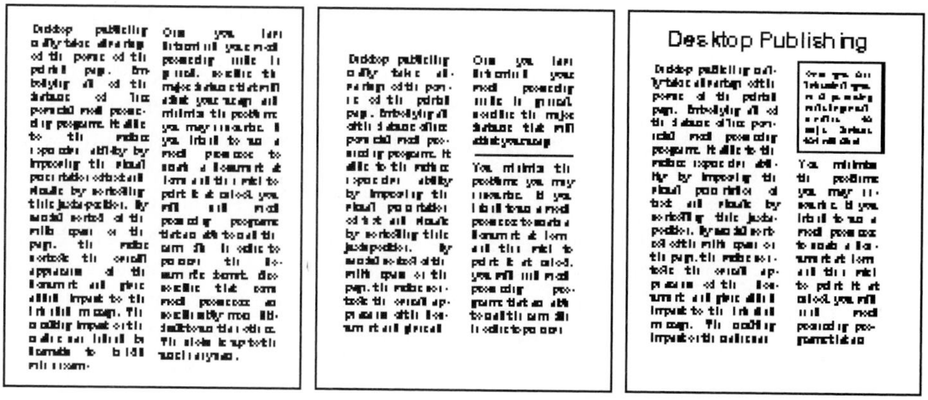

Figure 7–25
Examples of a few desktop publishing tools

DESKTOP PUBLISHING ORGANIZATION TOOLS

Headlines entice people to read an article. They should be designed for impact and should stand out from the text of the article (often by using a contrasting typeface in a larger size). Sans serif bold typefaces are usually used. Avoid long headlines in uppercase type. They are difficult to read.

Captions relate illustrations to the content of the article. They summarize important points. Captions should be treated the same way throughout a publication.

Boxes can highlight parts of a publication. They often contain short, related articles.

Lines are used to separate parts of a publication. Horizontal lines usually separate different topics within the same column. They are often used to draw attention to short sentences ("pull-quotes") that summarize the key points of an article.

Margins determine the relationship of text and graphics. There should always be ample "breathing room" between the content and the page edge. Wide margins promote a "lighter or brighter feel" to the publication.

Columns organize the horizontal placement of content. Text is usually arranged in one or more columns on a page. The space between columns is called the gutter. Narrow gutters often make a publication more difficult to read, because the reader's eye tends to jump between columns.

Column width influences a publication's readability. Readers scan groups of words. Wide columns are more difficult to read because a reader's eyes have to shift several times when reading each line.

Symbols such as bullets and numbers organize lists of items. Use bullets (•) or asterisks (*), or other like symbols ($\sqrt{}$, °, Δ) when all items in the list are of equal importance. Numbers suggest a linear order.

Figure 7–26
Desktop publishing organization tools

Full-featured desktop publishing word processing programs can be expensive and quite complex for the average user. Less-expensive desktop publishing programs are available with a reduced set of features, making them easier to use. These have found favor with teachers and students who use them to prepare newsletters and bulletins and even to lay out yearbooks. A program such as The New Print Shop Deluxe® is a fully featured desktop publishing program aimed at students at all levels from grades 1 through 12. Greeting cards, signs, calendars, banners, certificates, and simple newsletters are some of the projects easily accomplished with this program. Kid Works Deluxe combines a word processor and a paint program and allows PreK through fourth graders to produce multimedia books, awards, and other projects. At the other end of the continuum are desktop publishing programs such as PageMaker®. This fully featured professional desktop publishing program can be mastered by students in high school with some practice and effort.

THE WORD PROCESSOR AS A PRODUCTIVITY TOOL

The computer is a tool, and word processing is one of the most popular and powerful tool uses. Seat work, homework, exercise sheets, lesson plans, bibliographies, class notes, reports, essays, compositions, memos, letters to parents—the list of practical word processing applications goes on and on. It is easy to understand why most people purchasing a personal computer do so primarily to use it as a word processor.

The argument can be built that the word processor and not the computer itself is in fact the productivity tool. Software indeed transforms the hardware. Using the best software appropriate for a given task makes the computer far more effective or productive than using poorly designed or inappropriate software. Once software is loaded into the hardware, perhaps we should no longer refer to it as a computer but, rather, call it a word processor, database manager, drawing table, and so on.

To gauge the word processor value as a productivity tool, the following questions must be answered. Does using the word processor increase my accuracy? Does it ease my task? Does it increase the speed at which I can complete a task? Does it allow me to accomplish something that I might otherwise find impossible? In other words, does it contribute to my efficiency or effectiveness?

INTO THE CLASSROOM:
Putting It All Together

Making one-page magazine-style advertisements engages small groups of upper-elementary students in a variety of team activities. It leads to high motivation, knowledge and skill sharing, and observable achievements in the language arts, mathematics, and computer literacy.

Collaborative ad-making involves use, sharing, and development of academic and so-cial skills. The task involves "authentic learning," especially when ads are made for actual home and school use, though many students are even more highly motivated when their products or services are fanciful. Students have applied the ad format to making posters for other purposes, for example, to make appeals for emergency relief when natural dis-asters occur around the world. Many students have expressed interest in doing new ads when they returned to school the following year.

Objectives of the Lesson

1. To develop number sense: accurate estimates of costs of common goods and services, correct decimal notations for dollars and cents, and mental calculations of multiples of simple whole or two-place decimal numbers.
2. To practice and expand desktop publishing skills: keyboarding, selecting fonts and graphics, and designing page layout for clarity and attractiveness.
3. To practice and develop small-group collaborative decision-making skills: dividing re-sponsibility for individual tasks and combining efforts into a final product.
4. To practice process writing skills: prewriting text elements, keyboarding, reading criti-cally, editing, printing, sharing, and revising.
5. To promote self-assessment: students examine products in relation to explicit criteria (clarity, attractiveness, creativity, complexity, accuracy), other groups' work, and exem-plary models.

Prerequisite Skills

Students must be familiar with the basic operation of computers, whether Mac or Win-dows, and with a word processing program such as The Student Writing Center (second graders may use Kid Pix). Also, they must have previously learned how to work effectively within a small group, recognizing their division of roles and collective responsibilities.

Sequence of Activities

(Daily or one-a-week, 50-minute sessions may be abridged or expanded.)

Session 1: The teacher displays and describes magazine ads and asks students to discuss the characteristics and purposes of the ads. Students select two peers to form small groups to examine sample ads and to make a list of features.

Session 2: The teacher asks students what they recall about purposes and characteristics of ads while sketching an ad on markerboard accordingly. The teacher then challenges them to make ads of their own and clarifies which software is to be used and what com-ponents and qualities will be expected (real or imaginary products or services; prices for one, two, or three discounts; etc.). Groups of three or four students begin drafting their own ads, while the teacher provides guidance as needed.

(Continued)

Session 3: Students examine and revise their first drafts. The teacher provides guidance concerning product or service and prices. Members of the group take turns keyboarding text and share in decision making about fonts, colors, graphics, and layout.

Session 4: Students revise according to posted criteria, print in draft mode, share, edit, print in color, take home, share with family and friends, and solicit suggestions.

Session 5: Group members discuss suggestions received, make final revisions, print color version, post on bulletin board, or place in approved locations.

Evaluation

Students examine their draft and final ads in relation to posted criteria—clarity, attractiveness, creativity, complexity, and accuracy. They compare their ads with those of their peers and with exemplary models provided by the teacher. The teacher assesses quality of interactions among students in each group, interest and engagement displayed during production, quality of products, and application of skills acquired to related tasks, transfer of skills to new tasks, and subsequent eagerness to use skills for their own purposes.

Steven Hackbarth
Elementary Computer Specialist Teacher
P.S. 6 and P.S. 116
New York City, New York

SUMMARY

This chapter addressed the value of using a word processor in the classroom as a tool to facilitate written communication. Studies have shown that the use of word processing by students increases their motivation to write and expands their vocabulary.

Features that might be considered when choosing a word processor were examined. The more sophisticated, and usually more expensive, programs are expected to contain a greater number of features. After writing needs are determined, a program can be selected that has an appropriate set of features.

Representative editing functions were examined that allow the user to navigate through the document, adding, deleting, finding, replacing, inserting, and moving information at will. In addition, print commands were acknowledged that allow the user to describe paper size; margins; character typeface, size, and style; and right, left, center, or full line justification. Lettering guidelines were suggested in order to take full advantage of the visual impact of print generated from a word processor.

Teacher applications were explored, using the word processor as a tool to save time and effort and to personalize communications. A process called mail merge integrates information from a data file into a word processed document. Material that is used repeatedly without modification is known as a boilerplate and can be incorporated into documents, thereby saving a good deal of time.

Collaborative writing, a technique that allows more than one student at a time to engage in a writing activity, is greatly facilitated by a word processor. New software allows students sitting at computers on a network to write and to edit each other's documents as they write them.

Examples of student applications were presented in a cross-disciplinary fashion in order to stimulate the reader's imagination and encourage unique creative applications.

CHAPTER EXERCISES

To complete the specified exercises on-line, go to the Chapter Exercises Module in Chapter 7 of the Companion Website.

1. Examine computer magazines, journals, and catalogs. List advertisements for at least three of the various entry devices available for the computer. Discuss briefly the features that are being promoted.

2. Many programs in the school setting currently use keyboard input from students. There has been a good deal written in the past several years on the subject of keyboard instruction. Write a two- to three-page paper discussing the issue of teaching typing starting at an early level. At what grade level would you begin teaching keyboarding skills? Defend your position. Check your library to review any research on this subject. Cite your sources.

3. Describe at least five examples of how you might use word processing in your work as a teacher. Develop a sample of one of them.

4. Many word processors automatically reformat and check spelling and grammar as words are typed into the computer. How does this help your students? How could this be detrimental to your students?

5. Which features found in word processing programs would you find indispensable? What feature would you like companies to add to a word processor?

6. Using a word processor, write a two- to three-page reaction paper to the concept of collaborative writing. Include a bibliography listing at least three sources.

7. Using a word processor, write a few paragraphs about the motivation that is prompting you to enter the teaching profession and save the file. Exchange your file with a friend who has written a similar one. Finish the document you have received by adding a few paragraphs of your own describing what you hope to accomplish as a teacher. Edit the entire document for consistency of style. Once again exchange it with your friend and compare the documents.

8. Pick a partner and together choose a topic on which to write. After agreeing on an outline, divide the writing task between yourselves. After completing your independent writing assignment, merge your files. Edit the entire document for consistency of style.

9. Obtain an educational software catalog that contains software for students with special needs. (Don Johnson is one, among others.) Describe how word processing programs for students with special needs might be used to help students who are physically challenged or learning disabled.

10. How might lack of access to a word processor at school or home affect the education and future prospects of a student from a poorer school district?

PORTFOLIO DEVELOPMENT EXERCISES

To complete this exercise on-line, go to the Digital Portfolio Module in Chapter 7 of the Companion Website.

One of the NETS•S standards covered in this chapter was "Students are proficient in the use of technology" under *Category 1: Basic operations and concepts.* Begin to develop your own portfolio of lesson plans that demonstrates your ability to have your students reach the NETS•S standards.

1. Design a lesson plan activity for elementary, middle school, or high school students in which they use a word processing program to write a report on a subject that you will be studying. Try to combine several tools found in word processing programs. The number that you use should depend on the grade level. Younger students may only use simple tools (bold, italics, font change, etc.). Older students will be required to use more sophisticated tools (boxes, numbering or bulleting, hanging indents, paragraph or document formatting). This lesson should demonstrate that your students have achieved the standard. Be sure to include a system of evaluation for your students' understanding and competence to ensure that they have met this standard.

2. Adapt the lesson plan activity you developed in exercise 1 for students to evaluate each others' work.

For more information on developing digital portfolios go to the Digital Portfolio module on the Companion Website www.prenhall.com/forcier

GLOSSARY

boilerplate Material, such as paragraphs of text, that can be used repeatedly in many documents without modification.

desktop publishing Usually refers to the use of software that contains an extensive set of text and graphics manipulation commands and includes advanced page layout capabilities.

font The collection of characteristics applied to a typeface in a particular size and style.

mechanical spacing Letter spacing that requires letters within a word to be equally distant from each other regardless of the letter shape. This results in unequal surface areas in the spaces between letters.

monospaced See *mechanical spacing.*

optical spacing Letter spacing that requires letters within a word to have equal surface areas in the spaces between each other, thereby taking letter shapes into account. Distances between letters will vary.

orphans Single lines of text that occur at the bottoms of pages.

print formatter The part of a word processing program that delivers the text file to the printer and ensures that it is printed correctly on paper.

proportional-spaced See *optical spacing*.

size The height of a letter expressed in points (1 point equals 1/72 of an inch).

stationery Sometimes used as a replacement for template.

style (1) A set of characteristics (left aligned, 10 point, Times, 0.5 inch first line indent, exact line spacing, for example) that can be applied to text in a word processor. (2) When dealing strictly with the appearance of text, style pertains more narrowly to the appearance of a particular typeface (plain, bold, italic, outline, shadow, and underline).

template See *boilerplate*.

text editor The part of a word processing program that allows the user to manipulate text on a screen display. It is used during the text entry phase to help add, change, and delete text, as well as to locate words or phrases.

text-wrapped graphics The format feature that allows the program to wrap lines of text around the edges of graphics.

typeface The design or appearance of a particular letter type and the name given to that design (Bookman, Geneva, New Century Schoolbook, Palatino, Times, etc.).

widows Single lines of text that occur at the tops of pages.

word processor Software, with accompanying hardware, used primarily to facilitate the creation, editing, formatting, saving, and printing of information in electronic and hard copy form.

word wrap A process of monitoring the entry of words so that words are not split on the right side of the screen. If a complete word will not fit on the current line, the complete word is moved to the next line.

WYSIWYG (what you see is what you get) Pronounced "wizzy wig," the exact screen replication of what will be printed on paper.

REFERENCES & SUGGESTED READINGS

Baugh, I. W. (1999–2000, December/January). To keyboard or not to keyboard. *Learning & Leading with Technology, 27*(4), 28–31.

Bowman, M. (1999, May). Children, word processors and genre. *Scottish Educational Review, 31*(1), 66–83.

Campbell, G. (2000, July). The future is here: Self-typing text. *PC World, 18*(7), 222.

Hayden K. L., Norman, K. I. (2002, July). K–12 Instruction in the United States: Integrating National Standards for Science and Writing through emerging technologies. Descriptive report. 12. ERIC NO: ED469626.

Kiefer, K. (2002, March). This isn't where we thought we were going: Revisiting our visions of computer-supported writing instruction. Opinion paper. 12. ERIC NO: 46843.

Lang, M. (1999, May–June). Electronic learning. Write on! *Instructor, 108*(8), 70–71.

Levin, M. (1997). *Kids in print: Publishing a school newspaper*. Parsippany, NJ: Good Apple. Electronic Learning, 4.

Raef, C. (1996, April). Improving student writing skills through the use of technology. Master's thesis, St. Xavier University, ERIC NO: ED399537.

Tolly, K. (2002, July). Words matter. *Network World*, 14.

1. What is a spreadsheet and how does it work?

2. How are text and values entered in a spreadsheet?

3. How are formulas created in order to manipulate values?

4. How can a spreadsheet be used to sort textual information?

5. How can problem-solving strategies be applied to designing spreadsheets?

6. How might you as a teacher use a spreadsheet as a productivity tool in multidisciplinary lessons and activities to keep and sort records, calculate numerical data, forecast results of decisions, and analyze information?

7. How can charts be generated from spreadsheet data?

8. Following a linear problem-solving approach, how can a grade book system be developed on a spreadsheet?

This chapter contains information needed to meet standards listed under three NETS•S categories. Standards under *Category 3: Technology productivity tools* are easily met with information found throughout the chapter. Spreadsheets increase productivity and can help you and your students creatively solve problems and produce documents and projects. Spreadsheets are another media format that helps students communicate information and ideas effectively thereby meeting one standard under *Category 4: Technology communications tools*. Students learn how spreadsheets can be used as a research tool to process data and report results. NETS•S *Category 6: Technology problem-solving and decision-making tools* standards are met as students learn about a new tool to aid in problem solving and making decisions and develop strategies for solving problems in the real world. Spreadsheets are a wonderful tool for you as a teacher. They automate and simplify number processing in the form of budget data or student grades. Learn to use a spreadsheet. Incorporate them into your curriculum and student assignments. They are fun and easy to set up and use, and you never can tell when its power will become a real ally to you, your class, and your students.

The term **spreadsheet** originated in the accounting world to refer to data entered in columns and rows on a wide sheet of paper. The data was "spread" across columns in the same row. This ledger sheet, or spreadsheet, as it became known, was in fact a two-dimensional paper grid of rows and columns. Spreadsheets can be used for a wide variety of activities, but most applications of spreadsheets focus on generating numeric information from other numeric information such as creating budgets and income projections and forecasting needed amounts of equipment or supplies based on a number of factors. Some use spreadsheets as preformatted databases where stored data can easily be sorted. This may be useful when you want to examine the entire set of data. It is not as useful when you need to search for or select specific data related to an individual item. Many teachers use spreadsheets in place of grade book programs to keep track of student and class progress and grades.

NETS•S Standards Addressed in This Chapter

3. Technology productivity tools
    • Students use technology tools to enhance learning, increase productivity, and promote creativity.
    • Students use productivity tools to collaborate in constructing technology-enhanced models, prepare publications, and produce other creative works.

4. Technology communications tools
    • Students use telecommunications to collaborate, publish, and interact with peers, experts, and other audiences.
    • Students use a variety of media and formats to communicate information and ideas effectively to multiple audiences.

6. Technology problem-solving and decision-making tools
    • Students use technology resources for solving problems and making informed decisions.
    • Students employ technology in the development of strategies for solving problems in the real world.

 A list of the ISTE/NCATE standards addressed in this chapter is available in the Standards Module on the Companion Website www.prenhall.com/forcier

The present-day electronic spreadsheet lets the user enter text and values and create formulas that set up relationships between values, which may be governed by the simple arithmetic operators of $+$, $-$, $*$, and $/$ or by sophisticated functions that are expressions of more complex mathematical and statistical formulas. The spreadsheet automatically recalculates all related values as new data entries are made, thereby revealing relationships instantaneously.

Why would a teacher use a spreadsheet instead of a commercial grade book program? Teachers manage grades in many different ways. All too often, a grade book program forces teachers to change their grading methods to adapt to the grade book program purchased. A spreadsheet, on the other hand, can be custom-designed to the teacher's system.

Consider the teacher-made grade book spreadsheet example in Figure 8–1. As the classroom teacher uses this grade book spreadsheet by inputting or changing grades, the spreadsheet program will continually calculate the students' total point accumulation and display a final score in column G. This spreadsheet is also designed to keep the statistics on each class activity, identifying the highest, lowest, and average score on the activity, giving the teacher information by which to assess the activity. Any change in any score will automatically update any of this information linked to that score. The rows may be sorted in alphabetical order by the student names in column A at any time; so, as new students are added, the grade book is sorted once again.

USING A SPREADSHEET

The illustrations used in this chapter to explain the operation of spreadsheets are actual screens of *Microsoft Excel*™. This is a very popular spreadsheet program that is part of the *Microsoft Office* suite and available in both Windows and Mac OS. It is

◇	A	B	C	D	E	F	G
1	**Name**	**Lab 1**	**Lab 2**	**Test**	**Midterm**	**Portfolio**	**Grade**
2		10	1	100	100	100	100
3	Alderson, Kathy	9	7	78	75	80	78
4	Chagnon, Laura	7	8	80	80	80	79
5	Hall, Andrea	10	9	98	90	95	95
6	Hall, Les	9	10	92	80	90	89
7	Heilman, Jacob	8	10	90	80	80	85
8	McKinley, Rich	8	8	82	70	90	81
9	Prosser, Peggy	7	8	80	80	85	81
10	Strasbaugh, Kristin	10	7	98	90	95	93
11	**Highest Score**	10	10	98	90	95	95
12	**Lowest Score**	7	7	78	70	80	78
13	**Average**	8.5	8.4	87.3	80.6	86.9	85.1

Figure 8–1

A spreadsheet used as a grade book

◇	A	B	C	D
1				
2		17		
3				
4				
5				

B2 ▼ ✗ ✓ ▦ = 17

Figure 8–2

Data entered in a cell and displayed in the formula bar

important to note that most spreadsheets, regardless of program or operating system platform, look and act very much alike. To help understand the capability of a spreadsheet, visualize a spreadsheet as a matrix of lettered columns and numbered rows. Take a moment to examine Figure 8–2 as you consider the following. The intersection of a column and a row is called a **cell** and is identified by a letter and a number, which is first the column notation (letter) and then the row notation (number) designation. The cursor can be moved around through this grid and positioned in any cell. When you click in a cell, an outline appears around it, indicating that it has been selected as the **active cell.** Notice that the name of the cell also appears in the upper left-hand corner.

When an entry (text or a value) is made from the keyboard, it appears in an area at the top of the screen called the **formula bar.** If you typed the value 17 in cell *B2,* that cell is identified in the upper left-hand corner of the figure as the active cell and the value that has been typed in that cell, *17,* also appears in the formula bar, the area across the top of the screen. For obvious reasons, this area is sometimes also referred to as the **data entry bar.** Notice the small square at the sections of *B2, B3, C2* and *C3*. This is called the fill handle and will be discussed later.

A primary task when working with spreadsheets is specifying the relationship between the cells. The data in one cell can be automatically replicated in another by making cells equal to each other. Data in one cell can be added to, subtracted from, and multiplied or divided by data in another cell. Complex mathematical relationships can be expressed in a group of cells. Built-in formulas, called **functions,** may be used or formulas may be created by the user, to express this relationship between cells.

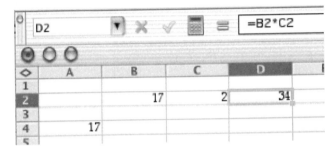

Figure 8–3
Relating one cell to
another by formula

Figure 8–4
Acting upon the
contents of two other
cells in a formula

Formulas entered begin with the *equals* sign and reference cells by their name. In Figure 8–3, the value *17* was entered in cell *B2*. The formula =*B2* was entered in cell *A4*. This formula will replicate in cell *A4* any entry occurring in cell *B2*.

Formulas may contain the arithmetic operations of addition, subtraction, multiplication, division, and exponentiation. These are represented by +, −, *, /, and ^, respectively. The operations are performed in the following order: (1) perform all operations inside parentheses, working from inside out if parentheses are nested within each other; (2) compute exponents; (3) perform all multiplications and divisions in order from left to right; (4) perform all additions and subtractions in order from left to right; and finally, (5) perform order operations (<, >, and =).

Examining Figure 8–4, we see that the value *17* was entered in cell *B2* and the value *2* was entered in cell *C2*. An additional cell, *D2,* was selected as the active cell and the formula entered in it was =*B2*C2* [cell *B2* (containing the value of *17*) * (multiplied by) cell *C2* (containing the value of *2*)]. Notice that the result of the formula *(34)* is displayed in cell *D2,* while the formula itself appears in the formula bar.

In this example, both *B2* and *C2* are known as relative references in the formula, since they actually relate to cells one position and two positions to the left of the active formula cell, *D2*. If, on the other hand, the formula is meant to always refer to an exact cell regardless of the placement of the formula cell within the spreadsheet, the reference is called **absolute,** or *fixed*. For example, if the formula must contain a reference to the top cell in the second column, the cell would be entered into a formula as a fixed reference and in most spreadsheets would be typed as *$B$1*. The dollar signs indicate that the column and row will not change. Should the formula be cut or copied to any other cell, no matter where it is located in the spreadsheet, the fixed reference would remain to cell *B1*.

To assist the user, the spreadsheet program contains a wide variety of built-in functions that can be used simply by referencing them in the desired formula, as well as the cells containing the related data. The following are common mathematical functions often used in formulas:

Sum (of values within a cell group)
Average (of values within a cell group)
Minimum (lowest of the values within a cell group)
Maximum (highest of the values within a cell group)
Standard Deviation (of values within a cell group)

The group of cells referenced by these functions are designated as a range from the first cell in the group to the last one. Within the formula, the first and last cells in the range are usually separated by a colon or an ellipsis, depending on the particular spreadsheet being used (e.g., *F9:F17* or *F9 . . . F17*), and enclosed in parentheses.

Let's take a look a brief look at the functions (formulas) that are included in *Microsoft Excel*. It is much easier and faster to use these built-in functions than to type in the formula every time. Returning to the grade book example used at the beginning of this chapter, to find the average for Lab 1 using the built-in functions, we type the equal sign in cell *B13* and then drag from cell *B3* to *B10* to highlight that range or selection. You can see in Figure 8–5 that we then choose *Function . . .* from the *Insert* menu. When the Paste Function menu appears, we select *Statistical* (fewer choices than *All*) and then the formula for *Average*. Notice that an explanation of the function chosen is presented at the bottom of the dialog box. The Paste Function menu contains many different function categories and function names. Clicking "OK" in the Paste Function dialog box will cause a window to open to show the formula and cells that we are using (Figure 8–6 left). We may edit this range of cells if we wish. Clicking "OK" on this screen will send us back to the spreadsheet now automatically showing the average for Lab 1 (Figure 8–6 right). To calculate averages for the remaining students, grab the *Fill handle* in the lower right corner of cell *B13* and drag across the row highlighting cells *C13* through *G13*. The other averages will be automatically displayed in the appropriate cells. Replicating the formula can also be achieved by selecting the *Fill* and *Right* commands under the *Edit* menu. *Fill Down, Up,* and *Left* are also available commands. The calculation of the highest and

Figure 8–5
Paste Function menu (right) accessed through the *Insert* menu (left)

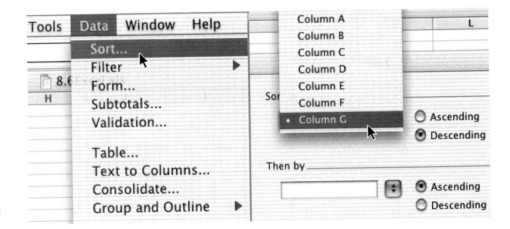

Figure 8–6
Spreadsheet formula (left) and calculated average (right)

Figure 8–7
Data menu (left)
used to access Sort
menu (right)

lowest scores are also achieved by employing the maximum (MAX) and minimum (MIN) functions built in to the spreadsheet and following the procedure just described for using the AVERAGE function.

Data can be sorted in many different ways. Notice that in Figure 8–6 the names in column *A* are in ascending alphabetic order. To sort by the *Grade* column (*G*), simply highlight the data you want sorted in columns *A* through *G* (drag from *A3* to *G10*—do not include the first two rows nor the last three) and open the *Sort* window, which is accessed through the Data menu (Figure 8–7 left). Select how you want to sort the data, in this case by column *G* (Grade) in descending order (Figure 8–7 right) and click OK. The result is displayed in Figure 8–8.

Spreadsheets are in fact highly specialized databases. They can store and manipulate text and numeric values and are sometimes used instead of database managers when their two-dimensional matrix format (columns and rows) lends itself to convenient data entry and when printed report requirements are minimal. The illustration in Figure 8–9 demonstrates the use of text both as **labels** in row *1* and as data

◇	A	B	C	D	E	F	G
1	Name	Lab 1	Lab 2	Test	Midterm	Portfolio	Grade
2		10	1	100	100	100	100
3	Hall, Andrea	10	9	98	90	95	95
4	Strasbaugh, Kristin	10	7	98	90	95	93
5	Hall, Les	9	10	92	80	90	89
6	Heilman, Jacob	8	10	90	80	80	85
7	McKinley, Rich	8	8	82	70	90	81
8	Prosser, Peggy	7	8	80	80	85	81
9	Chagnon, Laura	7	8	80	80	80	79
10	Alderson, Kathy	9	7	78	75	80	78
11	Highest Score	10	10	98	90	95	95
12	Lowest Score	7	7	78	70	80	78
13	Average	8.5	8.4	87.3	80.6	86.9	84.9

Figure 8–8
Data sorted in descending order by column G

◇	A	B	C	D
1	Name	Length	Weight	Diet
2	Tyrannosaurus	50	8 tons	Carnivorous
3	Allosaurus	25	4.5 tons	Carnivorous
4	Brachiosaurus	70	80 tons	Herbivorous
5	Triceratops	20	7 tons	Herbivorous
6	Stegosaurus	20	4 tons	Herbivorous
7				

Figure 8–9
Using a spreadsheet to sort text

to be manipulated in rows *2* through *6*. Spreadsheets are often used as powerful sorting devices to examine information grouped in a variety of ways. Each row in Figure 8–9 contains information about one dinosaur. A multilevel sort has arranged the information by (1) DIET in ascending alphabetical order, then within that first sort by (2) LENGTH in descending numeric order, and then within those two levels of sort by (3) WEIGHT in descending order. This ability to nest one sort within another adds versatility to the spreadsheet.

PROBLEM SOLVING WITH SPREADSHEETS

Consider that the process of problem solving might be approached in a nonlinear fashion by an individual with a random learning style. Figure 8–10 illustrates one such approach. "Given" is the information in your possession. "To Find" is the information you are seeking. What are the results you are trying to achieve? "Procedure" is the method you are going to employ to reach your goal. How will you achieve results?

Apply the problem-solving process just reviewed to the following simple word problem: A boy takes home $7.00 an hour from a weekend job. How many hours must he work in order to be able to purchase a $350 bicycle?

Given: Take-home pay is $7.00 per hour.
         Cost of the bicycle is $350.

To Find: Number of hours of work required to earn enough to purchase the bicycle.

Procedure: Divide the cost of the bicycle ($350) by the hourly take-home rate of $7.00.

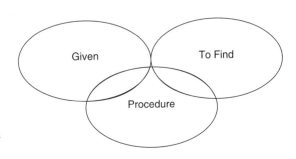

Figure 8–10
A nonlinear
approach to problem
solving

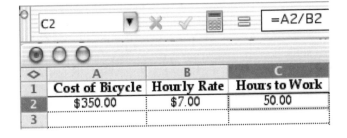

Figure 8–11
Using a spreadsheet
as an organizer and
a calculator

Figure 8–12
Using a spreadsheet
as a forecasting tool

In Figure 8–11, the cost of the bicycle (*350*) is entered in cell *A2* and the hourly take-home rate (*7.00*) is entered in cell *B2*. The formula = *A2/B2* (cost divided by hourly rate) is entered in cell *C2*. Upon completing the formula entry, the formula is displayed in the formula bar, and the value resulting from the formula as hours to work (*50*) is displayed in the cell.

Having discovered the number of hours necessary to earn the required amount, the boy might now wish to see the effect of moving to a higher-paying job and perhaps purchasing a slightly more expensive bike. He could play "what if" and forecast the results of change. As shown in Figure 8–12, by changing the data under "Hourly Rate" and/or "Cost of Bicycle," he could immediately see the impact on the number of "Hours to Work."

INTO THE CLASSROOM:
Spreadsheet Magic

I work as Computer Coordinator in a K–8 school, working with teachers to integrate technology across the curriculum. Students learn mathematics and other subjects as they use the spreadsheet tool. They are motivated to work on the computer and they take pride in the professional documents they produce. Mistakes can be easily corrected, and assignments can be modified for extension or remediation. Students as young as kindergartners use spreadsheets effectively as they use templates where the formatting of columns, rows, the grid, and print area has been done for them. Initially they learn to move around the spreadsheet, enter text, and duplicate graphics as they count to ten on the grid. Student skills improve gradually as they complete each assignment, and by eighth grade they can do their own formatting. If a template is used at all at this age, it is to save students time so that they can focus on learning and spend less time using the tool.

Students access data on the Internet and they need to interpret this and communicate what they have learned. They use spreadsheets to chart information, and they can then analyze their graphs; for example, they chart their own measurements. The spreadsheet grid provides a structure for organizing data. Students resize the cells to make calendars, multiplication tables, hundreds charts, and flash cards. Borders are selectively shown and hidden, and spreadsheets are used to teach concepts like fractions, decimals, number lines, time lines, and arrays. Learning is enhanced with visual cues as students fill cells with color and pattern, and they count to 100 on the spreadsheet and then fill multiples of threes with color, fives with pattern and see the intersection of the two. Number patterns become evident and they begin to count down rather than across on their hundreds chart. They also insert Clip Art to make pictographs, or an animal classification table.

Students use spreadsheets to sort data numerically and alphabetically; for example, they enter their spelling words and sort them alphabetically. Formulas are inserted in a template to make calculations for third grade students, who then focus on solving the problem of spending a target amount at the toy store while the computer does the calculations for them. Older students improve their understanding of abstract algebraic concepts as they make up their own formulas and then generalize them by filling down or filling right; for example, they use formulas to count the number of cells in the entire spreadsheet, or to make a calculator. They explore "What if . . . " type questions as they see how changing one variable affects the numbers that are generated by a formula.

The teachers at our school use spreadsheets as a utility tool: they record grades, make class lists, checklists, rubrics, seating charts. We make "digital worksheets" where students use a template with formulas that check numerical or one-word answers to questions, and gives instant feedback to the students.

(Continued)

I have written a book called *Spreadsheet Magic,* published by ISTE (http://www.iste.org). It includes instructions and national standards for 40 spreadsheet lessons for students in grades kindergarten through eighth grade, and a CD-ROM with templates and sample completed assignments. Teachers can access on-line tutorials for using spreadsheet programs like AppleWorks or Excel, on-line data sources, and mathematics resources. I have saved a collection of these links at Trackstar, http://www.digital-lessons.com/ at track 108349.

Pam Lewis
St. Luke School
Brookfield, WI

CURRICULUM APPLICATIONS OF SPREADSHEETS

We have described the spreadsheet as a matrix of interrelated columns and rows and have examined its operation. We understand that it can handle text and values, that it is founded on the ability to relate cells to each other, and that it has powerful built-in formulas. We are also beginning to explore some of the functional uses of spreadsheets to record, organize, and sort data (values and text); to calculate values; and to forecast results. As a recording tool, the spreadsheet allows us to alphabetize lists of names, track expenditures, analyze the performance of players in various sports, and manage a grade book. As a forecasting tool, the spreadsheet allows us to analyze the immediate impact of projected changes. We could, for instance, reveal the impact on a school district's budget of raising teachers' salaries by 5 percent, by 4 percent, by 6 percent, and so on.

The table below illustrates a number of spreadsheet applications in different curriculum areas and at various grade levels shown in Figures 8–13 through 8–21. This table summarizes the functional applications and possible curriculum areas of the lesson examples given.

Figure	Primary Function(s)	Curriculum Area
8–13	Measurement	Mathematics
8–14	Metric conversion	Mathematics
8–15	Calculation	Mathematics, home economics
8–16	Calculation, analysis	Mathematics, home economics
8–17	Calculation, analysis	Science, social studies
8–18	Recording, analysis	Social studies, mathematics
8–19	Recording, analysis	Athletics
8–20	Forecasting	Mathematics
8–21	Recording, calculation	Management

◇	A	B	C	D	E	F	G
1	Group	Estimate	Length	Width	Height	Volume	Difference
2	1	64	4.3	4.0	4.0	68.8	4.8
3	2	91	4.4	4.0	4.1	72.2	-18.8
4	3	43	4.2	3.9	3.9	63.9	20.9
5	4	64	4.4	3.8	4.1	68.6	4.6
6							
7							
8							
9							

SUGGESTED LESSON: Accuracy in estimation and measurement may be encouraged by having pairs of students estimate the volume of a cube and then measuring its dimensions.

The estimate and measurements from each pair may then be entered into a spreadsheet as illustrated above. Even a slight difference in the measurement of length, width, or height can result in a considerable difference in volume. Results from different student pairs are compared to stress importance of accuracy of measurement. The number in column G reveals the accuracy of the estimate.

The following formulas yield the necessary calculations in this example:

$Fn = Cn * Dn * En$ [n represents the number of the row]

$Gn = Fn - Bn$

Once the formulas are entered in cells $F2$ and $G2$, they are filled down in each column.

Figure 8–13
Using a spreadsheet to promote accuracy in measurement

◇	A	B	C	D
1	**Miles**	**Kilometers**	**Pounds**	**Kilograms**
2		0		0
3				
4	**Kilometers**	**Miles**	**Kilograms**	**Pounds**
5		0		0

SUGGESTED LESSON: This spreadsheet allows the quick conversion of metric to English or English to metric measurements of distance and weight. A value is entered into one of the clear cells (A2, A5, C2, or C5) and the conversion appears in one of the shaded cells.

Students could be asked to estimate the corresponding values and then use this spreadsheet to verify the accuracy of their estimates.

The following formulas yield the necessary calculations in this example:

B2 = **A2 * 1.602** [converts miles to kilometers]

B5 = **A5 * .06235** [converts kilometers to miles]

D2 = **C2 * .045454** [converts pounds to kilograms]

D5 = **C5 * 2.25** [converts kilograms to pounds]

Figure 8–14
Using a spreadsheet as a metric/English converter

◇	A	B	C	D	E
1				Serving Sizes	
2	Ingredients	Measure	6	15	24
3	Lean ground beef	Lbs.	1.5	3.75	6
4	Chopped onion	Cup	0.5	1.25	2
5	Canned corn	Oz.	14	35	56
6	Mashed potatoes	Cup	3	7.5	12
7	Grated cheese	Cup	0.75	1.875	3
8	Salt	tsp.	1	2.5	4
9	Pepper	tsp.	0.5	1.25	2

SUGGESTED LESSON: Adapting a recipe to a different number of servings is a common problem faced in preparing a meal. This illustrates how a recipe designed for a set number of servings can be adapted for any number. The example deals with serving sizes of 6, 15, and 24 but in reality any number may be used.

The formula must first calculate the unit measure by dividing the amount by the serving size given in the recipe. In this example, the amount of beef, onions, etc. is divided by 6, the serving size. The formula then multiplies the unit measure derived by the number of servings desired.

The following formulas yield the necessary calculations in this example:

D3 = **(C3/$C$2) * D2** [the $ represents an absolute reference]

E3 = **(C3/$C$2) * E2**

Once the formulas are entered in row 3, they can be filled down columns D and E.

Figure 8–15
Using a spreadsheet to calculate proportions

237

◇	A	B	C	D	E
1	Monthly income:		$4,000		
2		Transaction Categories			
3	Date	Food	Clothing	Entertainment	Balance
4	1-Mar	$53.50			$3,946.50
5	3-Mar		$189.00	$98.00	$3,659.50
6	6-Mar	$92.74			$3,566.76
7					
8					
9	Totals:	$146.24	$189.00	$98.00	$433.24
10	%	34%	44%	23%	100%

SUGGESTED LESSON: A personal finance discussion of budgeting could examine "Where the money goes" in a typical month. This spreadsheet could be used to illustrate some expenses made by a family and to explain the construction of a similar personal spreadsheet for each student.

Students' monthly income would be determined. Expenditure categories could be agreed upon and actual purchases recorded during one month. The proportion of expenses in each category would be revealed in the % row.

The following formulas yield the necessary calculations in this example:

E4 = **IF(A4>0,$C$1-SUM(B4:D4),C1)** establishes the initial balance once an entry is made on row 4.

E5 = **IF(A5>0,E4-SUM(B5:D5,"")** calculates a running balance as entries are made on the row. This formula is filled down the column for each row.

B9 = **SUM(B4:B6)** (repeated across columns) totals the amounts in each column.

E9 = **SUM(B9:D9)** this formula, located in column E, adds up the totals.

B10 = **IF(B9>0,B9/$E$9,"")** once an entry appears in the TOTAL cell above it, this formula divides that total by the sum of totals in column E. This formula is repeated for each column.

Figure 8–16
Using a spreadsheet as a personal budgeting tool

◇	A	B	C	D	E	F
1			City: Melbourne, Australia			
2	Date	High	Low	Mean	Amount	Days of
3		Temp	Temp	Temp	Precipitation	Precipitation
4	4/1/04	67	46	57	0.55	1
5	4/2/04	69	50	60	1	1
6	4/3/04	61	46	54	0.33	1
32	4/30/04	76	55	66	0	
33	High Temp	76				
34	Low Temp		46			
35	Average	68	49	59		
36	Amt. Precip.				1.88	
37	Days Precip.					3

SUGGESTED LESSON: Students enter high and low temperatures and any amount of precipitation each day. The spreadsheet performs all of the calculations. This information might be used in a science unit on weather or might be part of a social studies unit on climate as a component of geography. Data might be recorded from a number of different cities around the world with comparisons made and results analyzed. It's easy to see that it would lend itself readily to multidisiplinary unit.

The following formulas yield the necessary calculations in this example:

E4 = **IF(E4>0,1,"")** This formula generates a "1" if an entry appears in column E. It is repeated in each row.
B33 = **MAX(B4:B32)** [column B] returns the highest value in the column.
B35 = **AVERAGE(B4:B32)** [column B] returns the average of the values in the column.
C34 = **MIN(C4:C32)** [column C] returns the lowest value in the column.
C35 = **AVERAGE(C4:C32)** [column C] returns the average of the values in the column.
D35 = **AVERAGE(C4:C32)** [column D] returns the average of the values in the column.
E36 = **SUM(E4:E32)** [column E] adds the values in the column to generate a total.
F37 = **SUM(F4:F32)** [column F] adds the values in the column to generate a total.

Figure 8–17
Using a spreadsheet to calculate sums and averages in a cross-disciplinary science and social studies context

239

	A	B	C	D	E	F	G	H	I	J	K
1			Total # Died during the years					Total # Died during the years			
2	Age	Men	...-'75	'74-'50	'49-'25	'24-'00	Women	...-'75	'74-'50	'49-'25	'24-'00
3	0-10	0					0				
4	11-20	0					0				
5	21-30	0					0				
6	31-40	0					0				
7	41-50	0					0				
8	51-60	0					0				
9	61-70	0					0				
10	71-80	0					0				
11	81-90	0					0				
12	91-100	0					0				
13	Totals	0	0	0	0	0	0	0	0	0	0
14	Percentage										
15	Population*										
16		*population for the midpoint of each quarter century									

SUGGESTED LESSON: In exploring local history, students could be made aware of the value of a local cemetery as a primary resource. Data gathered from headstones could help the understanding of events and conditions prevalent in the local area. Students could first discuss the type of data available in which they might have an interest and formulate relevant questions. They might ask, for example, "How much longer did women live than men? Was there a period of unusually high mortality? How did life expectancy change over time?" and several other questions. Once prepared with data collection sheets and reminded of expected behavior in such a setting, teams of students could visit a local cemetery and gather data by tallying gender, age, and year of death of the deceased. Students would then enter data into a spreadsheet and search for trends and anomalies. The resulting information might generate additional questions requiring further research.

The following formulas yield the necessary calculations in this example:

B3 = **SUM(C3:F3)** and G3 = **SUM(H3:K3)** totals the number in columns C through F and H through K. These formulas are repeated in rows 4 through 12.

B13 = **SUM(B3:B12)** totals the values in the column and is repeated in columns C through K.

C15 = **C13/$B$13** and H15 = **H13/$G$13** repeated in the appropriate columns.

Figure 8–18

Exploring a local cemetery in a math and history lesson

◇	A	B	C	D	E	F	G	H	I	J	K	L	M
1	Player	Pos	Min	FGA	FGM	Pct	FTA	FTM	Pct	OR	DR	A	TO
2	Joe	C	30	12	7	58%	8	7	88%	8	14	3	2
3	Rich	C	10	5	3	60%	4	3	75%	3	6	4	1
4	Ryan	G	16	8	5	63%	4	3	75%	1	2	8	0
5	Patrick	G	14	5	3	60%	2	2	100%	2	1	6	0
6	Jake	G	10	3	1	33%	0	0	0%	0	1	4	2
7	Les	F	12	4	1	25%	0	0	0%	2	2	4	3
8	Paul	F	18	14	7	50%	6	2	33%	3	2	5	3
9	Mike	F	10	3	1	33%	0	0	0%	1	1	3	0
10	TEAM			54	28	52%	24	17	71%	20	29	37	11

SUGGESTED LESSON: Though this example deals with basketball, the recording and statistical analysis of player performance is applicable to all team sports. The coach or an assistant would enter data in columns A (Name), B (Position), C (Minutes played), D (Field Goals Attempted), E (Field Goals Made), G (Free Throws Attempted), H (Free Throws Made), J (Offensive Rebounds), K (Defensive Rebounds), L (Assists), and M (Turnovers) after the game. Formulas in columns F and I would calculate shooting percentages for each player. Additional columns could be added to analyze other facets of player performance. One or more formulas to calculate the ratio of assists to turnovers taking into account minutes played could focus on the players ball-handling skills.

The following formulas would yield the necessary calculations in this example:

Fn = **En/Dn** calculates field goal percentage [n represents rows 2–10]

In = **Hn/Gn** calculates free throw percentage [n represents rows 2–10]

D10 = **Sum(D2:D9)** calculates the total for the column
A similar formula is used for columns E, G, H, J, K, L, and M

Figure 8–19
Using a spreadsheet
to analyze player
performance statistics

◇	A	B	C	D	E	F
1	Profit	# of	List	Profit	Total Boxes	Boxes per
2	Goal	Students	Price	Margin	To Sell	Student
3	$500	30	$5.00	$2.00	250	8
4	$500	30	$6.00	$2.40	208	7
5	$500	30	$7.00	$2.80	179	6

SUGGESTED LESSON: A teacher may at times supervise activity to raise funds through a class project. Before deciding on a specific project, the class may want to consider alternatives with the hope of finding one that will generate the maximum income for effort spent.

For example, suppose one of the projects under consideration is the sale of candy. The list price, number of students available, and the target earnings could be set. The spreadsheet would let the class explore the required total sales and the number of units each student would have to sell at the list price. With this spreadsheet, the class could play "what if" and immediately see the results. Selling a more expensive product would reduce the required sales volume and therefore require a lower sales target per student in order to achieve comparable results.

Initial values are placed in columns A, B, and C. The spreadsheet will calculate the values for columns D, E, and F.

The following formulas would yield the necessary calculations in this example:

D3 = **C3*.40** (assuming 40% profit)

E3 = **A3/D3** [Profit goal divided by the profit margin]

F3 = **E3/B3** [Boxes to sell divided by number of students]
These formulas are filled down each column.

Figure 8–20
Using a spreadsheet to forecast sales in a class activity

◇	A	B	C	D	E	F	G	H	I	J
1	Serial	Item	Purch	Inflation	Purch	Expect	Age	Replace	Deprec	Replace
2	#	Type	Cost	Factor	Date	Life		Date	Value	Cost
3	10023	DVD	$389	0.02	9/9/02	7	2	9/9/09	$111	$443
4	10036	VCR	$235	0.02	8/10/00	5	4	8/10/05	$188	$259

SUGGESTED LESSON: This can be used to project the cost of replacing existing instructional equipment based on the purchase date, expected life of the equipment, original cost, and inflation.

Text or values are entered into columns A through F and the spreadsheet calculates the values in columns G through J.

An additional benefit of this exercise is the exposure to more complex formulas including the use of the TODAY() function.

The following formulas would yield the necessary calculations in this example:

G3 = **(TODAY()-E3)/365.25** The function TODAY() reads the computer's
internal clock/calendar. Subtracting the purchase date from TODAY()
yields the number of days which is then divided by 365.25 (accounting
for leap years) to return the number of years.

H3 = **E3+(F3*365.25)** The expected life (F3) is multiplied by 365.25 to yield
the number of days. This is added to the purchase date and the cell
(H3) is formatted as a date.

I3 = **C3*(G3/F3)** The purchase cost is multiplied by the fraction calculated
by (age/expected life).

J3 = **C3*(1+(D3*F3))** The purchase cost is multiplied by 1 plus the accumulated
inflation cost (inflation factor times the expected life).

These formulas are filled down each column.

Figure 8–21
Using a spreadsheet
to manage inventory
and to track
replacement needs

CHARTS AND GRAPHS

Abstract numerical data can be presented in a concrete, clear, and interesting manner by line or bar graphs, pie charts, and other pictorial means. Prompted in part by the significant increase in graphs in the popular media (newspapers, magazines, and television news), graphing is now being introduced to students at a much earlier age. Graphs can display relationships that would be more difficult to convey in a text or verbal mode. As visuals, they capture attention and promote greater retention of information.

Although graphs can certainly be informative, they have the potential of expressing a bias by the manipulation of scale. Thus, the analysis and interpretation of graphs has become an important subject in the K–12 curriculum. Students can be presented data and led through exercises designed to promote an understanding of those data. They can then be asked to select the most informative and accurate pre-

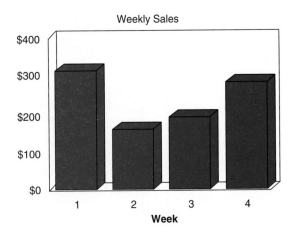

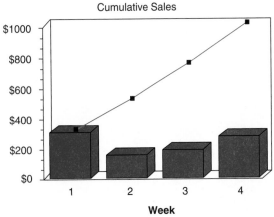

Figure 8–22
Examples of charts and graphs

Selection guidelines for charts and graphs may be examined at the Companion Website www.prenhall.com/forcier

sentation of the data. They may discover that, depending on the data, numeric tables show the most accurate, but also the most abstract and difficult to understand, relationships.

Line graphs, as shown in the upper left section of Figure 8–22, are ideal for displaying a continuous event or trends over time (e.g., growth or decline over time). Notice the steady increase in sales over the first four weeks portrayed on this graph. The rise and fall of the line on a graph easily portrays the fluctuations in value. Multiple trends can be compared simultaneously by plotting more than one line on the graph. *Area graphs* are variations of line graphs that are successful at depicting amount or volume. A line is plotted and the area below it is filled in with a selected pattern. Each data set creates a band, with each area being stacked on the preceding one. These graphs can be eye-catching, but, since they show cumulative results, they can, at times, be more difficult to understand.

Column graphs (vertical columns), as shown in the upper right section of Figure 8–22, and *bar graphs* (horizontal bars) present changes in a dependent variable over an independent variable and are excellent ways of comparing multiple variables with a common variable (e.g., different performances during the same time frame) but lack the feeling of continuity displayed by a line graph. Notice how the individual weeks stand out in this graph, making it easy to determine that the first and fourth weeks were the sales leaders. At times column graphs and line graphs can be combined effectively, as shown in the lower left section of Figure 8–22, to present both discrete and incremental views of the data. More elaborate graphs adding another variable (e.g., different performances at different locations during the same time frame) can be created by stacking the columns/bars.

Pie charts are the ideal way to display part-to-the-whole relationships, or percentages, as shown in the lower right section of Figure 8–22. The size of each slice shows that segment's share of the entire pie. As shown in Figure 8–23, a segment (pie slice) may even be dragged away from the center for emphasis and the chart displayed in three dimensions. Other, more esoteric charts and graphs can be created to display central tendencies, shared variables, and relationships to a common constant.

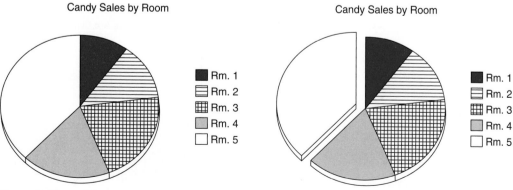

Figure 8–23
Pie chart in an exploded three-dimensional view

Several integrated software packages include a built-in graphing function. A number of other computer programs exist that allow a student to enter data directly or input them from a text file, determine the appropriate scale, and select the type of graph or chart to be generated by the computer. This allows the student to examine several graphic representations of the same data and choose the most accurate and informative one.

Graph Components

Graphs are composed of certain common basic components. Note the components as they are labeled in the column graph in Figure 8–24. The *title* announces what your graph is all about and often hints at the conclusion you want your viewer to draw. The title *Weekly Sales Are Climbing* is more suggestive of the conclusion you want drawn than would merely titling the graph *Sales*.

Data *elements* are the major components of the graph that represent the quantity of the data being portrayed. The elements in Figure 8–24 are columns. As we have seen, elements can also be bars, lines, areas, and wedges.

The *axes* are the vertical and horizontal dimensions of the graph. The horizontal axis is usually used to display the independent variable such as the *Weeks* shown in Figure 8–24.

The *scales* located along the axes indicate to the viewer how the data are measured. Scales usually begin at zero at the intersection of the *x* and *y* axes. The user can select the range, zero to the maximum amount, and the unit increments within the range. The graph in Figure 8–24 uses increments of 100.

Tick marks are short lines located on the axes to serve as visual reference points dividing the axes into evenly spaced units. They may be located on either side of the axis line or may cross through it. They are located at each major unit of scale and evenly distributed between them.

Labels may be applied wherever they are needed to identify other components. The word *Weeks* in Figure 8–24 designates the number of weeks along the horizontal axis.

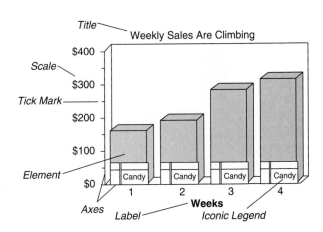

Figure 8–24
Components of a graph

The *legend* is usually a separate area of the graph that identifies the patterns or textures of columns, bars, or wedges and what they represent. The iconic legend may, however, be used as pictorial elements, similar to the candy boxes used in Figure 8–24, to strengthen the graph's message.

Graphs and How They Communicate

Let's explore graphs in a bit more detail. Figure 8–25 depicts population data in two different graphs, a line graph and a column graph. Both graphs use the same scale, represent data changing over time, and compare three quantities. The line graph clearly shows that population growth is leveling out in North America and in Europe, while it is increasing dramatically in Latin America. The column graph, though depicting the same data, does not show the trend as readily.

In 1950, North America and Latin America each had a population of approximately 165 million. In 1990, North America's population was 278 million and Latin America's was 447 million. Examine the line graph and area graph, shown in Figure 8–26, that portray these changes in population.

The line graph on the left of Figure 8–26 clearly demonstrates the regions' population trends. The area graph on the right effectively displays change in amount, but notice that the top sloping line represents the sum of the population in both regions, and the scale of the graph, therefore, has changed. Does it allow you to better understand the change within each region or is it more difficult to decipher? Which of the two graphs in Figure 8–26 is the most effective at communicating its information at a glance?

An inappropriate choice of scale can be very misleading. Consider the following hypothetical example. Five students received grades on an assignment; a perfect score was 10 points. Marci scored 8 out of 10, Kristin 9, Dick 7, Jerry 6, and Katie 9. The user must decide on the most accurate scale when graphing the data. Examine

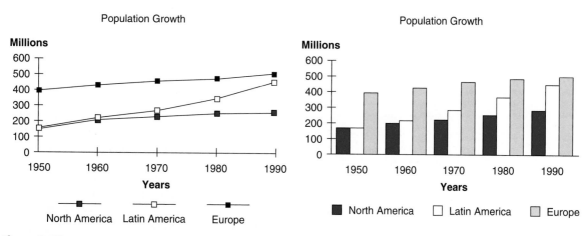

Figure 8–25
Line graph and column graph representing the same data

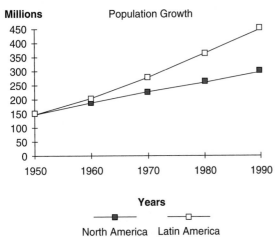

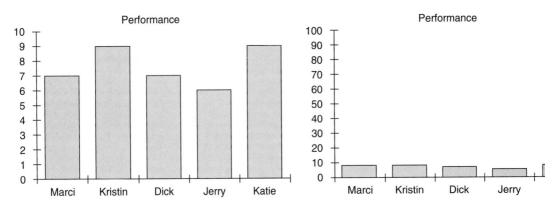

Figure 8–26
Line graph and area graph representing the same data

Figure 8–27
Column graphs demonstrating the impact of scale

the two examples presented in Figure 8–27. As demonstrated, selecting the wrong scale may be misleading. Since the perfect score on the assignment was 10, a scale of 0 to 10 was chosen for the graph on the left side of the figure. When this scale is employed, the differences between the students' scores on the assignment are accurately portrayed. It is easy to see at glance that scores for Kristin and Katie were 50 percent better than Jerry's score. The graph on the right shows the same data on a scale of 0 to 100. Notice how close all scores appear. The scale is too great to show clearly much differentiation and conveys the misleading impression at first glance that all scores were approximately the same.

CREATING A GRADE BOOK

Consider the creation of a computerized grade book to report student progress in your classroom. Employing the nonlinear problem-solving process discussed earlier in this chapter, how might we proceed?

Given: Student names
                Student performance on a variety of measures
                Target audience of students and their parents
To Find: Complete, accurate report of student progress
                Choose software that facilitates the selected presentation format.
                Organize relevant data clearly.
                Calculate and summarize results on performance measures.

A linear problem-solving strategy that might appeal more to a sequential learner consists of two phases, the *analysis* phase and the *synthesis* phase. In the analysis phase, we need to clearly examine the problem, define *what* must be done, and clearly identify the specific component tasks that relate to the problem. In the synthesis phase, we plan our strategy and carry out the solution to the problem. Evaluation provides feedback that could modify decisions made in both the analysis and synthesis phases.

In an effort to bring that linear problem-solving process into sharper focus, let's review the illustration in Figure 8–28 and consider once again the task of recording student progress in a computerized grade book.

Define the Problem

Develop a system to record grades given to student work and then to calculate an equitable and accurate score representative of the student's performance within the class.

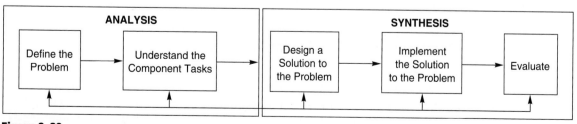

Figure 8–28
A linear approach to problem solving

Understand the Component Tasks

The following questions must be answered *before* you can sit down at the computer and begin to solve the problem:

- How will student names be entered (last name first)?
- How many different activity types will be allowed for each class (e.g., quiz, test, project, portfolio, lab)?
- How many different grades will be entered into each activity type?
- How are grades to be calculated (will they be weighted)?
- How are grades to be reported?
- What information will be calculated concerning class performance?

Design a Solution to the Problem

The primary purpose of the synthesis phase of problem solving is to help ensure that solutions designed to address the identified tasks are carried out in an effective and efficient manner and that the results are evaluated. Having defined what must be done and having identified tasks, we can now determine how each task can be carried out. The solution to this problem consists of designing labels as identifiers, creating appropriate formulas, and then entering accurate data.

Each operation must be written in a clear and effective manner.

- Student names will be entered in one column, last name first.
- Grades for two labs, one test, one midterm project, and one cumulative portfolio will be entered.
- Maximum raw scores are established for each activity as follows:
  Labs will have a maximum score of 10.
  The test will have a maximum score of 100.
  The midterm project will have a maximum score of 100.
  The cumulative portfolio will have a maximum score of 100.
- Grades will be weighted as follows:
  Labs will be equally weighted and will together account for 20 percent.
  The test will be weighted 25 percent.
  The midterm project will be weighted 25 percent.
  The cumulative portfolio will be weighted 30 percent.
- The final grade will be reported on a scale of 1 to 100 (a percent).
- The highest and lowest scores will be identified and an average calculated on all activities, as well as on the final grade.

Implement the Solution to the Problem

As illustrated in Figure 8–29, student names were entered in column *A,* last name first. They may be entered in any order and then sorted alphabetically by the spreadsheet. Grades for two labs with a maximum score of *10* each and a weighting of 10 percent each were entered in columns *B* and *C,* one test with a maximum score of *100* and a weighting of 25 percent was entered in column *D,* one midterm project with a maximum score of *100* and a weighting of 25 percent was entered in column

◇	A	B	C	D	E	F	G
1	Name	Lab 1	Lab 2	Test	Midterm	Portfolio	Grade
2		10	10	100	100	100	100
3	Alderson, Kathy	9	7	78	75	80	78
4	Chagnon, Laura	7	8	80	80	80	79
5	Hall, Andrea	10	9	98	90	95	95
6	Hall, Les	9	10	92	80	90	89
7	Heilman, Jacob	8	10	90	80	80	85
8	McKinley, Rich	8	8	82	70	90	81
9	Prosser, Peggy	7	8	80	80	85	81
10	Strasbaugh, Kristin	10	7	98	90	95	93
11	Highest Score	10	10	98	90	95	95
12	Lowest Score	7	7	78	70	80	78
13	Average	8.5	8.4	87.3	80.6	86.9	85.1

> The following formulas would yield the necessary calculations in this example:
>
> $G3 = B3+C3+(D3*0.25)+(E3*0.25)+(F3*0.30)$ adds the values in correct proportions for the Grade. This formula is filled down through row 10 in column G.
>
> $B11 = MAX(B3:B10)$ calculates the highest score in the column and is filled right through column G.
>
> $B12 = MIN(B3:B10)$ calculates the lowest score in the column and is filled right through column G.
>
> $B13 = AVERAGE(B3:B10)$ calculates the average score in the column and is filled right through column G.

Figure 8–29
Creating the grade
book/spreadsheet

E, and one cumulative portfolio with a maximum score of *100* and a weighting of 30 percent was entered in column *F.* The final grade will be calculated on the basis of *100* in column *G.* Examine the formula showing in the formula bar in Figure 8–29 that calculates this final grade. Functions named MAX, MIN, and AVERAGE were invoked in rows *11, 12,* and *13* to calculate the highest and lowest scores and an average on all activities, as well as on the final grade.

The formulas that calculate the maximum, minimum, and average scores are then repeated in columns *C* through *G.* Spreadsheets will allow the user to replicate the contents of a cell (text, value, or formula) automatically to the right across a row or down a column, often saving appreciable time. When a formula is created that has a blank (empty) cell as a divisor, many spreadsheets will generate a *#DIV/O!* message, indicating that they cannot divide by zero. As soon as a value is entered in the divisor cell, the message will disappear.

Having first analyzed the problem and then designed an acceptable solution to the problem, we must now execute the tasks to solve it. We must enter grades in our computerized grade book and print reports.

Evaluate

Debugging is the process of correcting logic and construction errors. An often-used debugging procedure is to give the program some test data that will produce known output over the entire range of use. Before entering your students' actual scores into

◇	A	B	C	D	E	F	G
1	Name	Lab 1	Lab 2	Test	Midterm	Portfolio	Grade
2		10	10	100	100	100	100
3	Alderson, Kathy	0	0	0	0	0	0
4	Chagnon, Laura	10	10	100	100	100	100
5	Hall, Andrea						0
6	Hall, Les						0
7	Heilman, Jacob						0
8	McKinley, Rich						0
9	Prosser, Peggy						0
10	Strasbaugh, Kristin						0
11	Highest Score	10	10	100	100	100	100
12	Lowest Score	0	0	0	0	0	0
13	Average	5.0	5.0	50.0	50.0	50.0	12.5

Figure 8–30

Debugging the grade book/spreadsheet

your grade book, you might enter score values that you can compute easily and verify that the computer results are as expected. In Figure 8–30, zero is entered as the score in each item for the first student on row 3, and the maximum (*10 or 100*) is entered for the second student on row 4. If the results are other than expected, debugging allows you to verify the correctness of your formula, the appropriateness of the functions you employed, and the logic of your design. A look at column *G* and at rows *11, 12,* and *13* verifies our expected results.

Documentation that accompanies a computer application provides valuable information for the user. The user of the grade book must clearly understand the intent of the program. Detailed written instructions about how to use the program can better ensure that the program is used effectively. The use of screen shots, such as those commonly found in software manuals, replicating what the user sees at any given point of using the program, is often helpful in illustrating the instructions. The instructions supplied with the grade book must clearly tell the user where and how to enter student names, the maximum scores allowed, where to enter the scores, how the scores will be weighted, and how the final grade will be calculated and reported.

As the classroom teacher uses the grade book/spreadsheet, it will continually calculate the students' total point accumulations and final scores and keep the statistics on each class activity. The rows may be sorted in alphabetical order by the data in column *A* at any time so, as new students are added, the grade book is sorted once again.

The grade book stores data about individual students but also reveals information about their progress and their comparative performance within the group. The results in Figure 8–31 also reveal that students had a bit more difficulty with the midterm project than either the test or the portfolio.

The grade book **template** (blank form) can be saved after labels and formulas are created but before any names or scores are put into the grade book. By loading the template, naming it with the course name, and resaving it, the teacher may use the same grade book template for many classes.

Space has limited the number of examples given in this chapter. Any calculations that are done regularly are prime candidates for spreadsheet applications. The user

◇	A	B	C	D	E	F	G
1	**Name**	Lab 1	Lab 2	Test	Midterm	Portfolio	Grade
2		10	10	100	100	100	100
3	Alderson, Kathy	9	7	78	75	80	78
4	Chagnon, Laura	7	8	80	80	80	79
5	Hall, Andrea	10	9	98	90	95	95
6	Hall, Les	9	10	92	80	90	89
7	Heihman, Jacob	8	10	90	80	80	85
8	McKinley, Rich	8	8	82	70	90	81
9	Prosser, Peggy	7	8	80	80	85	81
10	Strasbaugh, Kristin	10	7	98	90	95	93
11	**Highest Score**	10	10	98	90	95	95
12	**Lowest Score**	7	7	78	70	80	78
13	**Average**	8.5	8.4	87.3	80.6	86.9	85.1

Figure 8–31

Using the updated grade book/spreadsheet

needs only to set up a form that replicates the types of calculations that would have to be done by hand and then save the template. Whenever the calculation has to be done again, the template can be loaded and the problem addressed.

Commercially Available Grade Books

Now that we have examined the process of building an electronic grade book on a spreadsheet program, it would be worth our while to evaluate commercially available grade book software. The fundamental question we must ask is "Is the commercial product flexible enough to meet our needs?" Can we adapt the software to meet our requirements or will we have to change our grading system? Another question to ask is "Does it provide us with information about our students' performance beyond what is available in a grade book that we would create on a spreadsheet?"

Whether creating your own personalized grade book or purchasing one that is commercially available, it would serve your interests well to review the analysis phase of the problem-solving process. Clearly define the requisites of your grading system, understand all of its component tasks, and proceed as your grade requirements, time, budget, and personal preferences dictate.

For those choosing a spreadsheet rather than a grade book program, note that there are other spreadsheet programs currently available for use in the classroom in addition to *Microsoft Excel* and the programs found in *AppleWorks* and *Microsoft Works*. A top-selling one for elementary students in grades 3 and higher is *The Cruncher*™. In addition to the teacher- and student-friendly tutorial programs, this package contains 20 cross-curriculum learning projects and a host of ways to integrate spreadsheets into the curriculum.

SUMMARY

An electronic spreadsheet is a two-dimensional matrix of columns and rows. The intersection of a column and row is called a cell. The power of this software lies in the fact that cells relate one to another, allowing the contents of one cell to affect another cell. Cells may contain text, values, or formulas. Complex mathematical, statistical, and logical relationships can be described as formulas. Powerful functions are embedded in the software and can be called up by the user. Since the results of cell relationships are displayed and changing one cell immediately affects the results of the relationship, spreadsheets are often referred to as "what if" tools and are often used to make projections or forecast results.

Applying a nonlinear problem-solving approach allows us to appreciate that this approach permits divergent-thinking individuals to determine their own pattern without having a hierarchical structure imposed on them. A linear problem-solving strategy that might appeal more to a sequential learner was also examined and applied to the design of a grade book.

A number of examples were given in which a spreadsheet was used to predict results; to promote accuracy of the calculation of whole numbers and fractions; to calculate sums and averages; to generate graphs; to convert metric and English measurements; and, functioning as a database, to sort text.

Graphs can represent abstract numerical data in a concrete, clear, and interesting manner. They can display relationships that would be more difficult to convey in a text or verbal mode. As visuals, they capture attention and promote greater retention of information. The analysis and interpretation of graphs has become an important subject in the K–12 curriculum.

Ideally, a spreadsheet would become a tool for the teacher to examine options and to forecast results. It would be taught to a student, who could use it to answer "what if" questions in any academic discipline in which the act of problem solving dealt with the examination of comparisons. Along with graphics programs, word processors, and database managers, spreadsheets are programs that truly exemplify the concept of using the computer as a tool to extend our human capabilities.

CHAPTER EXERCISES

To complete the specified exercises on-line, go to the Chapter Exercises Module in Chapter 8 of the Companion Website.

1. Thinking of the computer as a management tool in education, describe the application of a spreadsheet to three management tasks faced by a teacher on a regular basis.
2. Thinking of the computer as a forecasting tool, describe the application of a spreadsheet to three tasks that a student might face.
3. Design a spreadsheet to record performances on a softball team. Calculate individual and team batting averages and on-base percentages for each game and for the season.
4. Design a spreadsheet to calculate a budget for the first Thanksgiving. From a reference source, identify the food items that were most likely present.

Estimate the number of portions needed. Calculate the cost in terms of today's prices.

5. Design a spreadsheet to convert your weight in pounds to kilograms, and your height in feet and inches to centimeters.

6. You are responsible for raising $2,000 in income for each home football game played. Explain your problem-solving strategy and design a spreadsheet to accomplish your goal.

7. Take a poll of your classmates to determine the five cities in which they would prefer to live. Assign a weighting of 5 for their first choice, 4 for their second choice, etc. Design a spreadsheet to record their preferences and identify an overall ranking for the cities chosen.

8. As a variation of exercise 7, design a spreadsheet to record the name and five livability factors for a city (e.g., population size, geographical location, climate, availability of public transit, education level). Rate each factor from one to five. Include a cell that averages these factors. Ask students to rate any five cities. Analyze the class results.

9. Record the gender of each student in your class and the length of time he or she has lived at the current address. Rank order the data from shortest to longest occupancy for each gender. Using the graphing capability of an integrated package or a stand-alone graphing program, create a line graph showing the occupancy ranges for each gender. Describe the results to a classmate.

10. The following problem is derived from an article entitled "Can You Manage?" (Hastie, 1992). Suppose you are a biologist responsible for managing a healthy, stable deer population in a given area. You must regulate the size of the deer herd according to the habitat that supports it. In other words, you must determine an annual deer harvest so as not to exceed the carrying capacity of the habitat and ultimately destroy it.

• Design a spreadsheet to manage four populations of deer. For Group One, hunters will be allowed to harvest 25 percent of the summer population; Group Two, 50 percent; Group Three, 75 percent; Group Four, 0 percent. Allow all groups to reproduce at a rate of 50 percent (new fawns equal one-half of the number of deer in the group each year).

• For each group, (a) start with 20 deer the first year, (b) for year two, remove number harvested, and (c) add the yearly fawn crop. Continue this process for three more years for a total of five years.

Answer the following questions:

• Which populations decreased in size? Which increased? Which remained the same?

• Suppose you determine the winter carrying capacity of each habitat to be 20 deer. Which harvest rate would allow you to do this and still maintain a reasonably stable population?

• Could you continue to harvest at the same rate each year or would you have to adjust the harvest rate in some years? If so, what rate would you use?

PORTFOLIO DEVELOPMENT EXERCISES

To complete this exercise on-line, go to the Digital Portfolio Module in Chapter 8 of the Companion Website.

One of the NETS•S standards covered in this chapter was "Students use technology resources for solving problems and making informed decisions" under *Category 6: Technology problem-solving and decision-making tools.* Begin to develop your own portfolio of lesson plans that demonstrates your ability to have your students reach the NETS•S standards.

For more information on developing digital portfolios go to Digital Portfolio Module on the Companion Website www.prenhall. com/forcier

1. Design a lesson plan activity for elementary, middle school, or high school students in which they use a spreadsheet program to examine and make a decision about a problem. Try to combine several functions found in spreadsheet programs. The number that you use should depend on the grade level. Younger students may only use simple tools (relating cells, simple math functions, etc.). Older students will be required to use more sophisticated tools (multiple functions, formulas, charting, etc.). This lesson should demonstrate that your students have achieved the standard. Be sure to include a system of evaluation for your students' understanding and competence to ensure that they have met this standard.

2. Adapt the lesson plan activity you developed in exercise 1 for students to evaluate each others' work.

GLOSSARY

absolute reference A formula is meant to always refer to an exact cell regardless of the placement of the formula cell within the spreadsheet. (Sometimes called fixed reference.)

active cell The cell that is selected and ready for data entry or editing.

cell The intersection of a row and a column in a spreadsheet.

data entry bar See *formula bar.*

debugging The process of removing all logic and construction errors.

documentation Written explanations supporting program maintenance and use.

formula bar The area at the top of the screen that displays the content of the active cell and that can be edited.

functions Built-in mathematical formulas used to calculate cell values.

labels The text descriptor related to adjacent data.

spreadsheet Software that accepts data in a matrix of columns and rows, with their intersections called cells. One cell can relate to any other cell or ranges of cells on the matrix by formula.

template A blank form in a spreadsheet or file manager program.

REFERENCES & SUGGESTED READINGS

Godson, S. (2002, December). Optimization analysis of projectile motion using spreadsheets. *The Physics Teacher, 40*(9), 523–26.

Goodwin, A. (2002, March). Using a spreadsheet to explore melting, dissolving and phase diagrams. *School Science Review, 83*(304), 105–8.

Hastie, B. (1992, May–June). Can you manage? *Oregon Wildlife,* 9–10.

Howell, D., Morrow, J., & Summerville, J. (2002). *Using Excel in the classroom.* Corwin Press, Inc.

Johnson, D. R. (2002, September). Use your spreadsheet as a project management tool. *School Business Affairs, 68*(8), 17–20.

Killmer, K., & George, N. (2002, February). Show and tell in real time: Link a spreadsheet to a PowerPoint slide for up-to-the-minute visuals. *Journal of Accountancy, 193*(2), 57–64.

Lewis, P. (2002, November). Spreadsheet magic: The basic spreadsheet is a powerful tool for teaching. *Learning and Leading with Technology, 30*(3), 36–41.

Paul, J., & Kaiser, C. (1996, May). Do women live longer than men? Investigating graveyard data with computers. *Learning and Leading with Technology, 23*(8), 13–15.

Riley, K. (2002, Fall). Using spreadsheets to estimate the volatility of stock prices. *Mathematics and Computer Education, 36*(3), 240–46.

9

Learning with Database Tools

1. What is a database?

2. What are its component parts?

3. How do you find information in a database?

4. What is a database manager and how does it work?

5. What are the important concepts related to data storage and retrieval?

6. How can you create and use files with a database manager?

7. How could problem-solving strategies be applied to designing databases?

8. How might you and your students use a database as a productivity tool to store, retrieve, and analyze information?

9. Following a linear problem-solving approach, how can a community resource file be developed in a database?

10. How might you develop a test item database to prepare objective exams?

This chapter covers information your students will need to meet standards in three NETS•S categories. Databases are wonderful tools to enhance learning, increase productivity, and produce creative works, thus meeting both standards found under *Category 3: Technology productivity tools.* Databases are a very important tool in research, and sections on database design and problem solving with databases fit neatly under standards found in both *Category 5: Technology research tools* and *Category 6: Technology problem-solving and decision-making tools.* Databases are one of the most useful and versatile tools about which you will ever learn. They can be used in your teaching and in your classroom in many ways. Introduce them to your students and incorporate them into your lessons. Databases are wonderful tools to store and manipulate data. They can also be used in association with a word processing application to quickly and easily merge data into documents and produce letters and envelopes using the word processor's mail merge feature. Databases are an important set of tools for your students to learn and understand.

Information is organized, structured data. Data are everywhere and in themselves, are useless. They are constantly flowing into our minds through our senses. Fortunately, we are very selective in attending to them and we ignore most of them. Our conscious and subconscious minds filter data, accepting some and rejecting the rest. We have the ability to organize the data we accept and give it meaning. Only then do data become information. Information is power. Information literacy is a survival skill we teach to our students. As they become increasingly information literate, they will

NET•S Standards Addressed in This Chapter

3. Technology productivity tools
   - Students use technology tools to enhance learning, increase productivity, and promote creativity.
   - Students use productivity tools to collaborate in constructing technology-enhanced models, prepare publications, and produce other creative works.

5. Technology research tools
   - Students use technology to locate, evaluate, and collect information from a variety of sources.
   - Students use technology tools to process data and report results.
   - Students evaluate and select new information resources and technological innovations based on the appropriateness for specific tasks.

6. Technology problem-solving and decision-making tools
   - Students use technology resources for solving problems and making informed decisions.
   - Students employ technology in the development of strategies for solving problems in the real world.

A list of the ISTE/NCATE standards addressed in this chapter is available in the Standards Module in the Companion Website www.prenhall.com/forcier

understand how data are organized and how to sift through and manipulate the data to access information. Information is purposefully structured data often stored in a database. As Figure 9–1 attempts to conceptualize, a database manager is software designed to structure aural, visual, and textual data and store, organize, access, and correlate it in order to produce information, thereby giving meaning to data.

Database managers not only allow us to input, store, and restructure information but they also give us the ability to pick and choose the parts of our information that we would like to display.

We commonly use databases in our everyday lives. Examples include an inventory sheet of sports equipment in the physical education department, the student records system at your school, and your holiday or birthday card list at home. One of the most ubiquitous databases is the telephone directory. It is a collection of data organized according to a clear structure. In order to derive useful information from this database, we must understand its structure. Our telephone directory (database) is a collection of facts (data) organized into a series of records that each contain an individual's, a family's, or an establishment's name, street address, and phone number. The phone number is a unique identifier. Only one person, one family, one institution, or one business can have that phone number. When we search the phone book, we are usually looking for someone's phone number. Using the alphabetical listing of names as the key, we find the name and corresponding phone number as part of each individual record. The record is composed of all of the data related to that individual entry (i.e., name, address, and phone number). It would be an extremely difficult task to

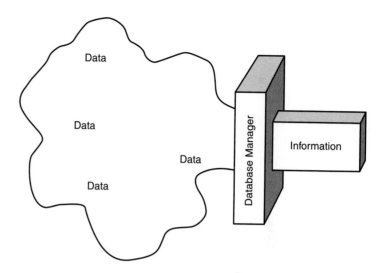

Figure 9–1
A database manager
transforms data into
information

find the phone number in a regular phone book if we knew only the address but not the name. Although the *purpose* of the phone directory is to list the telephone numbers, the name is the *key* to its successful use.

We have defined the concept of a tool as something used to facilitate the performance of a task. A database manager is an appropriate tool in the management of information if it meets one or more of the following rubrics:

- It increases the speed of information acquisition.
- It increases the ease of information acquisition.
- It increases the quality of the information acquired in terms of both accuracy and completeness.
- It improves the dissemination of information.

We owe it to our students at all grade levels to help them develop data management and information retrieval skills. We are fortunate to have at our disposal database managers designed for the personal computer. Microsoft Access™, FileMaker Pro, and AppleWorks are three commonly used databases in schools. The examples used in this chapter were created with FileMaker Pro, a popular, easy-to-use program available for both the Windows and Macintosh platforms. At this writing, it is by far the most popular database application, though Microsoft Access is gaining fast. Files created on one platform run seamlessly on the other.

We have watched third grade students use a FileMaker Pro file created by their teacher. This file related to fish that live in the ocean. The students entered data and then sorted the data and searched the database for specific characteristics such as the depth zone in which certain fish live. Insights were developed as different characteristics were compared. The interaction of these students provided a testimonial to the user-friendliness of this program.

This chapter deals with concepts related to understanding, creating, and using a data file. It examines a database manager and its component parts. It discusses Boolean logic and the searching and sorting of data to develop search strategies. Some concepts associated with database management are fairly abstract. In an effort to bring them to a more concrete level, we use examples created in FileMaker Pro.

Advantages of Developing and Using Databases

In designing a database, students are engaged in activities that contribute to the development of organizational skills and higher-order thinking skills. They refine a specific vocabulary. They research information on a given topic. They verify the accuracy of data, note the similarities and differences among data examined, and explore relationships. They classify information discovered. They consider how information might be communicated effectively to others.

In searching for information in a database, students develop and refine information retrieval skills. They improve their ability to recognize patterns, trends, and other relationships. They are encouraged to think critically by interpreting data and testing hypotheses. All of these skills have real-world applications and contribute to preparing students to take their place as productive members of society.

FILE/DATABASE MANAGERS

What is a database? A **database** is an organized, structured collection of facts about a particular topic. We studied spreadsheets in the previous chapter, which are also a structured collection of facts. Spreadsheets and databases differ in that spreadsheets are preformatted in columns and rows and are designed to deal mainly, though as we have seen, not exclusively, with numerical data. Spreadsheets also present broad information rather than focus on any individual entry. Databases are much more versatile. They are designed to deal with both text and numerical data and their reports can be formatted in a wide variety of ways. These reports can present data ranging from concern dealing with an individual record to summary information relating to the entire file.

At times the facts in a database are grouped together in subsets called **files.** A database may consist of a single file or a number of related files. Computer systems for file management are sometimes called **database managers.** The term implies the capability of managing a number of files of data simultaneously or at least in a closely related manner. Programs with this capability are properly called **relational database managers.** Software designed to manage a single file is properly referred to as a **file manager.** Through popular usage, however, distinctions have blurred and the terms have come to be used interchangeably, with file managers now being called database managers or simply databases. We accede to this change in terminology: When reference is made to *database,* we treat it synonymously with *file.*

Database Operation

What is a database manager and how does it actually work? Figure 9–2 presents the seven major functions of a database manager and indicates that database management software is designed to allow the user to create a structure for the storage, manipulation, and retrieval of data. Once data are entered into the file, the software allows the user to act on those data in a variety of ways. A good **file management** system lets you do four basic things: gather related data into a central collection, find specific data to meet a particular need, reorder those data in various ways, and re-

• **File design:**	Establishes structure of file by creating data fields of appropriate type
• **Form design:**	Creates a layout of fields and where they will appear displayed on the screen or printed on paper
• **Record editing:**	Allows data to be entered, altered, and deleted
• **Record finding:**	Facilitates the selection of certain records while ignoring others
• **Record sorting:**	Organizes records according to some field order
• **Report creation:**	Finds specific records, sorts them, and arranges them on a selected form
• **Report printing:**	Displays the information on paper or on the screen

Figure 9–2
Functions performed by a database manager

trieve the product of that reordering in a useful form. New data can be created through calculations based on existing data entered into the file. The products of file managers fall into two main categories: the real-time, "on-line" search for specific information; and the ability to print reports organized in a particular fashion.

File Design. The individual data item is the most discrete element of a database and is called a data field, or simply a **field.** In the case of the telephone directory, a phone number is an individual field, as is the address and the name. Fields can contain text, numeric values, dates, pictures, sounds, movies, and even links to Websites. Fields can contain calculations that perform mathematical operations on other numeric fields within the record and store the resulting values (e.g., multiplying the contents of two other fields). Fields can also contain summaries of data across a number of records and display the result (calculate the total or the average of specific field values for a group of records). After each field has been defined, this information is saved as the file structure (how the data in each record are stored).

Field **labels** are created to assist recognition of fields on the screen or in reports. Figure 9–3 illustrates fields and their labels. Keep in mind that labels simply identify or describe the fields where the data are actually stored.

The data record, or simply **record,** is the building block of the file. A record is composed of all the related fields. An individual record in the phone book contains all the data related to that entry (i.e., name, address, and phone number). A file is the aggregation of all the records. The phone book file is the collection of all the records for a city, town, or region. A file, then, is composed of individual records

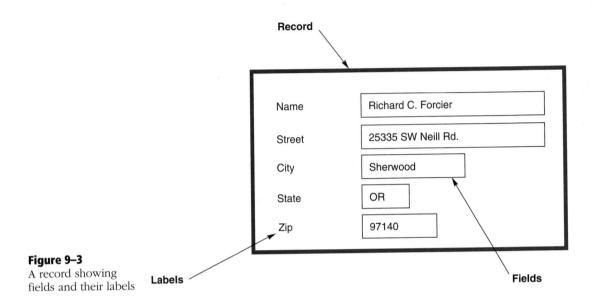

Figure 9–3
A record showing
fields and their labels

that are themselves composed of individual fields. A *database* may be made up of several files.

Form Design. As fields are defined, labels are created and grouped together, creating a **form,** or **layout,** which appears on the screen with areas where data can be entered. It is common to create several layouts for a file including a columnar one that is referred to as a *List View.* In this layout, a different record is displayed on each line. (This resembles a spreadsheet where a row represents one record and each column represents a different field in that record.) Records can be sorted on the basis of any field and in any order with the results displayed in a convenient way to scan through all, or selected records in the file.

Once data are entered, the layout that is selected or created can be thought of as a window through which to examine data in selected fields. Most file managers allow a good deal of freedom in custom designing a layout. Figure 9–4 shows a layout on the left, where fields and their labels are included to facilitate data entry; a second layout on the right containing only the fields to be used as a mailing label (notice that graphics such as the edge trim in this example may be added to a layout); and a third layout that is in list view. This last layout could be sorted by last name, by city, by phone, or by any other field that would yield useful information. Layouts are created based on the information required by the user. Fields are individually chosen to appear in a layout and their most appropriate position.

Data Entry and Record Editing. During data entry, the file manager displays the field labels on the screen, places the cursor at the first position in the first field, and facilitates the entry of data (e.g., letters, numbers, pictures, or sounds). The user is free to alter or change the data in any field in any of the records at any time. To edit records, you place the cursor in the appropriate field and type the change.

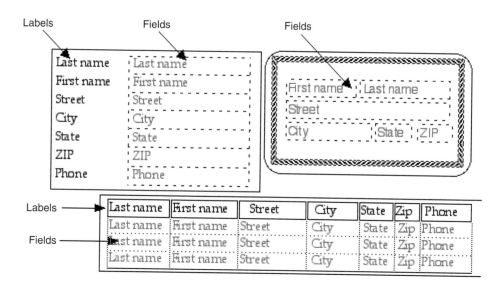

Figure 9–4
Three different
layouts

Record Finding and Sorting. The software allows the user to perform a **logical search,** sometimes called a **query,** to select records based on a wide range of criteria. For example, an *exact match* of a value in a field can be requested (e.g., find field value *equaling* "Francis" = *Francis*). *A match containing a value* in a field can be requested (e.g., find field value *containing* "Francis" = *Francis, Francis*can, San *Francis*co, etc.). Many other searches can be performed, including those greater than, less than, or not equal to a value. Searches can be performed on ranges of data by specifying the extremes of the range (i.e., minimum and maximum values). Searches can find all the records except those indicated to be omitted. Compound searches can be constructed to examine data in multiple fields using the **Boolean connectors** illustrated in Figure 9–5. The use of the AND connector restricts the search and makes it more specific. The use of the OR connector expands the search, making it less specific. The NOT connector removes those records having the second search criterion from the set of records otherwise found.

For example, as illustrated in Figure 9–6, one could search a student file by gender and address for all records of girls who live in Springfield, a specific town in the attendance area. The search would be "girls" AND "Springfield." *Both criteria* would have to be present in the same record in order to select that record. However, one could search the file for records of girls or records of all students (boys or girls) who

Figure 9–5
Boolean connectors

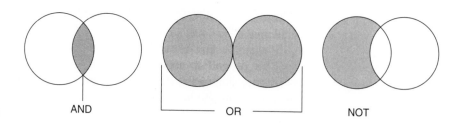

AND   OR   NOT

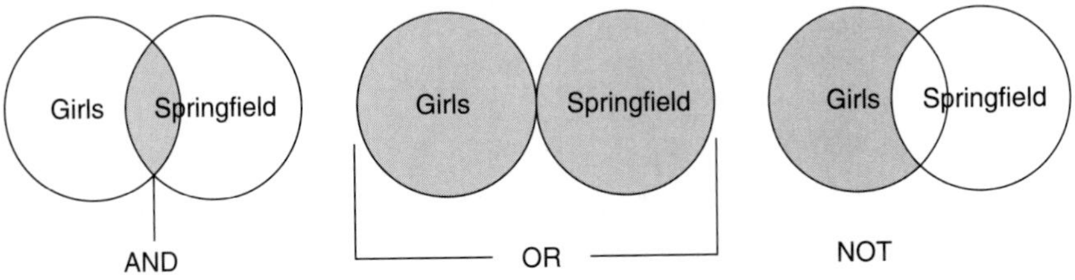

Figure 9–6
Selection results
using Boolean
connectors

live in Springfield. The search would be "girls" OR "Springfield." *Either criterion*
would have to be present in a record in order to select that record. All records of
girls plus all records of the specified town (both boys and girls) would be selected.
A popular way of distinguishing between the two selection connectors is to remember that "OR is more." The NOT connector would be used to find all girls who are
not living in Springfield.

Let's briefly review the effect of these Boolean connectors. When using the AND
connector, you are applying a subsequent criterion only to the information subset
created by previous search criteria, not to the total data pool. The resulting subset
will always be equal to or smaller than the previous one. The OR connector broad-
ens your search and includes the greatest number of items from the original data
pool. The NOT connector excludes items from the search. The AND and the NOT
connectors increase the specificity of the resulting information.

Data can be sorted or arranged in a prescribed alphabetic, numeric, or chronological order in either ascending (e.g., A–Z, 1–99, 1941–2000) or descending (e.g.,
Z–A, 99–1, 2000–1941) fashion. This organization of records within the file can be
based on any individual field. Most software also allows nested, or multilevel, sorts.
For example, one could sort a grade book in ascending alphabetical order by last
name and then as a second level, by first name. This would create an alphabetic list
of students by last name and then, if any students shared the same last name, the
sort would alphabetize those students by first name.

Report Creation and Printing. To develop a report for printing information from the
file, the user first selects the appropriate layout, then selects the records to be included
in the report (finds the records indicated by the search criteria), and, finally, designates
their order (sorts the records found in ascending or descending order in a particular
field). For example, to print a report consisting of students' first names, last names, and
birth dates, the user would:

- Designate the size of the page and create column titles that would serve as
  labels: *First Name, Last Name, Birth Date.*
- Choose the records to be printed: All records? Only those after a certain birth date?
- Define the order: Alphabetic by last name? Birth date order?

In this example, the report might be sorted by birth date, and, if two or more students had the same birth date, these names would be sorted alphabetically, by last
name. This technique is referred to as a **nested sort,** or **multilevel sort.**

Many different reports can be produced from the same file. In our example, another useful report would print mailing labels on adhesive label stock. Both the mailing labels and the student lists constitute reports. By adding fields for grade level and teacher's name, reports could be generated, presenting a list of students by grade or teacher, thereby increasing the usefulness of the file.

The power of database managers is in the fact that the information can be entered once, and many reports can be generated simply by instructing the software how to organize the data. You do not have to rework the collected information by hand. All of your time and energy goes into data entry and maintenance. Very little time is spent generating reports.

Another useful feature of a database is the ability to combine the information it contains with a word processing document using the mail merge feature of the word processing program. The mail merge feature allows specific database fields to be printed in specific areas of the word processing document. Using this feature it is very easy to produce customized letters, placeholders, reports, and so on.

Using a Database Manager to Develop a File

To make the best use of a file management system, you must be able to meet the following four requirements:

1. *Understand your information needs.* Know the information you want your system to manage. Analyze what you are doing, what information is used, and how it is being used. How could the processing of that information be improved?
2. *Specify your output needs.* Although you cannot predict everything you will need from your file, you know the reports that are commonly needed and the information that is frequently accessed. Design those report formats.
3. *Specify your input needs.* Once you have determined output needs, input needs become obvious. Take advantage of the features of your file manager that will simplify, expedite, and improve the accuracy of data entry.
4. *Determine the file organization.* Consider the file input and output requirements in completing the record design.

When contemplating the use of a file manager, analyze what you are doing and determine what you would like to do. If you cannot design a way to perform a task using paper and pencil, a file manager probably can't help you.

PROBLEM SOLVING WITH DATABASES

Let us review the linear problem-solving method discussed in Chapter 8 that might be used by an individual with a sequential learning style. Figure 9–7 illustrates the two phases of sequential problem solving, the analysis phase and the synthesis phase. In the analysis phase, we develop a clear definition and understanding of the problem and of the component tasks that relate to the problem. In the synthesis

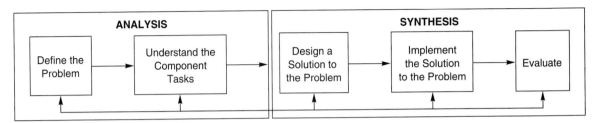

Figure 9–7
A sequential approach to problem solving

phase, we plan our strategy and carry out the solution to the problem. Evaluation provides feedback that could modify decisions made in both the analysis and synthesis phases.

Analysis

Remember that *analysis* is defined as the separation of a whole into its component parts for the purpose of examination and interpretation. The need is to clearly define the problem and clearly identify the specific tasks that must be accomplished. In defining the problem, you establish a need.

Problem Statement. *A teacher wishes to make the best use of the local resources in the community.*

In an effort to bring the problem-solving process into sharper focus and to understand component tasks, let's consider the management of some resources external to the classroom. Apply the problem-solving process just reviewed and illustrated in Figure 9–7 to accomplish the stated task. Begin by analyzing the required output and formulating questions, such as those that follow, to help determine what is necessary to produce this result.

Understanding Components. What are the resources? How do they align with the curriculum? How might they be accessed by teachers and students?

These items could certainly be further expanded, refined, and organized in outline fashion. Chapter 6 discusses effective outlining. An outlining strategy is often helpful in reaching a better understanding of the components. The top-down outlining approach illustrated in Figure 9–8 is one that proceeds from global to specific concerns and facilitates systematic analysis. As we attack the problem of managing external resources, we must make sure that we understand what is required of the software *before* we attempt to solve the problem. Otherwise, we might select the wrong software or spend a lot of time and effort producing something that will not meet our expectations. The outline presented in Figure 9–8 identifies type, curriculum areas, and access as the major headings in response to the preceding questions. It refines each heading using more specific subheadings and, in some instances, even more specific third- and fourth-level subheadings.

```
RESOURCES
    Type
                        Industrial corporations
                        Retail commercial ventures
                                Goods
                                Services
                        Government agencies
                        Nonprofit corporations
                        Individuals

    Curriculum areas
                    Occupations
                    Social studies/language arts
                    Science/mathematics
                    Performing arts
                    Health/physical education
    Access
                    Contact
                            Name, address, phone number
                    When available
                    Come to the school
                        To the classroom
                                    Speakers/demonstrations
                                    Film/video
                        To an assembly
                    Host on their site
                        Group size
                        Safety issues
```

Figure 9–8
Outlining
components of a
classroom resources
file

Synthesis

Synthesis is defined as combining elements to form a coherent whole. The primary purpose of the synthesis phase of problem solving is to help ensure that solutions designed to address the identified tasks are carried out in an effective and efficient manner and that the results are evaluated.

Field Definition. The solution to the information management problem just outlined involves designing a database to store relevant data and to allow easy retrieval of useful information. Referring to the outline developed in Figure 9–8, a resources file can be developed by defining appropriate fields.

Figure 9–9 presents the fields derived from the outline presented in Figure 9–8. Notice that a field to store the record entry date is also included so that the information can be examined on a periodic basis to determine its validity or usefulness. We cannot overemphasize the importance of first knowing how the data will be

Resource type	[ ]
Curriculum areas	[ ]
Contact name	[ ]
Contact address	[ ]
Contact phone number	[ ]
Available date	[ ]
Available time	[ ]
Location	[ ]
Presentation type	[ ]
Group size	[ ]
Safety issues	[ ]
Record entry date	[ ]

Figure 9–9
Fields defined for the classroom resources file

manipulated and reported. Will we be merging this data into a document? If so, should we have had separate fields for last name and first name? Title (Mr., Ms., Mrs., Dr.)? Will we ever have to sort by city or state?

Error Trapping. Accurate data entry is essential to the production of meaningful information from a database. Error trapping is a process of designing safeguards into your solution. In error trapping, a designer makes sure that the program does not accept entry of incorrect data. If certain values must be excluded when entering data into the file, then a technique must be used to ensure that the unwanted data cannot be entered, thereby preventing potential errors that could cause the program to yield faulty information.

Depending on the capability and sophistication of the software being used, the *Resource type* field in the *Resources file* example could present checkboxes on the screen, as shown in Figure 9–10, representing the available entries rather than depending on input typed from the keyboard. The *Curriculum areas* field might present the user with a predetermined list from which to make a selection. Checkboxes and predetermined lists also aid in sorting data at a later time by standardizing responses and limiting choices to set options. As illustrated in Figure 9–11, the *Available date* field might be restricted to accept only unique values to prevent double scheduling and dates that fall between 9/15/06 and 6/15/07, for example, to make sure that the date falls in the correct school year. It can prohibit a user from overriding the restriction and display an appropriate message when an attempt is made to enter incorrect data.

Another example of error trapping data entry in a student records database is to designate a range of values from 0 to 4.0 in a field designed to store a numerical equivalent of F to A course grades. Limiting data entry to this range would catch typing errors, such as a double-key press, that might attempt to enter a nonsensical value of 33, for example.

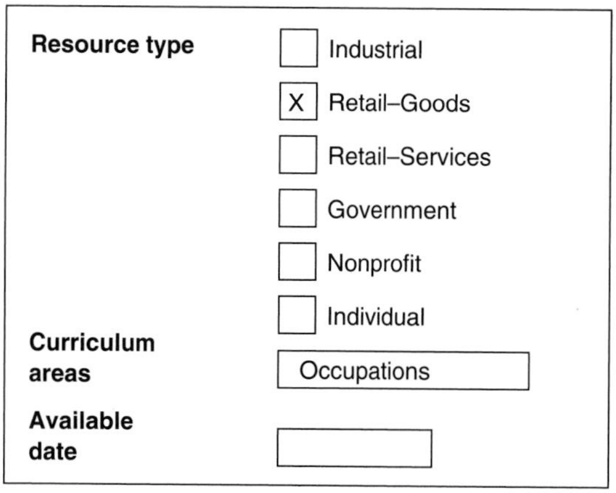

Figure 9–10
Checkboxes to
control data entry

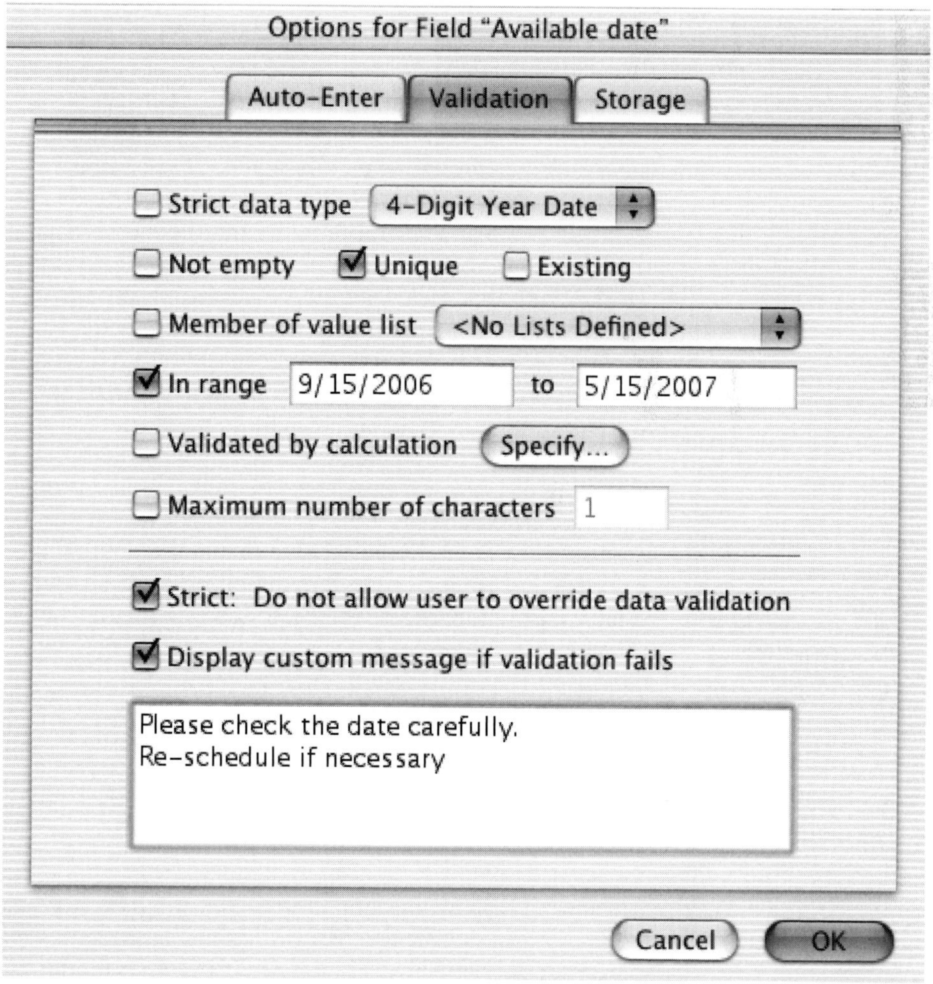

Figure 9–11
Field validation
controls designed
to trap errors

Debugging. Debugging is the process of correcting logic and construction errors. In designing a database, it is especially important to verify calculation and summary fields. As we have seen in the preceding chapter, an often-used debugging procedure is to give the program some test data that will produce easily verifiable output. If the results are other than expected, debugging allows you to verify the correctness of your data entry and calculations, the appropriateness of the functions you used, and the logic of your design.

REVIEW OF DATABASE FEATURES

Following are some features readily found on a number of database managers currently on the market.

- *Accuracy control.* Database managers should include the ability to restrict or evaluate data entry to ensure its accuracy.
- *Data entry automation.* Data, such as a serial number or the date, might be automatically entered when a new record is created. In order to simplify and control data entry, a layout might include checkboxes, pop-up lists, or buttons to be clicked with the mouse rather than requiring data always to be entered through the keyboard.
- *Field definition.* Fields should be able to be defined as text, number (value), date, time, picture, sound, movie, calculation, and summary.
- *Finding records.* The user should be able to find records using the Boolean connectors of AND, OR, and NOT as well as the operators < (less than), > (greater than), and = (exact match).
- *Layout.* The better database managers allow the user a great deal of control in designing the data layouts (forms or views). Some programs include a number of preformatted layouts along with graphics tools to enhance their appearance.
- *Sorting.* The user should be able to sort the entire file or a found set of records in ascending or descending order. Multiple-level or nested sorts are very useful. They allow records to be sorted first by the contents of one field (e.g., last name) and then by the contents of another field (e.g., first name).

A database manager evaluation form may be examined on the Companion Website http://www.prenhall.com/forcier

As is the case for word processors and spreadsheets, database managers are available either as individual programs or as part of integrated software packages.

CURRICULUM APPLICATIONS OF DATABASES

Teachers want help in alleviating the paperwork demands made on them. They want help accomplishing activities that do not involve students directly and are quite often done outside of actual class time. If the time required to perform these tasks could be decreased, the teacher would have more time to devote to working with students.

INTO THE CLASSROOM:
Using a Database to Bring Students Together

Why a database? My goal was to come up with a project for my fourth-grade student Travis, who has a hearing impairment, to work on with a hearing peer. I wanted Travis to have the opportunity to learn some new computer skills, do some problem solving with a peer, and practice his communication skills. I needed a problem-solving activity and I've been interested in investigating uses of databases with my elementary students. Learning ways to organize information is always a valuable activity for learners, as is analyzing and evaluating data. A bonus when choosing a database as an analysis tool is the opportunity for the students to grasp the importance of planning the structure of the database and making decisions about its contents before they actually set it up. My plan was to guide Travis and a partner of his choice in developing a class database. This type of project would involve the whole fourth-grade class in which Travis is mainstreamed. Travis and his partner would also serve in the role of mentors who would give their classmates their first exposure to the possibilities inherent with database use. The two mentors would design the database and learn the skills of entering and manipulating the data, and then share those skills with the rest of the class.

Travis chose Richard as his partner and both boys were enthusiastic about jumping right into the project, but this was their first exposure to a database and I wanted to make sure they really understood what a database is and what it can do. Starting with the concrete, I created a "paper database" with note cards to represent fields and labels. I showed Travis and Richard pictures of three children and asked them to tell me about them.

When they told me that one was a boy named Amos who was 8 years old and weighed 63 pounds, I put the information onto my note card "fields" and made a "record" about Amos. We repeated the procedure for Kate and Zoe and discussed number versus text fields. Cards enabled us to sort and find. I showed Richard and Travis a ClarisWorks database centering around Amos, Kate, and Zoe that I had created on the computer, and then the boys "challenged" the computer to find information as quickly and sort cards as accurately as they could. We discussed ascending and descending order and even arranged the fields in Browse and List views. During this activity, everything we did with the computer database, we mirrored with our paper database. It turned out to be a very successful unit!

Susan Monahan
Instructional Technology Facilitator
Austin Independent School District
Austin, Texas

Students need access to increasing amounts of information if they are to construct their own knowledge. Information organization and retrieval skills can be taught using databases. The database is an ideal tool for students to gather and arrange data, examine trends and relationships, and test theories.

We have described the file, a term that has become interchangeable with database, as an organized, structured collection of facts and have examined its operation. We understand that it can handle text and values, that it is founded on the ability to group data fields into records that can be selected and ordered. We recognize that database managers have powerful built-in formulas. We are also beginning to explore some of the functional uses of databases to record data, organize them according to specific criteria, calculate values, sort data, and print reports.

Several activities are presented to illustrate how a database might be used as a tool by the student or the teacher. The examples present database applications in a variety of subject areas and grade levels and can be easily modified and adapted to individual lessons or units of instruction. If students are to capitalize on the power of the database manager as a tool and use it with confidence, they must develop an understanding of its application and a reasonably high level of skill in its use.

The presidents file shown in Figure 9–12 gathers data relevant to each U.S. president's term of office and provides opportunity to generate interesting information. Many of the reports are in the List View format. Analyses could be made by home state, party affiliation, and prior employment for example.

The geography file suggested in Figure 9–13 might be set up for all countries of the world or only for countries in a specific geographic region. The process of entering data will require the students to conduct some research to gather the relevant facts. As information about the countries is studied, students could be encouraged to suggest additional fields for the database. Specific inquiries might be made, such as "Which country has the largest landmass? Which country has the highest population density? What countries have significant rivers or mountains? Which countries are Spanish-speaking? What countries have the same ethnic groups?" Once information is generated, relationships can be explored. Does the area of the country relate directly to its population density? Is climate related to population density? Referring to a map of the region, do any of the physical features (rivers, mountains, etc.) form political boundaries? Examining countries whose citizens speak the same language, do they share something else in common? Were they part of a political union or an empire? A number of other relationships can be explored based on the students' interest and need for information and the teacher's direction.

A travel agency classroom simulation could be designed to explore existing countries in the database and to determine interests of students. Students could ask to go mountain climbing, to spend time in the sun, or to go where they could practice a foreign language they are learning. As students reveal a variety of interests, additional fields could be added to the database on that basis.

As an extension of the example illustrated in Figure 9–13, a database could be designed and data entered by students who are using the program Where in the World Is Carmen Sandiego? The following fields could be defined: Country, City, Currency, Language, Chief Products, Points of Interest, Bodies of Water, Mountains, Deserts, and Miscellaneous. As students encounter clues, they could search the database and,

A 30-day demo copy of FileMaker Pro for Windows and Macintosh platforms and the actual files of the examples in this chapter are included for your use on the Companion CD. If this copy will no longer function, you may download another demo copy from the FileMaker Pro Website www.filemaker.com

Last Name [_____]
First Name [_____]
Party [_____]
Prior Employment [_____]
Vice President [_____]
Term of Office [_____]
Rank [_____]
Home State [___]
Event 1. [_____]
Event 2. [_____]
Event 3. [_____]

SUGGESTED LESSON: The process of entering data into the fields will require the students to conduct some research to gather the relevant facts. Students will be able to print out the following informational tables:

1. Chronological list of presidents
2. Alphabetical list by last names of presidents to find information pertinent to a specific president
3. List of presidents sorted by party to examine voting patterns
4. List of presidents sorted by home state to examine any geographical patterns
5. List of presidents and events to reveal expressions of party philosophy at the time
6. Alphabetical list of the prior employment of presidents or a selection of only one employment such as attorney

The following printouts could serve as games, as contests, and for drill and practice.

1. Leave a blank column for the president's name and print a column of events for a selected date range based on the term of office field. Students must indicate the president who was in office when each event occurred.

2. Print two lists in alphabetical order, one of the presidents and the other of events, with the objective being to match presidents and events.

3. Print any of the following reports with a blank column requiring information to be entered.

POSSIBLE REPORTS:

a. Rank	Term dates	First/last name	Party	Vice president
b. Last/first name	Rank	Term dates	Party	Vice president
c. Party	First/last name	Rank	Term dates	
d. Home state	First/last name	Term dates		
e. Last name	Party	Event 1_____		
		Event 2_____		
		Event 3_____		
f. Prior employment	President	Term dates		

Figure 9–12
Presidents file

if results were not achieved, they could research the relevant information and create a new record in the database. The database grows more powerful as more clues are encountered, and students refine their information-gathering skills.

The recommended books file suggested in Figure 9–14 would be created by and for students. Unlike the previous examples, it would be used mainly for on-line searching. It is not intended to replace a library automation system's public access catalog but, rather, to be a file of student opinion regarding books in the school library.

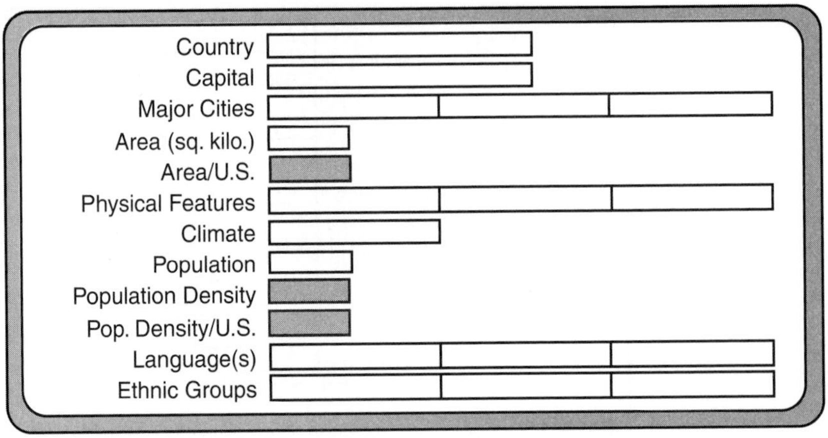

SUGGESTED LESSON: The database contains three calculation fields: Area/U.S. field (Area field/area of the United States expressed as a ratio); Population Density field (Population field/Area field expressed as a ratio); and, Pop. Density/U.S. field (value calculated in the Population Density field/population density of the United States expressed as a ratio). Four fields (Major Cities, Physical Features, Language(s), and Ethnic Groups) are defined to be able to store up to three different values. Students can print out the following informational tables:

1. List by country to find information about cities in a specific country.
2. List by country to find landmass, population, and comparison to the United States
3. List by country to find climate and physical features of a specific country
4. List by country to find ethnic groups and languages in a specific country
5. List by ethnic group to determine countries
6. List by population density to view rank order of countries

POSSIBLE REPORTS:

a. Country		Capital	Major cities	
b. Country	Area	Area/U.S.	Population	Pop. density Pop density/U.S.
c. Country		Climate	Physical features	
d. Country		Ethnic group(s)		Language(s)
e. Ethnic group		Country		
f. Pop. density		Country		

Figure 9–13
Geography file

Data would be gathered by students and, for some, might serve as motivation to read. The data could be gathered as part of a school library's reading promotion effort. The data entry itself might be restricted to a few students in order to control the integrity of the file. An **authority list** (a list of approved headings) might be used for the subject/genre field to facilitate accurate retrieval of information. To accomplish this, the computer could present the user with a predetermined list of entries.

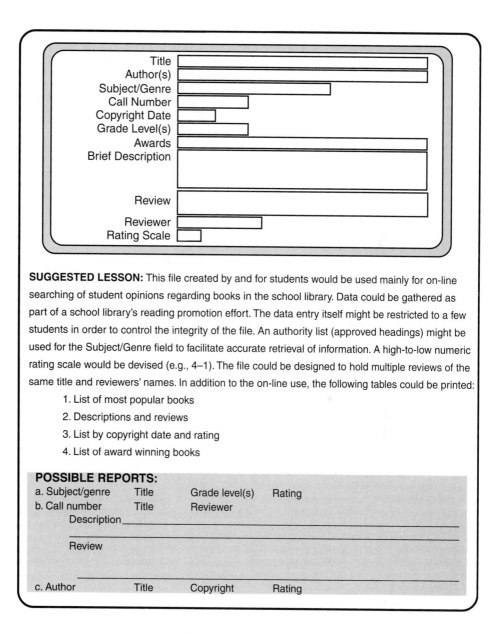

Figure 9–14
Recommended
books file

SUGGESTED LESSON: This file created by and for students would be used mainly for on-line searching of student opinions regarding books in the school library. Data could be gathered as part of a school library's reading promotion effort. The data entry itself might be restricted to a few students in order to control the integrity of the file. An authority list (approved headings) might be used for the Subject/Genre field to facilitate accurate retrieval of information. A high-to-low numeric rating scale would be devised (e.g., 4–1). The file could be designed to hold multiple reviews of the same title and reviewers' names. In addition to the on-line use, the following tables could be printed:

    1. List of most popular books

    2. Descriptions and reviews

    3. List by copyright date and rating

    4. List of award winning books

A high-to-low numeric rating scale would be devised (e.g., 4–1). The file could be designed to hold multiple reviews and reviewers' names.

Students might query the database by a specific subject/genre, asking for a list of titles at a particular grade level, and then sort the list in descending order by rating scale. They would then be able to find the most popular books in their area of interest.

Once having selected a group of records to examine, students could change to a layout that would let them read a brief description, review, and reviewer name in order to choose a book that appealed to them. The addition of the call number in the layout would help students find the book on the library shelf. A student could search for a favorite author and get a list by title, copyright date, and rating scale to find the most recent and popular work by that author.

A layout that listed the awards (e.g., Caldecott, Newberry, Young Reader's Choice Award), the rating scale, and the reviewer name for each title would allow students to form their own opinion of a reviewer's judgment when compared against a broader measure.

It's easy to see the computer as a creative graphics tool in the visual arts and a composition tool in music but we should not ignore the fact that the computer is a wonderful manager of information. A database manager, such as suggested in Figure 9–15, could be created to store data concerning art and music history. Research could be divided by time period or by medium and assigned to teams of students. Images could be either photographed with a digital camera or scanned into the file. Short excerpts of sound recordings could be imported as well. As data was gathered, it would be entered into the database. Artists working in specific media could be examined. Specific works could be found and examined. Searches could be initiated to examine the art and music of specific time periods and reports prepared. An extension of the example in Figure 9–15 might include a comment field where a teacher's commentary might be stored or students might be encouraged to develop their own comments based on readings done about a particular work.

Databases as Managers of Digital Portfolios

As we have discussed, teachers have become increasingly interested in authentic assessment measures and techniques, and the portfolio has surfaced as an interesting alternative. Typically, the portfolio is seen as an attempt to gather evidence of a student's performance. This evidence can take the form of tests, written assignments, exercises, projects, and audio and video projects completed by the student. By comparing like measures over time, growth can be observed in the individual's performance.

Manual portfolios are difficult to manage and cumbersome to store. As more and more performance evidence is gathered, portfolio management and the analysis of like measures become more and more difficult. The shear size of the container for the documentary evidence grows to the point that storage becomes an issue for the teacher and for the school administrator.

Digital portfolios may present an answer to the problems created by manual versions. Written documents and photographs can be scanned into electronic files. Digital pictures can be recorded. Videotaped sequences can be converted to digital formats. Many types of software can be used to tie everything together: HyperStudio, PowerPoint, and Microsoft Word are three examples. A database manager such as FileMaker Pro can also provide the management needed to organize the various artifacts collected and can provide efficient analyses of like measures over time. Each student's digital portfolio can be stored on a recordable CD-R or DVD-R.

Artist's Name
Artist's Photo

Medium
Style
Title of Work
Photo of Work
Sound Sample of Work
Date of Work

Suggested Lesson: This database file might be used in the study of art history. As the students conduct the research and enter data into this file, they could search the file in a number of different ways. A search by Title would reveal the Artist's Name, the Work, Medium, Style, and Date of one work. A search by Artist's Name could reveal all of the artist's works and their dates. A search by Date could reveal all works across all media to help make comparisons. A search by Medium could focus on just one medium over time.

The following fields would be defined in the database.

Field Name	Type	Entry Option	
Artist's Name	Text	Required value; Do not allow user to override Indexed	
Artist's Photo	Container		
Medium	Text	Indexed; Value List:	Painting Drawing Sculpture Photography Instrumental Music Vocal Music
Style	Text		
Title of Work	Text		
Photo of Work	Container		
Sound Sample/Work	Container		
Date of Work	Date		

Figure 9–15
Art and music history file

Commercially Available Databases Related to Curriculum

A number of commercial databases are being marketed to address specific content areas. Databases of scientific facts (e.g., periodic table, scientists, inventions), historical facts (e.g., famous people, events, time lines), and geographic facts (e.g., map locations, climates, migration) are becoming readily available from various publishers of educational software.

The examples that follow as Figures 9–16 through 9–18 are taken from an award-winning program called MacGlobe[Reg] (also available as PC Globe[TM] for

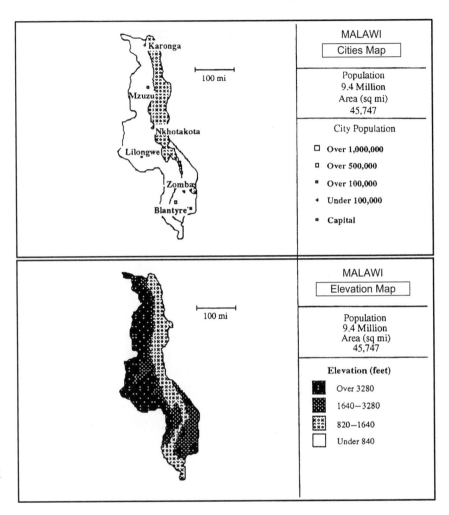

Figure 9–16
Map screens from MacGlobe (Reprinted with permission of Broderbund, Inc.)

Windows), which is a rich database of geographical facts covering every country in the world. It begins with a world map and lets the user choose from regional maps (e.g., continents, political and economic alliances), country maps (e.g., political divisions and elevation), and thematic maps (e.g., population, natural resources, agricultural production, education). The user can paint selected countries or regions in a chosen pattern and return to the world map to observe the results. The program can also display the flag of any country and can display distances, currency conversions, and a number of charts revealing information about each country.

Programs such as this one present the student with a valuable resource of information with which to make comparisons, draw inferences, and construct knowledge. After examining Figures 9–16 through 9–18, what would you say in describing

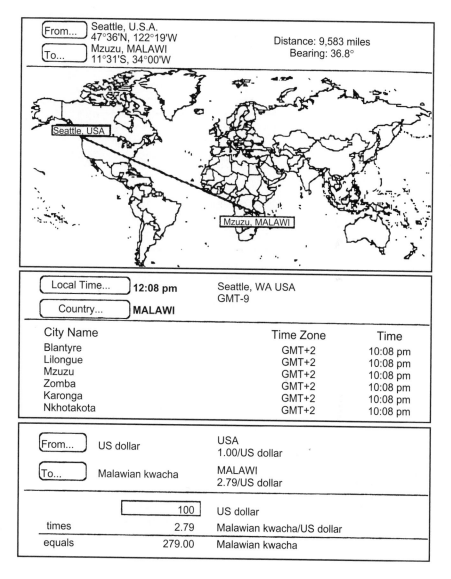

Figure 9–17
Map screens from
MacGlobe (Reprinted
with permission of
Broderbund, Inc.)

Malawi to another student? How is it similar to and how is it different from the United
States? What else do you want to know about Malawi?

The top screen in Figure 9–16 shows the location and population of the major
cities of the African country of Malawi. The bottom screen shows the elevation of
the different regions in the country. Figure 9–17 explores differences.

The top screen gives the user a sense of the distance from the West Coast of the
United States to the African country of Malawi (distance can be calculated between
any two points on the globe). The middle screen reveals time differences between

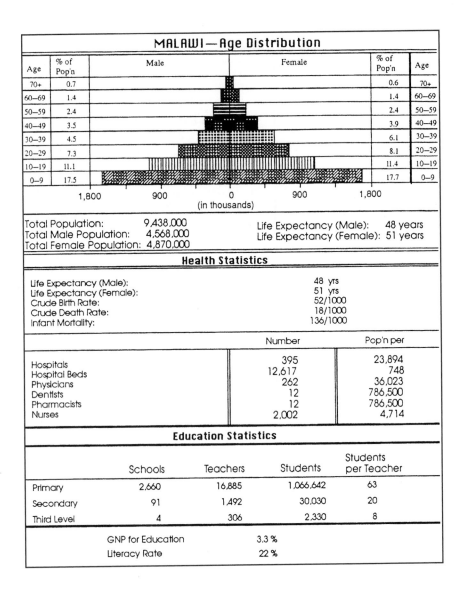

Figure 9–18
Statistics screens from MacGlobe (Reprinted with permission of Broderbund, Inc.)

the local point and the distant country. The bottom screen converts currency between the two countries. The three screens in Figure 9–18 reveal statistics about the age, health, and education of the Malawi population.

A multimedia, CD-ROM-based literature database called Find It! Science makes it possible for students to search by topic, to view a science book's cover in full color, to see a content summary, and to search for related titles among more than 3,000 award-winning science books. Find It! Science can produce bibliographies on a range of topics, selected by type (fiction, biography, reference), author, awards won, and other criteria.

OPTIONAL EXERCISE: DESIGNING A TEST ITEM DATABASE

Objective exams have often been prepared with the use of a word processor. A test item file, however, would allow a teacher the highest degree of flexibility in test construction for a paper-and-pencil exam as well as being a great time saver. We will design such a file following the four requirements outlined earlier in this chapter.

A demo copy of FileMaker Pro for Windows and Macintosh platforms and a working copy of this file replete with 20 sample questions is included for your use on the Companion CD. If this copy will no longer function, you may download another demo copy from the FileMaker, Inc. Website www.filemaker.com

1. *Understand our information needs.* We wish to print master copies of exams to be duplicated that will include midterm, final, and perhaps, more than one version of each. The questions must be reasonably current and must relate to specific topics and/or textbook chapters. We must be able to easily select the questions we wish to use.

2. *Specify our output needs.* The exams must include true/false and multiple-choice questions. Appropriate layouts must be created for each type of question and must include directions for the students. We must also be able to view a question selection screen and print an answer key.

3. *Specify our input needs.* The following fields and their labels will be required: *Question #, Question Type, Question, Answer, Modification Date, Topic, Chapter, Exam, Select?* and *Instructions.* Appropriate layouts must be created.

4. *Determine the file organization.* The *Question* field will be the primary field in the record and it will be set as a unique field in order to prevent inadvertent duplication. The file will be indexed by this field, as well as by *Topic* and *Chapter* fields, in order to speed the sorting of the file. The *Question Type, Topic,* and *Exam* fields will contain predetermined lists to simplify and safeguard data entry.

Preparing a File. This file was built in FileMaker Pro and was begun by defining the fields according to the list presented in Figure 9–19. Notice several fields have predetermined value lists, sometimes called **authority lists.** The complete file including 20 questions can be found on the Companion CD along with a trial version of FileMaker Pro 6.0. This is a full-blown version of the software but it is set to expire 30 days after you first use it.

Once fields are defined, layouts must be prepared. The *Data Entry* form displayed in FileMaker Pro's *Layout* view shown in Figure 9–20 would include a Question field; Answer fields for multiple-choice elements; Answer Key fields for both multiple-choice (radio buttons) and true/false (checkboxes) questions to store the correct response; a Chapter field correlated to the text being used; and a Topic field. Notice that the two fields (Date and Instructions) automatically generated by the computer are not found on this layout.

Figure 9–21 shows an exam question as it would appear in the question selector layout. Notice that the *Select?* box offers the choice of M (Midterm) or F (Final). This field could be used to note different exams or different forms of the same test. This could obviously be changed to meet an instructor's need for any exam or quiz. Figure 9–22 shows the same question in the multiple-choice question exam printing layout.

Field Name	Field Type	Formula/Entry Options
Question #	Number	
Question	Text	Indexed
Question Type	Text	Value List:
		True/False
		Multiple-Choice
Chapter #	Number	Range: 1–12
		Indexed
Topic	Text	Indexed
Select?	Text	Value List:
		Yes
		No
MC Answer a.	Text	
MC Answer b.	Text	
MC Answer c.	Text	
MC Answer d.	Text	
MC Answer Key	Text	Value List:
		a.
		b.
		c.
		d,
TF Answer Key	Text	Value List:
		T
		F
Date	Date	Auto-enter: Modification Date
Instructions	Calculation	= if(Question type="Multiple Choice", "Select the one best answer for each question and respond on the answer sheet provided", "Select T if the answer is completely true or F if any part of the answer is false and respond on the answer sheet provided")

Figure 9–19
Field definitions for a
test item file

While an *Answer Key* layout might contain the question, the answer choices provided and the key to the correct answer, an abbreviated *Answer List* is shown in Figure 9–23.

If you use the file found on the Companion CD, add as many questions to the file as you'd like. FileMaker Pro saves itself automatically when it is idle. Clones (copies of the file without any data) can be renamed and saved, if you want to use this file for other classes.

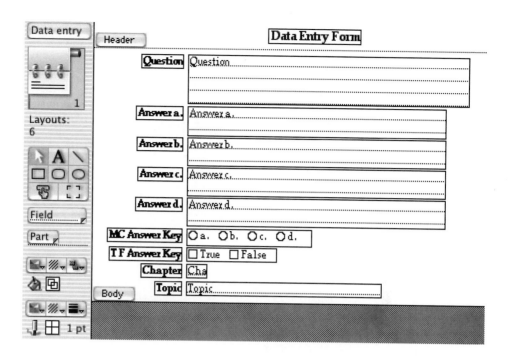

Figure 9–20
Data entry layout

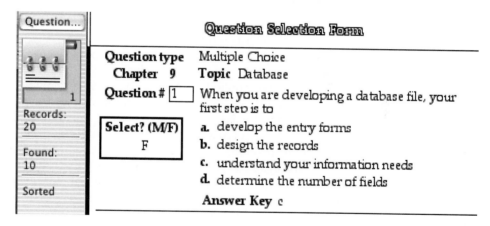

Figure 9–21
Question selection
layout

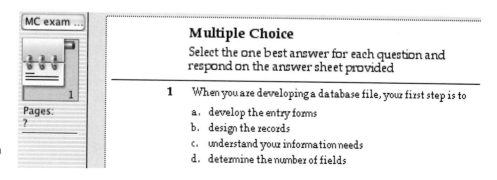

Figure 9–22
Multiple-choice exam
printing layout

Answer list		
	Question #	**MC Answer Key**
	1	c
10	2	c
Records: 20	3	b
	4	b
Found: 10	5	d
	6	b
Sorted	7	b
	8	a
	9	b
	10	b

Figure 9–23
Multiple-choice
answer list layout

SUMMARY

A database manager is software designed to structure data to produce information. It is an information management tool with the potential to increase the speed of information acquisition, the ease with which information is acquired, and the quality of the information acquired in terms of both accuracy and completeness. A database may consist of a single file or a number of related files. Database management software is designed to allow the user to create a structure for the storage, manipulation, and retrieval of data. The products of file managers fall into two main categories: the real-time, on-line searching for specific information and the ability to print reports organized in a particular fashion.

The individual data item is the most discrete element of a database and is called a field. Fields can contain text, numeric values, dates, pictures, sounds, and calculations that perform mathematical operations on other numeric fields within the record and can store the resulting values. Fields can also contain summaries of data across a number of records and can display the result. Field labels are created that identify or describe the fields where the data are actually stored.

The record is composed of all the related fields. A file is the aggregation of all the records. As fields are defined, labels are created and grouped together, creating a layout that appears on the screen. Once data are entered, the layout that is selected or created can be thought of as a window through which to examine data in selected fields.

The database manager software allows the user to search for and select records based on a wide range of criteria. Compound searches can be constructed to examine data in multiple fields using the Boolean connectors AND, OR, and NOT. Data can then be sorted or arranged in a prescribed alphabetic, numeric, or chronological order in either ascending or descending fashion based on any individual field. Most software also allows nested, or multilevel, sorts.

To develop a report for printing information from the file, the user first selects the appropriate layout, then selects the records to be included in the report, and, finally, designates their order. Information can be entered once, but many reports can be generated.

To make the best use of a file management system, you must be able to meet the following four requirements: (1) understand your information needs, (2) specify your output needs, (3) specify your input needs, (4) determine the file organization.

Teachers want help in addressing their information needs and alleviating the paperwork demands made on them. Students need access to increasing amounts of information if they are to construct their own knowledge. Information organization and retrieval skills can be taught using databases.

Digital portfolios provide for the storage of written documents, images, and video. A database manager can organize the various artifacts collected and can provide efficient analysis over time. Portfolios can be stored on a removable magnetic medium or on a recordable CD-ROM.

CHAPTER EXERCISES

To complete the specified exercises on-line, go to the Chapter Exercises Module in Chapter 9 of the Companion Website.

1. List at least three database management applications for each of the following and explain how the database addresses a particular productivity need.
   Student
   Teacher
   School administrator
2. Look at your personal tax or budget records. To what areas might you apply a file manager? Do you have records in a paper format that could be stored and manipulated electronically? What would be the advantages and disadvantages of doing this? Would it make you more productive?
3. Develop a file that would include all the information you would need on the students in a given class. Determine the kinds of reports you would need from this file.
4. Determine the kinds of reports you would need if the entire student population of your school were put on a database. What kind of information would have to be placed in the database and how often would this information have to be updated?
5. Using a word processing program, write a letter (holiday, seasonal, how you are doing, family news, job application request, etc.). Leave at least four blank spaces in the letter that will be filled with receiver specific information (person's name, title, location, hobbies, pets, etc.). Develop a database of at least four individual recipients that contains fields for each of the blank spaces. Merge and print the four letters.
6. Select one of the database examples illustrated in Figures 9–12 through 9–15 and create a similar one. Add, delete, or change the fields suggested in

order to modify the database to suit your particular needs. Enter sample data and prepare a user's guide so that a classmate can run some reports.

7. Design a database application for a model digital portfolio. In addition to identification and date fields, include all fields necessary to capture required documentation in text, audio, picture, and video formats. Develop two sample reports that would support comparison of like measures.

8. After examining Figures 9–16 through 9–18 as products of the software MacGlobe, write a brief description of Malawi. Be sure to point out similarities to and differences from the United States. Indicate what else you would like to know about Malawi.

9. List two different database activities that you might use in your future class that would actively involve all of the students. Explain your answer to the class and change ideas if needed.

10. Many times teachers use information gathered from the class to add interest to the database assignments (i.e., age, gender, favorite color). List several types of information that may be too sensitive or objectionable from the students', parents', or administration's view to solicit from your students. Defend the items on your list. Discuss the lists in class.

PORTFOLIO DEVELOPMENT EXERCISES

 To complete this exercise on-line, go to the Digital Portfolio Module in Chapter 9 of the Companion Website.

One of the NETS•S standards covered in this chapter was "Students use technology tools to process data and report results" under *Category 5: Technology research tools.* Begin to develop your own portfolio of lesson plans that demonstrates your ability to have your students reach the NETS•S standards.

1. Design a lesson plan activity for elementary, middle school, or high school students in which they use a database program to assemble and record data and report results. Some examples may include a database of individuals that you might study during the year, a database of teachers in the school, a database of friends and relatives, or a database of something that the students like to collect. Have students sort the data in at least two ways and report their results. Try to combine several tools found in the database programs. The number that you use should depend on the grade level. Younger students may only use simple tools (list function, etc.). Older students will be required to use more sophisticated tools (design multiple layouts, etc.). This lesson should demonstrate that your students have achieved the standard. Be sure to include a system of evaluation for your students' understanding and competence to ensure that they have met this standard.

2. Adapt the lesson plan activity you developed in exercise 1 for students to evaluate each others' work.

GLOSSARY

authority list A list of approved headings, names, terms, and so on designed to control what is entered into a field.

Boolean connectors Words such as AND, OR, and NOT used to connect search terms. These will restrict or increase the number of items found by the search.

database The collection of related data records stored and accessed electronically by computer. By popular use, now used interchangeably with the term *file.*

database manager Software that is designed to manage electronic files. The term is often used interchangeably with *file manager.*

field The group of related characters treated as a unit within a record—for example, the last name of a student. The smallest, most discrete element of a file.

file A collection of related records treated as a unit.

file management A systematic approach to the storage, manipulation, and retrieval of information stored as data items in the form of records in a file.

file manager Software designed to manage a single database file.

form See *layout.*

label The descriptor related to a data field.

layout The selection and positioning of fields and their labels for screen or printed use.

logical search The ability to apply logical operators to a search—for example, "Find all words that contain 'th' " or "Find all values greater than 100."

multilevel sort A series of second, third, and so on levels of sorts performed after a primary one has been performed—for example, sorting a group of students by first name after they were first sorted by last name.

nested sort See *multilevel sort.*

query See *logical search.*

record A group of related fields treated as a unit. For example, in a student file, a record might be all the information stored relating to a given student. A group of records constitutes a file.

relational database manager Software designed to manage a collection of related electronic data files.

REFERENCES & SUGGESTED READINGS

Arnone, M., & Small, R. (2001, November). *S.O.S. for information literacy: A tool for improving research and information skills instruction.* Paper presented at the National Convention of the Association of Educational Communications and Technology. ERIC NO: ED470194.

Brown, J., Fernlund, P., & White, S. (1998). *Technology tools in the social studies curriculum.* Wilsonville, OR: Franklin, Beedle, & Associates.

Loertscher, D. (2003, June). The digital school library. *Teacher Librarian, 30*(5), 14–25.

Peck, J. K., & Hughes, S. V. (1997, January–February). So much success . . . from a first-grade database project! *Computers in the Schools, 13*(1–2), 109–16.

Repp, R. (1999, March). The World Wide Web: Interfaces, databases, and applications to education. *Learning & Leading With Technology, 26*(6), 40–41.

Storey, V., Goldstein, R, & Ding, J. (2002, January–March). Common sense reasoning in automated database design. *Journal of Database Management, 13*(1), 3–15.

10

Learning with Multimedia Tools

1. What is multimedia and how can it be effective?

2. What are hypertext and hypermedia?

3. How could we incorporate multimedia into our teaching and curriculum?

This chapter contains information that will help your students meet standards found under two NETS•S categories. NETS•S *Category 3: Technology productivity tools* and NETS•S *Category 4: Technology communications tools* are both covered with information throughout the chapter. The advent of hypertext and hypermedia has changed the way information and ideas are organized and presented. No longer do we have to use complicated and technical tools to infuse various media formats into a presentation. The advent of digital media and computers has simplified all of this. Multimedia applications are great productivity tools for you and your students. They help to organize thoughts and ideas and communicate them to others in ways that have never been able to be done before. This chapter contains very important segments shaping the role of technology in your students' lives.

Many years ago, Edgar Dale (1969) developed a model for learning that became known as the "Cone of Experience." This model, as shown in Figure 10–1, illustrates a continuum from direct, purposeful experiences directly involving the learner, located at the base of the cone, to abstract symbols that learners passively observe at the top of the cone. *Multimedia* was missing when Dale constructed this model in 1946, but it fits neatly in the midsection of the cone. The term *multimedia* surfaced several years later in the 1950s as educators combined various media in support of each other to heighten the effect on learning.

For more than 50 years, educational researchers have been telling us that people learn better when they are involved in their learning, and that involvement increases as more senses are used by the learner to acquire information. Thus, multimedia technologies, which can provide stimulating and interactive multisensory experiences to learners, can help teachers improve the quality and the appeal of their instruction.

Many times we hear the terms *multimedia, hypermedia,* and *hypertext* discussed together, often by different people meaning the same thing. Even people in the field find the words hard to distinguish (Tolhurst, 1995). **Multimedia** simply means a presentation that contains several types of media such as still and moving graphics, text, sounds, and animations used to communicate information. **Hypermedia** refers to linked media. In a hypermedia presentation, it would be possible to move from one form of media to another through the use of buttons or mouse clicks. **Hypertext** refers to hypermedia links that are textual in nature. Recently this definition has gotten even fuzzier because links found on Web pages, be they textual, images, or buttons, are now referred to as *hypertext links.* We will discuss this in greater detail later.

291

A list of the ISTE/NCATE standards addressed in this chapter is available in the Standards Module in the Companion Website www.prenhall.com/ forcier

---

NETS•S Standards Addressed in This Chapter

3. Technology productivity tools
   - Students use technology tools to enhance learning, increase productivity, and promote creativity.
   - Students use productivity tools to collaborate in constructing technology-enhanced models, prepare publications, and produce other creative works.

4. Technology communications tools
   - Students use a variety of media and formats to communicate information and ideas effectively to multiple audiences.

Members of the Association for Educational Communications and Technology (AECT), as professional educators, have led the way in showing the power of various instructional media (sounds and projected and nonprojected images, for example) on learning. Multimedia is certainly multidimensional and multisensory and has great potential for involving the user. Multimedia has now gone digital! The familiar "low-tech" slide series accompanied by synchronized audiotapes with perhaps film clips thrown in have given way to personalized "high-tech" experiences of sounds, images, animation, and movies presented to the user on a computer screen or projected in the classroom. The impact of digital technology on multimedia is impressive. Digital multimedia has made it possible for the learner to navigate through combinations of sights and sounds as never before. For educators, the opportunity to involve students so directly in learning and problem solving is one of multimedia's most appealing qualities. Multimedia software has been developed over the past several years that enable children as young as the first grade to develop multimedia projects with ease. Students can incorporate text, graphics, video, and hyperlinks in reports and projects as never before. *Kids Media Magic*™ and *Kid Pix 3rd Edition*™ allow students to add text and pictures as well as video, sound, music, and animations to projects to help instill a new excitement into learning. *Multimedia Workshop*™ includes photographs, sound effects, music, and even *QuickTime*™ movie clips for students to add to their presentations and projects. More sophisticated programs such as *HyperStudio* and the very versatile *Movieworks* add even more features such as pop-up text and menus, hypertext links, image, movie, and sound editing and easy interface with CD-ROMs, laser disks, and other programs such as *Kid Pix Studio Deluxe*. Even the new *Microsoft PowerPoint* presentation software package contains everything needed to make a sophisticated multimedia presentation.

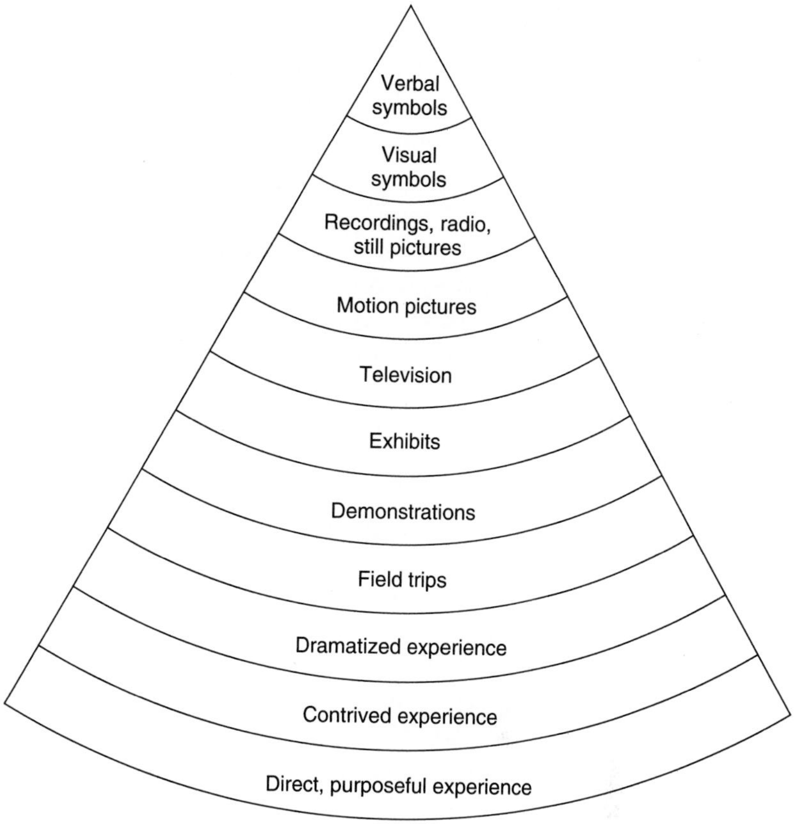
Verbal symbols
Visual symbols
Recordings, radio, still pictures
Motion pictures
Television
Exhibits
Demonstrations
Field trips
Dramatized experience
Contrived experience
Direct, purposeful experience

Figure 10–1
Dale's Cone of Experience ("Cone of Experience" from *Audio-Visual Methods in Teaching,* 3rd ed., by Edgar Dale, copyright © 1969 by Holt, Rinehart & Winston, reproduced by permission of the publisher.)

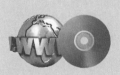

INTO THE CLASSROOM: Starting Early with Multimedia

At our small suburban elementary school, we use multimedia software regularly to integrate technology into the curriculum. One of our favorite programs is *Kid Pix Studio Deluxe.*

We use this program in a variety of ways, starting with our kindergarten students. They become acquainted with the drawing tools (usually one or two at a time) until they are comfortable in using them. Teachers introduce these tools and then allow the students to explore, followed by a more directed activity. They use it for graphic arts as well as simple

(Continued)

activities such as reinforcing phonics. For example, the students might use the letter stamp and the typing tool to type their "letter of the week" and then find stamps and draw objects that begin with the same sound.

By the time students reach grade one, they are familiar with this program and are ready to try more complex ideas such as building simple slide shows. We have done slide shows in primary grades where each student makes one slide, then it is put together as a class celebration and publication of their learning.

Our students also enjoy creating class books on topics of interest, and this works well because they can use the software to compose their ideas and then use the graphic tools to make accompanying drawings. My students recently finished a science unit on "Rocks and Minerals" and they composed poetry, which was written and illustrated using *Kid Pix*. The laminated covers were coiled together to make a very polished-looking product for our classroom library.

Students in older grades use this program to create more sophisticated multimedia reports with voice-overs, scanned and imported artwork, and graphic arts to share their learning on a particular topic.

By the time our students finish grade six they are comfortable in using graphic and multimedia tools. The tool bars and processes they have been using are very similar to those in other programs such as *HyperStudio* and *PowerPoint*, so these skills will transfer easily to their work in other settings.

Joni Turville
Elementary Teacher and Technology Mentor
Ronald Harvey School
St. Albert, Alberta, Canada

MULTIMEDIA: HYPERTEXT AND HYPERMEDIA

Multimedia in its simplest definition means "many media" or "a combination of several media." Something as simple as a slide presentation with taped audio is "multimedia." **Digital multimedia,** on the other hand, is a relatively recent development that allows a computer user to combine and control a number of instructional resources in order to present information. Its power lies in its ability to network information resources and to provide ready access to the learner. As suggested by Figure 10–2, some multimedia computer programs may be used to control the presentation of video, graphic, audio, and textual information from external sources such as videotape, CD-ROM, or DVD. This audio and video information is presented to the user under the control of the computer. Other programs may be totally self-contained, with all data stored on an optical disk and the information presented to the user through the computer's monitor and speaker.

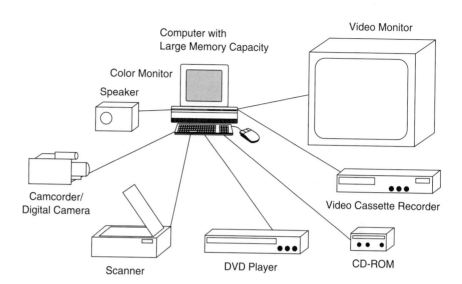

Figure 10–2
Equipment
supporting
multimedia

Multimedia presentations can create multisensory learning experiences for students. Using an instructional program, developed and played on a multimedia computer system, students are able to jump from medium to medium at the will of the developer utilizing the best medium available to illustrate a particular objective. As a teaching tool, commercially prepared or teacher-designed multimedia programs might include the use of textual, graphic, audio, and video materials to convey information to the user, who would interact with it by reading, listening, observing still and moving images, and navigating through options presented on the screen. As a learning tool, not only can students navigate through this rich medium as they search for information from which to construct knowledge, but they can also express themselves in a number of ways as they author multimedia reports. Features that underlie the power of multimedia as a teaching and learning tool are listed in Figure 10–3.

Multimedia allows students to create their own visuals and incorporate them into their products and to navigate in original and customized ways through existing resources. It gives the student control of powerful tools in the exploration and creation of information. A camcorder, digital camera, optical scanner, CD-ROM drive, and DVD and video cassette recorders all become potential information-gathering tools. Multimedia tools allow a student to create a complex statement that might include computer-generated sound, graphics, and animation, along with sound and visual forms stored in another medium such as video cassette or CD-ROM.

While normal text written on a page is designed to be read in a linear fashion from beginning to end, hypertext is a nonlinear way of representing text. Because the meaning of the text in this new medium doesn't depend on sequential ordering, readers can access information according to their own interests and needs, thus giving them much more control in the reading process.

To understand how hypertext works, think of the analogy of a Rolodex address wheel. Each *information screen* is seen as a card containing a person's name, address,

Text	Text can be presented in an attention-getting manner. Text may be selected and made into a *button* or *link*.
Graphics	Graphics can be created or imported. Photographs, video still frames, scanned images, and Web images can be imported as well.
Animation	Graphics and text can be animated to illustrate concepts.
Sound	Digitized sounds can be captured from a microphone, audio recorder, audio-CD, and Internet sources. Sounds can be used for an attention-getting effect or to clarify a concept.
Video	Digitized video, a powerful instructional medium, can be captured from a camcorder, VCR, CD-ROM, and other sources.
Data Storage	Database capabilities allow the student to search for information, or they can be used by the teacher to record and analyze a student's performance.
Integration	Integration with audio and video storage devices and with the Internet facilitates direct access to information by the user.
Navigation	The user controls the pace and many times the level of difficulty of the material covered using responses ranging from simple keystrokes or mouse clicks to text entry and evaluation. Links can be established to take the student to other information within the presentation, external information on video and CD-ROM, for example, and information around the world with links to the World Wide Web.

Figure 10–3
Features found in
multimedia programs

phone number, etc. Cards can be arranged in any order and a user can navigate among the cards in a nonlinear manner, perhaps looking up the phone number for Forcier first, followed by Descy, and finally Stollenwerk. Cards are grouped into logical units, or stacks, and a user can navigate between stacks in a seamless fashion. This is exactly the same method of navigation that you have used on the World Wide Web. In that case, clicking on an underlined part of the text on a Web page, called a hypertext link, transports the user to other information on the same or a distant Web server. Navigation in a multimedia presentation, in most instances, is accomplished by clicking on objects called **buttons.** Buttons can be visible objects that look, in fact, like a button or hidden (invisible) objects that could be specific areas of the screen, often covering images or text. Button destinations or **actions,** such as playing a sound or video or moving to another location, can be programmed very simply in a matter of seconds using pull down menus, mouse-clicks and/or typing the desired actions, or perhaps just clicking and checking a box listing the desired action. Each screen on a multimedia presentation may be called a **card,** a screen, or a slide and complete groups of these cards or slides are usually called a **stack** or a slide show.

Hypermedia embeds hypertext elements into multimedia. The cards in a hypermedia stack might contain text, but they also might provide users with information in other forms. Hypermedia programs can contain text, graphics, and sounds on their cards, and even animation sequences and digitized video clips. They can even reach into cyberspace by sending a URL to a Web browser such as *Internet Explorer* which will open the Web browser and display the page. The term *hypermedia* has largely given way to *multimedia*. Digital multimedia programs contain all the navigation control elements of hypermedia.

To illustrate this concept, imagine that you are using a multimedia geography program and that you are looking at a screen of information about a country. Buttons on that screen may lead you to additional text-based information about that country such as lists of products exported, population statistics, or climate conditions. Other buttons could also lead you to graphical information in the form of topographical or political maps, to an audio clip playing a traditional song, or to a digitized video clip on the World Wide Web recorded from yesterday's evening newscast of the country's president delivering a speech to the United Nations Assembly.

APPLICATIONS OF MULTIMEDIA IN EDUCATION

More and more classrooms are acquiring the software and equipment to allow teachers to produce and use multimedia presentations as a method of instruction and to support student development of multimedia projects. Data gathered by Quality Education Data (1997) found that multimedia software is one of the fastest growing segments of the market. The U.S. Department of Education recently outlined a goal of one multimedia computer to every five students. Because these technologies are interesting, interactive, multidimensional, and student-controlled, they are ideally suited for educational purposes. Learners are engaged by the exciting technology, and they can explore information at their own pace and according to their own interests and needs.

Multimedia authoring can be approached from both the teacher's and student's perspective. The teacher can select and create material, addressing instructional needs ranging from discrete projects aimed at specific facts and concepts to be taught to complete lessons. A chemistry teacher might design a multimedia periodic table of the elements that would allow a user to select an element; identify its atomic number, atomic weight, and discoverer; see an illustration of its atomic structure; and then see a picture of the discoverer and read a brief biography. An English teacher might create a simple multimedia program that would present the student with lesson objectives, ask specific questions to focus the student's attention, and give the student a brief introduction to a work of Shakespeare being studied and a link to the *Complete Works of William Shakespeare* Website (http://www.thetech.mit.edu/Shakespeare/works.html). A teacher of English to Speakers of Other Languages (ESOL) might create a multimedia vocabulary program that would allow a student to see a word and hear it pronounced. An image of an object representing the word might also be displayed. At the simplest authoring level, a teacher of any subject at any grade level might create bookmarks appropriate to the World Wide Web browser being used that would allow students to interact with multimedia Websites related to current lessons being taught.

From the student's perspective, multimedia authoring presents a rich environment in which to explore information and construct knowledge. As an example, students might be assigned the task of developing a multimedia project describing the early settlement and subsequent development of their community. The resulting product might be text gleaned from official records, pictures found in a museum or library, and audio clips from live interviews with senior citizens, accompanied by their photographs.

Advantages of Multimedia Presentations

- *Active learning:* Creating and using multimedia presentations actively involves the learner in the process.
- *Creativity:* Students have a wide variety of input and output mechanisms available to them as they design their learning activities.
- *Collaboration:* Ample opportunity is afforded for collaborative projects as each student uses their strengths and weaknesses in developing a single group effort.
- *Communications:* From the initial planning stages through the final project presentation, students are able to develop communications skills with each other and the final audience.
- *Constructivist:* Students are able to access a wide variety of knowledge and knowledge presentation techniques and construct a learning environment appropriate for themselves and others.
- *Control:* Many multimedia presentations have multiple channels to the same end. Students are able to control pacing, and in some cases information, to meet their individual learning style. Students can control the choice of media they place in presentations that they develop.
- *Feedback:* Feedback loops can easily be built into multimedia presentations.
- *Flexibility:* Presentations are able to incorporate several paths or learning options to achieve the same outcome.
- *Fun:* Students enjoy the ease with which they can develop and use multimedia presentations.
- *Individuality:* Presentations and responses are able to incorporate many of Gardner's "intelligences" allowing tailor-made learning activities for each student.
- *Motivation:* Students are kept interested by the varied delivery and response methods relieving the boredom so often found in single medium, single response presentations.
- *Multisensory:* Multimedia presentation can involve text, sounds, static and moving visuals, animations, and movies.
- *Reinforcement:* Positive reinforcement can be built in with positive messages, diversions, and explorations of topics in greater depth as the need arises.
- *Remediation:* Remediation is easily built in to catch problems early and help students with difficult information or concepts on an as-needed basis.

- *Technology application:* Students apply new and different technologies in an active learning setting.
- *Thinking skills:* The process of planning, designing, and producing a multimedia project involves higher-order and critical thinking skills as students deconstruct and reconstruct knowledge to meet the project goals and objectives.

Discipline Specific Multimedia Ideas and Software

- *Art:* Art is a wonderful place for students of all ages to incorporate multimedia into their studies. Drawing and painting come to mind first, followed by the integration of several forms of media to produce a media-collage on a specific subject. Multimedia tours of great museums, architectural wonders, and tours of artist's home areas add concrete referents to learning. *Fun with Architecture*™, *Kid Pix Studio Deluxe, Pablo-Internet Edition*™, *Paint, Write & Play*™, *Print Shop Deluxe, With Open Eyes: Images from the Art Institute of Chicago*™.
- *Creativity:* Creativity with multimedia crosses all disciplines. Creating multimedia presentations involves the senses, critical thinking skills, collaboration, individual and group work, and practice in the ability to bring together material to construct a unique learning situation. *Hollywood High*™, *HyperStudio, Imagination Express (Destination: Castle, Neighborhood, Ocean, Pyramids, Rainforest, Time Trip USA), Kid Pix Studio Deluxe, Leonardo's Multimedia Toolbox*™, *Print Shop Deluxe, Storybook Weaver Deluxe*™, *Student Writing & Research Center*™.
- *Critical thinking:* Viewing and developing multimedia presentations of all types help students prepare for the future by reinforcing creativity, critical thinking skills, logic, memory retention, mind mapping, problem solving, and reasoning. *Inspiration*™, *Memory Challenge!*™, *Revenge of the Logic Spiders*™, *Strategy Challenges (1, 2)*™, *Super Solvers Midnight Rescue!*™, *Thinking Things Collection (1, 2, 3, Sky Island Mysteries, Galactic Brain Benders, etc.)*™, *ThinkAnalogy Puzzles*™, *Thinkology*™.
- *Early learning:* Add fun and interest to reading, math, science, and social studies. Students interact with the media. Interactive books make stories come alive because students are able to interact with the characters and environment. *Blue's Clues 1–2–3*™, *Interactive Math Journey*™, *McGee Visits Katie's Farm*™, *The Playroom*™, *Sammy's Science House*™, *Stanley's Sticker Stories*™.
- *Language arts:* Students can take just about any topic that they would ordinarily have to write a paper for or present an oral report and make it into a multimedia presentation. Multimedia storybooks, discovery projects, and newsletters all fit here. Students love interactive storybooks. *The Amazing Writing Machine*™, *Bailey's Book House*™, *Storybook Weaver Deluxe*™, *Student Writing & Research Center*™, *Ultimate Writing & Creativity Center*™.
- *Math:* Many math projects can be presented using a multimedia format. Photos, diagrams, charts, and movies can be added to illustrate mathematical concepts. Skill building and problem solving are easily built in. *Carmen Sandiego Math Detective*™, *Logical Journey of the Zoombinis*™, *Math Concepts in Motion*™.

- *Music:* Students are able to learn about composing and actually compose their own music. Musical instruments can be discovered and explored using their sounds and shapes. Rhythm and melody can be explored. *Juilliard Music Adventure*™, *Making Music*™ and *Making More Music*™, *Microsoft Musical Instruments*™, *Songworks*™.
- *Reading:* Students have fun as they learn to read using interactive story books, phonics games, and vocabulary builders. Self-pacing assures success for even slow readers. *Let's Go Read! (An Island Adventure, An Ocean Adventure)*™, *Read, Write & Type*™, *Reader Rabbit's (Interactive Reading Journey, Kindergarten, Learn to Read, Reading 1, 2, 3)*™, *Reading Blaster (Ages 4–6, Ages 6–9, Ages 9–12, Vocabulary)*™, *Spelling Blaster*™, *Stickybear's (Reading Comprehension, Reading Fun Park, Reading Room Deluxe, Spelling)*™.
- *Science:* Produce multimedia projects illustrating science concepts bringing in sounds, graphics, and video. Produce interactive lessons on cycles, gravity, motion, the periodic table, and much more. View and interact with information and content safely. Manipulate variables to view outcomes. *A.D.A.M. The Inside Story*™, *Canoma*™, *Interactive NOVA Animal Pathfinders*™, *My Amazing Human Body*™, *Sammy's Science House*™, *Schoolhouse Rock: ScienceRock*™, *Thinkin' Science*™ *Virtual Labs: (Light, Electricity)*™.
- *Social studies:* Design interactive field trips using maps, video, audio with full interactivity. Trace histories of people and places. Produce interactive timelines. Follow the path of explorers. Tour historic sites. Produce newsletters and newspapers. *Culture World*™, *Native Americans*™, *Oregon Trail*™, *Point of View*™, *Timeliner*™, *TripMaker*™, *Where in the (World, U.S.A., Time, etc.) Is Carmen Sandiego?*
- *Special needs:* Multimedia allows special needs students to master their own world at their own pace using programs designed to meet their needs and learning styles. They are fun and exciting and build knowledge and confidence as they problem solve, increase manual dexterity, and become immersed in their own learning. Satisfaction and self-confidence grows as they make professional looking presentations with simple tools. *Ace Reporter*™, *Big:Calc*™, *Co:Writer*™, *Easy Street*™, *Knowledge Adventure Bricks*™, *ULTimate (Reader, KidBooks)*™, *Write:OutLoud*.

Virtual reality (VR) is a term referring to computer-based technologies ranging from sophisticated 3-D simulations to full immersion experiences in which the participants find themselves in a highly interactive, multisensory, artificial environment so vivid that it appears real. It is the ultimate multimedia experience, with elements so carefully and convincingly synchronized that computer-generated audio and visual messages appear to be real.

Multimedia technologies allow users to experience and express information in many ways, including allowing them to interact with this information by creating, or authoring, programs and presentations combining original or ready-made text, graphics, and video clips. HyperStudio, a multimedia authoring tool, was the most popular single piece of educational software sold to schools in the mid-to-late 1990s. Inspiraton and Kidspiration have since knocked it down to number three. Multimedia technologies give the teacher or student control of powerful tools in the exploration and creation of information. A camcorder, digital camera, optical scanner, CD-ROM drive, and video recorder all become potential information-gathering, composing, and presentation tools. Multimedia tools allow a student or teacher to compose a complex curriculum aide that might include computer-generated sound, graphics, and animation, along with sound and visual forms stored in another medium such as videotape, CD-ROM, or DVD.

Because multimedia involves the combination of more than one medium into a form of communication, there are many different types of multimedia productions. Thus, a variety of programs that help users to create multimedia products and presentations are available.

DESKTOP PRESENTATION AUTHORING TOOLS

Desktop presentation is the design, creation, and display of textual and graphic information under the control of a personal computer and so may be considered a form of multimedia. It has gained favor in boardrooms and business and community meetings, as well as in elementary, secondary, and college classrooms. Desktop presentation is quickly replacing traditional overhead transparencies and photographic slide shows as a medium of projected visual information. To take advantage of this new electronic medium, the user must have access to presentation software that permits the creation or import of text and graphic images and their subsequent organization and display. The medium also requires appropriate hardware such as a computer and projector to display the images to the selected audience. Newer versions of desktop presentation software have become true hypermedia tools. Rather than just a linear display of slides containing multimedia (drawings, images, video, sound, etc.), the developer can easily add hypertext and hyperlinked buttons that allow the user to present the slides in a nonlinear fashion, move between presentations, and open Web pages or other programs at will.

Presentation Software

Presentation software such as *Microsoft PowerPoint* provide the user with word processing, outlining, drawing, graphing, presentation management tools, and the ability to move through the presentation in a branching as well as linear fashion. Any piece of text can be changed into a hypertext link that will move the presentation on to any other page in the presentation, or even onto the Internet (Figure 10–4). Presentation software also readily accept existing material originally prepared by other word processor, spreadsheet, and graphics programs. In addition, movies, sounds, text and graphic animations, hyperlinked buttons, and text can be placed in the presentation making it a truly nonlinear presentation. The software also allows the user to print outlines of the presentation, speaker's notes, and handouts.

The software usually allows the user to switch among five different views as the presentation is being created. These five views are the *Normal View,* showing the

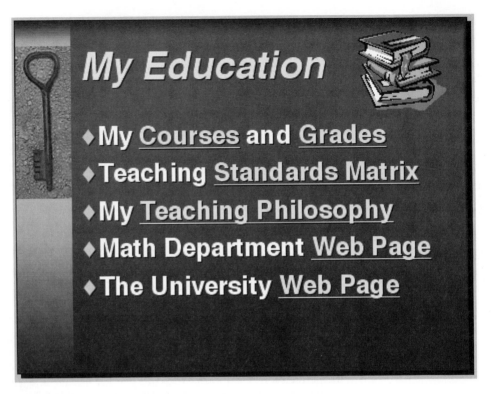

Figure 10–4
PowerPoint slide
with hypertext links.
Each underlined
word takes the
reader to a new slide
or Web page

actual slide being developed (Figure 10–5), the outline to the left, and a window to type teaching notes under the slide; the full presentation in *Outline View;* the *Slide Sorter View,* showing a thumbnail of each slide in order (Figure 10–6); and the *Slide Show View* that allows the developer to view the slide on the full screen in the actual presentation mode. Each view can be accessed at any time by clicking the boxes that can be seen in the lower left of each screen illustration in Figures 10–5 and 10–6. The illustration of those four views, shown in Figure 10–5 and Figure 10–6, were prepared using *Microsoft PowerPoint* and are representative of those created by other desktop presentation programs.

We usually work in the slide view adding text, graphics, sounds, hyperlinks, etc., as we deem necessary. The outline view is good for handouts and as a display of the text found on the slides. The slide sorter view is very handy. The order of the slides in the presentation can be changed by simply clicking on the slide and dragging it to the desired location. Transitions (how one slide changes to another) and text animation (how the text first appears on the screen, i.e., from the right, for example) are also added using this view just by highlighting the desired slide or slides and finding the desired transition and text animation on the toolbar directly above the slide sorter view.

PowerPoint allows the user to select transition effects from a wide variety of **wipes** and **dissolves** between visuals. A wipe is a transition effect that allows a second visual to gradually replace the first one being viewed. In a *wipe left* transition, the fol-

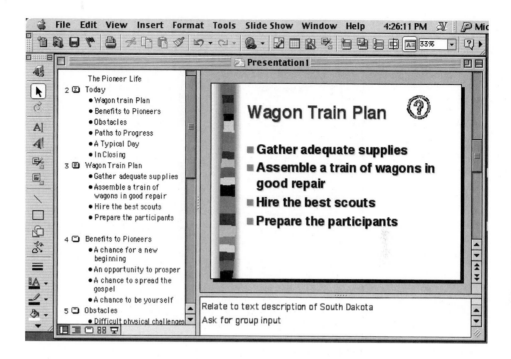

Figure 10–5
Normal view with outline and teacher notes

lowing visual will enter the screen at the right and move leftward across the preceding visual. Other common wipes include a *scroll,* acting either vertically from top or bottom of the screen or from side to side; a *barn door,* acting horizontally from or toward the center of the screen; a *venetian blind,* acting as its name implies by breaking up the image in horizontal slats and introducing the new one; and an *iris,* which is a circular effect acting from or toward the center of the screen.

Actual development of a desktop presentation is quite simple. We will continue to use *Microsoft PowerPoint* as an example since it is the most popular desktop presentation tool. Macintosh and PC versions of that software have screens and techniques that are almost identical. Upon opening PowerPoint, we would suggest that the reader look at the information available under the "help" menu on the menu bar.

The first screen that you see should look similar to Figure 10–7. Open up "Presentations" "Designs" on the left menu. A screen (Figure 10–8) should appear.

Click on the various templates, choosing the one that you would like to use. Keep in mind that it is best to have a solid color background, preferably in a dark color with light text. We are using "Dad's Tie," a template with a white background, for ease of illustration in the text. We do not recommend that you use this one because of the light background. After you have chosen the template, a screen as in Figure 10–9 should appear.

We have chosen "Bulleted List" to illustrate formatting the slide master but you probably want to choose the one in the upper left (Title Slide) first. The screen as in Figure 10–10 should appear. Note all of the different menus in this figure. If all of these horizontal menus (called *toolbars*) do not appear, access them through the "Toolbar" menu under the "View" menu at the top of the screen. We are using the

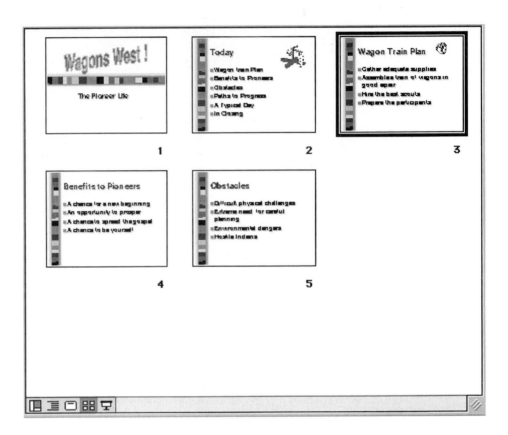

Figure 10–6
Slide sorter view

"Standard," "Formatting," and "Drawing" toolbars. Many students also place the "Common Task" toolbar on the screen. As you drag the mouse over each icon on the toolbars, a little explanation window should appear.

STOP!!! Before you click in the boxes and add information, we must show you how to reformat the text defaults first. Unless told otherwise by your instructor, you must change the defaults. *PowerPoint* defaults are not good examples of proper graphic technique! Go to the "View" menu, move down to "Master" and over to "Slide Master." A screen as in Figure 10–11 should appear. Changing a format on this slide will change the format (font, font size, font and background color, text location on slide, footer, etc.) on all of the slides in the series except the title slide.

It is quite easy to change the format. Just pretend it is a word processing document. Highlight the words you want to change on the slide master and use the "formatting" toolbar, second toolbar from the top (directly over the screen), to make changes. Make the following suggested changes or other changes as directed by your instructor:

1. Change the font to an easy-to-read sans serif font. (Helvetica is a good one.)
2. Change the font style to bold. (Easier to read.)

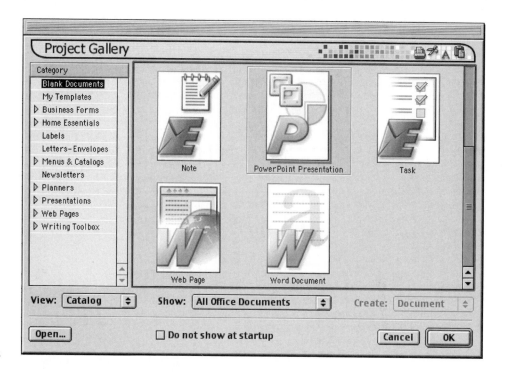

Figure 10–7
Introductory
PowerPoint™ screen

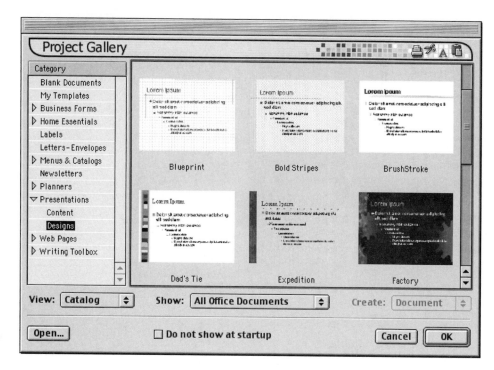

Figure 10–8
Presentation Designs
screen

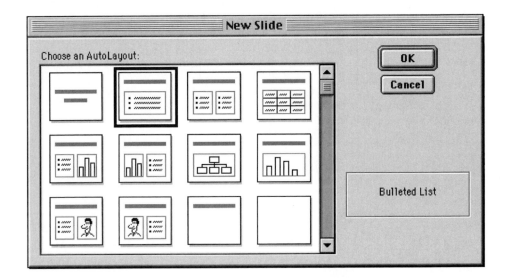

Figure 10–9
AutoLayout screen
(Reprinted with
permission from
Microsoft®, Inc.)

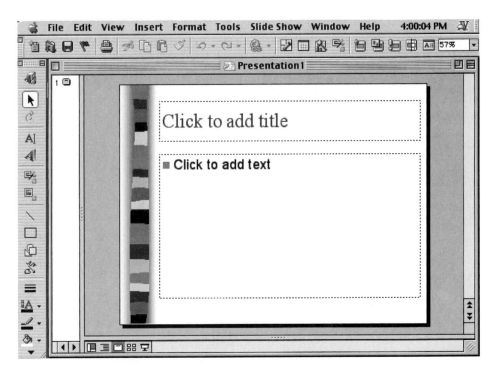

Figure 10–10
Full PowerPoint™
screen shot

3. Increase the size of the title to 48 (44 minimum). (The default is too small.)
4. Increase the size of the first regular line of type in body to 36. (Again, the default is too small and body should contain about five or six lines of type, each with a maximum of five or six words.)

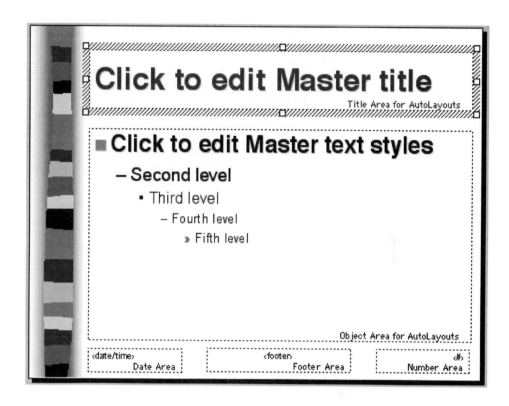

Figure 10–11
Slide master screen

5. Change the font color if need be to the highest contrast possible. (Unless it is on a very dark background, never use yellow as a text color—its nearly impossible to read.)

6. Remember that we are using a light background for clarity of text illustration. Dark backgrounds with high contrast lettering are easier to see by your audience.

Once the defaults have been changed, access the screen shown in Figure 10–10 through the "View" and "Slide" menu. When you have completed a slide and want to make another, just go back up to the top menu, choose "Insert" and "New Slide." Or choose "New Slide" from the "Common Tasks" toolbar.

Now you are on your own! If you want to insert something, just click on "Insert" on the top menu bar. *PowerPoint* is very intuitive and the toolbars are very similar to the ones found on *Microsoft Word* and *AppleWorks*. Experiment with the bottom (drawing) toolbar. The title "Wagons West!" seen on slide 1 previously in Figure 10–6 was made with the *PowerPoint WordArt*™ feature accessed by clicking the "slanted A" in the center of the drawing toolbar.

Following the guidelines in Figure 10–12 will ensure a more effective presentation. Remember that the visual dimension is an important part of the presentation but you, as the presenter, are the most significant element.

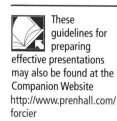

These guidelines for preparing effective presentations may also be found at the Companion Website http://www.prenhall.com/forcier

---

Guidelines for Effective PowerPoint Presentations

General Guidelines
- Begin your presentation with a blank screen to control your audience's focus on your first slide.
- Use an attention-grabbing title screen.
- Use a single background or frame throughout your presentation.
- Avoid a complex background. Keep it simple.
- Place headings at the same location in successive screens.
- Use generous margins to help focus attention on the content.
- Limit yourself to one idea per slide.
- Select transition effects carefully to create a graceful style and to help your audience follow your train of thought. Avoid mixing transition effects.

Lettering Guidelines
- Limit yourself to one or two typefaces throughout the presentation.
- For maximum visibility and to minimize the amount of text per slide, choose a type size of 24 points or larger.
- Avoid ornate typefaces.
- Use all uppercase letters only in major headings and make them a slightly larger type size.
- Use single words and concise phrases to make a point about which you will supply the details verbally.
- Check carefully to eliminate any spelling/typing errors.

Color Guidelines
- Limit yourself to two or three colors per slide.
- Use the same colors throughout the presentation.
- Use bright colors to emphasize important points.
- Use color contrasts effectively (e.g., yellow on dark blue is highly visible, while red on black is barely readable).

Graphics Guidelines
- Keep any background graphics or text simple and restrict it to the same screen position.
- Use dingbats (bullets, checkmarks, and other symbols) to organize lists.
- Use drop shadows and gradient fills judiciously.
- Remember that graphics, sounds, and special effects can often distract from the purpose of the presentation. Less is often more!

Figure 10–12
Guidelines for preparing effective presentations

Desktop Presentation as a Tool

Desktop presentation, with its ability to design, create, and display information under the control of a personal computer, is a tool that extends the capability of the user to communicate. This electronic medium requires users to access software that permits them to design and create the message and to use appropriate hardware to display the message effectively. The presentation, once created, may be saved in a single file on disk, making it a very portable presentation indeed. It also may be saved as a Web presentation able to be accessed from almost any part of the globe. Once again, as we note decreasing equipment size and increasing portability, we see evidence of the paradigm shifts described in Chapter 1: Compare a presenter carrying file folders full of overhead transparencies or carousel trays full of slides to one carrying a floppy disk in a pocket or purse.

Desktop presentation tools can also be utilized in the classroom in a number of different ways. We shall discuss several at the end of the chapter. Teachers with an Internet connection should access the Microsoft Website (http://www.microsoft. com/education/tutorial.classroom/default.asp) for a step-by-step tutorial on the use of *PowerPoint.*

INTO THE CLASSROOM:
A Multimedia Project

Students use *HyperStudio* to draw maps of Alaska identifying geographical regions of the state, significant topographical features such as mountain ranges and bodies of water, animal distribution, population centers and cultural groups. Some students scan images and record sound into their *HyperStudio* stack. I encourage them to then write adventure stories that provide multiple pathways and optional endings.

Fred Ross
Sixth Grade Teacher
Bering Strait School District
Unalakleet, Alaska

HYPERMEDIA AUTHORING TOOLS

HyperCard, a program introduced in 1987 by Apple Computer, is said to have opened the door to multimedia as we know it today. The program has now been surpassed by a number of others, most prominent among them *HyperStudio,* which works on both the Macintosh and Windows platforms. Unlike *HyperCard,* which was not an easy program to master, *HyperStudio* affords the novice user the satisfaction of creating a multimedia product with ease. Other high-end, sophisticated, and expensive authoring programs such as *Macromedia Director*™ and *Authorware Professional*™ are more useful to experienced and professional multimedia programmers.

Figure 10–13 presents various multimedia applications created in HyperStudio. The HyperStudio home stack title page is located at the top center. Top-left is a geography stack on Australia; top-right is a look at the people of Rwanda; bottom-left and bottom-center are examples of electronic portfolios; bottom-right is a storybook created by elementary students that is complete with picture and with text that can be read aloud by the computer; in the center of this collage is a QuickTime™ movie welcoming people to the NECC conference in Minneapolis. Not only does Hyper-Studio allow the user to create buttons that link to the World Wide Web through Netscape™, but it is designed to let users publish their multimedia projects over the

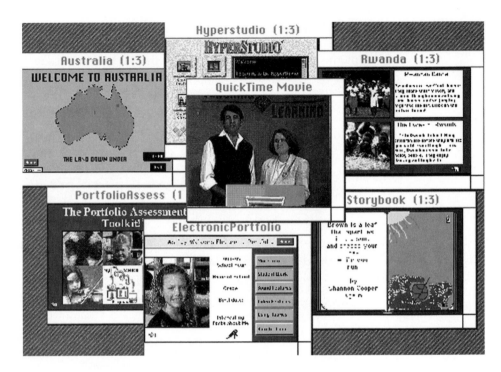

Figure 10–13
A variety of
applications created
in HyperStudio®
(Reprinted with
permission from
Knowledge
Adventure, Inc.)

World Wide Web as well. A HyperStudio window can be embedded in a Web page
or the complete HyperStudio created display can be an entire Internet document. In
many ways, multimedia is a marriage of technologies that allows information to be
presented locally to an individual or to groups and globally to anyone accessing the
World Wide Web.

Even though HyperStudio is used in such varied locations as the Royal Bank of
Scotland, Jimmy Buffett's enhanced music CD, and hundreds of colleges and universities, it is simple enough to allow even first-graders to make multimedia presentations with ease. Version updates, project information, training material, and even a
free fully-functional CD are available through the HyperStudio Website at http://
www.hyperstudio.com

Designing a HyperStudio Stack

Before you or your students design a HyperStudio stack, preplanning should take
place. Students love to dive in (And . . . You and I!) but unfortunately, a slow start
and careful planning will make the development process more efficient and far less
frustrating. Follow the tips listed in Figure 10–14.

As you will notice in Figure 10–14, there are several types of cards that will be
produced. The first is a *title card*. It is important that this card be lively and interesting. It should be designed to gain attention with perhaps a bright, eye-catching
visual. The *introduction card* may follow the title card. This card contains introductory material to familiarize the audience with the topic. Branching may start at this

---

Overall Considerations

Define intended audience.
Identify size of presentation audience.
Determine time frame for project completion.
Access production materials.
Ascertain size of project group (individual or group).

Preplanning

Determine outline content to be covered.
Develop a card map showing cards and links (make sure that there are no dead ends).
Sketch each card in a storyboard.
List media required for each card.
Make a citation card for each piece of medium not produced by the group.
Sketch each card in detail citing each piece of medium.
List all assignments and responsibilities, due dates, and so on.
Gather materials.

Basic Cards Required

Title card.
Introduction card.
Index or menu card (may be part of Introduction card).
Stack cards.
Credits card(s) (citations, acknowledgments, student names, bibliography).

Figure 10–14
Steps in preplanning a multimedia presentation

card or may be followed by either an *index card* or *menu card*. If branching has not started, it usually starts with the index card or menu card. A variety of *stack cards* follow. Be very careful that there are no dead ends. Each card should link to another card if only to an index or menu card. *Credits card/s* with information such as stack authors, citations, acknowledgments, bibliography should close the stack and link back to the title card.

INTO THE CLASSROOM:
Immunization for PowerPoint Poisoning—Creating Conditions for Powerful Presentations

PowerPoint is such a potent multimedia tool that it is tempting for teachers and students to overuse the program's strong capabilities. The effect may be to distort, undermine, and distract from the real message of the presentation. Here are five practical steps that we

(Continued)

tell teachers and students to follow so that they all effectively immunize their presentations against *PowerPoint Poisoning*.

Five Powerful Steps:
1. Plan It!
2. Storyboard It!
3. PowerPoint It!
4. Rehearse It!
5. Present It!

The best immunization for PowerPoint Poisoning is to focus up-front attention and energy on planning, organization, and content.

Plan It!
1. Determine who your audience will be.
2. Determine the purpose and content of the presentation.
3. Review, reevaluate, and revise.

Storyboard It!
1. Organize the information in a logical, understandable sequence for your specific audience.
2. Define the major and minor points of the presentation.
3. Write each major point on a sticky note.
4. Storyboard your sticky notes in logical sequence. Reorganize and rearrange as necessary.
5. Review, reevaluate, and revise.

PowerPoint It!
(The authors suggest following the guidelines presented in Figure 10–12.)

Rehearse It!
1. Practice—practice—practice.
2. Critically evaluate and adjust your PowerPoint presentation in terms of your purpose.
3. Critically evaluate its effectiveness.

Present It!
The proof is in the presentation. Successfully present the final powerful version of your PowerPoint presentation to an enthusiastic audience in your classroom.

Michael S. Houser, Ed.D.
Educational Technologist (retired)
Heidelberg District Superintendent's Office
Department of Defense Dependents' Schools—Europe
Hanau, Germany

Information on where you can obtain a free examination copy of HyperStudio can be found at the Companion Website http://www. prenhall.com/forcier

Simple HyperStudio Stack Construction

It is very simple to produce a simple HyperStudio stack. First, find the HyperStudio program on your hard drive or on the CD-ROM that came with this book and open it up. The first screen that you see should be similar to Figure 10–15. This screen and all of the other information screens were made using *HyperStudio!*

You may want to take a few minutes to familiarize yourself with the information on this screen. The three scroll boxes contain menus to help you learn about HyperStudio. To access some of the information on the menus you must have the *HyperStudio* CD in the CD-ROM drive. The "Learn" menu contains all of the tutorials to help you learn how to use the program. The menu in the *Discover* box contains general information about many of the new features in *HyperStudio* 4.x and are accessed by clicking the "HS4 Preview Menu" here. Further down this same menu are sample lesson plans and school projects. The "Excel" menu contains information on professional development and using the Internet with *HyperStudio*. Press *Open Stack* to open a stack that is made or being made (or, of course, you can simply double-click on the stack to open it). *Quit* does just that. To make a new stack, press the *New Stack* button. Let us start there. Now click "OK" on the next box.

Now go to "Edit" on the top menu and down to "Preferences." Make sure that the box in front of "I'm an experienced HyperStudio user" is NOT checked. This will make sure that the help boxes appear each time to activate a function. If you can see your computer's desktop behind the HyperStudio slide box, click "Presentation Mode," choose a background color to your desktop (use black since this will be the least distracting), click "OK" to close this box and "OK" to close the "Preferences" box. If your desktop was visible, it is now covered in black. Click "OK" to close this box. Now, go back up to the top menu, click and hold down the mouse on "Tools." A drop-down palette will appear. Drag it down onto the screen. Do the same with the "Colors" palette. If the "Extras" and "Shortcuts" palettes are not visible, go to "Extras" on the top menu and click on "Navigation" and "Shortcuts." On the "Options" menu, click on "Show Media Window" if it is not on the screen. Your desktop should be similar to Figure 10–16 at this point. We will put together a simple card. You will notice at each step of the way that we are not going into much detail. Rest assured, you will have time to experiment with *HyperStudio* on your own.

Adding a Background. Make sure that the mouse cursor is an arrow. If it is not, click on the arrow icon (top right) on the "Tools" palette. Select a color for the background from the selection on the "Colors" palette. Choose a very light or very dark color. High contrast with the lettering is very important! Click on a color that you would like for your background on the "Colors" palette, move the arrow cursor back up to the paint bucket icon on the "Tools" menu and click. Now move the arrow cursor onto the card and click the mouse. Since we are going to link a card and our card backgrounds should all be similar, go to the "Edit" menu and "Copy Card," release and "Paste Card." The card on the screen should be "Untitled Card 2." Press the "Back" button on the "Navigation" palette to go back to card 1.

Adding Text. It is easiest to add text using the "Add Text Object" from the "Shortcuts" menu. When this is clicked, a box will appear. Read this box and click "OK."

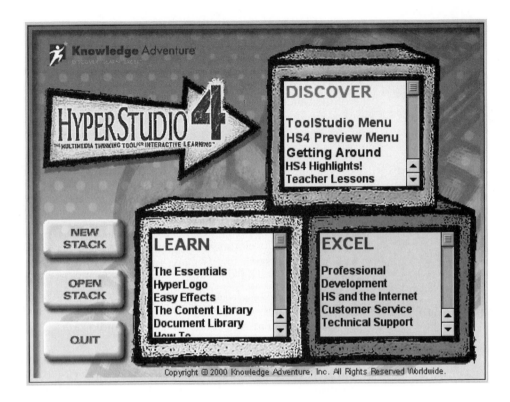

Figure 10–15
HyperStudio home
screen
(Courtesy of
Knowledge
Adventure, Inc.)

Position the text box and click outside the box. The "Text Appearance" box will appear (Figure 10–17).

Notice the four boxes below the "Name:" box. Use these if you do not want a frame or scroll bar on the card. Press the "Style..." button. The "Text Style" box (Figure 10–18) should appear.

Choose a minimum text size of 24, bold, and a sans serif font such as "Charcoal." The text box will be white unless you change the background color now. Choose a text color that will be of high contrast with the background. Click "OK" twice and type text into the text box. If you ever want to change the size of the box or any of the settings, just click on the arrow cursor and double-click on the text box. This will reactivate all of the above screens.

Adding Graphics. Press "Add Graphic" from the "Shortcuts" menu. Find "HS Art" and open "Addy." Use the lasso tool to draw a circle around Addy and click "OK." Place Addy where you want her on the card and click on the card outside of her image. Just click "OK" when the "Graphic Appearances" box appears. (We are adding Addy as a graphic instead of clip art because we can later go back and move a graphic. Clip art is painted onto the background and can't be moved.)

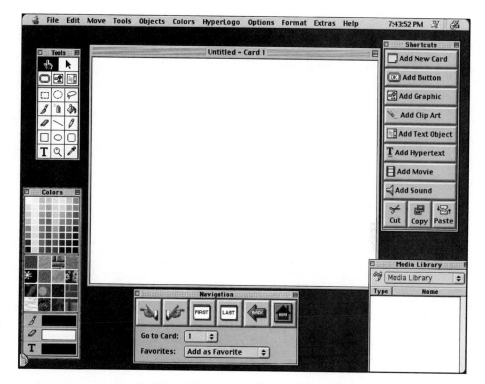

Figure 10–16
HyperStudio desktop
(Courtesy of
Knowledge
Adventure, Inc.)

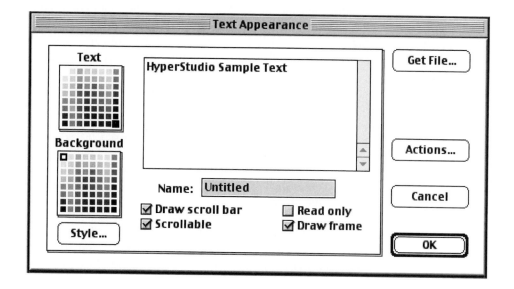

Figure 10–17
HyperStudio® Text
Appearance box
(Reprinted with
permission from
Knowledge
Adventure, Inc.)

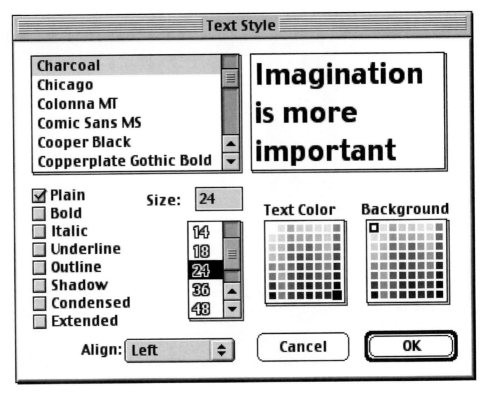

Figure 10–18
HyperStudio® Text
Style box (Reprinted
with permission from
Knowledge
Adventure, Inc.)

Adding a Button. Press "Add Button" on the "Shortcuts" menu. Type in "Next Card" in the "Name" text box. Click "OK." Position the button where you want it and click outside the button. The "Actions" box will appear (Figure 10–19). This is the most powerful box in the entire program. It adds Hyper to *HyperStudio*.

Notice that the right column adds actions to the button and the left column moves changes to another card, stack, or program. It is possible to pick one move from the left column and multiple actions from the right column for each button. For simplicity, just click on "Next Card" in the left-hand column. A "Transitions" box will appear. This is how one card blends into the next. Choose the one you would like and "Try It." "Fast" is usually too fast for me. Click "OK." Now change your arrow to a pointing finger by pressing the pointing finger icon on the "Tools" palette. Your card is complete. When you press the "Next Card" button, the next card will appear.

We have made a very simple stack. Everything in HyperStudio is that easy. If we had more space, we could have added a movie and sound. *HyperStudio* is very powerful but it is really very simple to use. It is possible to save *HyperStudio* presentations in a format so that they can be accessed and shown on the Web. A special *HyperStudio* plug-in must be downloaded and placed in the plug-ins folder of your browser. Remember you can always download a trial copy or request another trial CD-ROM for yourself at the *HyperStudio* Website (http://www.hyperstudio.com).

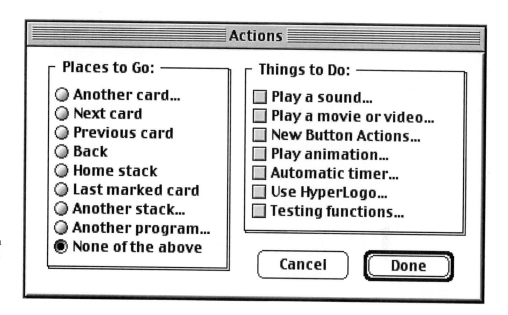

Figure 10–19
HyperStudio® action box (Reprinted with permission from Knowledge Adventure, Inc.)

MULTIMEDIA IN A CONSTRUCTIVIST CLASSROOM

Susan K. Arnold (1996) set out to prove that using multimedia technology as a tool for accessing information and demonstrating knowledge would improve self-directedness in learners. Her research took place in a suburban elementary school of 14 mixed-age classrooms, with an average of 26 students in each class. Her sample population consisted of 51 students in two fourth-/fifth-grade classes. The students were placed in two heterogeneous groups, with consideration given to balancing the variables of grade level and students with special needs.

The groups were assigned a four-week research project on the topic of United States immigration. Group A was taught how to use electronic technology to retrieve information and produce a multimedia report in *HyperStudio*. Group B was restricted from using electronic technology. At the end of four weeks, the groups were assigned another four-week research project; this time on famous Americans. Group A was restricted from using electronic technology and Group B was taught how to use electronic technology to produce a multimedia report. At the end of the eight weeks, the students presented the results of their projects to their peers, teachers, parents, and invited guests.

The analysis of the data focused on differences within each group, not on differences across the two groups. Class mean scores using the Oregon Department of Education Student Self-Directed Learning Scoring Guide showed substantial improvement when students had access to electronic technology. The table presented as Figure 10–20 summarizes multimedia technology's impact on the students.

	More When Using Technology (%)	More When Not Using Technology (%)
Effective Work Habits		
Focused attention on research	73%	27%
Used time wisely	69	31
Set goals each day	69	31
Had better work habits	67	33
Followed a Work Plan		
Enjoyed researching and gathering materials	57	43
Did a better job finding resources	62	38
Hardest work	65	35
Best-quality work	76	24
Self-Reflection		
Felt responsible for getting work done	72	28
Project that communicated information best	73	27
Project liked doing best	90	10
Proudest of project	79	21

Figure 10–20
Technology's impact on student self-directedness

Students took a good deal of pride in the multimedia presentations they had prepared. Students who had been identified as "At Risk" were observed being significantly more involved during the electronic technology treatment and exhibiting a higher degree of personal responsibility. These are the feelings students had about their exposure to multimedia technology, captured in their own words (Arnold, 1996):

"I really took time to do a good job. I stayed in at breaks to finish it."

"I worked longer on the technology project and it wasn't just slopped together."

"It's like it's easier to stick to the project."

"My tech project shows my hardest work. It looks a heck of a lot better. I worked hard to make it neat, interesting, and fun for the person looking at it."

"My technology project looks more professional."

"When I use technology I feel . . . powerful and different. Learning's more fun."

"I feel privileged because in other generations people were not able to do this. We're lucky!"

Multimedia technology can be a catalyst for change, helping teachers alter their approach to teaching and learning from passive learning to active learning. Roblyer (1999) found that one of the benefits of multimedia is that it gives students a chance to experience and process information through any of several multiple channels. This "may have unique capabilities to facilitate learning because of the parallels between multimedia and the natural way people learn" (Bagui, 1998, p. 4).

Technology can lead teachers to develop more learner-centered environments. Students learned more than was expected and also developed new competencies like the ability to collaborate, to recognize and analyze problems as systems, to acquire and use large amounts of information, and to apply technology to solve real-world problems (Dwyer, 1996).

SUMMARY

Multimedia employs more than one way of conveying information in a multisensory manner. Multimedia computer programs are used to control the presentation of video, graphic, audio, and textual information from external sources such as videotape, CD-ROM, and DVD. Hypermedia uses a nonlinear method of conveying multimedia information.

Multimedia authoring tools allow students and teachers to create and compose desktop presentations, hypertext and hypermedia documents, Web pages, and other multimedia productions. These creations might include computer-generated sound, graphics, and animation, along with sound and visual forms stored in another medium such as videotape or CD-ROM.

Presentation software makes it possible to index slides, view thumbnail representations in a slide sorter format, and prescribe their subsequent viewing in a specific sequence.

Multimedia technology can be a catalyst for change, helping teachers to alter their approach to teaching and learning from passive learning to active learning. Students take a good deal of pride in preparing multimedia presentations. Students' self-directedness and other study and learning habits may show substantial improvement when students have access to multimedia technology.

CHAPTER EXERCISES

To complete the specified exercises on-line, go to the Chapter Exercises Module in Chapter 10 of the Companion Website.

1. Evaluate a multimedia program from your school's software collection. Did it take full advantage of the multimedia format? What were its strengths and weaknesses? Can you suggest a better way to convey the same information?
2. If your principal told you that you could buy any two multimedia software packages to use in your class, which ones would you choose? Write a short paragraph explaining your choices to the principal.
3. Log on to the *HyperStudio* Website. Review the information and projects available on the site. Write a short paragraph telling how this site may be helpful to you in your teaching. What are some of the problems you foresee in trying to add multimedia presentations to your teaching.
4. If you have not already done so, obtain some software catalogs that list software sales such as the one from Learning Services™ (1-800-877-3278). Review the types of software being purchased today. How many of the popular ones do you recognize? How many have you tried firsthand?

What conclusions can you make regarding the types of software being purchased?

5. Search AskERIC or another lesson plan archive for lesson plans using multimedia software. Present your findings to the class.

6. Search the electronic database of educational periodicals in your school's library for articles discussing multimedia use and multimedia software. Write a short review of one of the articles. Discuss your review with the class.

7. Ask a student teaching supervisor, mentor teacher, cooperating teacher, etc., about the multimedia software found in the schools in your area. What software seems most popular? What obstacles do they see that might inhibit its use in the school? Discuss your findings with the class.

8. Design a multimedia project for the grade level you wish to teach. How many types of media can you incorporate into the project? Discuss your project with the class.

9. Look again at the project that you designed above. Can it be used with handicapped students or students with limited English proficiency? What could you do to make it more accessible?

10. Search the electronic database of educational periodicals in your school's library for the five most recent articles on multimedia in the classroom. What do the authors believe is the apparent impact on education?

PORTFOLIO DEVELOPMENT EXERCISES

To complete this exercise on-line, go to the Digital Portfolio Module in Chapter 10 of the Companion Website.

One of the NETS•S standards covered in this chapter was "Students are proficient in the use of technology" under *Category 1: Basic operations and concepts.* A second one was "Students evaluate and select new information resources and technological innovations based on the appropriateness for specific tasks" under *Category 5: Technology research tools.* Begin to develop your own portfolio of lesson plans that demonstrates your ability to have your students reach these NETS•S standards.

For more information on developing digital portfolios, go to Digital Portfolio Module on the Companion Website www.prenhall.com/forcier

1. Design a lesson plan activity for elementary, middle school, or high school students in which they will work in groups to design and produce a multimedia presentation about your class, a subject they have or will be studying, or their school. They should use a form of HTML editor, PowerPoint, or HyperStudio. This presentation should be designed to be presented to a group other than their own classmates, such as their parents, religious or community organization, or school board. This lesson should demonstrate that your students have achieved the standard. Be sure to include a system of evaluation for your students' understanding and competence to ensure that they have met this standard.

2. Adapt the lesson plan activity you developed in exercise 1 for students to evaluate each others' work.

GLOSSARY

action The programmed result of clicking on a hypermedia button.

button A visible object or an invisible area of the screen, often covering images or text, that can be programmed using a scripting language to perform certain actions.

card One screen or frame of a hypermedia presentation.

desktop presentation The design, creation, and display of textual and graphic information under the control of a personal computer.

digital multimedia A multimedia design that allows a computer user to combine and control a number of instructional resources in order to present information.

dissolve Moving from one screen to the next by having one visual fade out as the second fades in.

hypermedia A multimedia presentation that contains links or buttons that will allow the product to be presented in a nonlinear fashion.

hypertext A term synonymous with hypermedia but emphasizes textual links instead of buttons.

multimedia A technique that conveys information in a multisensory manner. It might include the use of textual, graphic, audio, and video materials to convey information to the user, who would interact with it by reading, listening, and observing still and moving images.

stack A group of cards linked together to form a complete hypermedia presentation.

virtual reality (VR) Computer-based technologies ranging from sophisticated 3-D simulations to full immersion experiences.

wipe Moving from one slide to the next by having one slide replace the next by covering it across the screen as from left to right or top to bottom.

REFERENCES & SUGGESTED READINGS

Arnold, S. (1996). *Effects of integrative technology on student self-directedness at Mountain View Elementary School.* Unpublished thesis for a Master of Education degree in Information Technology, Western Oregon University.

Bagui, S. (1998). Reasons for increased learning using multimedia. *Journal of Educational Multimedia and Hypermedia, 7*(1), 3–18.

Dale, E. (1969). *Audio-visual methods in teaching* (3rd ed). New York: Holt, Rinehart and Winston, 108.

Dwyer, D. (1996, Winter). Apple classrooms of tomorrow, the first ten years. *Apple Education Digest.* (*http://www.info.apple.com/education/acot.menu.html*)

QED. *Educational technology trends 1997.* Denver: Quality Education Data, 1997.

Roblyer, M. D. (1999). Our multimedia future: Recent research on multimedia's impact on education. *Learning and Leading with Technology, 26*(6), 51–53.

Tolhurst, D. (1995). Hypertext, hypermedia, multimedia defined? *Educational Technology, 35*(2), 21–26.

11

Learning with Internet Tools

1. What is the Internet and how did it develop?

2. What kinds of resources are available on the Internet?

3. What are some tools that increase the user's productivity when using the Internet?

4. What is the World Wide Web and how does it relate to the Internet?

5. How does one publish on the World Wide Web?

6. How are advances in telecommunications affecting the teaching/learning process?

7. How can a user maximize the World Wide Web's potential as an information source?

8. What are some styles for citing references to information obtained on the World Wide Web?

9. What are some copyright and ownership concerns regarding information, either textual or graphical, obtained from the Internet?

In Chapter 11 we cover parts of all of the NETS•S categories. We continue with our coverage of *Category 1: Basic operations and concepts* with a discussion of the Internet and the various tools that are available to use it effectively. Standards listed under *Category 2: Social, ethical, and human issues* are covered here as we discuss filtering and intellectual property. *Category 3: Technology productivity tools* are covered as students use the Internet to enhance learning, increase productivity, and prepare and produce creative projects. *Category 4: Technology communications tools* is covered as we discuss some of the ways that students and teachers can use the Internet to collaborate, publish, and interact with individuals from around the world. The Internet fits closely into any coverage of *Category 5: Technology research tools.* Our discussion covers all of the tools that a student would use while using the Internet for research along with ways that a student can evaluate Internet information. In addition, the Web page construction and HTML editor discussion shows how students can process the data gathered over the Internet and use the Internet as another form to report their findings. This fits nicely into *Category 6: Technology problem-solving and decision-making tools* as students are given more tools to find and process information found on the Internet. As you read this chapter, it is important for you to be aware of the NETS•S standards that your students will have to meet, just as it is important for you to be aware of the standards you need to meet as a teacher. Incorporating these standards into your classroom will help you to develop lesson plans and activities and learning environments that will not only benefit your students, but yourself as well.

NETS•S Standards Addressed in This Chapter

1. Basic operations and concepts
    - Students demonstrate a sound understanding of the nature and operation of technology systems.
    - Students are proficient in the use of technology.

2. Social, ethical, and human issues
    - Students understand the ethical, cultural, and societal issues related to technology.
    - Students practice responsible use of technology systems, information, and software.
    - Students develop positive attitudes toward technology uses that support lifelong learning, collaboration, personal pursuits, and productivity.

3. Technology productivity tools
    - Students use technology tools to enhance learning, increase productivity, and promote creativity.
    - Students use productivity tools to collaborate in constructing technology-enhanced models, prepare publications, and produce other creative works.

4. Technology communications tools
    - Students use telecommunications to collaborate, publish, and interact with peers, experts, and other audiences.
    - Students use a variety of media and formats to communicate information and ideas effectively to multiple audiences.

5. Technology research tools
    - Students use technology to locate, evaluate, and collect information from a variety of sources.
    - Students use technology tools to process data and report results.

6. Technology problem-solving and decision-making tools
    - Students use technology resources for solving problems and making informed decisions.
    - Students employ technology in the development of strategies for solving problems in the real world.

 A list of the ISTE/NCATE standards addressed in this chapter is available in the Standards Module on the Companion Website www.prenhall.com/forcier

THE INTERNET

It would be impossible, within a single chapter of a textbook, to thoroughly describe all of the features of a topic so far-reaching and as constantly changing as the world-wide collection of computer networks known as the **Internet.** It is without a doubt the best-known network today. In reality, though, it is not a network of computers but rather a network of computer networks. The beginnings of this super-network, called ARPAnet (Advanced Research Projects Agency network), named for the agency that designed it, was a Cold War attempt by the U.S. Department of Defense in the mid-1960s to build a decentralized network linking government installations in the hope that such a network would survive a nuclear attack on the United States. The diffuse nature of the network did not rely on a single pathway to move data but rather contained multiple pathways between each point. If one route (such as a telephone line or fiber optic cable) is busy or destroyed, files or pieces of files called packets are simply transmitted over other routes until they all arrive at their destination, where they are reassembled into the complete file. A set of standards, called **Transmission Control Protocol/Internet Protocol (TCP/IP),** was developed to allow different networks and different types of computers to interconnect. As long as the computer, regardless of operating system (Windows, MacOS, Linux, etc.) runs a version of TCP/IP software, it can send packets to any other computer over the Internet. The commercialization of the Internet in the late 1990s caused such an explosion in interest that the Internet now spans the globe and serves hundreds of millions of users. The original, decentralized design of the Internet with no one central hub and no centralized control has interesting ramifications. The Internet was originally intended to facilitate the free exchange of ideas and information in a military, and later an academic, context. This tradition of free exchange is a major reason why most longtime Internet users resist most forms of regulation or censorship, including governmental regulations governing pornographic sites, taxation of products bought over the Internet, and ownership of audio, video, text, or graphics posted on the Internet. Now that commercial interests have become such an important part of the Internet, copyright and intellectual property laws have become increasingly important. Because of this, you must remember that *everything on the Internet is owned by the person who placed or contracted to have it placed there.* You cannot download text, graphics, movies, etc., from the Internet without considering the legal implications. Luckily, there are many sites on the Internet that contain huge amounts of free graphics, movies, and sounds for teachers to download and use for nonprofit purposes. Just place the words *clip art* and *education* into a search engine and look at the results.

Most people see the Internet as an enormous and immediate source of information, while others see it as an expansive channel for profitable sales of goods and services. Many are concerned about some of its content or about the social inequities of access to its potential. Regardless of personal viewpoint, the Internet will stand alongside Gutenberg's printing press as one of the greatest change agents in human history.

For educators, the Internet offers many opportunities to access an ever-increasing base of knowledge, resources, and people on a global scale. Students may search extensively for information relevant to their lives and aspirations, may increase or refine their communication skills, and may practice critical evaluation of the information available to them. In addition, the Internet provides a rich environment for students to discuss, display, and transmit the knowledge they have constructed with others outside of their immediate community. It also contains many hazards ranging from fictitious information designed to deceive people, to pornography and other material not fit for children and young adults. In fact, 60 percent of teen Internet users surveyed said that they have been contacted by strangers (Poftak, 2002). Regardless of the diversity of opinion about its uses, the Internet is rapidly expanding as a dynamic repository for human knowledge and experience, and it will continue to have a profound influence on both the form and the content of human communications.

The students in your classes will not be strangers to the Internet. Students ages 12 to 17 with Internet access spend an average of 7 hours, 36 minutes on-line from home; 1 hour 36 minutes on-line from school; and 1 hour, 6 minutes on-line from a friend's or relative's home per week (Poftak, 2002). Many of them have been on the Internet most of their lives. Don't be afraid to ask them for help and assistance!

INTERNET RESOURCES AND APPLICATIONS

As one would expect with the world at our fingertips, the amount of information available is staggering. Internet software is user-friendly and allows even a novice user to send and receive e-mail, search and surf the Web, and download everything from clip art to software at the click of a mouse. As a result, 71 percent of teen Internet users say that they choose the Internet over going to the library to complete school projects even though only 51 percent of the students believe that "most or all" of the information on the Web is accurate (Poftak, 2002). Material on the Internet is not filtered for truth, bias, or accuracy as it would be in a real library. Because of this, it is imperative that information found, posted on, or transmitted through the Internet be subject to the same critical evaluation for accuracy and reliability that we might give to any other unfiltered media. This is a wonderful opportunity for us as educators to incorporate training and practice in critical thinking and information evaluation skills within any classroom activity that involves use of the Internet.

Let us take a look at the range of Internet applications available. Each application is a tool that has its own unique features and ways that it can be used in the curriculum. As we have said, good tools, chosen wisely, help us work more efficiently and effectively. Learning should always drive the use of technology and not vice versa.

Electronic Mail

Electronic mail or **e-mail** has become a part of everyday life for many of us. E-mail allows users to exchange messages with others, whether they are right next door or around the globe. All that is needed is an Internet connection, an e-mail program or Web browser, and the recipient's e-mail address. Free e-mail accounts are available on the World Wide Web from such places as yahoo.com, msn.com, hotmail.com, and even sites like I-love-dogs.com, to name just a few. [A survey of teen Internet users found that 56 percent of them have two or more e-mail addresses (Poftak, 2002)!] The number of e-mail messages sent surpassed those sent by regular postal delivery way back in 1995!

E-mail has phenomenal holding power. Students eagerly spend time each day reading and writing at the computer. What an opportunity for a teacher to develop language arts skills! Once the novelty and electronic pen-pal syndrome wear off, students might see e-mail as a means of accessing information on specific topics and learning about different cultures. A study of college students suggested that an e-mail journal helped students to increase self-assessment skills and synthesize their learning better than traditional journaling.

Let us take a quick look at e-mail addresses. The authors' addresses are RPForcicr@AOL.com and DDescy@yahoo.com. These addresses are composed of two basic parts (1) the *user ID* (mailbox) and (2) the *domain* and *subdomains* (name and location of the computer). These two parts are separated by an @ symbol. So an e-mail address is really *mailbox(at)computerlocation*. E-mail addresses are not case specific.

Typical e-mail addresses are shown in Figure 11–1.

Reading the addresses from right to left, .net on the forcier address represents one of the major domains on the Internet and identifies the site as a network. On the descy address, *.edu,* represents another major domain on the Internet and identifies the site as a post-secondary educational one. Some other domains are government agencies (.gov), commercial vendors (.com), and organizations (.org). International sites are frequently identified geographically by two characters representing the country in which they are located—for example, Canada (.ca), United Kingdom (.uk), and Australia (.au). Because of the phenomenal volume of new users joining the Internet, the convention of using geographic identifiers within the United States is supplementing the use of .edu and similar domain names. Many public schools in the United States have addresses that include the school, grade level, state, and country. For example, the e-mail address for Pinellas Central Elementary School in Florida is (person's name) @pinellas.k12.fl.us. Each part of an address is separated by a dot (period).

Again, reading the forcier address from the right, the next part of the address, *AOL,* identifies the subdomain name of the network provider subscribed to (sometimes called the **Internet Service Provider** or simply **ISP** for short). On the descy address, *yahoo,* is the subdomain name identifying a computer located at yahoo. com. The symbol @ separates the leftmost part of the address, which is the user ID

Figure 11–1
Parts of Internet e-mail addresses

> - E-mail is not private. Write only what you would not mind others reading.
>
> - E-mail written on school or business computers may be the property of that school or business.
>
> - Many times deleted e-mail is not deleted but is still on your hard drive or backed up and stored by your network or service provider.
>
> - Place only general information in your e-mail signature. Personal information such as home phone or home address should be avoided.
>
> - If you receive unsolicited advertisements, chain letters, junk mail (called Spam), do not reply to ask to be taken off their mailing list. You are telling the Spamer that your mail account is active and your reply message may lead to even more Spam.
>
> - Choose a password that is easy to remember but is difficult to link to you.
>
> - Never give your e-mail password to others.

Figure 11–2
E-mail safety
practices

(or mailbox), RPForcier or DDescy. Now that you know our addresses, we hope to hear from you with your comments and suggestions related to this book. We do read them all and, many times, incorporate reader suggestions into new editions of the text.

Practice sessions provide the opportunity to stress proper communication rules and mitigate what some believe to be e-mail's negative effect on writing habits and skills because of its informal nature. It is always prudent to keep in mind the safety practices listed in Figure 11–2.

Many e-mail programs now contain spelling and grammar checkers. If this is not the case with the one that your students are using, they might want to compose their communication off-line on a word processor, following guidelines for grammar and spelling, then copy and paste their message into the message area of the e-mail program. Figure 11–3 reviews some e-mail etiquette (called netiquette!) that users should follow.

E-mail Discussion Groups (LISTSERVs)

E-mail discussion groups, sometimes called *mailing lists* or **LISTSERVs.** (LISTSERV™ is a trademark for a particular brand of e-mail discussion group software. It can only be legally used when that software is being used for the e-mail discussion group.) An e-mail discussion group is an automated mailing list that accepts incoming messages from a person whose e-mail address is on a master mailing list and forwards it to all of the other e-mail addresses on the master list. The process of adding your e-mail address to an e-mail discussion group is called *subscribing*. E-mail discussion groups develop around common interests (i.e., Shakespeare, ESL, English teachers, Bedlington terriers, or perhaps there is one for your own class). It is very easy to join an e-mail discussion group. In many cases it is just a matter of sending

Figure 11–3
E-mail "netiquette" network communication etiquette

NETIQUETTE

- Compose all but brief messages off-line to minimize network traffic.
- Limit each message to one topic and keep it succinct.
- Use subject headings that are very descriptive.
- Reply promptly to messages received.
- When replying, restate only enough of the message to clearly identify context.
- Treat e-mail to you as you would a regular mail letter. Do not forward it to others without the writer's permission.
- Delete messages once you have read them.
- Don't be vulgar or offensive.
- Don't attempt to represent yourself as someone you are not.
- Don't criticize ("flame") others on the network.
- Supply clues if you are intending to write using humor, irony, sarcasm, or emotion. Your intent may not be obvious to the reader. Using all uppercase in a word or phrase SHOUTS. Try :-) for a sideways smile or ;-) for a wink.
- Use a signature footer that includes your name, school, and e-mail address.
- Practice safe communications. Don't spread viruses! Check downloaded executable files.
- Consider yourself a guest on the system and behave accordingly.

---

a message such as *subscribe* to the group address. E-mail discussion groups are usually run by a computer with no human help; therefore, you must follow the *subscribe* and *unsubscribe* procedures and directions on how to send messages and reply directly to others exactly.

E-mail discussion groups are a wonderful place to gather information, keep up-to-date with happenings and news in your field, find answers to questions, and meet people with your same interests. When you ask a question on an e-mail discussion group, you are accessing the minds of hundreds of colleagues from all over the country and perhaps even the world. It is very easy to set up your own discussion group for free for a club or organization you belong to. One such free site is yahoogroups.com.

 Information and representative e-mail discussion groups for educators can be found at the Companion Website http://www.prenhall.com/forcier

Many e-mail discussion groups have a *digest feature* that collects all of the messages each day and just sends you one large message containing all of them. Do join an e-mail discussion group of interest. Don't oversubscribe to multiple e-mail discussion groups though. You will find that they require considerable time just to read or delete the messages!

Internet Relay Chat (IRC)

Internet Relay Chat (IRC) is a real-time public discussion. Individuals log onto a specific site or *chat room* and watch as others type in messages to other people also in the "room." A chat room does not exist as a physical room but rather the term is a metaphor for the specific location on the host computer where all of the messages for a particular group pass through. The individual may join the conversation by typing in messages that will also be displayed on the screen for others in the room to read. It is also possible to hold a private conversation with another individual in the chat room. There are hundreds of chat rooms around the world covering just about all areas of interest. Many of you, as college students, know of friends who spend hours in chat rooms every week. Many public schools limit student access to chat rooms since there is no real way to identify who the students are chatting with or what their intended purposes may be. Several screened chat rooms for teenagers can be found at Teen Chat Center (http://www.teenchatcenter.com/).

Instant Messaging

Instant messaging is like IRC but it is carried on between two individuals or a small group of people using software that each have on their computer. As one person types on their computer, the typing is also displayed on the other person's computer. Individuals using cell phones and pagers can also join in. Many instant messaging programs are available free on-line from such places as AOL/Netscape, Microsoft, and Yahoo. Along with conversation, photos, audio, and live Web cams can be used with most programs. Interactive themed backgrounds are available in a variety of subjects from cartoons to movies to animals and nature. Many programs allow the typist to take on the appearance or role of one of the characters in the theme. A survey released in November 2002 found that nearly 87 million people in the United States were using instant messaging (Anthony, 2002).

World Wide Web

Many people confuse the Internet with the **World Wide Web.** The Web is defined as "a global hypertext system that uses the Internet as its transport mechanism" (Pfaffenberger, 2000). Just as a telephone line can carry your conversation, FAX messages, and computer traffic, the Internet can carry e-mail, instant messages, and Web pages.

Web pages are written in a "code" called **HTML** (HyperText Markup Language) that will be discussed later in the chapter. You probably noticed that all Web page addresses start with "http." **HTTP** (HyperText Transfer Protocol) is the set of rules that govern how Web pages are written, transferred, and displayed. HTTP assures anyone following this protocol that their pages can be accessed, transferred, and displayed by everyone else following the same protocol regardless of the platform they are using (Windows, Macintosh, Unix, etc.).

Two pieces of software are required to view a Web page. These are **Web server** software and **Web browser** software. Web server software is located on a computer, called the *host,* that contains the Web pages. Server software is needed to access the Web pages on the host computer and to transmit the Web page over the Internet to other computers. Web server software is very easy to set up and use. It must be placed on a computer with a permanent Internet address that can be left on at all times. Apache^{TM}, Microsoft IIS^{TM}, Netscape-Enterprise^{TM}, and WebStar^{TM} are a few popular Web server software packages. A Web browser is software that runs on the user's machine, translates HTML code received from a remote Web server, and displays the Web page on the user's machine. Common browsers are Internet Explorer^{TM}, Netscape Navigator^{TM}, and Apple Safari^{TM}. Web browser software must be on the receiving computer to receive and display the Web page.

The World Wide Web is comprised of many Websites, each having a unique address called a **Uniform Resource Locator (URL)** (see below). Each Website contains at least one Web page. The main page of a Website is the one usually accessed first and is called its **home page.** A Website may have a number of pages, each capable of displaying text, graphics, and dynamic links to other pages, other sites, sounds (audio), movies (video), etc.

Mosaic™ was the first graphic browser. A graphic browser displays pictures, backgrounds, etc., along with the text. Netscape Navigator was derived from Mosaic. Microsoft Internet Explorer is the most popular Web browser in use today. Apple Safari, first released in 2003, is designed to make full use of the new Macintosh OS X operating system and is said to be the fastest browser for the Macintosh.

Internet Explorer allows us to create **favorites** (called **bookmarks** on the Netscape and Safari browsers) to identify sites so we can return to them easily. Favorites, in fact, become a personalized directory of your favorite Web pages. The favorite file is saved on our computer as an individual file that can be transferred electronically to another computer and then used to call up the Website on the new computer. Remember that when we purchase a new computer, you just have to transfer your favorites file from your old computer to your new computer. The help menu on the browser should explain how to perform this task. In addition, the entire set of favorites for a given computer can be saved as an HTML file that can be opened and viewed as a document in another computer's browser, complete with the individual favorites linked to their URLs. Educators can utilize these capabilities to provide for Internet-based lessons, with students directed to specific Web locations in the order desired by the instructor.

Features common to most Web browsers include the ability to print out the Web page, giving students the means to capture information from the Web. This print capability is important in a classroom or media center setting, where there are many students yet fewer computers with Internet connections, because it allows students to progressively get on-line, download some information, and free up the computer for another student. An even more efficient feature is the ability of most browsers to copy both text and images to temporary memory and save to disk. This is usually accomplished by highlighting the text desired and then using the Edit . . . Copy command to place the text in temporary (RAM) memory, and then using the Edit . . . Paste command to place the text into, for instance, a word processing document or e-mail message. Images can also be copied into memory or saved to disk by simply pressing down the right mouse button on Windows computers as the pointer rests on the image (pressing the mouse button on the Macintosh will do the same thing). Again, we will stress that items posted on the Web are automatically owned (copyrighted) by the person who posts them, providing they were not taken illegally from somewhere else. Students should always properly cite their Web sources, using the appropriate electronic citation style (presented in a section later in this chapter). Most Web browsers also include a mail and instant messaging function.

Uniform Resource Locator. The World Wide Web is a disjointed array of billions of Web pages located on Web servers all over the world. Even though these pages are scattered around with little or no order, it is possible to access many of them (we cannot access some military, government, and commercial Web pages for obvious reasons). We can do this because each and every Web page has a unique address called the Uniform Resource Locator (URL). Typing the Web page's unique URL in the proper location in a browser sends the browser off to that location to retrieve the Web page. The browser connects with the Web server only long enough to retrieve the Web page. It then frees the Web server up to serve the page to other individuals. Parts of the Web page are stored in the browser on your computer in a storage area (file) called the **cache**. This speeds up loading of the page next time by using the information stored in the cache rather than retrieving it from the distant computer again. The parts of a URL are explained in Figure 11–4. It is imperative that the user types in the URL exactly, noting the use of either uppercase or lowercase letters in the URL to the right of the single slash following the name of the host computer, along with the use and placement of characters such as the colon, slash, period, tilde, and underscore.

Searching the Web. As we said before, there are billions of Web pages scattered on computers all over the world. Think of the volumes of information available to you with just a few taps on the keyboard! All you need to know is the URL of the page you want! Unfortunately, it is not that easy because there is no master list from which to just look up the URL. According to data gathered by Notess in 2000, Fast™, the largest search engine, had a database of 300 million URLs. Today, the largest is Google™ with well over 3 billion URLs (Notess, 2002). That may sound impressive but Notess found that over 22 percent of these URLs are dead (no longer accessible) and up to 25 percent of the URLs are listed in the database but not yet cataloged or described. So what are we going to do? First, we can keep our own record of URLs. Many times a bookmark file in our browser is not enough. It may soon become overcrowded and unmanageable. We can use file cards or lists created with a word processor. Better yet, we can create a computer database file of our favorite URLs identifying them by type or category. We can make note of any useful URLs as we read professional journals, magazines, and newspapers. We should also ask our colleagues (and students!) for their favorite URLs.

Search tools are various software programs located on the Internet designed to make finding information on the Internet easier. There are two basic categories of search tools: *search engines* and *directories*. **Search engines** index the contents of

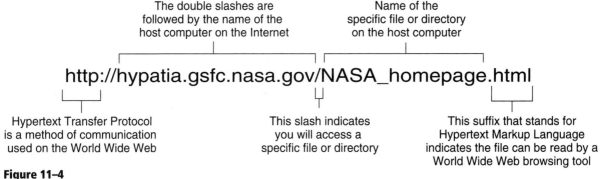

Figure 11–4
The component parts of a URL

Websites using words contained on the site and allow the user to search for information based on a set of search criteria, including keywords and logical connectors (e.g., AND, OR, NOT). **Directories** or catalogs (subject directories, subject guides, and specialized databases) are organized by subject areas. Search tools do not go out and actively search the Web for us each time we type in a keyword. This would be very time-consuming and difficult. If this were the case, the search tool would have to search all of the millions of computers on the Web to find accessible Web pages and then search all of these pages for the keyword(s) we typed in. Rather, each search tool relies on a database of Websites that they are cataloging from the Web. Websites listed in *subject directories* such as Yahoo™ are usually hand-selected by reviews and editors and carefully arranged into subject categories. Search engines, on the other hand, utilize software programs, called **spiders** or **robots** that travel the Web, usually by following links on known pages, adding new pages and keywords at every step of the way. This finding and cataloging process goes on with very little human interaction. Even with all of this, only about 20 percent of the Web is cataloged in all of the search tools around the world combined!

The process of searching is fundamentally similar to that used to search through databases or in on-line library catalogs. That is, the user enters a search term, and then the directory or search engine looks through its database of Internet sites for the best matches. We should caution you not to just look at the first matches or *hits* since some search engines and directories charge money to display certain Web pages at the top of the list. Directories such as Yahoo (http://www.yahoo.com) provide additional categories and subcategories of information to assist in narrowing down the search. Search engines such as Google (http://www.google.com) search Web pages in their database for a match with any of the words posted on these pages and rely on logical connectors, as well as other qualifiers to narrow the search. Meta-search engines, such as MetaCrawler™ and DogPile™, search other search engines. For example, MetaCrawler (http://www.metacrawler.com) searches About.com, Ask Jeeves, Excite Precision Search, Fast, FindWhat, Google, Inktomi, Looksmart, OpenDirectory, Overture, and Sprinks all at the same time! At first glance, it would seem that meta-search engines are the ones to use. Unfortunately, meta-searches are superficial (see Figure 11–5), barely finding 10 percent of keyword citations from each search engine they visit. Only about 40 percent of the results found in one search engine may be unique to that search engine. About 60 percent will overlap with results of other searches.

With so many Web pages in the world, it is not very easy to find the one that you may want. Note the number of hits in Figure 11–5 that a simple search using the keyword phrase *lesson plans* found. Interestingly, MetaCrawler was searched five times in rapid succession and produced 77, 69, 88, 85, and 66 hits! Adding the search terms *elementary* and *civil war* reduced the number of hits considerably. Unfortunately, the number of hits was still staggering for the most part. Each of these particular search tools are programmed to list their results by "relevance," even though some, as we have said, had paid sites listed first. The terms *lesson plans* and *civil war* were grouped by quotation marks so they would be interpreted by the search tool as one term. We entered *"lesson plans" elementary "civil war"* in the search box in each tool. The order of our three terms did not matter. It is important to look at

Search Tool	"lesson plans"	"lesson plans" elementary "civil war"
AllTheWeb	2,011,752	38,411
AltaVista	631,297	7,107
Dog Pile*	2,686	36
Google	1,309,000	9,470
Lycos	2,009,312	38,426
MetaCrawler*	77	50
MSN	731,852	6,149
Yahoo (search)	1,290,000	9,130
Yahoo (directory)	31	0

*Dog Pile and MetaCrawler search multiple search engines

Figure 11–5
Hits for different search phrases using popular search tools

sites deeper into the list and not just on the first page. It is also important to use several search tools. It is interesting to note that the two meta-search tools had the fewest hits even though they advertise that they use several search tools in each search. The meta-search tool Dog Pile found only 10 sites through Google. Using the same terms, Google by itself found 9,470!

Teaching search strategies to students will pay off in a more efficient use of their time while on-line and will give them experience in the logical cognitive process of defining and narrowing a search for information. We strongly encourage you not to ever do a search for the first time in class or hand out a search assignment that you have not rechecked within the past 24 hours. There are many sites on the Web that you would not want your students to stumble into or have them tell their parents that you stumbled into. It is not uncommon for you to do a search on a term one day and find good sites and a few days later do the same search and find some inappropriate sites.

If we were to state two rules about searching, they would be: (1) *Don't limit* your search to a "favorite" search engine or directory. Always use several engines and directories for each of your searches. (2) *Read* the information on how to use that particular search engine or directory. Each search tool uses a slightly different method to search its database.

The Invisible Web

The *visible Web* is defined as that part of the Web that is searchable by regular search engines. The **invisible Web** is defined as that part of the Web that is unable to be searched by regular search engines.

Most of the invisible Web is made up of the contents of thousands of specialized *searchable databases* that can be searched via the Web. BrightPlanet™, a research company specializing in searching the invisible Web, estimates that the invisible Web with its over 350,000 specialized databases is 500 times larger than the visible Web (Bergman, 2003)! If you can search for books in your college library, you are searching one of these databases. Along with library holdings, other databases include newspapers and other publications, museums, medical information, yellow pages, classified listings, job databases, travel schedules, shopping and auctions, and many other databases containing specialized listings. These databases construct the Web page with your results on the fly after you type in the search terms. The page you will see does not exist until after you press enter. At that time, the computer searches for what you are looking for and constructs a Web page with the results. This is called a *dynamic* Web page as opposed to a *static* Web page that already exists. The second group of Web pages that make up the invisible web are *excluded pages*. Excluded pages are pages that Web search engines are not programmed to search or the search engine owner does not want it to search for some reason. Pages are usually excluded because of format. Examples of excluded formats include PDF, Flash, Shockwave, Word, WordPerfect, and PowerPoint (Google now catalogues several of these). Pages may also be excluded if the page contains script-based commands. Script is a programming language. You can tell a script-based page if the URL contains a "?".

Since the largest search engines such as Google or NorthernLight™ index no more than 16 percent of the visible Web, we are only searching 0.03 percent of the Web or one in 3,000 pages that are really out there (BrightPlanet, 2001).

How do we find information that is held in the invisible Web? As you may have noticed as you read some of the descriptions of the "invisible" databases above, Web pages like yahoo.com have links to some of these at the bottom of their pages. Jobs, airline schedules, auctions, people, etc., are just a few that they list. You can also enter the search term *invisible Web* into a search engine. Many of the hits will contain lists of invisible, but searchable databases.

Due to the character of the Internet, definite rules should be followed when students are searching on-line. Figure 11–6 suggests some of these rules.

Filtered Search Engines

Several search engines (Google and Yahoo, for example) offer filtered search modes. We can turn the filters on and off by clicking on a menu that can be accessed through the "Advanced Search" feature of these search engines. Each one filters a little bit differently. With some we are even able to set and password protect the filtering parameters. No Internet filtering device is perfect though. Some good sites may be filtered out and some inappropriate sites may not be filtered. Figure 11–7 identifies a student-friendly Website for kids to use for searching (*Ask Jeeves for Kids*™ and *Onekey*™ are other examples).

Citing Internet Resources

The citation form varies for information retrieved from the World Wide Web, on-line chats, e-mail discussion groups, e-mail, on-line databases, and on-line encyclopedias. The basic form of APA (American Psychological Association) citations as we are writing this for the World Wide Web contains the same format used for a print source

On-line searching rules

1. Require students to have very specific search objectives in mind. Never give students free time to just "surf the Web".

2. Always "pre-search" the Web using keywords and phrases that the students may use.

3. Require students to write down full citations of any sites that they use in their reports or presentations.

4. Require a bibliography including citations for all pictures, diagrams, sounds, and movies.

5. Don't send all of your students to view the same site at the same time.

6. Always reexamine sites you will show in class beforehand as close to class time as possible. Have a list of alternate sites on hand.

7. Require students to cross-reference information using another medium (e.g., print) whenever possible to help insure accuracy.

Figure 11–6
Rules to follow when searching online

Figure 11–7
Yahooligans is a great place for young students to start their search. (http://www.yahooligans.com)

with the Web information placed in a statement at the end of the reference. Using the page we found as an example:

Electronic references. (n.d.). Washington, DC: American Psychological Association. Retrieved January 19, 2005 from http://www.apastyle.org/elecref.html

Users of the Modern Language Association (MLA) style can find current general information on the MLA Website in the "frequently asked questions" section. The basic form of MLA citation for the World Wide Web is as follows: Author's name with full first name. "Document title." *in title of complete work* date of publication/last revision/site update. Organization or publisher. date visited <URL>. Using the above as an example:

"Electronic reference." APAstyle.org 23 Dec. 2001. American Psychological Association. 26 Jan. 2005 <http://www.apastyle.org/elecref.html>

APA Style:
      Schrock, K. (1995, June 1). *Kathy Schrock's guide for educators.*
Retrieved Month Day, Year from
http://www.school.discovery.com/schrockguide/

MLA Style:
      Schrock, Kathleen. <u>Kathy Schrock's Guide for Educators.</u> 1
June 1995. Day Month Year Accessed
<http://www.school.discovery.com/schrockguide/>.

Figure 11–8
APA and *MLA citation styles* (http://school.discovery.com/schrockguide)

More information on citing Internet resources can be found at the Companion Website http://www.prenhall.com/forcier

Figure 11–8 illustrates both APA and MLA citation styles for information found on *Kathy Schrock's Guide for Educators* Website.

The Internet is still relatively new and citations are in a state of flux. You may want to check University of Iowa "Guide to Citation Guides," which is part of the "Journalism Resources" compiled by Karla Tonella at the University of Iowa: (http://bailiwick.lib.uiowa.edu/journalism/cite.html) for any changes in APA or MLA style.

Web Page Construction. A favorite activity of students in many schools around the country is the design and construction of one or a series of Web pages. At first, the predominant student page was one devoted to themselves. Teachers are moving away from that activity now and are using their students' time more productively. They are using Web design and construction as a means of knowledge transfer from their class and students to the world (see WebQuests below). Rather than posting personal pages, students and groups of students are posting projects, term papers, and their own research on the Web. Until just a few years ago, Web construction was done by hand using a mark-up language named **(HTML) HyperText Markup Language.** HTML is a series of tags (enclosed in brackets < >) that tells the browser (Internet Explorer, Netscape, etc.) how to display the page on the computer screen. Examples include <center> to center the text, <I> to change the text to italics, and <b> to make the text bold. We now have applications called **HTML editors** that do all of the "tagging" for us.

HTML Editors. There are three general categories of HTML editors. Some of them are designed specifically for that purpose such as *Microsoft FrontPage*™, some are included in regular word processing programs such as *Microsoft Word*™, and some are free software that can be downloaded from the Web as part of a browser package such as *Netscape Composer*™. HTML editors all work about the same, and if you have ever made a word processing document into which you have added graphics, you really know all of the basics. Developing a word processing document and making a Web page using an HTML editor are very similar processes. You just type on the page using the menu found at the top (not very different from a word processing menu) to change the font, font size, font color, and other attributes (bold, underline, italics, etc.). Graphics are added in a similar way that you might use to add graphics to any word processing document. Figure 11–9 shows the top and bottom menus for the free HTML editor Netscape Composer. We have pancaked the figure so just these menus are

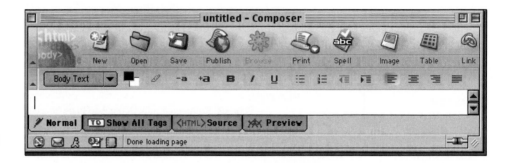

Figure 11–9
Top and bottom
menus on Netscape
Composer

Figure 11–10
Top menus on
Microsoft FrontPage

visible. (We are using the latest version available at press time. Your version may differ slightly because it is a different version or because you are using a different platform.)

Let us take a look at the very top menu line in Figure 11–9. Starting from the left, we can see the following buttons: new page, open file, save file, publish (sends the page to a predetermined Website), browse {light gray} (opens up Navigator and shows Web page), print page, spell check, insert image, insert table, make link (from highlighted text or image). The second menu from the top has the following buttons: body text (puts in preformatted styles, i.e., paragraph, headings, address, etc.), black box (click to choose text color) and white box (click to choose background color), light gray slash (click to choose text highlight color), −a (decreases text size), +**a** (increases text size), **B** (bold text), *I* (italic text), U̲ (underline text), bulleted list, numbered list, move text to left, move text to right, align left, align center, align right, justify. The second menu from the bottom from left to right: display as working page (this is where you construct the page), show working page with tag icons, show HTML tags, show page as it would look in a Web browser. The very bottom menu is used to navigate around Netscape and is not needed to compose a Web page. The icons are from left to right: display Netscape, display mail and newsgroups, display instant messaging, display composer, display address book. Figure 11–10 shows the top menus for Microsoft FrontPage. If you have used Microsoft Word, notice how similar it is to FrontPage menus and Netscape Composer menus (Figure 11–9).

Web Page Construction Using Netscape Composer

Now let's make a Web page using Netscape Composer. Later we will make the same page using Microsoft Word. As you may remember, Netscape Composer can be downloaded when you download the Netscape Communicator™ Web browser. We will use Composer because it is free, available for Windows and Macintosh, and easy for your students to use. Before we start, we searched Google.com for "clip art" and "backgrounds." We found one site that had both (http://www.hellasmultimedia.com/

webimages/). We found some images of clip art, backgrounds, and lines that we wanted to use in our example; we put the mouse cursor over the image, held down the right mouse button (the mouse button on Macs) and a menu popped up. We chose "Download image to disk" and downloaded the images to a folder on our hard drive. The images that we will use are shown in Figure 11–11.

Open Netscape, go to the top menu bar on your computer screen and click on "Window" and "Composer." This will open up a new Netscape Composer page. [It should be a longer version of Figure 11–9 ;-).] Now save this blank page to the same directory (folder) where your images are stored. Remember to save your work often, just in case. Later, when you want to move your Web page, you can just move the whole directory or folder. If you just move your Web page and not the images (background and pictures), your images will not show up on your page. Unlike a word processing document where the images actually become part of the word document file, a Web page does not contain images but rather points to where the images can be found. The browser then goes out, finds the images, and places them on the page where needed.

The first thing that we will do is put in a background. We want to use the one on the upper right in Figure 11–11, but before we do, let's talk about background images. Unless we have an image that will completely fill the background of the page, like an image of your school seal, we place a very small image in the background and the browser automatically tiles it across and down the page. If we place

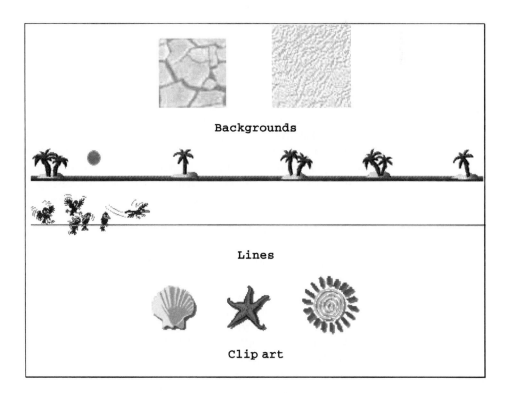

Figure 11–11
Backgrounds, lines, and clip art downloaded from http://www. hellasmultimedia. com/webimages/

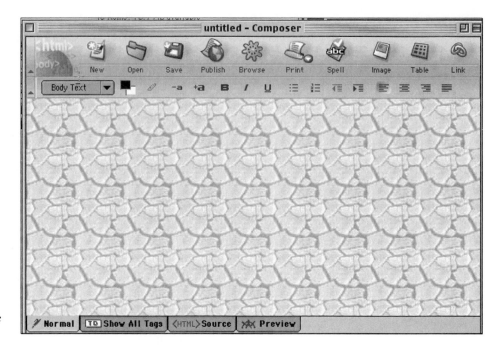

Figure 11–12
Small background images are tiled across and down the page

the left background image (the one that looks like a dozen or so flat stones) on a Web page, it will be tiled across and down the page to look like the background in Figure 11–12. You can see that it is the same little background image pattern used over and over again.

That background is too busy for us because it will not print very well in the following figures so we will place the background on the right in Figure 11–11 on the page. To do this, we first go to the "Format" "Page Colors and Background . . . " (Figure 11–13 left). The "Page Colors and Background" box will appear (Figure 11–13 right). In this box, click on "Choose File . . . " and find the background image you want for your Web page. When you click on "Open," the chosen background will appear in the window in the action box. If the default text (Normal, Link, Action, Visited) colors shown in small window do not show up against the background, or you would rather have a solid color background, choose "Use custom colors:" and click on the box to the right of the text description and/or "Background" to change the color. "Normal" text is the regular page text color, "Link" is the color your hypertext link will be (normally blue), the "Action" color can be seen only while you are pressing the link, and the "Visited" text color is the color of the link after you have visited it and have come back to your page (usually purple).

Now let's type in a title. Our page should look like the one in Figure 11–12, except it will have the different background tiled across and down the Web page. Going across the lower top menu from left to right: choose "Body Text" "Heading 1," click on the **B** to make the text bold, click on the "Align Center" (third box from right). This should give us a large, bold title in the center of the first line in Composer. We have typed in "Forcier and Descy" in our example. Press the "return" key.

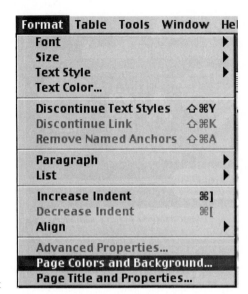

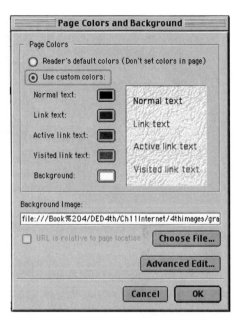

Figure 11–13
Format background
menu and action box

Now let's add an image line. Click on "Image" on the top menu. An "Image Properties" box will appear (Figure 11–14). Type a few words that describe the image in the "Alternate text" box. This is *very important*. If a visually impaired person is viewing this page with text reader software, the software will read the words you put in the box that describes the picture so the person will know what it is. You must do this for your school pages. It is the law. It is a good idea to automatically do this for any Web page you or your students construct. Now click on "Choose File" and find the image you want to use.

In this case, we are using the bottom image above "Lines" in Figure 11–11. Click "OK" and when you return to the Composer screen, you will see the image line on the screen; press the "return" key twice. "Align left" the text (fourth button from the right) and type in three lines of text. You will note in our example that we pressed the *"I"* button found on second from the top menu line to type in some text in italics. Press the "return" key. Now we will center the curser and add the top image above "Lines" in Figure 11–11. We do it the same way that we added the first image; then we typed in "chain of islands" for our "Alternate text." It is difficult to place images and text on the same line. We will do this by making a table and placing images in some boxes and text in others. Press the "Table" button. The "Insert Table" box will appear (Figure 11–15). Note that we want 1 row, 4 columns, and the table border of 0 pixels (0 pixels will give us a table with no borders). We will see a red dotted line in the Composer window where the table is when "Normal" is clicked on the bottom menu. To see how it will look on the Web without borders, click on "Preview" on the bottom menu. Now we will place the curser in the first table box on the left, center the curser, and insert an image just as we added the image lines above. We will repeat this in the next three boxes to the right. We could also have

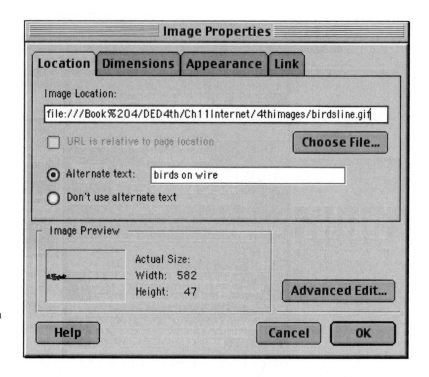

Figure 11–14
Image Properties
box. You must fill in
the "Alternate text"
and choose the
image file

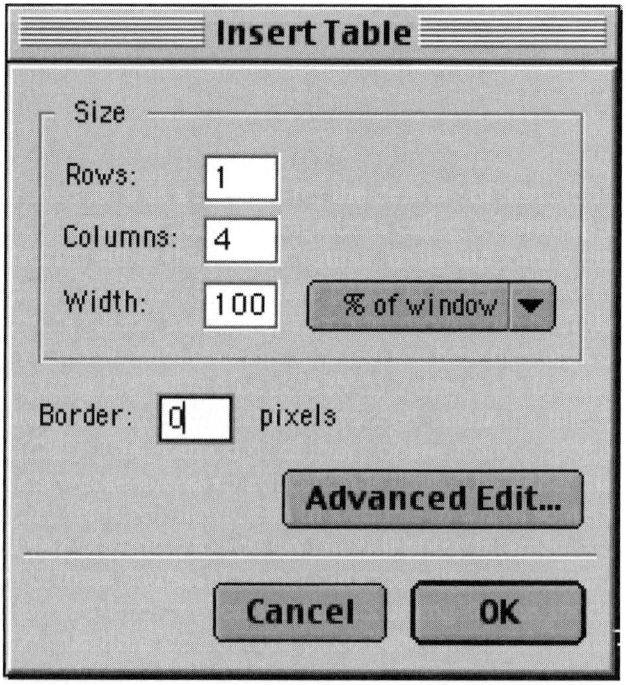

Figure 11–15
Insert Table box

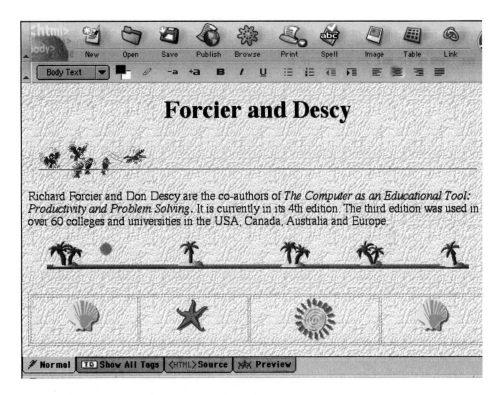

Figure 11–16
Composer screen in "Normal" view showing table cells

typed text in any of these boxes. The bottom of the Composer window will look like Figure 11–16. Note again that you can see the cell borders in the "Normal" view.

Before we click on "Preview" on the bottom menu to see how our completed page will look on the Web, let's add a hyperlink. We will make the title of the text a hyperlink that, when clicked on, will take us to the textbook Website. First, we will highlight the title of the textbook. Now press the "Link" button on the top menu. The "Link Properties" box will appear (Figure 11–17). We typed the location of the Prentice Hall Website in the box provided. If we wanted to go to another page we made, we would simply use the "Choose File . . . " box to choose the Web page we want.

Click "OK." The highlighted title of the text is now underlined and blue. Now we will click "Preview" at the bottom to see how our page will look on the Web (Figure 11–18). It is too bad that the book is not printed in color. It looks really nice!

Web Page Construction Using Microsoft Word

The most common word processing program is Microsoft Word. Let's make the same Web page as above, but this time we will use Word. Again, your version may look a bit different. Open Microsoft Word. If a blank document does not appear, go to "File" "New Blank Document." First, let's put in our background. Go to the top menu and press "Format" "Background" (Figure 11–19 left). A "background" box will open (Figure 11–19 middle). Here is where you can choose a background color or by pressing "Fill Effects"

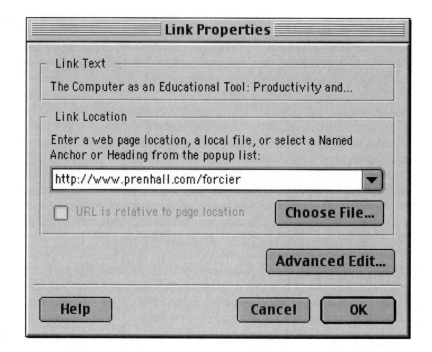

Figure 11–17
Link Properties box

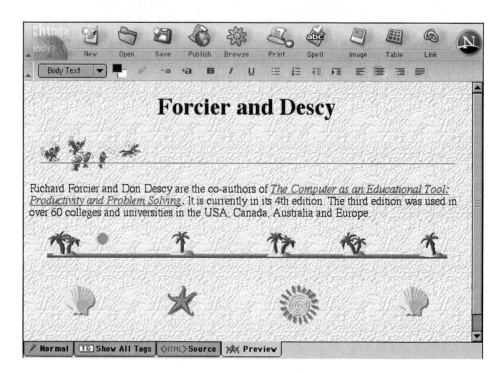

Figure 11–18
Composer screen in "Preview" view showing borderless table cells

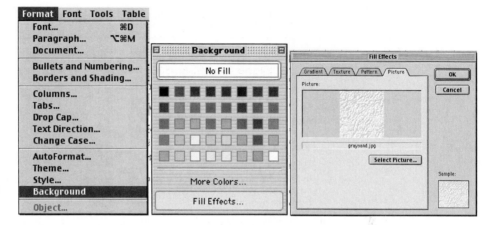

Figure 11–19
Format, Background, and Fill Effects menus

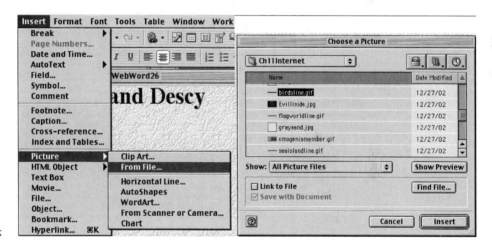

Figure 11–20
Insert menus and Choose a Picture box

and "Select Picture" in the box that appears (Figure 11–19 right), you are able to choose the background that you want. Again, we are choosing the same background as we did earlier. We now set "Times" font, "36" point size, **B**old and "Center" align and type our title. We press the return key twice. We do not change "Center" align and go to "Insert" "Picture" "From File" (Figure 11–20 left). In the "Choose a Picture" box that appears (Figure 11–20 right), we find the image (the "bird line" image) that we want to insert and press "Insert."

Press the return key once. We set the text to "14" point size, "Left" align and type in the same text that we did in the previous example. To make the title of the text into a hyperlink in Word, we highlight the text, and go to "Hyperlink" at the bottom of the "Insert" menu (Figure 11–20 left). The "Edit Hyperlinks" window will appear (Figure 11–21). Type the location of the Website you desire in the "Link to" box.

Press "OK." Now we press the return key twice. We will now place the "Islands line" image on the page. First, we press "Center" align and follow the steps above

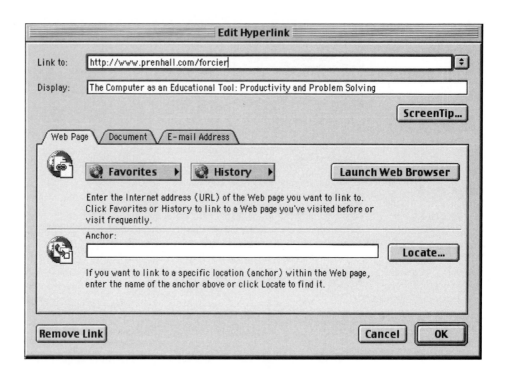

Figure 11–21
Edit Hyperlink box

that we did to place the "bird line image" using the menus in Figure 11–20. Now we again press the return key twice. On the top menu bar we can choose "Table" "Insert" "Table" or we can press the Table icon on the top Word menu bar (seventh one from the right—it looks like a calendar). In the "Insert Table" box (Figure 11–22) that appears, type in "4" columns, "1" row, and press "OK."

Now place the curser in first table cell (make sure that it is centered in the cell) and insert a picture as did above (see Figure 11–20 for help). When you have placed all of the images in the table cells, click to the left of the table to highlight the table. Now press the small downward facing arrow to the right of the "Box Border" (third icon from the right). A second box will appear (Figure 11–23). Click on the second icon (gray box) in the second row to remove the table outline.

If you have not done so, save this file to your disk by going to "File" "Save." Also save it as a Web page by going to "File" "Save as Web Page." Let's take a look at how it will look on the Web. It is really very simple. Just go to "File" "Web Page Preview" and Word will open up Internet Explorer and present your page! The one that we were working along on as we typed this is shown in Figure 11–24. You may want to compare this with Figure 11–18.

The major difference between a Web page made with an HTML editor or Microsoft Word and a regular word processing document is something that goes on in the background. As we construct our Web page using the HTML editor, the editor is also generating a whole other page containing all of the HTML tags needed to display the

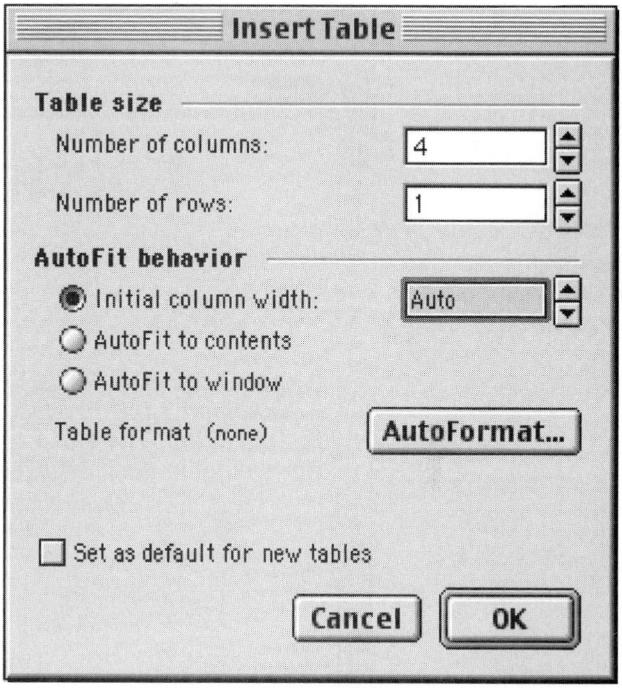

Figure 11–22
Insert Table box

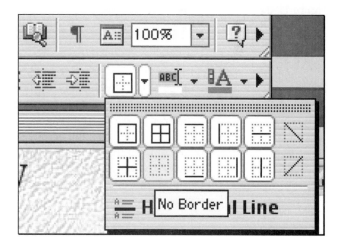

Figure 11–23
Format Border
window

page on a browser the way we are constructing it. The HTML tags are also generated when we save our Word document as a Web page. Figure 11–25 shows the tags Composer generated in the background as we developed our page shown in Figure 11–18. Notice the third button from the left (<HTML> Source) on the bottom Composer menu is activated to obtain this view.

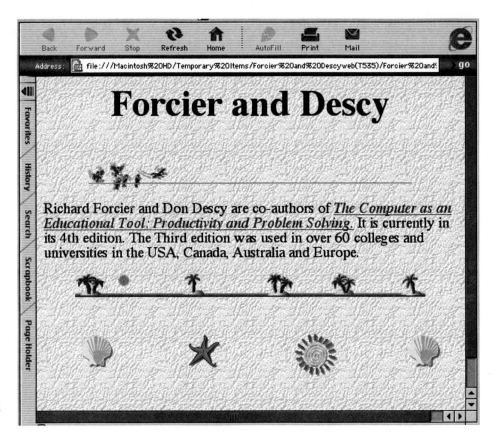

Figure 11–24
Web page made with
Microsoft Word

Tags written by the HTML editor, though similar, seem to be more confusing than
handwritten ones. This is because HTML editors add many other tags that are not
necessary to display the page on a browser. Pages made with HTML editors are said
to be "dirty" because they contain these extra tags. The fundamental approach is to
begin publishing on the Web using a simple page and then to elaborate as your
skills or content needs develop. Publishing on the Web is far more than just another
mode of expression; it provides opportunities for interaction among individuals. A
few words of caution: Since publishing on the Web is much like publishing in any
other medium, the person or student group posting a Web page is responsible for
the accuracy of the content, which should be free of bias or at least with any biases
clearly stated, and should have sources of information such as text and graphics accurately cited. It is also very helpful to the viewer of the page to be able to see the
name of the person who developed the page, the date on which the page was
posted or last revised, and an e-mail address so that the viewer of the Web page
can contact the developer directly. Unless there is a very good reason, students
should never post their photographs and personal information such as complete
names and addresses.

Figure 11–25
HTML tags generated by Netscape Composer

SUMMARY

The Internet is a network of networks that spans the globe, serving millions of users. The primary resources available are e-mail, e-mail discussion groups, and information posted on World Wide Web pages. The World Wide Web is a global hypertext system that uses the Internet as its transport mechanism. HyperText Markup Language (HTML) provides the coding to display both text and graphics, along with dynamic links both within the document and to other external Internet sites. Each site also has its own Uniform Resource Locator (URL), or address.

Web browser software on the user's machine communicates with Web server software at a remote site and receives images and HTML that it puts together to display the Web page. Each Web server has at least one HTML document, referred to as a Web page. The main page of a Website is the one usually accessed first and is called its home page.

Search engines are commonly employed to assist the user with the task of finding specific information on the Internet. The user enters a search term or terms, and then the search engine looks through its database of Internet sites for the best matches.

Publishing on the World Wide Web begins with a simple page and then elaborates as the user's skills or content needs develop. HTML editors and many word processing applications make it easy for anyone who can use a word processor to also construct a Web page. The person or group posting a Web page is responsible for using accurate content, free of bias, or at least with any biases clearly stated, and with sources of information such as text or graphics accurately cited.

CHAPTER EXERCISES

 To complete the specified exercises on-line, go to the Chapter Exercises Module in Chapter 11 of the Companion Website.

1. Research the early history of the Internet. What was the original purpose? How has that changed?
2. Pick out a topic or theme that you wish to explore, and then compare several Internet search engines for their ease of use, cataloging of sites, speed of finding information, and use of logical terms to help narrow your search.
3. Design a form for students to use in evaluating Internet sites for content accuracy or completeness, currency of information, purpose of the site, authorship, date of posting or most recent revision, degree of interactivity, appropriate use of graphics, and useful links to related sites.
4. Using an HTML editor or word processing application, design your own class World Wide Web page that includes a title, some text, two images, and a hyperlink to another Web page.
5. Download demonstration copies of one of the Internet filtering software packages such as CyberPatrol, NetNanny, or Surf Watcher. Compare their claims about ease of operation, methods of filtering (e.g., keyword), appropriate settings for use, and the relative completeness of filtering inappropriate sites. Would you recommend using one of these packages at your school? Defend your answer.
6. Some people are for and some are against Internet filter applications. Explore the issue, decide which point you seem to favor, and write a short paper defending the opposite view.
7. Team up with a group of students in your class. Have an equal number of groups design a lesson involving the Internet. Share these lessons with the class. Which approach do you prefer? Defend your position to the class.
8. List and discuss four or five ways you could involve your class in Web design activities when you are a classroom teacher. What do you feel will be the barriers that might develop to hinder your plans?
9. In Chapter 2 we discussed equitable Internet access. List several ways that lack of Internet access might affect the quality of education in a school or district. Can you think of any ways to work around these problems? Discuss your thoughts with the class.
10. How do you think that the Internet and World Wide Web may change by the time a child born today enters first grade?

PORTFOLIO DEVELOPMENT EXERCISES

To complete this exercise on-line, go to the Digital Portfolio Module in Chapter 11 of the Companion Website.

One of the NETS•S standards covered in this chapter was "Students use telecommunications to collaborate, publish, and interact with peers, experts, and other audiences" under *Category 4: Technology communications tools.* Begin to develop your own portfolio of lesson plans that demonstrates your ability to have your students reach the NETS•S standards.

 For more information on developing digital portfolios, go to the Digital Portfolio Module on the Companion Website www.prenhall.com/forcier

1. Design a lesson plan activity for elementary, middle school, or high school students in which they interact with peers, experts, and other audiences. This should be a project that could involve individuals in other schools in this country and abroad. How would you go about facilitating this project? How would you go about finding other groups to participate in this project? This lesson should demonstrate that your students have achieved the standard. Be sure to include a system of evaluation for your students' understanding and competence to ensure that they have met this standard.

2. Adapt the lesson plan activity you developed in exercise 1 for students to evaluate each others' work.

GLOSSARY

bookmarks A feature of World Wide Web browser programs that allows the user to save and organize the URLs of desired Internet sites. Also called *favorites.*

cache A Web file storage area on the hard disk.

directories (subject directories, subject guides, and specialized databases) These are catalogs of Internet sites organized by subject areas.

electronic conferences Electronic forums usually organized around specific topics designed to allow the exchange of information by a number of simultaneous users.

e-mail (electronic mail) The electronic transfer of messages and files from one person to another over a computer network.

e-mail discussion group (mailing list) A group of e-mail addresses given a single name on a computer. Messages sent by the owner of one of the e-mail addresses in the group is automatically forwarded to all other e-mail addresses in the group.

favorites See *bookmarks.*

home page Usually the first Web page accessed at a Website, it often includes links to other Web pages within that site or at other Websites. This term is also given to the Web page that may be specified to be accessed by a Web browsing program when that program is first opened or when the "home button" is selected within the program.

HTML (HyperText Markup Language) A programming language that allows the user to post a World Wide Web document with text, graphics, and dynamic links to other Websites.

HTML editor A program designed to streamline the process of building a Web page through the automation of adding certain HTML language code. Many editors provide the ability to visualize what the Web page will look like when opened in a Web browser.

HTTP (HyperText Transfer Protocol) The format by which World Wide Web documents are transferred over the Internet (every WWW address begins with "http://. . . ").

Internet The Internet is a worldwide network of networks based on the TCP/IP protocol.

ISP (Internet Service Provider) The organization or business that connects individually or group-owned computers to the Internet backbone.

invisible Web That part of the Web that is unable to be searched by regular search engines.

LISTSERV™ A registered trademark for a particular brand of software used to create and run e-mail discussion groups.

robots See *spiders*.

search engines Computer applications that automatically search World Wide Web pages and store keywords and text from each page.

spiders Programs used by search engines to travel the Web, usually by following links on known pages, to add new pages and keywords at every step of the way.

Transmission Control Protocol/Internet Protocol (TCP/IP) A set of standards developed to allow different networks to interconnect electronically.

Uniform Resource Locator (URL) The address of any site on the Internet, including gopher and the World Wide Web sites.

Web browser Software that finds and displays Web pages.

Web server Software that allows Web pages to be broadcast to the Web.

World Wide Web An Internet navigation system that allows users, through a graphic browser interface, to access information organized on hypertext-linked screens called pages.

REFERENCES & SUGGESTED READINGS

Anthony, T. (2002, December 24). 'IM here'—keeping in touch online. *The FreePress, 119*(222), 8C.

Bergman, M. K. (2003). *The deep web: Surfacing hidden value.* Retrieved 17 Feb. 2003 from *http://brightplanet.com/deepcontent/tutorials/DeepWeb/index.asp*

BrightPlanet. (2001, February 22). *The deep web.* Retrieved 17 Feb. 2003 from *http://brightplanet.com/deepcontent/tutorials/DeepWeb/index.asp*

Descy, D. E. (1999, September). HTML editors: Web pages in minutes. *Tech Trends, 43*(4), 5–7.

Notess, G. R. (2002). *Search engine statistics: Database relative size.* [Online] Available *http://www.notess.com/search/stats/size.html*, January 19, 2000.

Notess, G. R. (2000). *Search engine statistics: Database relative size.* Retrieved 21 Feb. 2003 at *http://www.searchengineshowdown.com/stats/size.html*.

Pfaffenberger, B. (2000). *Webster's new world computer user's dictionary* (8th ed). New York: Macmillan.

Poftak, A. (2002, August). Net-wise teens: Safety, ethics, and innovation. *Technology & Learning, 25*(1), 36–49.

CHAPTER **12**

Internet Applications
in Education

1. What kinds of resources are available on the Internet?

2. What is an Acceptable Use Policy and why is it important for a school to have one?

3. How will filtering software affect many schools?

4. How can students evaluate materials found on the World Wide Web?

5. How can teachers incorporate both directed and exploratory learning styles using the World Wide Web?

6. What are some examples of good Web-based learning activities?

7. How can instruction be delivered over the Internet?

In this chapter we cover parts of all of the NETS•S categories. We continue with our coverage of *Category 1: Basic operations and concepts* with a discussion of the various tools available for use on the Internet. Standards listed under *Category 2: Social, ethical, and human issues* are covered here as we discuss acceptable use policies, and the credibility of Web resources. *Category 3: Technology productivity tools* are covered as students use the Internet to enhance learning, increase productivity, and prepare and produce creative projects. *Category 4: Technology communications tools* is covered in depth as we discuss some of the ways that students and teachers can use the Internet to collaborate, publish, and interact with individuals from around the world. The Internet is just one of a variety of media formats that is used to communicate information and ideas to others around the corner and in distant lands. The Internet fits closely into any coverage of *Category 5: Technology research tools.* Our discussion covers all of the tools that students and teachers will use when they use the Internet for research along with ways that a student can evaluate Internet information. This fits nicely into *Category 6: Technology problem-solving and decision-making tools* as students are given more tools to find and process information and determine the credibility of Web resources. As you read this chapter, it is important for you to be aware of the NETS•S standards that your students will have to meet, just as it is important for you to be aware of the standards you need to meet as a teacher. Incorporating these standards into your classroom will help you to develop lesson plans and activities and learning environments that will not only benefit your students, but yourself as well.

NETS•S Standards Addressed in This Chapter

1. Basic operations and concepts
   - Students demonstrate a sound understanding of the nature and operation of technology systems.
   - Students are proficient in the use of technology

2. Social, ethical, and human issues
   - Students understand the ethical, cultural, and societal issues related to technology.
   - Students practice responsible use of technology systems, information, and software.
   - Students develop positive attitudes toward technology uses that support lifelong learning, collaboration, personal pursuits, and productivity.

3. Technology productivity tools
   - Students use technology tools to enhance learning, increase productivity, and promote creativity.
   - Students use productivity tools to collaborate in constructing technology enhanced models, prepare publications, and produce other creative works.

4. Technology communications tools
   - Students use telecommunications to collaborate, publish, and interact with peers, experts, and other audiences.
   - Students use a variety of media and formats to communicate information and ideas effectively to multiple audiences.

5. Technology research tools
   - Students use technology to locate, evaluate, and collect information from a variety of sources.
   - Students use technology tools to process data and report results.
   - Students evaluate and select new information resources and technological innovations based on the appropriateness for specific tasks.

6. Technology problem-solving and decision-making tools
   - Students use technology resources for solving problems and making informed decisions.
   - Students employ technology in the development of strategies for solving problems in the real world.

 A list of the ISTE/NCATE standards addressed in this chapter is available in the Standards Module on the Companion Website www.prenhall.com/forcier

EDUCATION AND THE INTERNET

Telecommunication offers significant advantages to classroom teachers and other educators because it allows them to transcend the isolation that typifies their profession. Teachers of art and music, library media specialists, and other faculty and special subject teachers, who are frequently one of a kind in their buildings, may feel less isolated by sharing teaching strategies and curriculum ideas with distant peers in a daily electronic "convention."

Information is broadcast across electronic networks sooner and in greater quantity than in any other publication medium. Social studies and foreign language teachers are enthusiastic about wide-area computer networking because it facilitates significant cultural exchanges. Science teachers can expand the scope of their data collection far beyond their local environment by collaborating with classrooms across the country or, indeed, the world.

Telecommunications supports the reform movement in education by facilitating cooperative and interactive learning. Since distance, personal appearance, physical disabilities, and special needs are invisible on the network, students who are set apart from their classmates can participate as equals. Many who are reluctant participants in the classroom become eager contributors when they can compose their inquiries and responses on their own time.

Keep in mind the paradigm shifts explored in Chapter 1 and the dramatic changes in schooling. Telecommunications allows educators to create a virtual classroom without walls, bringing global resources and experiences to their students. Students have access to information resources as never before as they develop their problem-solving skills and construct their own knowledge.

EVALUATING INTERNET INFORMATION

More information on evaluating Web sites can be found at the Companion Website http://www.prenhall.com/forcier

Media literacy applies as much to the Internet as to any other medium such as television or print. Once information has been located, students should have the opportunity to develop skills in evaluating the accuracy of the information, as well as the way it is displayed on the Internet site in order to become critical readers of Web pages. A teacher-generated checklist or survey document can assist the students in making their evaluation. Figure 12–1 contains a rather thorough and sophisticated set of guidelines to evaluate on-line resources.

Several excellent sites exist on the Internet to provide examples of evaluation devices and strategies. A Web search will find many articles and discussions about Web credibility.

Guidelines for Evaluating Internet-based Resources

Author: Who are the authors in the field? Does this author list any affiliations? Is there a "mail-to" or an e-mail address included? Have you tried to find other information about this author by searching *Who's Who in Education*, Educational Resources Information Center (ERIC), *Journals in Education (JIE)*, or *Current Index to Journals in Education (CIJE)?* Is the author the creator of the information or a compiler of other information resources? Can you find a personal home page or a campus listing for this author?

Producer: Is the producer/affiliation of the page clearly noted? Was it produced by an organization? Is it a well-known professional organization or is it a relative unknown? Are the members professionals, advocates, or consumers? Does this organization have an inherent bias? Is there a way to contact the producer?

Site: Is the URL clearly noted? What is the ending suffix (.edu, .com, .org, .net, and so forth)? Can you find out where it is located? Does it seem to make sense that a producer such as this one would reside on a site such as this?

Publication: Is it a single page or part of a series? Is the remainder of the series by the same author, a collection of authors, or an organization? Is it an abstract or the full text of an article or presentation? Where was the article published or the presentation given? Was is published by or presented at a nationally known organization or conference?

Purpose: What was the purpose of the document? Was it designed to inform others of new research, summarize existing research, advocate a position, or stimulate discussion?

Date of publication: When was the page placed on the Internet? When was it updated?

Arrangement: How difficult was it to find information related to the six guidelines presented earlier in the chapter? Was the information clearly presented in a conspicuous place or was it missing altogether?

Intended audience: Who is the intended audience of this page (professionals, advocates, consumers, and so on)? Would the intended audience change the scope or slant of the information?

Coverage: Does the page cover the information that you need? Does the page include links to other references or backup information? Does the page itself contain substantive information or is it simply a collection of links to other sources?

Writing style/reasoning: Is the information presented in a thoughtful, orderly, well-reasoned manner? Does the information appear to be well researched? Are assumptions and conclusions well documented? Is the information presented as fact or opinion? Can you detect any bias? Do the words used tend to evoke strong emotions?

References: Is the page well documented? Are there links to any primary sources? Is the page referenced to information on the same server or to servers at different sites? How current or relevant are the references?

Figure 12–1
Guidelines for evaluating Internet resources [Adapted from Descy (1996 September), *Tech Trends,* copyright 1996 by the Association for Educational Communications and Technology. Reprinted with permission.]

INTO THE CLASSROOM:
Checking Internet Credibility

The Internet is a great source for a wide range of school projects. Students love to use it, but the problem is that there are no editors or librarians to check the quality of information that is found. Anyone can put anything they like on the Internet. As a result, students sometimes inadvertently use biased or inaccurate sources in their research.

Teachers and library media specialists must help students understand that information on the Internet may not be what it seems. It is essential for students to realize that being on the Internet does not make a Website true or useful. To help students choose the best sources for their projects, it is necessary to assist students in learning to evaluate Websites before they use the information that they contain for their papers and projects.

I use both formal and informal methods to help students evaluate Internet sources. I created a Website discussing evaluation techniques at <http://www.crcs.k12.ny.us/lib/hs/evaluating_internet_%20site.htm> to aid in this evaluation. Teachers and media specialists can use this for whole-class lessons, as well as for independent work by students (and other faculty). Besides deciding whether a page appears to be accurate and make sense, there are several other important questions to ask about a Website:

- What is the purpose of the page? Is it to inform, persuade, sell, or explain?
- Does the information on the site agree with other information I have found?
- Does the information appear to be fact or opinion?
- Does the content of the page seem to be biased or stereotyped?

Asking these and similar questions should help students avoid the accidental use of biased, incorrect, or fake information.

To answer these questions, students should look at the address (URL) to try to learn about the sponsor and location (is it at a .com, .edu, .gov, etc. site) of the page, check the background and credentials of the author, and find out if a site is current and up-to-date. The address (URL) gives important information about the sponsoring organization of a site. Information about the background of the author of a page is usually found on the bottom of a page. The date the page was created or last updated should also usually be found on the bottom of a page. This is a great opportunity to have the students cross-check what they found on the Web using other print and nonprint sources. After evaluating the quality of a Website, the most important question a student should ask themselves is whether a site is useful for his or her project. Students should never forget that they are trying to find the BEST material for their projects.

Joanne Parnes Shawhan, Ph.D.
Media Specialist
Cobleskill-Richmondville High School
Cobleskill, New York

INTEGRATING INTERNET-BASED TOOLS INTO THE CURRICULUM

The Internet is opening up whole new worlds and information resources for both classroom teachers and their students. Many teachers have used the power of its many tools to supplement classroom goals and objectives in many different ways. We will discuss some of the many ideas in this chapter. How we use the Internet in our classrooms is only limited by our imagination.

E-mail

E-mail can be used as a means of connecting teacher to teacher, class to class, and student to student. Don't feel that e-mail cannot find a place in your curriculum if you only have one computer and one e-mail account. Proper sharing of this account can make it very useful. Many sites such as Yahoo.com, hotmail.com, and I-Love-Dogs.com offer free e-mail accounts to anyone who can access them with a Web browser.

E-mail is a wonderful collaborative tool. Students can meet other students, learn about different lands, and share customs and ideas on-line. Many students have written autobiographies and descriptions of their towns, and even exchanged prices on a shared grocery list with other students and classes around the globe. It is a wonderful way for students to practice writing and collaboration skills. Students have also shared the adventures and communicated with explorers in Africa and the Arctic using e-mail.

Internet Pen Pals (Keypals)

Students can learn about other people and other cultures by writing letters and by exchanging journal entries and school and local news. Nationwide, continent-wide, and worldwide projects can be carried out using e-mail and key-pals. History, geography, science, and writing skills are but a few of the areas where Keypal correspondence can be utilized. The Keypals site from Pitsco, Inc. illustrated in Figure 12–2 is a good place to start.

Mentor Projects

You may want to start closer to home by linking up students to students or students to adults as mentors and helpers. Do this by establishing an on-line mentorship program. Pair up high school students to help younger students with their homework or adults to help middle school students for guidance and help. Establish a mentorship program with a college or university class to aid and guide your K–12 students.

THE WORLD WIDE WEB

The World Wide Web is probably one of the easiest tools to integrate into your curriculum. There are numerous opportunities to search the Web for information needed for reports or for students' own personal use. Web searching presents us with a wonderful opportunity to integrate a whole series of important lifelong learning

Figure 12–2
The Keypals™ site helps find friends all over the world (http://www.keypals. com) (Reprinted with permission from Pitsco Inc.)

activities into our classes, including searching techniques (accessing information, searching techniques, limiting searches, reasons for multiple searches, search tool capabilities), and critical evaluation (site and source credibility, author searches, critical reading skills, using non-Internet sources to back up findings). We are able to tap all of our students' higher-order thinking skills as described in *Bloom's Taxonomy* (Figure 12–3).

Multicultural Understanding

Students are able to achieve a better understanding and appreciation of other peoples and cultures using the vast array of information available on-line. Students from a small town in New York have found that they have a great deal in common with American Indian students living in South Dakota after examining the Indian School's Website. E-mail correspondence followed. Other classes have celebrated country specific holidays found through the Internet as they study cultures around the globe. The Worldwide Holiday and Festival Site (Figure 12–4), the Today's Calendar and Clock Page (http://www.ecben.net/calendar.html), and the Kidlink Multicultural calendar (http://www.kidlink.org) are good places to look for information.

Group Projects

Schools in many parts of the country and the world have worked together gathering information on weather patterns, insect migration, costs of a set of products in a supermarket, and civil war history. Each school researches the part of the topic

Figure 12–3
Levels of Learning
within Bloom's
Cognitive Domain

> **Category:** *verbs* (Questions)
>
> **Knowledge:** *list, memorize, name, recognize, recall, repeat, reproduce, state.* (What is this information I found?)
>
> **Comprehension:** *describe, discuss, explain, recognize, restate, select.* (I have a problem. What exactly is it? How do I solve it?)
>
> **Application:** *choose, interpret, solve, use.* (How do the pieces fit together? How can I organize and present this information in an appropriate and meaningful way?)
>
> **Analysis:** *analyze, discriminate, distinguish, examine, test.* (What is it exactly that I'm trying to discover? What are the most efficient and effective search methods and tools to use?)
>
> **Synthesis:** *arrange, construct, create, design, organize.* (How can I integrate and summarize this information into a usable form?)
>
> **Evaluation:** *appraise, assess, compare, defend, evaluate, judge, predict, support.* (Is this credible information? Are there any underlying biases or motives present?)

Figure 12–4
The Worldwide
Holiday and Festival
Site helps bring other
cultures into the
classroom (http://
www.holidayfestival.
com) (Reprinted with
permission from
Prescott-Decie
Services S.A.R.L.)

The Worldwide Holiday & Festival Site

Introduction
Countries
Religions
This Month
Search
Explanation
Accuracy
Links
Bookstore
Buy Data
Just for Fun
For Kids!
Awards
Credits
Disclaimer
Contact Us
About Us

Afghanistan
Aland Islands
Albania
Algeria
American Samoa
Andorra
Angola
Anguilla
Antigua and Barbuda
Antilles, see Netherland Antilles
Argentina
Armenia
Aruba
Austral Islands, see French Polynesia
Australia
Austria
Azerbaijan
Bahamas
Bahrain
Bangladesh
Barbados
Belarus

Macau
Macedonia, Former Yugoslav Republic of
Madagascar
Maiao, see French Polynesia
Makatea, see French Polynesia
Malawi
Malaysia
Maldives
Mali
Malta
Malvinas, Islas, see Fakland Islands
Man, Isle of
Manuae, see French Polynesia
Marshall Islands
Martinique, see France
Maupelia, see French Polynesia
Maupiti, see French Polynesia
Mauretania
Mauritius
Marquesas or Marquises Isles, see French Polynesia
Mayotte, see France

362

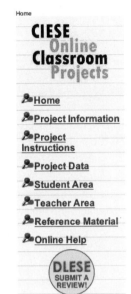

Figure 12–5
"Down the Drain": Internet project from Stevens Institute of Technology in Hoboken, New Jersey (http://www.k12science.org/curriculum/drainproj/)

Home

CIESE Online **Classroom** Projects

🔖**Home**
🔖**Project Information**
🔖**Project Instructions**
🔖**Project Data**
🔖**Student Area**
🔖**Teacher Area**
🔖**Reference Material**
🔖**Online Help**

DLESE SUBMIT A REVIEW!

🔖**Project Overview**

How much water do you use everyday in your home? Would you be surprised to learn that according to the USGS the average American uses between 80-100 gallons (approx. 300 - 375 liters) of water per day? Do you think people in other parts of the world use more or less water than Americans? Well, this collaborative project will help you find out the answers to these questions. By collecting data on water usage from people around the world you will be able to see how your water use compares to others and determine what you might do to use less water.

START HERE
(For First Timers Only)

germane to its particular region. The combined data has helped the students understand a product, event, or process from a global perspective. The CIESE Online Classroom Projects site (Figure 12–5) is worth a look.

Project Center (www.hmco.com/hmco/school/projects/index.html), Global SchoolNet Projects (www.gsn.org/pr/index.html), and Project Zone (www.cccnet.com/success) may also give you ideas and contacts for group Internet projects.

Electronic Field Trips

It is possible for students to tour distant places through many sites on the World Wide Web. Distant countries, cities, museums, monuments, zoos, underground New York, and even the sewers of Paris can be toured on-line. On-line maps and weather sites can also be used. Other technology including video and computer programs such as *Where in the World Is Carmen Sandiego?* can also be interwoven into these activities. Virtual Tours (http://www.virtualfreesites.com/tours.html) contains links to over 300 virtual tours of museums and exhibits around the world, 100 cities, and many U.S. government buildings. The Weather Channel (http://www.weather.com) and Mapquest (http://www.mapquest.com) both contain useful information to utilize in creating virtual field trips for your students. With just a little typing and a few clicks of the mouse, students can visit their nation's capital and take a virtual tour of the Institute and Museum of the History of Science in Florence, Italy (Figure 12–7).

Research Projects

The Internet allows for up-to-the-minute research on many topics. Newspaper and television Websites offer current news and information. Museums and archeological

INTO THE CLASSROOM:
Mrs. McGowan's First Grade Website

The main purpose of our classroom Website (Figure 12–6) is to provide authentic communication opportunities for my students. It's the "home base" for all our daily Internet activity. Students turn the computers on when they arrive and navigate to our Website. The children access information from various other Websites that I have previewed, and saved links to, on our site. A morning weather report, reached from an image link on the homepage, is a good example. Numerous seasonal, thematic, and subject pages are made available through this linking procedure.

We also get on-line information about other places in the world through class e-mail, our Website guest book, and participation in collaborative on-line projects. One year our class had e-mail pals with a school in Western Australia. My students learned what it's like to have your school built on stilts in case of flooding and what it's like to ride your horse to school instead of taking a car ride or school bus!

However, the main way we communicate with other classes and the general public is by publishing student work on our Web page. The children love seeing their writing and drawings on the screen. So do their families! Some of the most appreciative responses to our Website have come from grandparents living far away. Knowing that so many people will be seeing their work helps motivate the children to do their best.

Our Website also has been hosting collaborative literacy projects. These projects primarily are designed to provide a rich source of on-line reading material for young students. The project resource pages stay on-line as well and can be utilized by other teachers.

I also use the Website for pages to extend specific classroom lessons. There are on-line quizzes for compound words or math riddles and lists of spelling words to drag and drop into ABC order. Some activities I create and others are shared by teachers from all over the country.

Finally, the Website has become a "supermarket" of resources for students, parents, and other teachers. Our spelling lists, word wall words, schedules, and flashcards are all there for home use. It's a convenient place to find tips on reading with children, critical thinking questions using Bloom's Taxonomy, our state standards, Website building information, holiday puzzles, math projects, rubrics, book lists, and links to other teacher Websites—just to name a few!

Marci McGowan
First Grade Teacher
H. W. Montz Elementary School
Spring Lake, New Jersey

Figure 12–6
Mrs. McGowan's First
Grade Web Page
(http://www.
mrsmcgowan.com/
index.html)

Mrs. McGowan's First Grade
Spring Lake, NJ

Spring Lake
Weather

Search This Site

Favorites From Room 104

Winter Fun

Winter Poetry Project

February Spotlight

Internet Projects

Student Showcase

Our Classroom

Spelling Lists

Parents and Teachers

Kids Corner

Month by Month

Welcome to our first grade class at H.W. Mountz Elementary School in Spring Lake, NJ. We're located in the central part of the state, just a few blocks from the beach and ocean.

This website highlights new student work, Internet projects, class activities, and online resources for parents, children, and visitors. We update frequently, so please come back often.

February Fun

This is the *how do we fit it all in* month! To help, we're featuring resources for Chinese New Year, African-American History, Groundhog Day, Dental Health, Valentines Day, 100th Day of School, and online interactive activities. You'll be directed to our own latest published work and winter collaborative poetry project as well. Busy month!

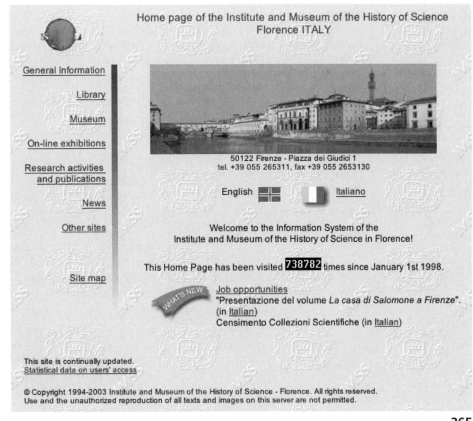

Figure 12–7
Students can take a
virtual tour of the
Institute and Museum
of the History of
Science in Florence,
Italy (http://www.
imss.fi.it/)

Home page of the Institute and Museum of the History of Science
Florence ITALY

General Information

Library

Museum

On-line exhibitions

Research activities
and publications

News

Other sites

Site map

50122 Firenze - Piazza dei Giudici 1
tel. +39 055 265311, fax +39 055 2653130

English   Italiano

Welcome to the Information System of the
Institute and Museum of the History of Science in Florence!

This Home Page has been visited 738782 times since January 1st 1998.

WHAT'S NEW   Job opportunities
"Presentazione del volume *La casa di Salomone a Firenze*".
(in Italian)
Censimento Collezioni Scientifiche (in Italian)

This site is continually updated.
Statistical data on users' access

sites offer glimpses into the past. Libraries and historical sites, and universities and government archives contain records and information needed for research reports.

Parallel Problem Solving

Students in several parts of the country can independently work on the same or similar projects assigned through e-mail, e-mail discussion groups, or the Web. Upon completion, they can exchange methods and results with the other groups.

WebQuests

Bernie Dodge and Tom March developed the WebQuest concept in 1995. WebQuests are "inquiry-oriented activities in which most or all of the information used by the learner is drawn from the Web" (Dodge & March, 1999). WebQuests may be teacher- or student-designed activities and can last from a few hours to a few weeks. They may be worked on individually or by a group of students. The group approach will also foster teamwork, sharing, and individual responsibility as well as responsibility to the group as a whole. This directed-learning approach guides the student through the Web as they try to find answers and draw conclusions while helping them avoid many of the pitfalls found in general Web surfing. WebQuests fit very nicely into a constructivist classroom atmosphere as students synthesize their own knowledge using a teacher-guided set of activities. "There are wonderful, award-winning WebQuests for every grade level (even PreK)" (Summerville, 2000). The WebQuest shown in Figure 12–8 is a great starting point.

Well-designed WebQuests contain six or seven parts:

1. *Introduction:* The purpose of this section is to hook and prepare the student for the WebQuest. It should be interesting and make the student want to go on.
2. *Task:* The purpose of this section is to focus the students on what they are going to do as the culminating product or performance. This should be an interesting and different assignment, not just write a report or give an oral report. Students reading *The Ugly Duckling,* for example, might have to write a letter to the duckling explaining how swans are special birds. Students studying states may have to give a talk designed to make other students in the class travel to that state.
3. *Process:* This section outlines how the student will accomplish the task in a step-by-step fashion. Links to reviewed on-line resources will be given along with links to Web pages that the teacher/students may have developed. Other forms of print and nonprint resources may also be included such as books, videotapes, filmstrips, etc.
4. *Evaluation:* This section describes the evaluation criteria that will be used to grade the student. Rubrics are often used to help the student meet content and performance standards.
5. *Conclusion:* This section encourages reflection and brings closure to the WebQuest. Additional links and rhetorical questions encourage students to extend their thinking and encourage further study.

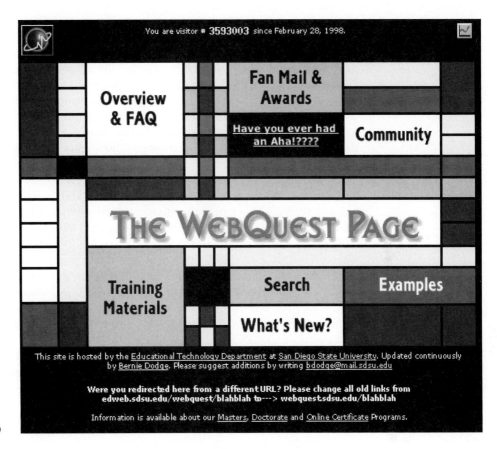

Figure 12–8
The WebQuest Page at San Diego State University (http://webquest.sdsu.edu/)

6. *Teacher Page:* This section includes much of the systematic design work including standards, target audience, notes on teaching the unit, problems, and questions that may arise and sometimes examples of finished products.

Many people place "Resources" as number 6. Here they list other information and Websites for students to look at for more information on the subject. The first five (and number 6 if it is "Resources") are usually placed on one Web page with links to other Websites and Web pages that the author has constructed. The "Teacher Page" is usually a separate Web page. Don't be afraid to use WebQuests in your classroom. There are three accepted ways to go about using them. First, it is perfectly OK to go out on the Web and use a WebQuest that someone else has made—just be sure to give the author full credit. It is also permissible to use someone else's as a starting point and modify it to meet the needs of your class, curriculum, and/or location. If you do this, you should e-mail the developer, thank them for their ideas, and share your WebQuest with them. Lastly, you can make your own WebQuest. WebQuests are also good projects for a student or group of students to develop for a final unit project.

 More information on WebQuests can be found on the Companion Website http://www.prenhall.com/forcier

Scavenger Hunts

More specific searches can be accomplished by several strategies. One such strategy is the *scavenger hunt*. In this strategy, the students are given a list of terms or concepts to search for that perhaps all relate to the same topic or theme. The students are asked to report back on specific information, along with the URL where they located it. For example, when asked to find the number of airports in Burkina Faso, students must determine what Burkina Faso is, where it is, and the search tool that would most likely yield the answer. Though such a question might relate to a geography lesson, its primary purpose may be to refine search skills and acquaint the students with new information resources. A second strategy is to give students a specific set of bookmarks that they are to locate and then to provide specific questions or responses to which the students need to respond. Many Internet sites are particularly targeted to students and can provide interactive lessons of their own. Bookmarks can be distributed as simply as having the URLs typed on a handout, or more efficiently in a HTML document that could provide a given order for access along with some teacher annotations. Web pages can even be *whacked*—that is, copied—while on-line to have their images stored in a data-storage device (e.g., a hard-drive) for later instructional use by students viewing specifically saved sites. An interesting collaborative strategy is to give individual students, or teams of students, specific portions of an overall task and then to have them e-mail each other to share and combine what they have found. This furthers the concept of knowledge as a shared process of interaction that combines multiple sources and interpretations of information.

Website Displays

Students can research areas of local, national, and international interest and post their research and findings on the Web. Students at Dakota Meadows Middle School in Mankato, Minnesota did just that. So far they have developed and posted sites on the Holocaust, the Dakota Indian Uprising (Figure 12–9) around the Mankato area during the middle 1860s, and journals—first-hand accounts and stories from people who lived through World War II either at home or in the armed services. While students read the narrative and view colorful images, they can listen to a traditional Dakota song.

If you are still wondering how to get started or how to design customized Internet lessons for your particular curriculum, Pacific Bell's Knowledge Network Explorer contains a tool called Filamentality (http://www.kn.pacbell.com/wired/fil/#intro). Filamentality is a fill-in-the-blank interactive Web tool that will guide you as you pick a topic, search the Web for suitable sites, and build Web-based activities appropriate for your class.

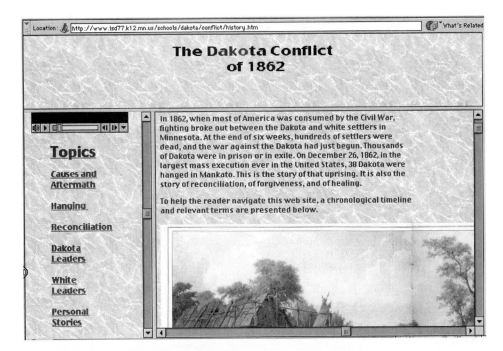

Figure 12–9
Students can post research projects such as this on the World Wide Web (http://www.isd77.k12.mn.us/schools/dakota/conflict/history.htm) (Reprinted with permission)

INTO THE CLASSROOM:
Meaningful Student Web Projects

Today's students are not intimidated by technology; rather they expect to have access to it and use it. Dakota Meadows Middle School opened in 1993 with the goal of integrating computer and other emerging technologies into the student learning experience. Internet technologies help students gain access to information and provide students an opportunity to share their work with others in the school, community, and around the world. Our students use computers, digital video and still cameras, digitizers and scanners, and a wide variety of computer software and programs for producing educational Websites.

Students are more motivated and learning is more effective when they know that their product will be viewed by someone other than the teacher. Students know they must stand behind their work before the world when it is produced for distribution on the Internet.

(Continued)

Our grade 8 English students are required to write for an audience other than their teacher. One way to do this is through a student-constructed Web. This project motivates students to write clearly, without error, and to use a vocabulary that can be understood by a world-wide audience. Students have constructed Websites on mini-mysteries (http://www.isd77.k12.mn.us/schools/dakota/mystery/contents.html) and community memories of World War II (http://www.isd77.k12.mn.us/schools/dakota/war/worldwar.html). In the latter, they interviewed local veterans and individuals living during the 1930s and 40s.

Students further improved their research and writing skills when building *The Dakota Conflict 1862* Website. This Website documents a major local Native American uprising. I had students work in teams against a deadline to produce their piece of the project. Students had to resolve time, as well as content issues within their individual teams. For a number of students, *The Dakota Conflict 1862* project was their first experience with fieldwork and interviewing as information gathering tools. Students learned the history of the *Conflict* and subsequent efforts at native and immigrant reconciliation. This engaged them in an examination of their ideas and attitudes about other times and other peoples. Students also learned to use Website building technologies in order to tell their story. *The Dakota Conflict 1862* Website has been featured in local television and print media and was entered in the *International Schools CyberFair*. Here it won first place in the History category among competing entries from schools from around the globe. Positive community, national, and international feedback has provided students with an incentive to continue designing and producing projects in order to share their work with others beyond the school's walls.

Beth Christensen
Eighth Grade English Teacher
Dakota Meadows Middle School
North Mankato, Minnesota
Minnesota Teacher of the Year, 1996–1997

Prescreened Collections of Websites

One of the first places to look when you are preparing a lesson is one of the Websites that contain lists of prescreened sites. These sites usually list the sites by subject and topic. They are a good place for you to find information and also a wonderful place to find Websites to send your students to. Many times outright Web searching is not carried on in the lower grades; instead, teachers send students to particular sites to find information. Many teachers also develop their own Web pages containing lists of prescreened sites for students to use in their search for knowledge.

Ed's Oasis is a huge site containing a great deal of information for teachers. The *Treasure Zone* (http://www.connectedteacher.com/library/bestofweb.asp) at that site is billed as the "Best Websites for K–12 Classroom Use." This site also contains information on Websites evaluation.

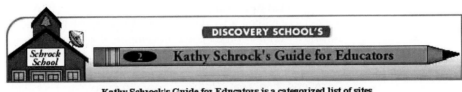

Kathy Schrock's Guide for Educators is a categorized list of sites useful for enhancing curriculum and professional growth. It is updated daily to include the best sites for teaching and learning.

Site of the School Day (SOS) | Audio Welcome | Kathy's Books | E-mail Kathy

SUBJECT ACCESS

- Agricultural Education
- Art and Architecture
- Business Sources/Grants
- Education Resources
- Entertainment & Travel
- Health, P.E., & Fitness
- History & Social Studies
- Holidays
- Internet Information
- Kidstuff
- Literature/Language Arts
- Mathematics
- News Sources/Magazines
- Organizations/Government
- Performing Arts & Music
- Reference & Librarians
- Science and Technology
- Shopping
- Special Ed Resources
- Sports
- Vocational Education
- Weather Info & Maps
- World Languages/Regions

ADDITIONAL ACCESS

- Alphabetic Index to Sites
- Full Text Search (coming soon!)
- Interactive Site Map

KATHY'S PICKS

- Site of the School Day Mailing List
- New Sites This Month
- Favorite Content-Rich Sites

TEACHER HELPERS

- Kathy's Books
- Upcoming Workshops
- Slide Shows for Teaching
- Assessment & Rubric Information
- Critical Evaluation Tools
- Short Circuits™ Newsletter
- WebQuest Information
- TeacherQuest™ Information
- Fry's Readability Graph
- Bulletin Board Ideas
- Other Useful Books

Figure 12–10
Kathy Schrock's Guide for Educators is a must-see Website for every teacher and preservice teacher (http://school. discovery.com/ schrockguide/) (Reprinted with permission by Kathy Schrock)

Kathy Schrock is the Technology Coordinator at Dennis-Yarmouth Regional School District on Cape Cod, Massachusetts. She has put together a huge site (now sponsored by Discovery Channel School), appropriately called *Kathy Schrock's Guide for Educators* (Figure 12–10). This site should be a required stop for all pre- and in-service teachers. Not only are there thousands of prescreened sites here but also search tools and information, slide shows for training, bulletin board ideas, assessment rubrics, readability graphs, and much more.

Yahooligans!™ (http://www.yahooligans.com) is a site for students, parents, and teachers. Not only can you find a vast number of prescreened sites for students but also many student activities. The Yahooligans Teachers' Guide contains information on teaching Internet literacy, Acceptable Use Policies, citing Internet sources, and evaluating Websites.

Educational and Learning Networks

A number of networks aimed primarily at K–12 education have developed during the past few years.

Classroom Connect. (http://www.classroom.com) is a free site, although you have to register, containing a wealth of information on teaching and learning. *Connected University,* an on-line professional development area and other areas containing on-line resources for K–12 teachers are found here.

DiscoverySchool.com. (http://school.discovery.com) is a service of the Discovery networks (Animal Planet, Discovery Channel, Discovery Health, TLC: The Learning Channel, Travel Channel) dedicated to making teaching and learning a rewarding and exciting adventure for teachers, students, and parents. It contains resources for students, teaching materials for teachers, and information for parents about helping their children enjoy learning and excelling in school. Kathy Schrock's guide is located here.

Scholastic Network. (http://teacher.scholastic.com) is another free registration site created by the commercial software company of the same name. There are sections here specifically designed for teachers, students, and parents. You will find wonderful lists of teacher resources, student activities, lesson plans, a *Web Guide* containing thousands of reviewed Websites, curriculum integration ideas, and more. Live interviews with such notables as J. K. Rowling (the author of the *Harry Potter* series) and General Colin Powell (for a Black History Month Special) were presented as well as live practice interviews for prospective teachers.

A list of educational networks may be examined at the Companion Website http://www.prenhall.com/forcier

Internet Archives (Databases)

The Educational Resources Information Center (ERIC). (Figure 12–11) provides Web access to its extensive collection of education-related literature, archives of educational LISTSERVs, a huge archive of lesson plans, and electronic library listings. Many of you have probably used articles and reports in the ERIC database in a library as a basis for reports and presentations in your college courses. It is possible to e-mail inquiries directly to AskERIC@ericir.syr.edu.

The Library of Congress (LOC). (http://www.loc.gov) is a wonderful site to visit. Even though only a portion of its 95 million maps, images, audio recordings, and 17 million books are accessible on-line at this time, the array of information is both interesting and mind-boggling. American Memory, an ongoing project to digitize the LOC's American historical holdings, and THOMAS, a congressional database, are easily accessed here. Another interesting literature site to view is the *University of Virginia Library's Electronic Text Center* (http://etext.lib.virginia.edu). This site contains one of the largest collections of electronic texts in over 13 languages!

One Internet database useful to math and science educators is *The Eisenhower National Clearinghouse (ENC)* (http://www.enc.org/index.htm) for Mathematics and Science located at Ohio State University and funded by the U.S. Department of Education. Its purpose is to improve access to the most current materials in math and science resources in the nation. Descriptions and evaluations are available.

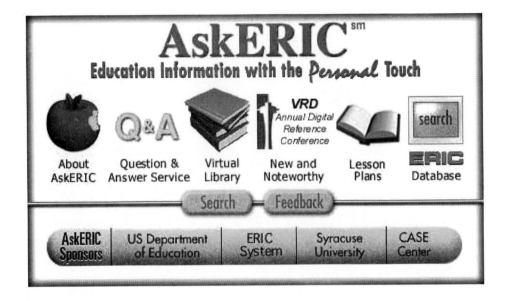

Figure 12–11
AskERIC™ contains a wealth of information for teachers. (http://askeric.org) (Reprinted with permission from AskERIC.)

WEB PORTALS

A Web portal, sometimes just called a *portal,* is a service or Website that offers a broad range of services and resources such as e-mail, e-mail discussion group development, forums and chat, search engines, travel information, yellow and white pages, and on-line shopping malls. Portals can be paid services, free services, and even special pages set up by schools and businesses. They usually act as the first or home page for the particular user's computer. The first portals were paid services such as America Online™, CompuServe™, EarthLink™, and Prodigy™.

Though most of these commercial companies offer a wide variety of services, their biggest draw is the ability to access the Internet through the service. This industry has been in a state of flux. More and more people are becoming comfortable with telecommunications and are demanding more and faster services. Established companies have gone bankrupt or have merged or been bought out by others. Now many people buy their Internet service from telephone companies or their local cable television system and because of this, free portals such as Netscape, MSN (also has a paid service), and Yahoo (Figure 12–12) offer many of the same services as the paid portals. Most services also allow the user to customize the main page with weather, news, and other information of interest to the user. Note the wide variety of information available for you to customize your portal homepage.

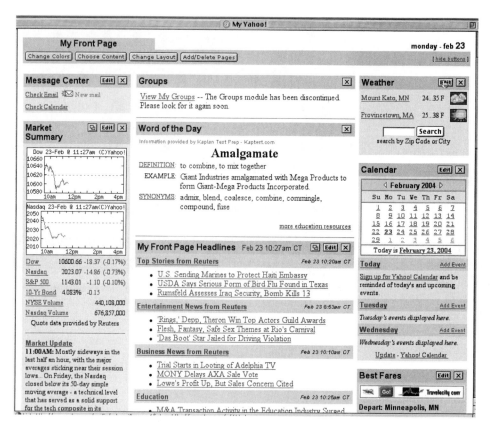

Figure 12–12
My Yahoo page of
one of the authors.
Just under 100
categories may be
added including such
items as lottery
results, pregnancy
calendar, and
package tracking

THE INTERNET AS A DISTANCE LEARNING TOOL

One of the newer uses of the Internet is as a medium for the delivery of instruction. A growing trend in electronic distance education (sometimes called *e-learning*) is to encourage instructors to present either their entire course, or its supporting materials, by means of a Web page. Students access these pages in order to read instructional materials, download or submit assignments, communicate with both the instructor and other students via e-mail, take tests and quizzes, see how they are doing in class, and just about anything they would be able to do if they were in a real classroom. E-learning software is so inclusive that it is grouped under the title of *Course Management System (CMS)*. This method of delivery opens many opportunities for instruction of students whose access to education is limited by either distance or physical impairment. Perhaps you have been in a course in which some, if not all, of the course material was presented to you on-line. All of the Internet tools we described may be utilized in these courses. Internet distance education communications tools are usually divided into two categories according to the mode. Asynchronous modes of communications do not take place between parties simultaneously. Examples include e-mail, e-mail discussion groups, Web pages, and dis-

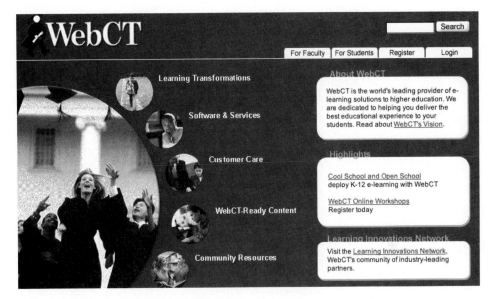

Figure 12–13
Opening screen of a sample WebCT™ course (http://webct. com)

cussion boards that enable students to access them at different times throughout the day and night. Synchronous modes are real-time communications in which the interaction between participants takes place simultaneously, perhaps during a set class time. Synchronous tools would include chat rooms, white boards, live Web cams, etc. Students are on-line in this mode and participate in learning and discussions together as a group. E-mail is usually used to keep students and teachers in touch with each other. Bulletin boards may be used to post information. Chat rooms and forums may be used to exchange questions and comments. The World Wide Web seems to be used most of all. Complete Web-based software packages can seamlessly integrate all of the above Internet tools to produce a comprehensive course. Figure 12–13 shows an introductory screen for WebCT™, one of these course management programs.

OTHER WEBSITES AND CURRICULUM INFUSION IDEAS

A number of Internet activities have already been mentioned. Student and teacher use of e-mail to communicate with peers or with experts in a given field extends the classroom experience to begin the realization of what is rapidly becoming a "global schoolhouse." Databases or archives and search engines assist both students and teachers in utilizing the encyclopedic quality of the vast array of content available on the Internet. WebQuests enable students to learn in a safe environment. However, just as it is a myth that merely placing a student in front of a computer will result in substantive learning, it is equally a myth that merely having access to the Internet will result in productive student acquisition and use of information. The immediacy of access, the sheer volume, and the dynamic quality of the information available is very different from that of previous media for storing and displaying knowledge.

Classroom or media center access is usually through the channel of modem-based communications or via a "hard-wired" cable in a local-area network. The main differences are the provider costs to the school district, long-distance fees if by modem connection, the speed of information transfer, and the number of connected computers in any given setting. Speed of transfer is often crucial (this is where networked cable communications have the advantage), especially where the number of computers or the time available for student on-line access is limited. Teachers need to plan the time allotted to Internet access, as well as the placement of connected computers within a classroom. If there is a single computer, then the logistics of providing equity of access to all students or a display that can be viewed by the entire class become very important. Equality of access means that students are not limited by such features as age, gender, socioeconomic background, and experience in working with computers.

Teachers should plan the use of the Internet as they would any other media, with a clear set of objectives, appropriate preparation and integration into the unit of study, and methods of assessing and reporting student performance.

Generalized searches of the Internet are often useful for determining just what is available. Teachers should assist the students beforehand in the ways of stating terms that narrow and define their search if they are to avoid "information overload." Additionally, students need to understand the appropriate methods of citing electronic information, paying special attention to the person or organization posting that information, and when that information was posted or last revised.

The Internet is not just for student retrieval of information. There are many opportunities for educators to grow as professionals. E-mail communication with other teachers provides for sharing of lesson plans or the solutions to specific classroom problems and issues. Also, teachers in many different parts of the world can have their classes collaborate and share such things as environmental data, poetry and artwork, and discussions of various cultural points of view. Many professional organizations for educators have Web pages posted, and many educational journals and sources of research information (e.g., ERIC) can be obtained on-line. Specialized sources of data provide the raw material for building curriculum and assessment and keep the educator up-to-date with local, state, and national standards in their particular content area.

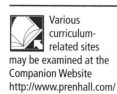
Various curriculum-related sites may be examined at the Companion Website http://www.prenhall.com/forcier

Figures 12–14 through 12–16 illustrate a few of the many Websites that are of particular interest to educators. The danger in identifying specific references on the Internet is that this dynamic structure is in a constant state of flux. New sites are added and existing sites are withdrawn. Hopefully, the sites represented in these illustrations possess a fair degree of longevity. Visit the textbook's Companion Website at http://www.prenhall.com/forcier to examine a host of curriculum-related sites.

The Children's Literature Web Guide (Figure 12–14) is a valuable resource of children's stories, authors, and book reviews. It contains excellent links to children's authors, stories, awards, movies, and television, as well as children's literature organizations.

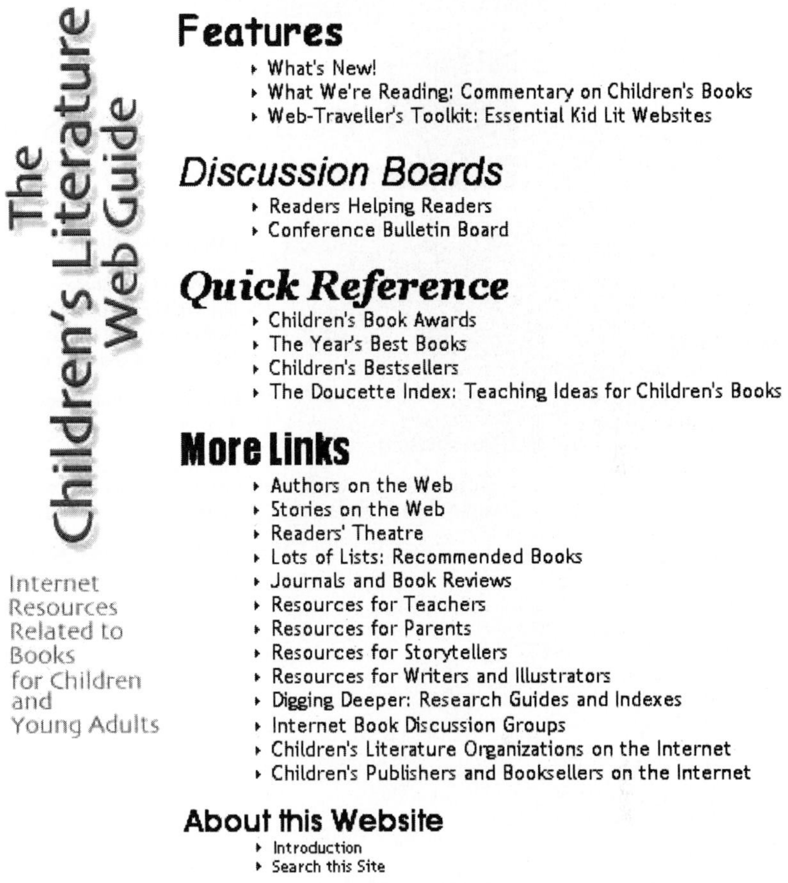

Features
▸ What's New!
▸ What We're Reading: Commentary on Children's Books
▸ Web-Traveller's Toolkit: Essential Kid Lit Websites

Discussion Boards
▸ Readers Helping Readers
▸ Conference Bulletin Board

Quick Reference
▸ Children's Book Awards
▸ The Year's Best Books
▸ Children's Bestsellers
▸ The Doucette Index: Teaching Ideas for Children's Books

More Links
▸ Authors on the Web
▸ Stories on the Web
▸ Readers' Theatre
▸ Lots of Lists: Recommended Books
▸ Journals and Book Reviews
▸ Resources for Teachers
▸ Resources for Parents
▸ Resources for Storytellers
▸ Resources for Writers and Illustrators
▸ Digging Deeper: Research Guides and Indexes
▸ Internet Book Discussion Groups
▸ Children's Literature Organizations on the Internet
▸ Children's Publishers and Booksellers on the Internet

About this Website
▸ Introduction
▸ Search this Site

The Children's Literature Web Guide

Internet Resources Related to Books for Children and Young Adults

Figure 12–14
The Children's Literature Web Guide is an extremely useful resource housed at the University of Calgary. (http://www.ucalgary.ca/~dkbrown) (Reprinted with permission of David K. Brown.)

CIA Publications (Figure 12–15), maintained by the Central Intelligence Agency, is an excellent resource for any geography or current events class. The high-quality maps are current and may be downloaded. The World Factbook alone is worth a visit to this site.

edHelper.com (Figure 12–16) is just one of the many sites for teachers. Here you can find lesson plans, worksheets and worksheet generators, WebQuests puzzles and exams and puzzle and exam generators, and a host of other teacher helpers divided into preK through twelfth grade areas. SAT and test prep worksheets are included along with links to the latest education news for teachers.

Perhaps most important, the Internet offers the means for the teacher to connect to a global educational system and to transition from being the source of any and all information in the classroom to being a facilitator of student skills in locating, retrieving, evaluating, assimilating, repurposing, and displaying the ever-increasing amount of information available on the Internet.

PUBLICATIONS & REPORTS

How to Purchase

Privacy and Security notices

About the CIA

What's New at CIA

Employment at the CIA

Publications & Reports

The World Factbook
Factbook on Intelligence

Speeches & Testimony

Press Releases &
Statements

CIA Publications

The World Factbook
The World Factbook is produced by CIA's Directorate of Intelligence. The Factbook is a comprehensive resource of facts and statistics on more than 250 countries and other entities.

Factbook on Intelligence
An overview of the Agency's organization, history, and mission.

Chiefs of State and
Cabinet Members of Foreign Governments
Updated: 20 July 2000

CIA Maps and Publications 2000
The Central Intelligence Agency's 2000 Maps and Publications Released to the Public is a listing of all unclassified maps and publications available to the public for purchase from GPO and/or NTIS.

Figure 12–15
CIA documents provide an excellent source of information on world geography. (http://www.odci.gov/cia/publications/pubs.html) (Reprinted with permission from the Central Intelligence Agency.)

Lesson Plans - Worksheets - Teacher's Lesson Plans - WebQuests - Primary Teacher Resources - Math Lesson Plans - Writing Lesson Plans - Reading Lesson Plans - Science Lesson Plans - Technology Lesson Plans - Social Studies Lesson Plans - ...

11443 Lesson Plans, **1296** WebQuests, **5000**
Free Worksheet Generators, 1600 Word and Critical Thinking Problems, Exams and Puzzles for Standardized Tests.

The spelling and vocabulary sections now include new worksheets and tools!
New Word Stories Math Problems Section!
Addition, Subtraction, Multiplication, and Division worksheets now use bigger fonts!
Language Arts Worksheets   Contractions
New **Animal Worksheets**   Solar System Worksheets   Weather Worksheets   Plants
New Biomes: Rainforests, Deserts, Polar Regions.
Reading + Math + Vocabulary + Spelling + Writing = **edHelper's New Reading Comprehension Section**
New Phonics Section with Printables and Worksheets

The Valentine
Scavenger Hunt
Now Playing!

January Theme Units   Winter Theme Unit   Penguins Theme Unit
February Theme Units   Groundhog Day   Valentine's Day   Black History

八百六十三   **Chinese New Year Theme Unit**
Using Chinese characters to learn about place value and more!

 Build a puzzle: **Use Your Own Words** (Build Spelling and Vocabulary Worksheets) | Word Find | Crossword | Spelling |
Math Crossnumber | Math Box | Math Sequences | Bingo | Number Word Searches | Missing Digits | Math Words |
Word Stories | **Critical Thinking Puzzles**

Figure 12–16
edHelper.com has thousands of lesson plans and teacher helpers. (http://www.edhelper.com/)

SUMMARY

Telecommunications offers significant advantages to the educator who wishes to collaborate with colleagues, access current information, and expose students to a broad range of cultures and curricular resources. Electronic networks overcome traditional barriers of social and geographic isolation, facilitate interactive and cooperative learning, and serve as highly effective motivators to reluctant writers. In particular, the Internet allows students to construct their own knowledge; promotes the use of technology as a powerful resource tool; enables collaboration between and among students through various projects and thematic units; provides a global perspective and interchange of ideas; allows teachers to individualize student instruction; and encourages the use of technology as a tool and enabler.

In order to take advantage of telecommunications, teachers must move from seeing the computer as a static piece of equipment they use to process data to seeing the computer as a vehicle capable of gathering information and transporting them and their students to distant places around the globe.

CHAPTER EXERCISES

To complete the specified exercises on-line, go to the Chapter Exercises Module in Chapter 12 of the Companion Website.

1. Put together an Internet scavenger hunt for a particular theme or content area. This should include descriptions of the relevant information to be found, a space for the answer, and another space for the recording of the URL. This activity may need to include instructions on appropriate search strategies.
2. Pick out a topic or theme that you wish to explore, find five appropriate sites, and discuss how you know that the information you found was credible.
3. Design a form for students to use in evaluating Internet sites for content accuracy or completeness, currency of information, purpose of the site, authorship, date of posting or most recent revision, degree of interactivity, appropriate use of graphics, and useful links to related sites.
4. Find a site on the World Wide Web that you know is fictitious but is designed to look credible. What techniques did the Website author use to try to fool you into believing the information is credible?
5. Write a short paper discussing the pros and cons concerning government mandated filtering of Websites. Be prepared to defend the side you disagree with in class.
6. Write a list of five to ten statements that you could post in your classroom regarding proper student use of the Internet.
7. Search the Internet for information about WebQuests. Using the grade level that you plan to teach, develop a short WebQuest that you might be able to use. Using what you learned in Chapter 11, could you make this WebQuest?

8. How will the Internet and/or the World Wide Web help your students understand cultural diversity in this country and around the world. Find and list several sites that might be helpful to you. Be prepared to share your comments and sites in class.

9. Explore *Kathy Schrock's Guide for Educators*. What feature of the site did you find most useful?

10. Search for a site that lists information that you can use in the grade level or subject you would like to teach after you graduate. Discuss this site with others in the class.

PORTFOLIO DEVELOPMENT EXERCISES

To complete this exercise on-line, go to the Digital Portfolio Module in Chapter 12 of the Companion Website.

One of the NETS•S standards covered in this chapter was "Students use technology to locate, evaluate, and collect information from a variety of sources" under *Category 5: Technology research tools*. Begin to develop your own portfolio of lesson plans that demonstrates your ability to have your students reach the NETS•S standards.

1. Design a lesson plan activity for elementary, middle school, or high school students in which they interact with peers, experts, and other audiences. This should be a project that could involve individuals in other schools in this country and abroad. How would you go about facilitating this project? How would you go about finding other groups to participate in this project? This lesson should demonstrate that your students have achieved the standard. Be sure to include a system of evaluation for your students' understanding and competence to ensure that they have met this standard.

2. Adapt the lesson plan activity you developed in exercise 1 for students to evaluate each others' work.

For more information on developing digital portfolios, go to Digital Portfolio Module on the Companion Website www.prenhall. com/forcier

REFERENCES & SUGGESTED READINGS

Brandt, D. S. (1996). Evaluating information on the Internet. *Computers in Libraries, 16*(5), 44–46.

Descy, D. E. (1996, September). Evaluating Internet resources. *Tech Trends, 41*(4), 3–5.

Descy, D. E. (2004, January). Organizing the Internet: Safe passage through a minefield of information. *Library Trends, 51*(4), 46–48.

Dodge, B., & March, T. (1999). *The WebQuest page*. Retrieved 15 July 2000 from the World Wide Web: *http://edweb.sdsu.edu/webquest/webquest.html*

Eastman, J. N., Nickel, T., Du Plessis, J., & Smith, L. D. (2000, April). An incremental approach to implementing a Web course. *TechTrends, 44*(3), 40–45.

Lamb, A. (1999). *Building treehouses for learning* (2nd). Emporia, KS: Vision to Action.

Poftak, A. (2002, August). Net-wise teens: Safety, ethics, and innovation. *Technology & Learning, 25*(1), 36–49.

Summerville, J. (2000, March). WebQuests: An aspect of technology integration for training preservice teachers. *TechTrends, 44*(2), 31–35.

A P P E N D I X

NETS•S Technology Foundation Standards for All Students

1. *Basic operations and concepts*
   - Students demonstrate a sound understanding of the nature and operation of technology systems.
   - Students are proficient in the use of technology.
2. *Social, ethical, and human issues*
   - Students understand the ethical, cultural, and societal issues related to technology.
   - Students practice responsible use of technology systems, information, and software.
   - Students develop positive attitudes toward technology uses that support lifelong learning, collaboration, personal pursuits, and productivity.
3. *Technology productivity tools*
   - Students use technology tools to enhance learning, increase productivity, and promote creativity.
   - Students use productivity tools to collaborate in constructing technology-enhanced models, prepare publications, and produce other creative works.
4. *Technology communications tools*
   - Students use telecommunications to collaborate, publish, and interact with peers, experts, and other audiences.
   - Students use a variety of media and formats to communicate information and ideas effectively to multiple audiences.
5. *Technology research tools*
   - Students use technology to locate, evaluate, and collect information from a variety of sources.
   - Students use technology tools to process data and report results.
   - Students evaluate and select new information resources and technological innovations based on the appropriateness for specific tasks.
6. *Technology problem-solving and decision-making tools*
   - Students use technology resources for solving problems and making informed decisions.
   - Students employ technology in the development of strategies for solving problems in the real world.

Index

ISTE National Educational Technology Standards for Teachers (NETS•T)

ISTE NETS for Teachers (NETS•T)* focuses on preservice teacher education. It contains fundamental concepts, knowledge, skills, and attitudes for utilizing technology in educational settings.

These standards may be divided into four profiles that correspond to four phases in a typical teacher preparation program. The four profiles are:

- General Preparation
- Professional Preparation
- Student Teaching/Internship
- First-Year Teaching

More information on these standards and the above four profiles may be found at the ISTE Website (http://cnets.iste.org/teacher/t_stands.html).

Educational Technology Standards and Performance Indicators for All Teachers

I. TECHNOLOGY OPERATIONS AND CONCEPTS

Teachers demonstrate a sound understanding of technology operations and concepts. Teachers:

A. demonstrate introductory knowledge, skills, and understanding of concepts related to technology (as described in the ISTE National Education Technology Standards for Students)

B. demonstrate continual growth in technology knowledge and skills to stay abreast of current and emerging technologies

II. PLANNING AND DESIGNING LEARNING ENVIRONMENTS AND EXPERIENCES

Teachers plan and design effective learning environments and experiences supported by technology. Teachers:

A. design developmentally appropriate learning opportunities that apply technology-enhanced instructional strategies to support the diverse needs of learners

B. apply current research on teaching and learning with technology when planning learning environments and experiences

C. identify and locate technology resources and evaluate them for accuracy and suitability

D. plan for the management of technology resources within the context of learning activities

E. plan strategies to manage student learning in a technology-enhanced environment

III. TEACHING, LEARNING, AND THE CURRICULUM

Teachers implement curriculum plans that include methods and strategies for applying technology to maximize student learning. Teachers:

A. facilitate technology-enhanced experiences that address content standards and student technology standards

B. use technology to support learner-centered strategies that address the diverse needs of students

C. apply technology to develop students' higher order skills and creativity

D. manage student learning activities in a technology-enhanced environment

IV. ASSESSMENT AND EVALUATION

Teachers apply technology to facilitate a variety of effective assessment and evaluation strategies. Teachers:

A. apply technology in assessing student learning of subject matter using a variety of assessment techniques

B. use technology resources to collect and analyze data, interpret results, and communicate findings to improve instructional practice and maximize student learning

C. apply multiple methods of evaluation to determine students' appropriate use of technology resources for learning, communication, and productivity

V. PRODUCTIVITY AND PROFESSIONAL PRACTICE

Teachers use technology to enhance their productivity and professional practice. Teachers:

A. use technology resources to engage in ongoing professional development and lifelong learning

B. continually evaluate and reflect on professional practice to make informed decisions regarding the use of technology in support of student learning

C. apply technology to increase productivity

D. use technology to communicate and collaborate with peers, parents, and the larger community in order to nurture student learning